D0118376

The HarperCollins Concise
ATLAS OF THE BIBLE

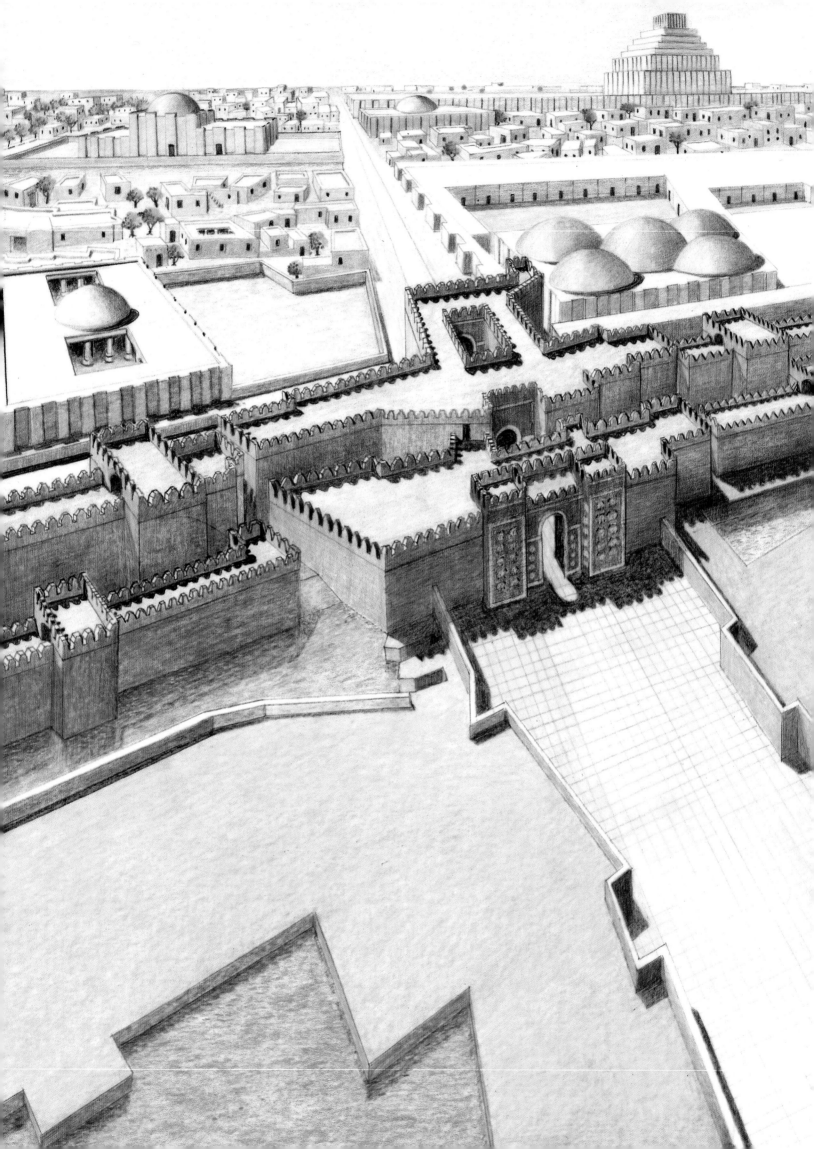

The HarperCollins Concise
ATLAS OF THE BIBLE

EDITED BY JAMES B. PRITCHARD

WITH
L. MICHAEL WHITE

HarperSanFrancisco
An Imprint of HarperCollinsPublishers

THE HARPERCOLLINS CONCISE ATLAS OF THE BIBLE
Copyright © 1991 by Times Books, London.
All rights reserved. No part of this book may be
used or reproduced without written permission
except in the case of brief quotations embodied
in critical articles and reviews. For information
address HarperCollins*Publishers*, 10 East 53rd
Street, New York, NY 10022.

First HarperCollins Paperback Edition
Published in 1997. Reprinted 1998, 2000, 2002

This book is published in Great Britain
by Times Books.

Artwork and typesetting
Swanston Graphics, Derby
Sue Paling
Andrew Bright

Color processing
Colourscan, Singapore

Design
Ivan Dodd

Editorial direction
Rosemary Aspinwall
Andrew Heritage

Alison Ewington
Ailsa Heritage
Isobel Willetts

Place name consultant, index
P J M Geelan

Printed in Singapore by Imago

ISBN: 0-06-251499-7

Acknowledgments
This atlas contains the work of many of the
contributors to THE TIMES ATLAS OF THE
BIBLE (1987) who are listed in that volume.
We also wish to thank the following:
L.M. White, Professor of Classics, University of
Texas at Austin

Inter-Testamental Period

New Testament

FOR CENTURIES a knowledge of ancient Hebrew and Greek has been the prime requisite for biblical scholarship. This continues to be true. Yet recently, approaches other than linguistic have come to play an increasing role. First came the discovery and decipherment of texts written by neighbouring Egyptians and Assyrians; then there was the archaeological recovery of how Israelites lived and worshipped; and most recently science has come to be used increasingly in getting at the biblical past. In 1987 *The Times Atlas of the Bible* sought to make use of these new approaches and grew into a large volume. About fifty specialists from a variety of fields contributed.

Understandably there are different levels of interest in detail among students and readers of the Bible. In the concise edition we have been able to produce a more compact atlas. Much of the text has been rewritten to exclude some peripheral matters and to present others in shorter form. New maps have been produced to combine information formerly given on two or more maps. The concise atlas has been designed to serve the reader or user who wants to get as quickly as possible to what is currently known about the historical geography of the Bible.

The general aim remains essentially the same as that of the larger work. It is to provide the geographical setting of such dramatic events as wars, military campaigns, destructions, rebellions; chart the routes of conquerors and exiles; mark the rise and fall of empires and the divisions of kingdoms; and locate the heroic deeds of patriarchs, judges and prophets.

In the process of condensing we have assumed that the Bible itself is of primary interest. What sheds light on its narratives is of major importance. We have introduced an index of biblical references, and another index to personal names found in the text of the atlas. A short bibliography is also a new feature.

For the sake of consistency we have made use of the dates given in the third edition of *The Cambridge Ancient History*, a widely used book of reference. We have followed the *Encyclopedia of Archaeological Excavations in the Holy Land*, vol. 4, edited by M. Avi-Yonah and E. Stern, 1978, for terminology and dates for archaeological periods from the Bronze Age onward.

The maps in this atlas have been specially designed in order to present the material in a clear and dynamic way. Many of the maps are based on recessive or unorthodox projections, and it is therefore not possible to provide scales for them – the distance between two places in the foreground, for example, will be considerably greater than that between two places near the horizon. In order to help the reader to interpret the maps, most of them carry longitude and latitude lines, in addition to an indication of the north-south axis. Further, an index of distances between principal biblical sites appears on page 138.

Again we are indebted to our former contributors, as well as to new ones, for their help in the production of this concise atlas, which, while resembling its parent, is not cast directly from the older mould.   J. B. *Pritchard*

September 1990

OLD TESTAMENT

c90,000 BC	Levant inhabited by small bands of hunter-gatherers
c12,500	Microliths and bone tools introduced
c8300	Wheat domesticated – oval houses
c7500	Agriculture – sheep herded – rectangular houses
c6000	Beginning of pottery in Syria
c3500	Copper metallurgy developed
c3800	Writing invented
c2500	Ebla archives
c2000	Potter's wheel in Palestine
c1792	Hammurabi's laws
c1665	Hyksos take control of Egypt
c1573	Kamose campaigns in Canaan
c1565	Amosis expells the Hyksos
c1530	Amenophis I campaign to Palestine
c1482	Tuthmosis III begins to build his empire in Palestine
c1482	Battle of Megiddo
c1400	Alphabetic writing at Ugarit
c1375	Beginning of Amarna correspondence
c1320	Sethos I's campaign to the coastland
c1300	Battle of Qadesh
c1280	Ramesses II's treaty with the Hittites
c1238 (?)	Merneptah's battle with 'Israel'
c1200	Invasions of the Sea Peoples
c1000	Phoenician trade begins in the Mediterranean
965	Solomon assumes the throne in Israel
931	Division of the Hebrew Kingdom
924	Shishak invades Palestine
853	Ahab defeated by Shalmaneser III at Qarqar
841	Jehu pays tribute to Shalmaneser III
738	Menahem's tribute to Tiglath-pileser III
734	Ahaz's tribute to Tiglath-pileser III
732	Tiglath-pileser III places Hoshea on throne
722	Fall of Samaria
712	Sargon II's campaign to Ashdod
701	Lachish attacked by Sennacherib
670	Manasseh pays tribute to Esarhaddon
612	Fall of Nineveh
609	Josiah slain by Necho II of Egypt
597	Nebuchadnezzar II conquers Jerusalem
597	Jehoiachin deported to Babylon

THE DATES assigned to the principal characters and events of the Bible can vary considerably. New discovery and the reassessment of older evidence make it difficult to have a consensus about chronology, particularly among the large number of contributors to the Atlas. In order to achieve something of a consistency in matters of terminology and date we have made use of the chronological tables in the third edition of the *Cambridge Ancient History*, now in the process of publication. Those who prefer another system of chronological notation can easily make adjustments from those available in the CAH. For the dates of the Babylonian and Assyrian kings not listed in CAH we have followed J. A. Brinkman in A. Leo Oppenheim, *Ancient Mesopotamia*, 1964, pp.341, 347; for the kings of Israel and Judah not yet appearing in the CAH volumes we have depended upon E. R. Thiele, *The Mysterious Numbers of the Hebrew Kings*, 1965, p.205.

The names and dates for the archaeological periods in Palestine are from two sources. For the earlier, prehistoric periods we have used those suggested by O. Bar-Josef in his contributions to this volume. The dates and designations for the Bronze Age and onward are taken from the chronological table appearing at the end of the *Encyclopedia of Archaeological Excavations in the Holy Land*, IV, edited by M. Avi-Yonah and E. Stern, 1978. However, it must be remembered that other terms and dates have had a wide use. For example, there are two other schemes for designating the periods from the latter part of the Early Bronze through the early Middle Bronze Age (c2350-1750). One divides the span into the 'Intermediate EB-MB Period' and a 'Middle Bronze I Period'. Yet another system makes use of 'EB IV A-C' for the period covered in our table by EB IV and MB I (2350-2000).

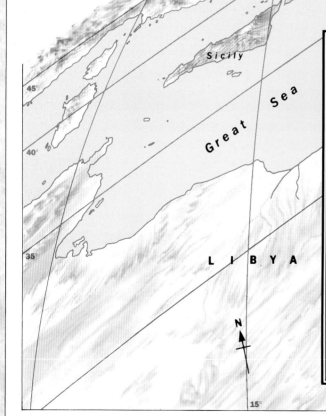

THE HASMONAEANS

Judas Maccabaeus	died 160
Simon Thassis	142-134
John Hyrcanus (Yehohanan)	134-104
Aristobulus I (Yehudah)	104-3
Antigonus (Mattityah)	died 104
Alexander Jannaeus (Yehonatan)	103-76
Alexandra Salome	76-67
Aristobulus II (Yehudah)	67-63
Hyrcanus II (Yehohanan)	63-40
Alexander	died 49
Antigonus (Mattityah)	40-37
Herod the Great	37-4
Aristobulus III	died 35

ROMAN EMPERORS

Augustus	27 BC-AD 14
Tiberius	AD 14-37
Gaius	37-41
Claudius	41-54
Nero	54-68
Galba	68-69
Otho	69-69
Vitellius	69-69
Vespasian	69-79
Titus	79-81
Domitian	81-96
Nerva	96-98
Trajan	98-117
Hadrian	117-138
Antoninus Pius	138-161
Marcus Aurelius	161-180
Commodus	180-193
Septimius Severus	193-211

KINGS OF EGYPT

Eighteenth Dynasty

Amosis	1570-1546
Amenophis I	1546-1526
Tuthmosis I	1525-c1512
Tuthmosis II	c1512-1504
Hatshepsut	1503-1482
Tuthmosis III	1504-1450*
Amenophis II	1450-1425
Tuthmosis IV	1425-1417
Amenophis III	1417-1379
Akhenaten (Amenophis IV)	1379-1362
Smenkhkare	1364-1361*
Tutankhamun	1361-1352
Ay	1352-1348
Horemheb	1348-1320

Nineteenth Dynasty

Ramesses I	1320-1318
Sethos I	1318-1304
Ramesses II	1304-1237
Merneptah	1236-1223
Amenmesses	1222-1217 (?)
Sethos II	1216-1210 (?)
Merneptah Siptah } Tewosret }	1209-1200

Twentieth Dynasty

Sethnakhte	1200-1198
Ramesses III	1198-1166
Ramesses IV	1166-1160
Ramesses V	1160-1156
Ramesses VI	1156-1148
Ramesses VII	1148-1147
Ramesses VIII	1147-1140
Ramesses IX	1140-1121
Ramesses X	1121-1113
Ramesses XI	1113-1085

*Co-regency with predecessor

BC	Event
539	Fall of Babylon
530	Cambyses becomes king of Persia
522-486	Darius
336	Alexander the Great
325	Beginning of rule of the Seleucids
305	Beginning of the Ptolemies
152	Hasmonaeans
	NEW TESTAMENT
67	Hasmonaean Civil War
64	Arrival of Pompey
43	Assassination of Julius Caesar
37-4	Herod, King of Judaea
AD	
6-41	Death of Herod the Great
6	Judaea under Procuratorial control
26-36	Tax census of Quirinius
34	Pontius Pilate, procurator
37-39	Death of Herod Philip
39	Removal of Herod Antipas
39	Herod Agrippa I
41-44	Pogrom against Jews of Alexandria, delegation of Philo to Rome
44-66	Paul in Aegean
50-60	Judaea under Procuratorial control
52-93	Herod Agrippa II
66-74	First Revolt against Rome
67	Fall of Galilee
68	Death of Nero, Year of 4 Emperors
70	Destruction of Jerusalem
74	Fall of Masada
c96	Death of Clement of Rome, John of Ephesus
c110	Ignatius of Antioch
c112	Pliny the Younger in Bithynia
115	Revolt of Jews in Egypt
132-135	Second Jewish Revolt (Bar Kochbah) against Rome
144-164	Justin Martyr, Marcion, and Valentinus in Rome
156	Martyrdom of Polycarp, bishop of Smyrna
193	Year of 3 Emperors
197	Persecution of Christians in Carthage
203	Persecution of Christians in Alexandria
c200	Rabbi Judah the Prince codifies Mishnah

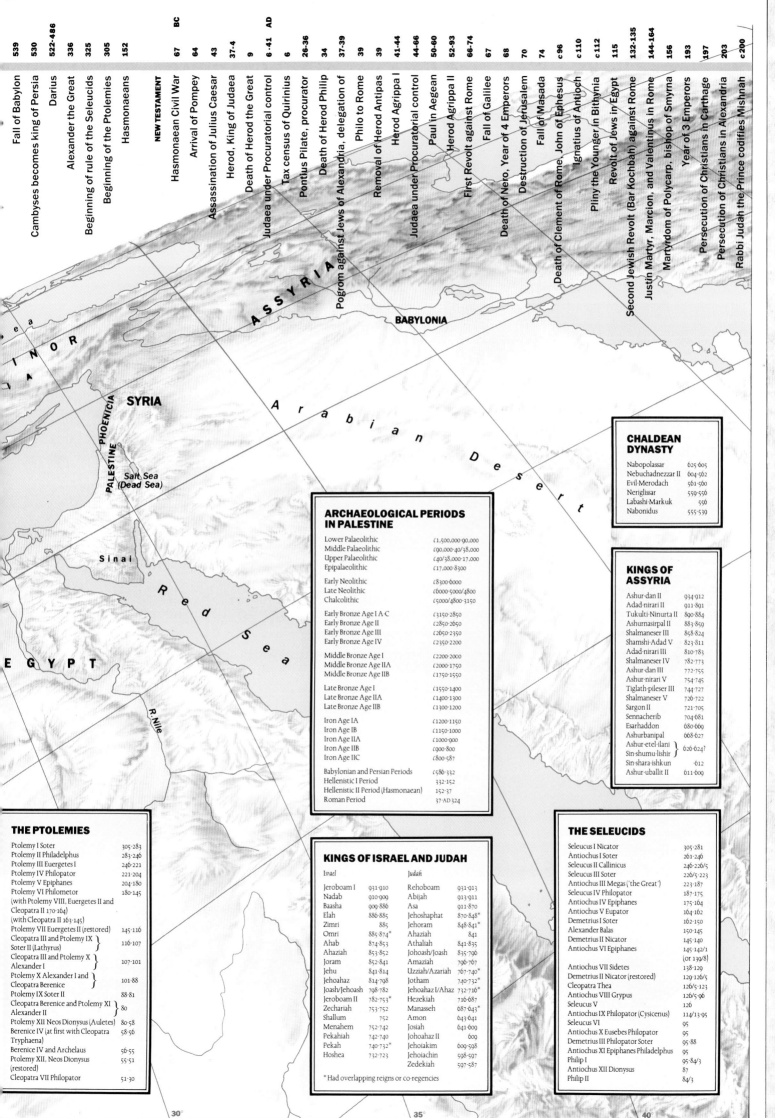

Map labels: ASIA MINOR · ASSYRIA · BABYLONIA · SYRIA · PHOENICIA · PALESTINE · Salt Sea (Dead Sea) · Sinai · Red Sea · EGYPT · R. Nile · Arabian Desert

CHALDEAN DYNASTY

Nabopolassar	625-605
Nebuchadnezzar II	604-562
Evil-Merodach	561-560
Neriglissar	559-556
Labashi-Marduk	556
Nabonidus	555-539

KINGS OF ASSYRIA

Ashur-dan II	934-912
Adad-nirari II	911-891
Tukulti-Ninurta II	890-884
Ashurnasirpal II	883-859
Shalmaneser III	858-824
Shamshi-Adad V	823-811
Adad-nirari III	810-783
Shalmaneser IV	782-773
Ashur-dan III	772-755
Ashur-nirari V	754-745
Tiglath-pileser III	744-727
Shalmaneser V	726-722
Sargon II	721-705
Sennacherib	704-681
Esarhaddon	680-669
Ashurbanipal	668-627
Ashur-etel-ilani } Sin-shumu-lishir }	626-624?
Sin-shara-ishkun	-612
Ashur-uballit II	611-609

ARCHAEOLOGICAL PERIODS IN PALESTINE

Lower Palaeolithic	c.1,500,000-90,000
Middle Palaeolithic	c.90,000-40/38,000
Upper Palaeolithic	c.40/38,000-17,000
Epipalaeolithic	c.17,000-8300
Early Neolithic	c.8300-6000
Late Neolithic	c.6000-5000/4800
Chalcolithic	c.5000/4800-3150
Early Bronze Age I A-C	c.3150-2850
Early Bronze Age II	c.2850-2650
Early Bronze Age III	c.2650-2350
Early Bronze Age IV	c.2350-2200
Middle Bronze Age I	c.2200-2000
Middle Bronze Age IIA	c.2000-1750
Middle Bronze Age IIB	c.1750-1550
Late Bronze Age I	c.1550-1400
Late Bronze Age IIA	c.1400-1300
Late Bronze Age IIB	c.1300-1200
Iron Age IA	c.1200-1150
Iron Age IB	c.1150-1000
Iron Age IIA	c.1000-900
Iron Age IIB	c.900-800
Iron Age IIC	c.800-587
Babylonian and Persian Periods	c.586-332
Hellenistic I Period	332-152
Hellenistic II Period (Hasmonaean)	152-37
Roman Period	37-AD 324

THE PTOLEMIES

Ptolemy I Soter	305-283
Ptolemy II Philadelphus	283-246
Ptolemy III Euergetes I	246-221
Ptolemy IV Philopator	221-204
Ptolemy V Epiphanes	204-180
Ptolemy VI Philometor	180-145
(with Ptolemy VIII, Euergetes II and Cleopatra II 170-164)	
(with Cleopatra II 163-145)	
Ptolemy VII Euergetes II (restored)	145-116
Cleopatra III and Ptolemy IX } Soter II (Lathyrus)	116-107
Cleopatra III and Ptolemy X } Alexander I	107-101
Ptolemy X Alexander I and } Cleopatra Berenice	101-88
Ptolemy IX Soter II	88-81
Cleopatra Berenice and Ptolemy XI } Alexander II	80
Ptolemy XII Neos Dionysus (Auletes)	80-58
Berenice IV (at first with Cleopatra Tryphaena)	58-56
Berenice IV and Archelaus	56-55
Ptolemy XII, Neos Dionysus (restored)	55-51
Cleopatra VII Philopator	51-30

KINGS OF ISRAEL AND JUDAH

Israel		Judah	
Jeroboam I	931-910	Rehoboam	931-913
Nadab	910-909	Abijah	913-911
Baasha	909-886	Asa	911-870
Elah	886-885	Jehoshaphat	870-848*
Zimri	885	Jehoram	848-841*
Omri	885-874*	Ahaziah	841
Ahab	874-853	Athaliah	841-835
Ahaziah	853-852	Johoash/Joash	835-796
Joram	852-841	Amaziah	796-767
Jehu	841-814	Uzziah/Azariah	767-740*
Jehoahaz	814-798	Jotham	740-732*
Joash/Jehoash	798-782	Jehoahaz I/Ahaz	732-716*
Jeroboam II	782-753*	Hezekiah	716-687
Zechariah	753-752	Manasseh	687-643*
Shallum	752	Amon	643-641
Menahem	752-742	Josiah	641-609
Pekahiah	742-740	Jehoahaz II	609
Pekah	740-732*	Jehoiakim	609-598
Hoshea	732-723	Jehoiachin	598-597
		Zedekiah	597-587

* Had overlapping reigns or co-regencies

THE SELEUCIDS

Seleucus I Nicator	305-281
Antiochus I Soter	261-246
Seleucus II Callinicus	246-226/5
Seleucus III Soter	226/5-223
Antiochus III Megas ('the Great')	223-187
Seleucus IV Philopator	187-175
Antiochus IV Epiphanes	175-164
Antiochus V Eupator	164-162
Demetrius I Soter	162-150
Alexander Balas	150-145
Demetrius II Nicator	145-140
Antiochus VI Epiphanes	145-142/1 (or 139/8)
Antiochus VII Sidetes	138-129
Demetrius II Nicator (restored)	129-126/5
Cleopatra Thea	126/5-123
Antiochus VIII Grypus	126/5-96
Seleucus V	126
Antiochus IX Philopator (Cysicenus)	114/13-95
Seleucus VI	95
Antiochus X Eusebes Philopator	95
Demetrius III Philopator Soter	95-88
Antiochus XI Epiphanes Philadelphus	95
Philip I	95-84/3
Antiochus XII Dionysus	87
Philip II	84/3

30° · 35° · 40°

9

THE beginnings of human culture, expressed genealogically in the list of sons of Adam and Eve – Cain, tiller of the ground; Abel, the shepherd; Enoch, the city dweller; Jabal, the nomad; Jubal, the musician; Tubal-cain, the smith – have also been investigated at numerous sites in the Holy Land. Man's presence in Palestine is attested for more than a million years before the Hebrews arrived.

An important change took place about 11,000 BC with the appearance of sedentary bases with houses, storage facilities, art objects, pounding and grinding tools and tools made from bone. The period is called Natufian after Wadi en-Natuf, in central Palestine, where remains were first discovered. Other sites provided more evidence: circular houses and lime-plaster for coating walls at 'Enan, carved gazelles on sickle handles of bone from El-Wad and a cave at Kebara with animal and human figurines. Natufian subsistence was based on hunting of gazelles, fallow deer, wild boar, fishing, trapping birds and gathering wild cereals, pulses and nuts. The Early Natufian base camps were the first relatively sedentary communities. Numerous burials within the settlement area as well as animals, such as house mice and sparrows, usually attracted by stores of food stuff, are indications of a sedentary way of life. With the increase in population Late Natufian communities expanded their territories and established new sites such as those at Mureybat and Abu Hureira on the Middle Euphrates and Rosh Zin and Rosh Horesha in the Negeb highlands. In Early Natufian there were common burials and the use of bone and shell pendants was common; in Late Natufian single burials were more common and body ornaments were rare.

Permanent settlements began to appear as early as the 9th and 8th millennium BC, such as those at Jericho and Nahal Oren in Palestine, Mureybat in Syria, Çayönü in Anatolia and Ganj Dareh in Persia. Permanent villages increased during the 7th millennium, due to the development of agriculture and animal husbandry, although most communities continued to rely throughout this period on hunting and gathering to supplement their diet.

The most intensive Neolithic settlement in Palestine occurred between c 7500 and 6000 BC, known as the Pre-Pottery Neolithic B period. Major settlements at Jericho, Munhatta, Beidha and 'Ein Ghazal show a general uniformity of culture. There were well built multi-roomed rectangular buildings with burnished lime-plaster on walls and floors. A group of male and female figures at 'Ein Ghazal suggests ancestor worship. Stone tools show continuity with those from the earlier period. The large flint blades probably indicate an increasing use of wood; flint arrowheads point to continuation of hunting. Most of these sites were abandoned around 6000 BC with cultivated cereals and domesticated animals becoming more important in Late Neolithic.

During the Chalcolithic period (5th–4th millennia BC) as food supply from agriculture and domestic animals increased so did permanent settlements. New building techniques, art and skills appeared, the most notable of which was metallurgy. Chalcolithic culture was first discovered at Teleilat el-Ghassul. This large site of some 60 acres has two spectacular buildings with wall paintings. One shows a procession of ceremonially dressed and masked human figurines approaching what is, perhaps, a shrine. The leader holds a sickle-shaped object over his right shoulder, an object similar in shape to an ivory sickle found at Horbat Zafad, near Beersheba. Some 40 burials of new-born infants beneath walls and floors may have been foundation sacrifices.

Recently, discoveries near Beersheba and at 'En-Gedi and Nahal Mishmar have greatly enlarged the earlier picture of Chalcolithic culture. Although only a few copper objects are known from the last settlement at Ghassul, Beersheba had a highly sophisticated metal industry. A hoard of copper objects from Nahal Mishmar remains the most remarkable collection of early metal objects yet found in the Near East. Other sites like those at Azor, Gilat and Megiddo have produced clay ossuaries (page 51), domestic house shrines, human and animal figurines. Toward the end of the 4th millennium new cultural traits appear that herald the birth of urban societies of the Bronze Age with its walled cities.

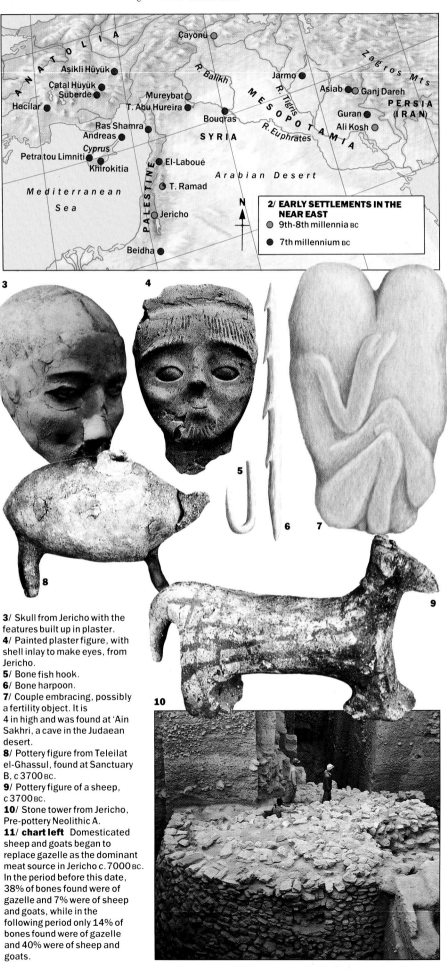

1/ **map right** Permanent settlement occurred in Palestine as early as the 10th-9th millennia BC.
2/ **below** Permanent settlement increased greatly in the 7th millennium BC due to the development of cultivated cereals and domesticated animals.

2/ EARLY SETTLEMENTS IN THE NEAR EAST
- 9th-8th millennia BC
- 7th millennium BC

3/ Skull from Jericho with the features built up in plaster.
4/ Painted plaster figure, with shell inlay to make eyes, from Jericho.
5/ Bone fish hook.
6/ Bone harpoon.
7/ Couple embracing, possibly a fertility object. It is 4 in high and was found at 'Ain Sakhri, a cave in the Judaean desert.
8/ Pottery figure from Teleilat el-Ghassul, found at Sanctuary B, c 3700 BC.
9/ Pottery figure of a sheep, c 3700 BC.
10/ Stone tower from Jericho, Pre-pottery Neolithic A.
11/ **chart left** Domesticated sheep and goats began to replace gazelle as the dominant meat source in Jericho c. 7000 BC. In the period before this date, 38% of bones found were of gazelle and 7% were of sheep and goats, while in the following period only 14% of bones found were of gazelle and 40% were of sheep and goats.

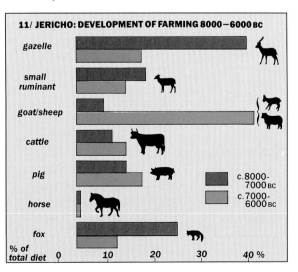

11/ JERICHO: DEVELOPMENT OF FARMING 8000–6000 BC

- gazelle
- small ruminant
- goat/sheep
- cattle
- pig
- horse
- fox

c. 8000-7000 BC
c. 7000-6000 BC

% of total diet: 0 10 20 30 40 %

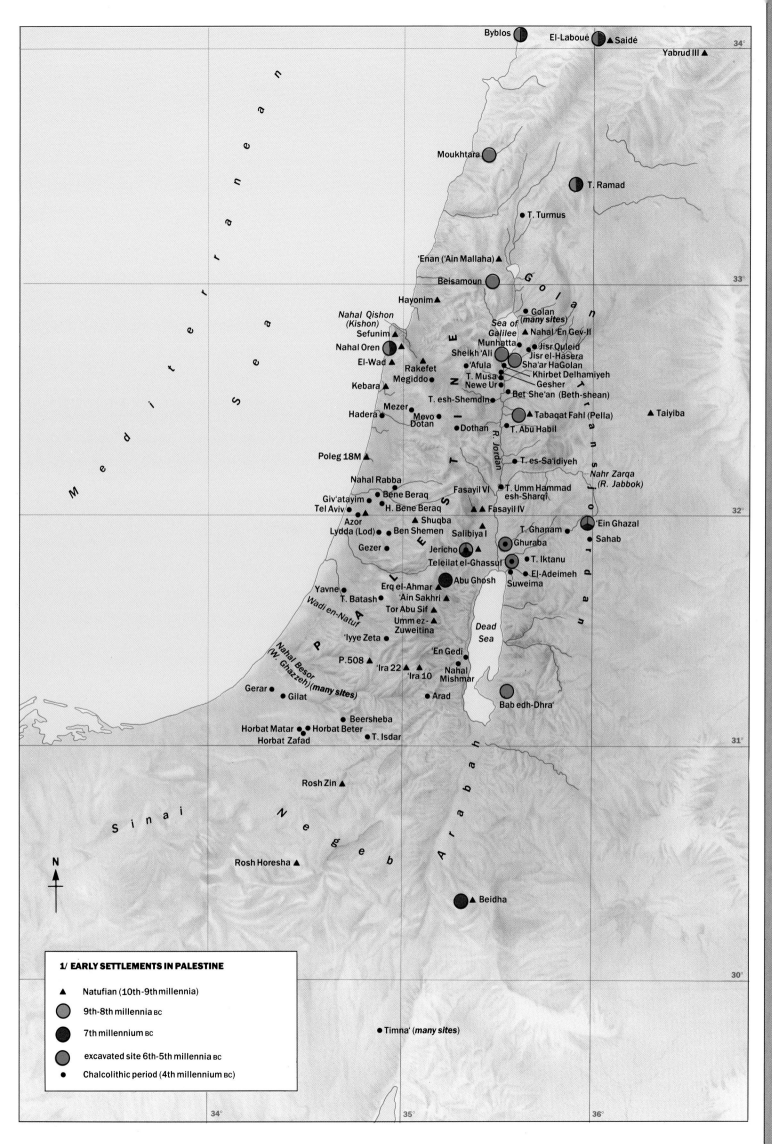

Byblos
El-Laboué   ▲ Saidé
Yabrud III ▲
34°

Moukhtara

T. Ramad

T. Turmus

'Enan ('Ain Mallaha) ▲
Beisamoun
Golan
33°
Hayonim ▲
Golan
(many sites)

Nahal Qishon (Kishon)
Sea of
Galilee   ▲ Nahal 'En Gev-II
Sefunim ▲
Munhatta
Jisr Quleid
Nahal Oren
Sheikh 'Ali
Jisr el-Hasera
El-Wad ▲
'Afula
Sha'ar HaGolan
Rakefet
Khirbet Delhamiyeh
Megiddo
T. Musa   Gesher
Newe Ur
Kebara ▲
Bet She'an (Beth-shean)
T. esh-Shemdin
Mezer
T. Abu Habil
Hadera   Mevo   Tabaqat Fahl (Pella)   ▲ Taiyiba
Dotan
Dothan
T. es-Sa'idiyeh

Poleg 18M ▲
Nahr Zarqa (R. Jabbok)

Nahal Rabba   Fasayil VI   T. Umm Hammad
esh-Sharqi
Giv'atayim   Bene Beraq
Tel Aviv   H. Bene Beraq   ▲ Fasayil IV
Azor
Shuqba   T. Ghanam   'Ein Ghazal
Lydda (Lod)   Ben Shemen   Salibiya I   Ghuraba   Sahab
Gezer
Jericho ▲   T. Iktanu
Teleilat el-Ghassul
Abu Ghosh   El-Adeimeh
Erq el-Ahmar   Suweima
Yavne   'Ain Sakhri ▲
T. Batash   Tor Abu Sif ▲
Wadi en-Natuf   Umm ez-
Zuweitina
'Iyye Zeta   Dead
Sea
Nahal Besor (W. Ghazzeh)   'En Gedi
P.508 ▲   Nahal
'Ira 22 ▲ 'Ira 10 ▲   Mishmar
Gerar   Arad
Gilat
Bab edh-Dhra'
Beersheba
Horbat Matar   Horbat Beter
Horbat Zafad   T. Isdar
31°

Rosh Zin ▲

S i n a i   *N e g e b*   *A r a b a h*

N

Rosh Horesha ▲

Beidha ▲

30°

1/ EARLY SETTLEMENTS IN PALESTINE

▲   Natufian (10th-9th millennia)

⬤   9th-8th millennia BC

⬤   7th millennium BC

⬤   excavated site 6th-5th millennia BC

•   Chalcolithic period (4th millennium BC)

Timna' (*many sites*)

M e d i t e r r a n e a n   S e a

34°   35°   36°

TOWARDS the end of the 4th millennium developments took place in the Levant which led, at the beginning of the Early Bronze Age, to the appearance of towns. The evolution of urban societies had a profound effect on civilization. Large buildings such as fortifications and temples were erected and this required a complex system of social, economic and political organizations. By about 3000 BC many Chalcolithic villages had been abandoned, to be replaced by a smaller number of walled towns, functioning, probably, as centres in a trading network linking Canaan with Egypt. Their most imposing feature was a defensive wall built of rough stones and mud bricks. At Arad, one of the best preserved sites, semi-circular bastions appear at regular intervals, exactly as those depicted in an Egyptian tomb of the 5th dynasty. At Jericho there were both rounded and square towers; and at T. el-Far'ah\(N) two square, mud-brick towers flanked the gateway. Incipient town planning may be seen at Arad, where a palace and a double temple appear to have been separated by a wall from the rest of the town. A large artificial reservoir to conserve the winter rains was also incorporated into the plan. The buildings themselves are of considerable diversity both in design and size, although one basic plan does seem to have been popular for temples and houses alike, namely a rectangular structure with the entrance in the long side and often with benches along the other three. Crafts and industries were at a comparatively low level. Artistic design was limited to cylinder and stamp seals, and the copper tools and weapons were cast in simple, open moulds. Only in pottery was there any real technological progress through the use of better clay, the wheel and better firing in a controlled kiln such as that discovered at T. el-Far'ah\(N). Ovoid jars of the period have been found in Egypt, providing tangible proof of the oil trade between the two areas.

The Early Bronze Age was not a peaceful period, to judge from the frequency of repair and strengthening of fortifications at

1/ map below Urbanization in the Early Bronze Age. Information about EBA Canaan comes from Pharaoh Phiops I's (c 2332-2283 BC) descriptions of his campaigns there.

2/ below left An artist's impression of the Beth-yerah granary. B. Mazar et al, who excavated this site, found enough evidence to produce a ground-plan of the structure, but could not attest its original shape. They theorized that it may have been a group of free-standing silos. However, one suggestion, illustrated here, supposes that the silos were encased within a larger structure. The building measured 100 x 130ft and had a capacity of 800 tons of grain. Each silo was about 30ft in diameter. The construction was of mud brick covered with plaster. The roofs were probably covered with reeds and mud.

3/ right At Arad, excavations have enabled a partial reconstruction to be made of the city. Evidence for town planning appears in the location of private dwellings in one quarter (top) and official buildings and temples in others. The black outline diagram shows the total area of the site. The semi-circular defensive towers accord well with Egyptian art (see **4**).

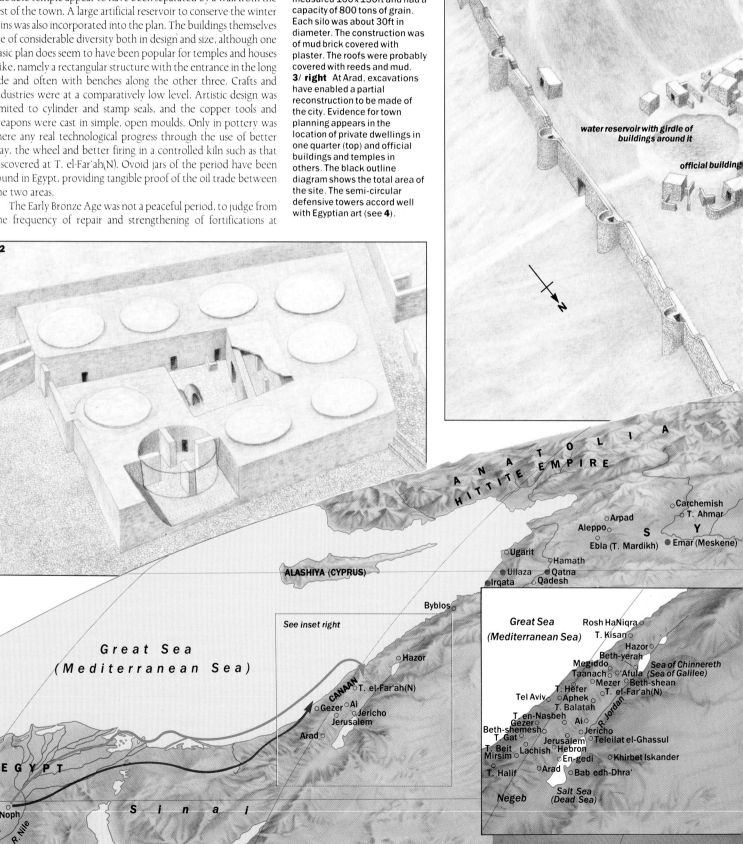

3/ RECONSTRUCTION OF ARAD

south-western gate

dwellings

water reservoir with girdle of buildings around it

official building

N

2

ANATOLIA

HITTITE EMPIRE

Carchemish
T. Ahmar
Arpad
Aleppo
S
Y
Ebla (T. Mardikh)
Emar (Meskene)
Ugarit
Hamath
ALASHIYA (CYPRUS)
Ullaza
Qatna
Irqata
Qadesh

Byblos

See inset right

Great Sea
(Mediterranean Sea)

Hazor

Great Sea
(Mediterranean Sea)
Rosh HaNiqra
T. Kisan
Hazor
Beth-yerah
Megiddo
Taanach
Sea of Chinnereth
(Sea of Galilee)
'Afula
Mezer
Beth-shean
T. Hefer
T. el-Far'ah(N)
Tel Aviv
Aphek
T. Balatah
T. en-Nasbeh
Ai
Gezer
Jericho
Beth-shemesh
Jerusalem
Teleilat el-Ghassul
T. Gat
Hebron
T. Beit
Lachish
En-gedi
Khirbet Iskander
Mirsim
T. Halif
Arad
Bab edh-Dhra'
Negeb
Salt Sea
(Dead Sea)

CANAAN
T. el-Far'ah(N)
Gezer
Ai
Jericho
Jerusalem
Arad

Great Sea
(Mediterranean Sea)

EGYPT

Sinai

Noph
R. Nile

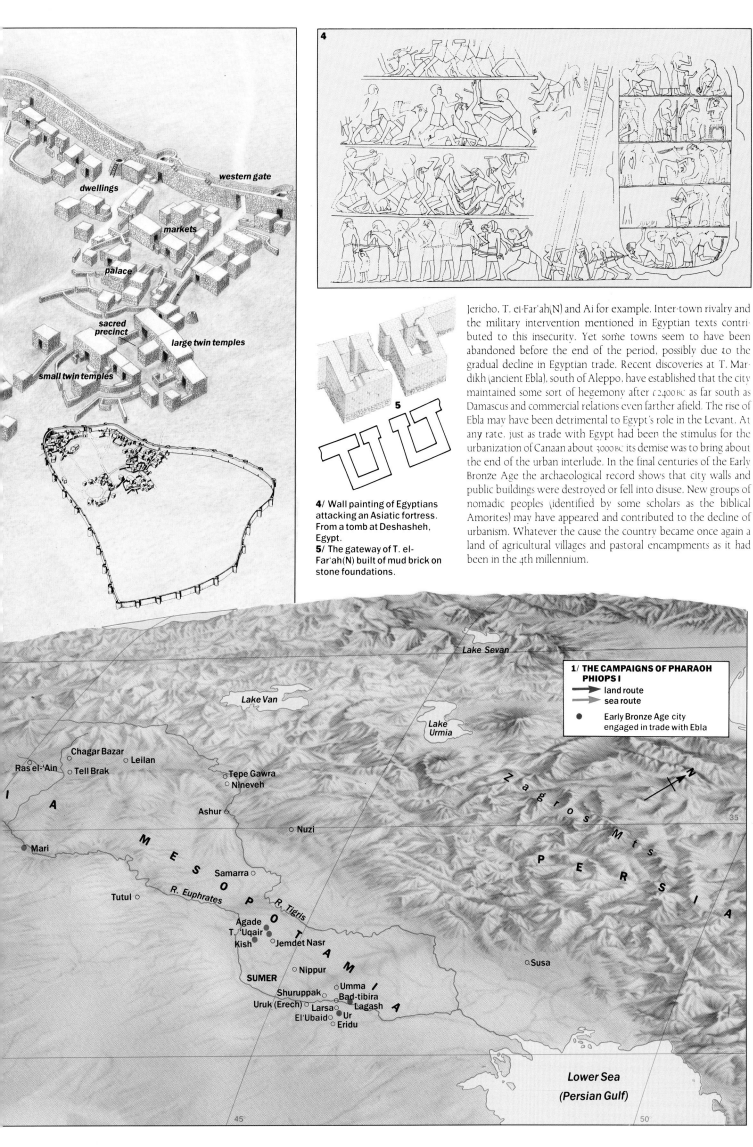

western gate

dwellings

markets

palace

sacred
precinct

large twin temples

small twin temples

Jericho, T. el-Far'ah(N) and Ai for example. Inter-town rivalry and the military intervention mentioned in Egyptian texts contributed to this insecurity. Yet some towns seem to have been abandoned before the end of the period, possibly due to the gradual decline in Egyptian trade. Recent discoveries at T. Mardikh (ancient Ebla), south of Aleppo, have established that the city maintained some sort of hegemony after c 2400 BC as far south as Damascus and commercial relations even farther afield. The rise of Ebla may have been detrimental to Egypt's role in the Levant. At any rate, just as trade with Egypt had been the stimulus for the urbanization of Canaan about 3000 BC its demise was to bring about the end of the urban interlude. In the final centuries of the Early Bronze Age the archaeological record shows that city walls and public buildings were destroyed or fell into disuse. New groups of nomadic peoples (identified by some scholars as the biblical Amorites) may have appeared and contributed to the decline of urbanism. Whatever the cause the country became once again a land of agricultural villages and pastoral encampments as it had been in the 4th millennium.

4/ Wall painting of Egyptians attacking an Asiatic fortress. From a tomb at Deshasheh, Egypt.
5/ The gateway of T. el-Far'ah(N) built of mud brick on stone foundations.

Lake Sevan

Lake Van

Lake Urmia

1/ THE CAMPAIGNS OF PHARAOH PHIOPS I
→ land route
→ sea route
● Early Bronze Age city engaged in trade with Ebla

Chagar Bazar
Leilan
Ras el-'Ain
Tell Brak
Tepe Gawra
Nineveh
Ashur
Nuzi

Z a g r o s   M t s

Mari

M E S O P O T A M I A

Samarra

R. Euphrates
R. Tigris

Tutul

P E R S I A

Agade
T. 'Uqair
Kish
Jemdet Nasr

Nippur

Susa

SUMER

Umma
Bad-tibira
Shuruppak
Uruk (Erech)   Larsa   Lagash
El'Ubaid   Ur
Eridu

Lower Sea
(Persian Gulf)

BRAHAM, the earliest of the Hebrew patriarchs, left his home in Ur, one of the principal cities of southern Mesopotamia, and journeyed to Haran ('crossroads') in the north and from thence to Canaan. From the biblical account of this decisive journey given in GEN 11.31-12.5 it is impossible to trace his specific route with any degree of certainty and scholars disagree as to the temporal setting (estimates range from 2000 to 1000 BC). However, commonly used trade routes between cities which flourished in the 2nd millennium BC are known from cuneiform sources and it is likely that a patriarchal caravan would have followed one of these. Among detailed surviving itineraries is one of an army or caravan moving by named stages from near Ur and up the R. Tigris, via Ashur and Nineveh, before striking westwards to Haran in the early 18th century BC. Another text describes the nine-month journey by Zimri-Lim, king of Mari, in c1760BC, up the R. Euphrates and R. Khabur, thence to Haran and on to Aleppo (Khalab). There is a well-attested route which extended from R. Balikh to Haran, south to Aleppo, and then via Qatna, Damascus and Hazor, along the Palestine ridge to Shechem, Hebron and Beersheba.

Already in the 2nd millennium major cities recorded their imports of non-local items such as gold, silver, precious stones and wine, together with the commodities essential to their industrial and technological processes (eg. copper, tin, oil) as well as luxury items, textiles, precious objects and furnishings. Valuable wood from Lebanon was floated down the coast or dragged to the major streams for transport to the eastern cities as tribute. In the north,

THE FLOOD FROM THE EPIC OF GILGAMESH

The Assyrian version of the story of the Flood was discovered on a clay tablet found at Nineveh (below). The tablet, now in the British Museum, is 6in high and forms part of an epic poem which is especially interesting when compared with some of the events in the book of Genesis.

Utnapishtim, the hero of the flood from Shuruppak, tells of the flood

Shuruppak – a city which thou knowest,
And which on Euphrates' banks is situate –
That city was ancient, as were the gods within it,
When their heart led the great gods to produce the flood.

The god Ea orders Utnapishtim to make preparation
'Man of Shuruppak, son of Ubar-Tutu,
Tear down this house, build a ship!
Give up possessions, seek thou life.
Forswear worldly goods and keep the soul alive!
Aboard the ship take thou the seed of all living things.
The ship that thou shalt build,
Her dimensions shall be to measure.
Equal shall be her width and her length.'

Utnapishtim proceeds to build the ship
On the fifth day I laid her framework.
One whole acre was her floor space,
Ten dozen cubits the height of each of her walls,
Ten dozen cubits each edge of the square deck.
I laid out the contours and joined her together.

I provided her with six decks,
Dividing her thus into seven parts.
Her floor plan I divided into nine parts.
I hammered water-plugs into her.
I saw to the punting-poles and laid in supplies.
All my family and kin I made go aboard the ship.
The beasts of the field, the wild creatures of the field,
All the craftsmen I made go aboard.

The rain-storm
Six days and six nights
Blows the flood wind, as the south-storm sweeps the land.
When the seventh day arrived,
The flood-carrying south-storm subsided in the battle.
Which it had fought like an army.

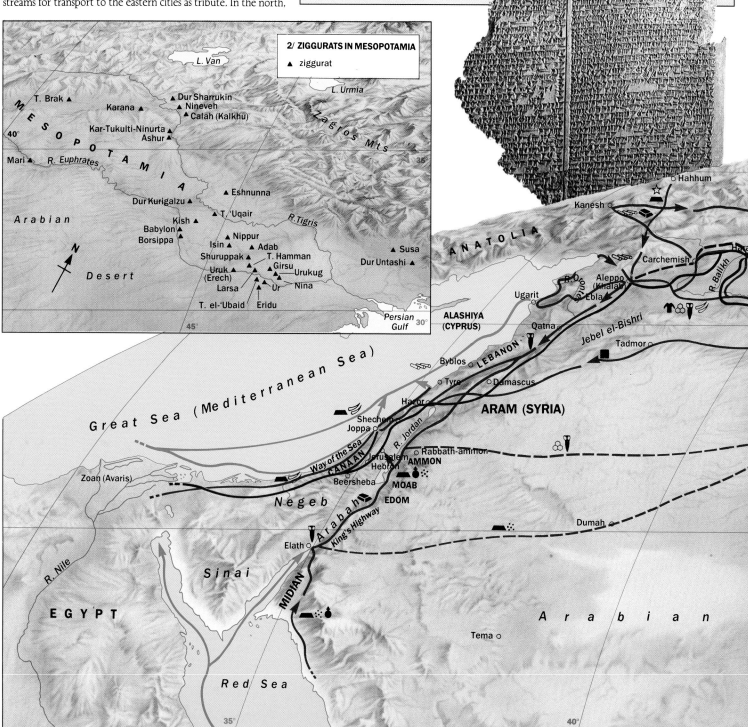

2/ ZIGGURATS IN MESOPOTAMIA

▲ ziggurat

tin from sources east of Mesopotamia was exchanged for copper, some tin reaching Canaan via Hazor and Mari. The major route followed in and near Palestine was named the 'Way of the Sea' and was the Philistine road from Egypt. It was supplemented by sea routes both to the Philistine coastal cities and to the northern ports such as Byblos, Tyre and Ugarit.

The particular tradition of Abraham, the Hebrew patriarch, coming from Ur in Mesopotamia is matched by certain more general links between the great centre of civilization to the east and the Bible. Details of the great flood described in GEN 6-8 resemble those found in the Gilgamesh epic from an earlier time. In the Mesopotamian epic of the flood the hero Utnapishtim is instructed in detail by one of the gods of the flood to build a ship to save himself and 'the seed of all living beings'. After six days of storm the sea grew quiet and the ship came to rest on a high mountain. A dove was released, then a swallow, and finally a raven which found the waters diminished enough for Utnapishtim to disembark and offer a sacrifice to the gods. Details of the more ancient tradition involving many gods are shared by the monotheistic flood story found in the Bible.

Abraham's journey from Ur to Canaan has left no visible traces along the route. Yet this memorable trek is deeply impressed into later tradition as an example of a bold adventure in obedience to a divine command. In later writings it is 'the God of Abraham', and the land which Israel later came to occupy is that which 'Yahweh gave unto Abraham'. But from a wider perspective there is the influence of Mesopotamian culture found in Israel. The tower in GEN 10.4 'whose top may reach unto heaven' is clearly a reference to the stepped temple tower, or ziggurat, which was seen throughout Mesopotamia. The flood story of Gilgamesh and the laws of Hammurabi, also attest these links. The story of Abraham's response to a call when he was 'beyond the River' has cast a long and decisive shadow over Jewish centuries, and even over those of the other faiths of Christianity and Islam.

THE MOSAIC LAW

The Lord said to Moses, 'Come up to me on the mountain, and wait there; and I will give you the tablets of stone, with the law and the commandment, which I have written for their instruction...'   EX 24.12

'...you shall give life for life, eye for eye, tooth for tooth, hand for hand, foot for foot, burn for burn, wound for wound, stripe for stripe.'   EX 21.23-25

'...But if the ox has been accustomed to gore in the past, and its owner has been warned but has not kept it in, and it kills a man or a woman, the ox shall be stoned and its owner also shall be put to death.'
EX 21.29

THE LAWS OF HAMMURABI

'I, Hammurabi, am the king of justice, to whom Shamash committed law. My words are choice; my deeds have no equal; it is only to the fool that they are empty...'

'If a seignior has destroyed the eye of a member of the aristocracy, they shall destroy his eye.'

'If he had broken another seignior's bone, they shall break his bone.'

'If a seignior's ox was a gorer and his city council made it known to him that it was a gorer, but he did not pad its horns or tie up his ox, and that ox gored to death a member of the aristocracy, he shall give half a mina of silver.'

1/ map below The ancient Near East was not a trackless waste but was covered with an extensive network of trade routes.
2/ map left Distribution of ziggurats or temple towers in Mesopotamia.

3/ above Black diorite *stela* inscribed with about 250 laws portraying life and society in Mesopotamia. The scene at the top shows the sun-god Shamash committing the laws to Hammurabi, king of Babylon, 1792-1750 BC. Height c.7ft.

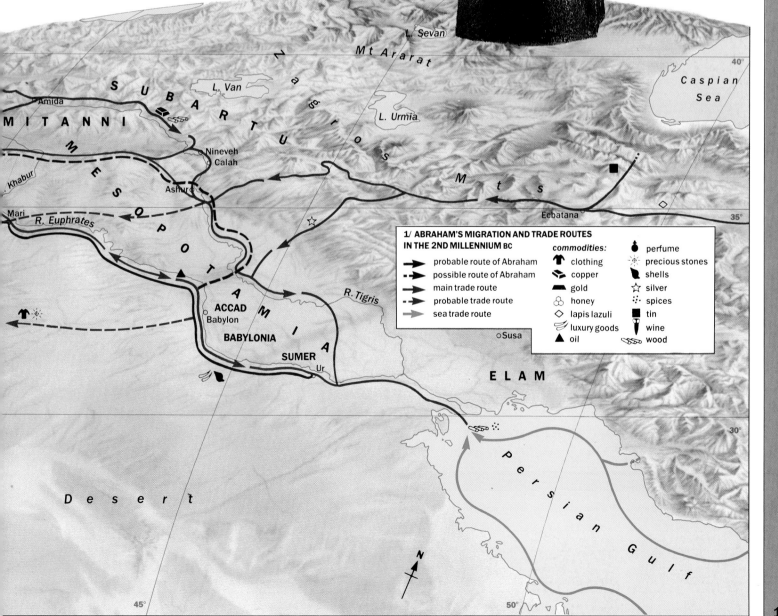

1/ ABRAHAM'S MIGRATION AND TRADE ROUTES IN THE 2ND MILLENNIUM BC

	commodities:	
→ probable route of Abraham	👕 clothing	🏺 perfume
⇢ possible route of Abraham	copper	precious stones
→ main trade route	gold	shells
⇢ probable trade route	🐝 honey	☆ silver
→ sea trade route	◇ lapis lazuli	⋮ spices
	luxury goods	▮ tin
	▲ oil	wine
		wood

THE HEBREW patriarchs, whose progeny was most closely associated with the land of Canaan, had strong ties with the distant Aramaean city of Haran. It was a stopping place for Abraham; Isaac took Rebekah for a wife there; and Jacob spent 20 years of his life tending the flocks of Laban in payment for his two wives, Leah and Rachel. Archaeology has revealed a great deal of the culture and history of this region over which the patriarchs are said to have travelled.

The patriarchs Abraham and Isaac generally confined themselves in their wanderings to the central hill country of Palestine, along the watershed route from Shechem to Hebron via Bethel and on to the biblical Negeb at Beersheba. The only forays toward the coast were to Gerar (GEN 20.26). Abraham made a military expedition to Dan and to near Damascus (GEN 14.14-15) but in general the patriarchs are portrayed as pastoralists who eschewed the urban life of Canaan.

Jacob went farther afield, even as far as Haran, a major city in north-western Mesopotamia. Haran had two claims to fame: its position on international trade routes (page 14), and as the centre for the worship of Sin, the moon-god. Haran is associated with the

1/ **map below** The wanderings of Abraham in Canaan; the wars of Chedorlaomer in Transjordan, the Dead Sea area and the south as related in GEN 14 (exact locations of peoples are conjectural); and settlement patterns in the Middle Bronze Age.

2/ **map right** GEN 28-29 describes how Jacob left Canaan and went to Haran, where he married his two cousins, Leah and Rachel. He eventually returned home over 20 years later and was united with Isaac at Hebron.

3/ **map left** Towns mentioned in Egyptian Execration texts.

4/ Execration figure. In this form of magic, a curse was made effective by smashing the figure. Such texts reveal the names of foreign rulers considered as enemies by the Egyptians.

5/ Zimri-Lim ruled Mari from about 1800 BC until his defeat in c1760 by Hammurabi of Babylon.

6/ Fresco from Mari showing a priest and sacrificial bull.

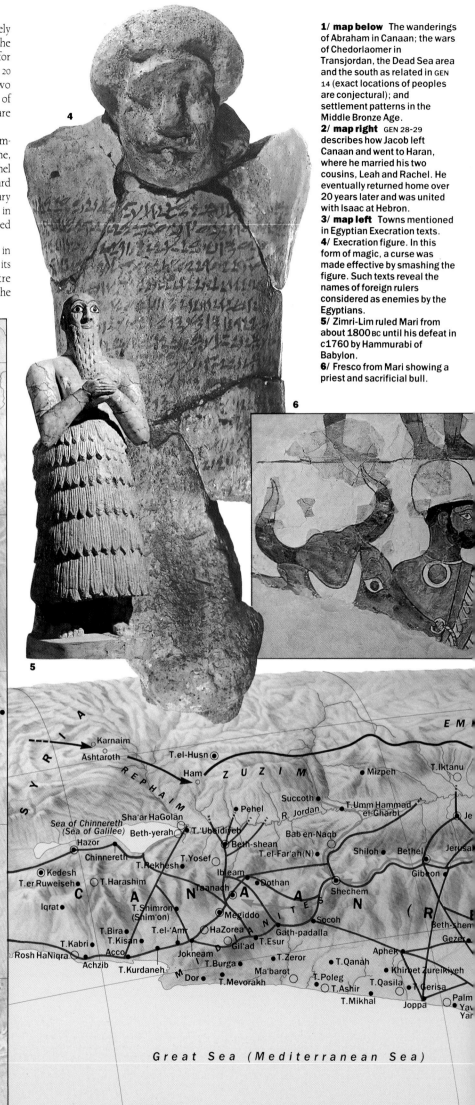

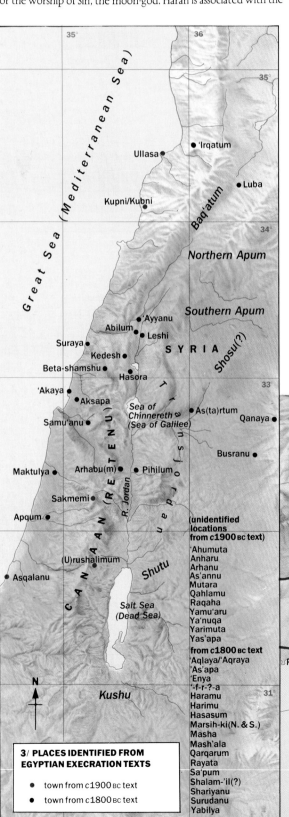

3/ PLACES IDENTIFIED FROM EGYPTIAN EXECRATION TEXTS

● town from c1900 BC text
● town from c1800 BC text

(unidentified locations from c1900 BC text)
'Ahumuta
Anharu
Arhanu
As'annu
Mutara
Qahlamu
Raqaha
Yamu'aru
Ya'nuqa
Yarimuta
Yas'apa

from c1800 BC text
'Aqlaya/'Aqraya
'As'apa
'Enya
'-f-r-?-a
Haramu
Harimu
Hasasum
Marsih-ki(N. & S.)
Masha
Mash'ala
Qarqarum
Rayata
Sa'pum
Shalam-'il(?)
Shariyanu
Surudanu
Yabilya

region Paddan-aram, the area between the R. Khabur in the east and the Euphrates to the west.

Jacob's journey from Beersheba was first to Bethel (Luz), the site of his famous dream of the ladder reaching to heaven and the divine promise of his destiny. From Bethel the road north passed through Shiloh, Damascus, Hamath and Carchemish, then turned east to Haran. Upon reaching Haran, Jacob married his cousin Leah, and seven years later, her sister, Rachel. After a dispute with his father-in-law, Laban, Jacob fled to Palestine via Transjordan. However, despite giving Jacob three days start, Laban caught up with him somewhere in the highland region of Gilead, covering the distance in a mere seven days. After a tense and ill-tempered confrontation, the two men concluded a covenant by heaping up stones at Galeed ('heap of witness'). From there Jacob continued toward Mahanaim and Penuel, where he had another divine encounter and became reconciled to his offended brother Esau. He proceeded on to Succoth, where he built a house and booths for his cattle (GEN 33.17). At Shechem he built an altar (GEN 35.7). When his wife Rachael died, Jacob buried her in Bethlehem and finally reached Hebron, some 20 years after starting his journey to Paddan-aram (GEN 31.38).

EGYPTIAN EXECRATION TEXTS

Important information about the towns of Palestine in the early 2nd millennium BC appears in an unusual collection of text written in Egyptian on small plates and figurines. Mentioned are potential enemies of the pharaoh, including the foreign rulers of Retenu (Canaan). Along with the personal names are their towns, many of which are known from the Bible and other texts. The pattern of settlement displays a concentration in the plains similar to that which continues into the Late Bronze Age. Only Shechem and Jerusalem are listed in the hill country and the smaller towns of Shiloh, Bethel and Beth-zur are not mentioned. Many locations from the earlier texts of c1900 BC are unidentified.

The history and distribution of settlements during the first half of the 2nd millennium BC is available from archaeological excavations. The semi-nomadic pastoralists of the MB I (c2200-2000 BC), known chiefly from burial sites, were succeeded during MB IIA (2000-1750 BC) by a settled population in urban centres which continued to flourish in MB IIB (1750-1550 BC). It is sometimes proposed that the patriarchs came into the land in the MB I Age, but there were then no city states, no known contact with Egypt and no settlements in the Beersheba area. Nor do the cities mentioned in the Bible, in connection with the wanderings of the patriarchs, fit into the map drawn from the Execration texts of the MB IIA Age. However, the biblical narratives mention peoples around about, such as the Philistines, Midianites and Ishmaelites, and the Edomites, Ammonites and Moabites, nations said to be descended from important figures in the stories themselves. These people belong to a period after the MB and LB Ages. Whenever it was that the patriarchs lived, the milieu of the biblical writings about them seems to derive from the end of the Bronze Age or the beginning of the Early Iron Age.

ARCHAEOLOGY AT MARI AND EBLA

Excavations at Mari on the Upper Euphrates and at Ebla in northern Syria, reveal a high culture and extensive trade in the Levant. The Palace of Zimri-Lim at Mari, discovered in 1933, provides a tangible record of life in this region during the first half of the 2nd millennium BC. The cuneiform tablets – some 25,000 texts have been found – are even more explicit. Mari traded with the cities of Canaan, Hattushash in Anatolia, and even with the centres of commerce in Alashiya (Cyprus) and Crete. Shipments of tin from Hazor and Laish (Dan) are also mentioned.

Contemporary with Mari was Ebla, discovered in 1964 at T. Mardikh. The site contained thousands of cuneiform tablets providing details about international trade and politics from Mesopotamia to Palestine between c2400 to 2250 BC. T. Mardikh was also occupied in the later Old Syrian period (c2000-1600 BC). Architectural features from this later period provide significant connections with Canaan.

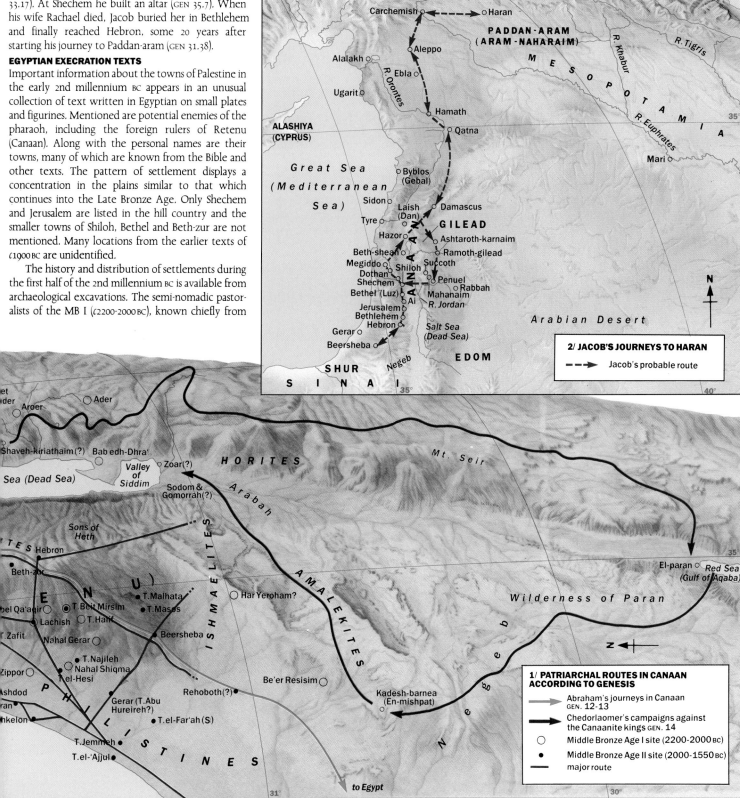

2/ JACOB'S JOURNEYS TO HARAN
- - - → Jacob's probable route

1/ PATRIARCHAL ROUTES IN CANAAN ACCORDING TO GENESIS
→ Abraham's journeys in Canaan GEN. 12-13
→ Chedorlaomer's campaigns against the Canaanite kings GEN. 14
○ Middle Bronze Age I site (2200-2000 BC)
● Middle Bronze Age II site (2000-1550 BC)
— major route

THE sojourn of Israel in Egypt is frequently referred to in the Bible and the deliverance from Egyptian bondage is a central theme in the ritual for the annual celebration of the Passover. GEN 37-50 recounts Joseph's entry into Egypt, his rise to power and the eventual settling of his family, the progenitors of the tribes of Israel, there to be saved from a famine in the land of Canaan. It is in these stories that Egyptian daily life is pictured in a detail found nowhere else in the Bible. Extra-biblical sources from Egypt provide significant parallels to the background pictured in the Joseph stories. However it must be kept in mind that Joseph is not mentioned in any of the Egyptian writings and that the biblical narratives are not specific as to the names of the pharaohs or to any datable events. Thus it is not possible to place Joseph with any degree of certainty within a definite historical period.

The Midianite or Ishmaelite traders (both names appear in the Bible) who brought Joseph to Egypt were one of many groups visiting Egypt during the first half of the 2nd millennium BC. The Canaanite towns of Shechem and Dothan which feature in Joseph's travels are also attested in external sources for this general period. It is significant that the list of one large Egyptian household of c1740 BC contained the names of 79 domestic servants, over half of them being 'Asiatics' with Semitic names. While many Asiatics spent their life in Egypt in this humble fashion, others, however, are known to have reached very high office, just as Joseph is said to have done eventually.

Prominent in the Joseph narratives is the account of his brothers coming to buy grain at the time of famine in their own land. As a fertile country Egypt would normally produce crops in excess. There are records of starving foreigners arriving to ask for assistance. However, sometimes the harvest failed repeatedly and an event such as this may be the basis for the tradition of 'seven lean years' which also appears in the Joseph narrative (GEN 41).

Many other biblical details reflect Egyptian practices. A section of an ancient prison register and other monuments reflect the Egyptian system at work. Major prisons had a director (cf the role of the captain of the guard in GEN 40.3 and keepers like the keeper or warder of GEN 39.22). Such prisons 'filed' inmates under seven entries from name and sex through to a final discharge tick, equivalent to 'case closed'. The initial cause of Joseph's imprisonment was the evidence and lies of his owner's wife (GEN 39). The Papyrus D'Orbiney, dated about 1225 BC, tells of the attempted seduction of a moral young man by his elder brother's wife. Having had her advances angrily rejected she then accuses the young man of attempting to rape her. This part of the story bears a marked resemblance to the biblical incident of Joseph's rejection of the advances of Potiphar's wife (GEN 39.7-18).

Butlers or cupbearers were prominent at the courts of the pharaohs, and came to play important roles in administration at the king's direct command. So the appearance of a royal butler and baker in the Joseph narrative is no surprise. Joseph's reported ability to interpret dreams accords with Egyptian beliefs in the importance of such practices and there exist manuals which give instruction in this art. When he was appointed to high office he was given a collar of gold and the royal seal. This was a regular custom. Finally the manner in which Joseph was embalmed and laid in a coffin was not a Hebrew custom but was typical of the practices of the Egyptians (GEN 50.26).

THE COMING OF THE HYKSOS

In Egyptian history the most prominent and best remembered incursion of a Semitic people into the land was that of the Hyksos. Scholarly attempts have been made to find a connection between the entry of Joseph into Egypt with the history of the Hyksos invasion, but the problems of such a connection have become increasingly complex so that agreement can only be reached upon the fact that foreigners did enter Egypt from Canaan over an extended period of time. The coming of the Hyksos, however, is the most fully documented example of this movement of people from the hills and desert of Canaan to the fertile land of Egypt.

From the 19th and 18th centuries BC, in the later 12th dynasty, a growing number of Semitic foreigners (Hik-shos, meaning 'chiefs of foreign countries') found places in Egyptian society, high or low, attached to households or serving such institutions as temples and their administrations. During the 13th dynasty the flow increased, and eventually there appeared one pharaoh with a Semitic name (Khendjer, cf Semitic hanzir, 'boar'). During 1750-1650 BC, one or more West-Semitic chiefs may have succeeded in becoming local ruler of part of the East Delta (the so-called '16th dynasty'). As the 12th and 13th dynasty kings had the key centre of Ro-waty (and possibly a summer residence there), adjoining Avaris, such local 'naturalized' foreign chiefs may have become involved with Egyptian royal politics of the day. Certainly, at about 1674 BC, one of these Hyksos rulers finally took the Egyptian throne not only in the East Delta but back in Memphis itself (with Itj-towy, its administrative satellite 'new town'), founding a new regime, the so-called 15th or Hyksos dynasty.

The new rulers imposed their control over all Egypt, treating as vassals both the line of the 13th dynasty, restricted to Thebes and the south, and a shadowy 14th dynasty in the West Delta. The summer capital was extended (or changed) to Avaris itself, centre of the worship of the god Seth, nearest equivalent to the weather gods of the Levant such as Baal, Teshub, or Adad.

The Hyksos kings adopted Egyptian royal style and retained a basically Egyptian bureaucracy, but introduced fellow-foreigners into the administration. The extent of the authority of the Hyksos kings in Canaan is uncertain; the concept of a vast 'Hyksos empire' lacks sufficient factual foundation. Certainly King Apophis was termed 'Ruler of Retenu' by his opponent Kamosis of Thebes; this could imply rule of part of Palestine. The distribution of Hyksos royal scarab-seals in Canaan, plus a broken stone lintel with remains of royal titles of about this age from near Yibna, would combine to suggest a sphere of direct rule as far north as Joppa, and reaching along the western foothills of Canaan from Gezer to Tell Beit Mirsim. Stray finds would extend communications as far as Jericho and Carmel. Much more distant trade or diplomacy might lie behind the objects naming King Khyan found in Crete and at Boğazköy in Asia Minor.

2

2/ Relief of starving people from the temple causeway of King Unis.
3/ List of servants in an Egyptian household c 1740 BC.
4/ Weather god Baal, equated with Seth who was worshipped at Avaris.
5/ Relief of an Egyptian official, Paset, being promoted to high office under Sethos I.
6/ Wall painting, from Khnumhotep's tomb, of Asiatics bringing eye paint. Their beards and coloured garments set them apart from the white-skirted Egyptians. Height of figures c 1ft 6in.

3

5

6

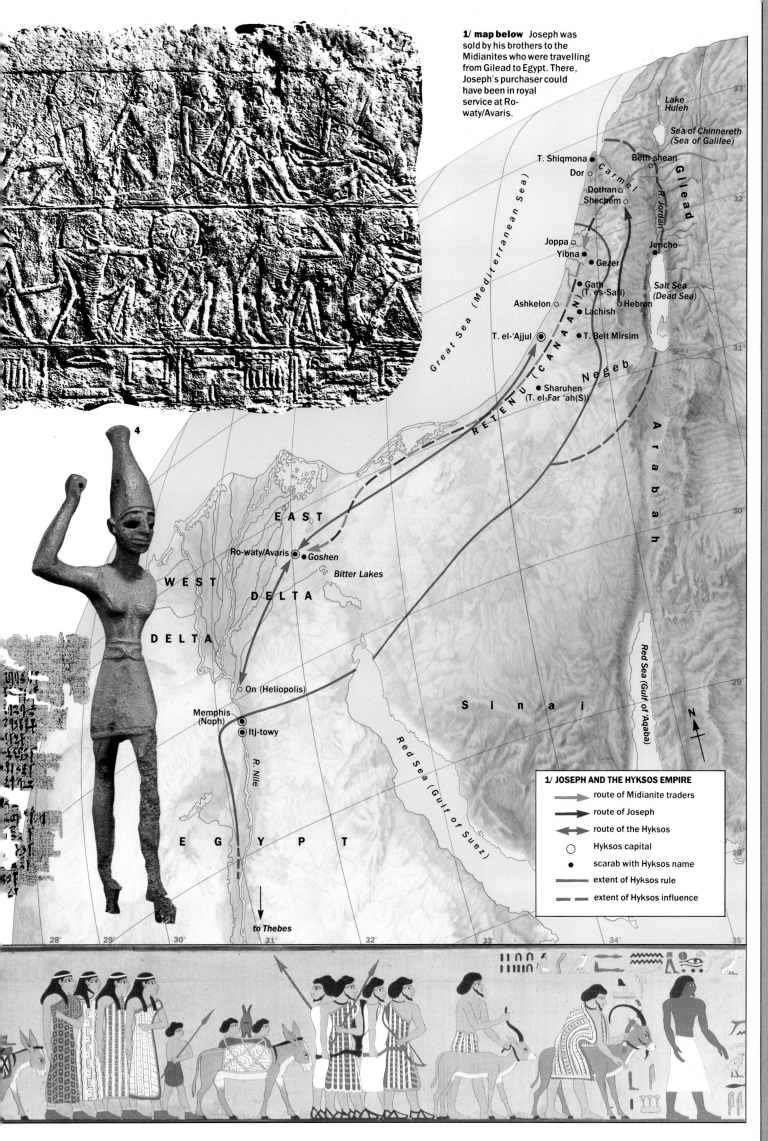

1/ map below Joseph was sold by his brothers to the Midianites who were travelling from Gilead to Egypt. There, Joseph's purchaser could have been in royal service at Ro-waty/Avaris.

1/ JOSEPH AND THE HYKSOS EMPIRE

→ route of Midianite traders

→ route of Joseph

↔ route of the Hyksos

○ Hyksos capital

● scarab with Hyksos name

— extent of Hyksos rule

- - - extent of Hyksos influence

THE patriarchal stories mention but a few cities in Palestine and only about a dozen of these can be identified on a map. The book of Genesis ends with the Hebrews settling down to live in Egypt. Their story continues in the book of Exodus with their oppression and departure – one tradition is that they were in Egypt for 400 years (GEN 15.13) – and eventual conquest of many strong Canaanite cities of the Promised Land. In the Bible itself there is no clue as to what happened in the land of Palestine or what the patterns of settlement were between the time of the patriarchs' entry into Egypt and the Exodus. These blank pages in the historical geography of the land have been filled in from sources found in Egypt. Eight of the pharaohs made military expeditions into Palestine and Syria that cover a period of about 300 years (c1500-1200 BC). In their lists of cities conquered and the routes of their marches there appear the names of about 90 cities and towns of Canaan, many of which figure large in the subsequent history of Israel.

The struggle to free Egypt from Hyksos rule (pages 18-19) began in Thebes, when Kamosis, the third king of the 17th dynasty, attacked Hyksos protégés in Middle Egypt and made an unsuccessful attempt to take Avaris, the Hyksos capital. His brother Amosis I did take Avaris in his eleventh year, pursued the Hyksos and captured the stronghold of Sharuhen (T. el-Far'ah) after a three-year siege.

It was Tuthmosis III (1504-1450 BC) who established Egypt's control over Canaan by making campaigns into Asia almost annually during the 20-year period from the 22nd to the 42nd year of his reign. In the so-called 'annals', carved on the walls of the Temple of Amon at Thebes as a memorial to the god who had given him victory, Tuthmosis is responsible for one of the most factually reliable sources for the geography and history of Palestine.

The account of the battle of Megiddo is unique in the amount of topographical detail provided. This sweeping victory of Tuthmosis III over a Syrian coalition led by the king of Qadesh, in mid-May 1482 BC, displays the tactical genius and daring of the pharaoh. The Canaanite coalition had gathered on the plains of Megiddo and occupied the best tactical position. Not knowing by which of the three possible routes the Egyptians intended to negotiate the Carmel range, the Canaanites chose to block with their troops the two most obvious routes. Tuthmosis, however, rejecting his officers' more cautious advice, decided to march his army single file through the narrow pass directly to Megiddo, taking the enemy completely by surprise. At noon the vanguard debouched into the plain, and an hour later Tuthmosis planted his headquarters on the bank of the brook south of Megiddo. Eventually the Canaanites broke ranks and ran. Megiddo was placed under siege, and six months later it capitulated. Subsequent Egyptian activity was directed towards reducing the power of Tunip on the Middle Orontes, and checking the spread of the Mitannian empire from beyond the Euphrates.

In his seventh year of reign, Amenophis II, son of Tuthmosis III, began his 'first campaign' (as sole ruler) against his arch-rival Mitanni. The first encounter took place at Shemesh-adam (Shamshu-'Adam), and the northernmost town mentioned is Aleppo (Khalab). He arrived at Niyi where he was received with fawning respect. An intelligence report which he received indicated a local attempt to dislodge an Egyptian garrison at a place, the name of which can possibly be taken as Ugarit. Amenophis went in person to that city, quelled the rebellion. Ten days after his arrival at Niyi he camped at Salqa, a town which was known to belong to the kingdom of Alalakh. After plundering the village of Mansatu, Amenophis was cordially received at two unidentified towns north of Qadesh. Afterwards, Amenophis went hunting in the forest of Lebo (Lebo-hamath) and then proceeded to put down resistance at Khashabu, in the Lebanese Beqa'a Valley.

In year 9, Amenophis II was again on the road to Retenu (Canaan), visiting Aphek, Socoh, Yaham, Adoren and through the valley of Jezreel to Anuhartu and Geba-somen where the ruler was summarily arrested and a new ruler was appointed.

In addition to geographical information, the inscriptions of Amenophis II also give a glimpse into the social strata of the Levant during the 15th century BC. Along with lists of booty are also rulers, the oligarchs who supported them, including the chariot warriors, and the names of geographical groups such as Canaanites, the people of Nukhashshe (Syria north of Tunip), bedouin and the 'outcasts' ('apiru).

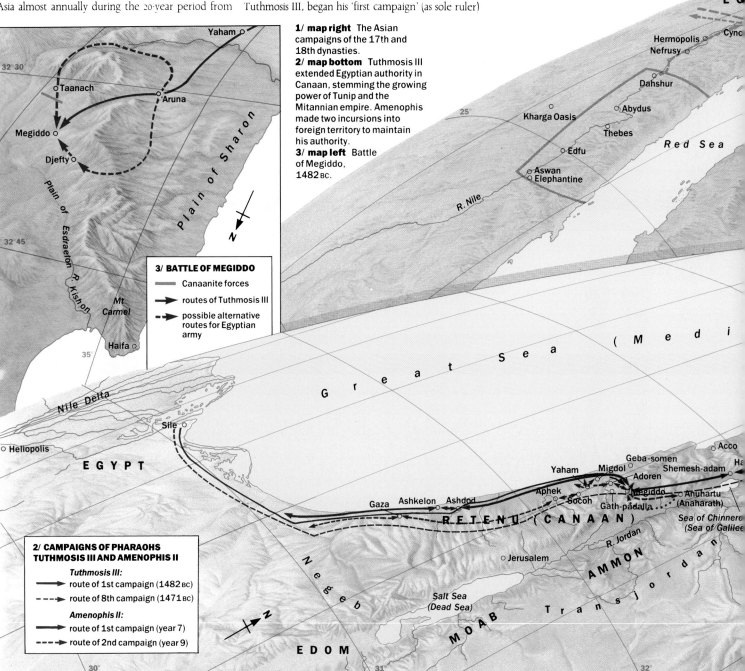

1/ map right The Asian campaigns of the 17th and 18th dynasties.
2/ map bottom Tuthmosis III extended Egyptian authority in Canaan, stemming the growing power of Tunip and the Mitannian empire. Amenophis made two incursions into foreign territory to maintain his authority.
3/ map left Battle of Megiddo, 1482 BC.

3/ BATTLE OF MEGIDDO
— Canaanite forces
→ routes of Tuthmosis III
⇢ possible alternative routes for Egyptian army

2/ CAMPAIGNS OF PHARAOHS TUTHMOSIS III AND AMENOPHIS II

Tuthmosis III:
→ route of 1st campaign (1482 BC)
⇢ route of 8th campaign (1471 BC)

Amenophis II:
→ route of 1st campaign (year 7)
⇢ route of 2nd campaign (year 9)

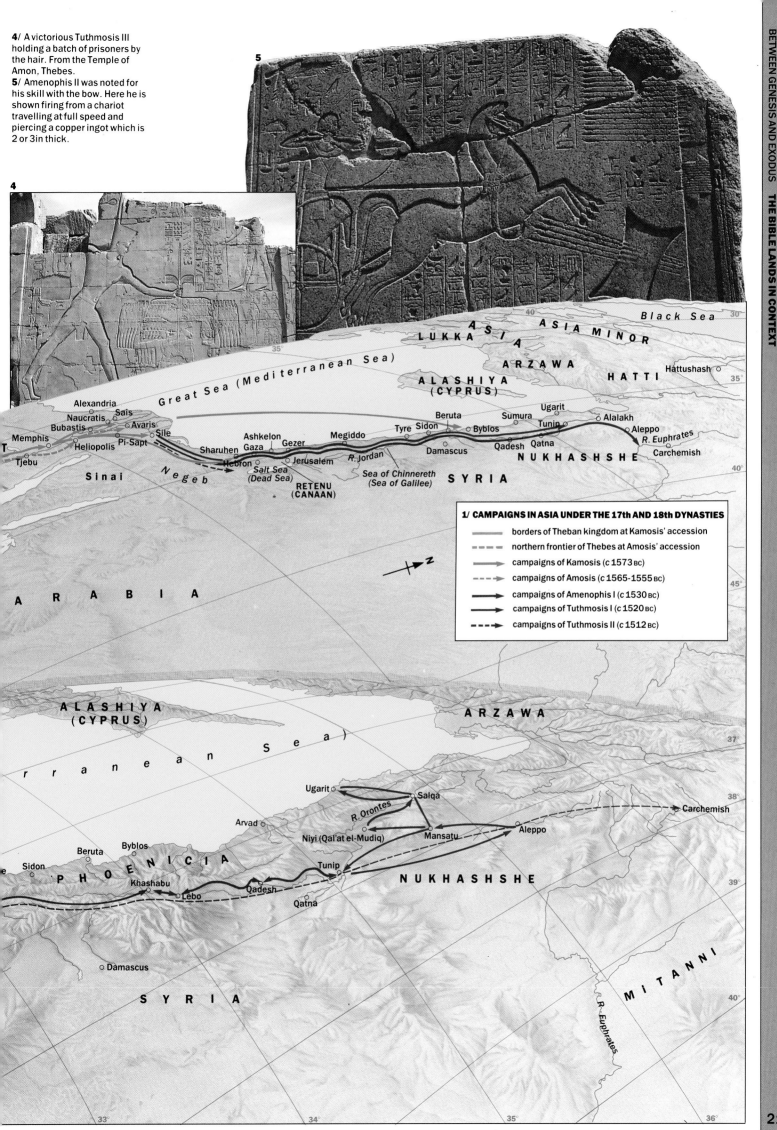

4/ A victorious Tuthmosis III holding a batch of prisoners by the hair. From the Temple of Amon, Thebes.

5/ Amenophis II was noted for his skill with the bow. Here he is shown firing from a chariot travelling at full speed and piercing a copper ingot which is 2 or 3in thick.

1/ CAMPAIGNS IN ASIA UNDER THE 17th AND 18th DYNASTIES

borders of Theban kingdom at Kamosis' accession

northern frontier of Thebes at Amosis' accession

campaigns of Kamosis (c 1573 BC)

campaigns of Amosis (c 1565-1555 BC)

campaigns of Amenophis I (c 1530 BC)

campaigns of Tuthmosis I (c 1520 BC)

campaigns of Tuthmosis II (c 1512 BC)

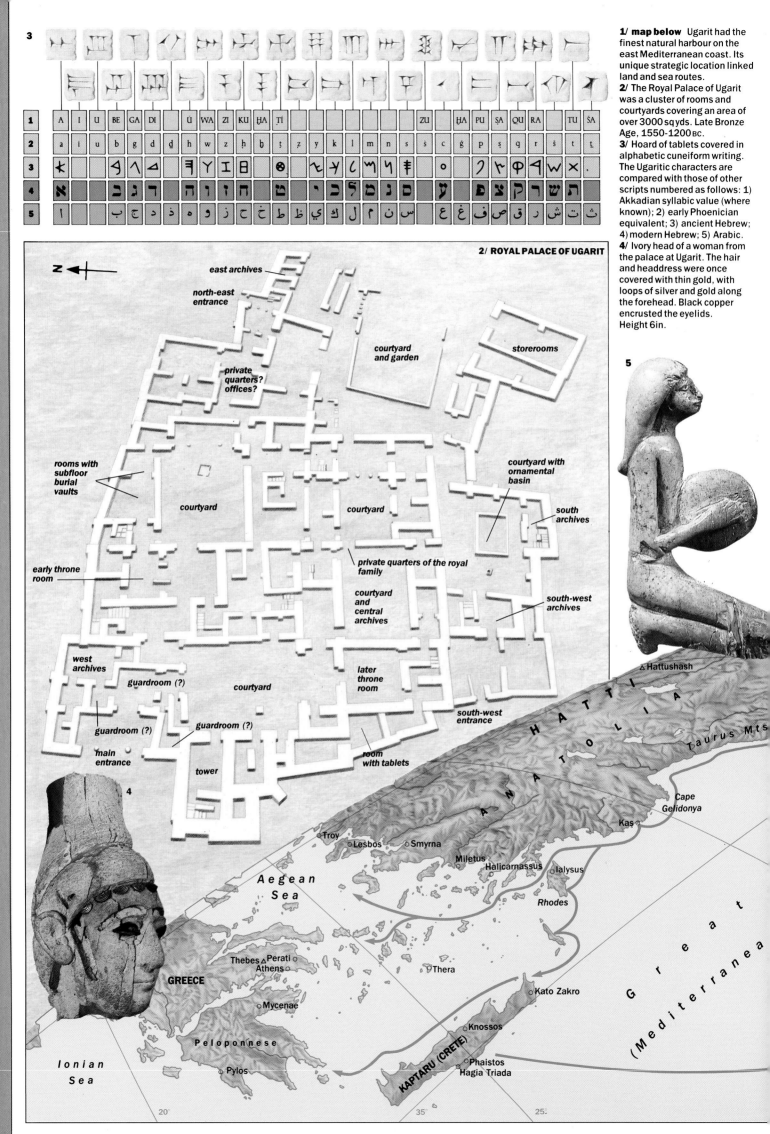

3

1	A	I	U	BE	GA	DI		Ú	WA	ZI	KU	ḪA	TI					ZU		ḪA	PU	ṢA	QU	RA	TU	ŠA
2	a	i	u	b	g	d	ḏ	h	w	z	ḥ	ḫ	ṭ		z	k	l	m	n	s	ṣ	c	ǵ	p	ṣ	q	r	ġ	t	ṯ
3																										
4																										
5																										

1/ map below Ugarit had the finest natural harbour on the east Mediterranean coast. Its unique strategic location linked land and sea routes.

2/ The Royal Palace of Ugarit was a cluster of rooms and courtyards covering an area of over 3000 sq yds. Late Bronze Age, 1550-1200 BC.

3/ Hoard of tablets covered in alphabetic cuneiform writing. The Ugaritic characters are compared with those of other scripts numbered as follows: 1) Akkadian syllabic value (where known); 2) early Phoenician equivalent; 3) ancient Hebrew; 4) modern Hebrew; 5) Arabic.

4/ Ivory head of a woman from the palace at Ugarit. The hair and headdress were once covered with thin gold, with loops of silver and gold along the forehead. Black copper encrusted the eyelids. Height 6in.

2/ ROYAL PALACE OF UGARIT

east archives

north-east entrance

courtyard and garden

storerooms

private quarters? offices?

rooms with subfloor burial vaults

courtyard

courtyard

courtyard with ornamental basin

south archives

private quarters of the royal family

courtyard and central archives

south-west archives

early throne room

west archives

guardroom (?)

courtyard

later throne room

south-west entrance

guardroom (?)

guardroom (?)

main entrance

tower

room with tablets

5

4

△ Hattushash

H A T T I

A N A T O L I A

Taurus Mts

Cape Gelidonya

Kaş

Troy

Lesbos

Smyrna

Miletus

Halicarnassus

Ialysus

Rhodes

Aegean Sea

Thebes △Perati

Athens

Thera

Kato Zakro

GREECE

Mycenae

Peloponnese

Knossos

Phaistos

Hagia Triada

KAPTARU (CRETE)

Ionian Sea

Pylos

G r e a t M e d i t e r r a n e a (Mediterranea

20°   35°   25°

5/ Ivory figurine of a kneeling woman holding a set of cymbals, from Ugarit.
6/ Ivory panel from the headboard of a bed depicting a king, or other royal person, embracing his consort. 1400-1350 BC, height 9.5in.
7/ Clay tablet from Ugarit, inscribed with the earliest known alphabet written in cuneiform.
8/ Late Bronze Age bilingual seal of a Hittite king, from the royal palace at Ugarit.
9/ Weight shaped like a man's head, from Ugarit.

URING the two centuries documented for Ugarit's civili-zation (1400-1200 BC) no city of the ancient Near East has provided such a diverse and rich profile. Indeed the disasters at the end of the 13th century which brought to an end most of the great Bronze Age civilizations of the Levant snuffed out the glory of Ugarit at its peak. It would be centuries before the Phoenician cities of the south would once again mirror the sophistication of Ugarit's culture (pages 56-57). It was here that a hoard of alphabetic cuneiform tablets was found which relate to the language and subject matter of the Old Testament. Ugarit and its port of Makhadu (modern Ras Shamra and Minet el-Beida) formed the centre of a trading network covering the Levant, Anatolia and Greece. The remarkable Near Eastern culture is known from archaeological records discovered at Ras Shamra itself, and from written records found in Ebla, Mari, Egypt and the Hittite capital of Hattushash (modern Boğazköy). The city was already established in the 25th century BC when it was referred to in the Early Bronze Age records of the city of Ebla. The kingdom of Ugarit, with a heavily fortified capital of over 52 acres, extended over some 1300 square miles of fertile countryside.

Donkey caravans converged on the city from Syria, Mesopota-mia and Anatolia to exchange goods with merchants from Canaan and Egypt as well as the maritime traders who arrived by ship from Alashiya (Cyprus) and Kaptaru (Crete) and the Aegean. Ugarit's industries – textiles, ivory, metal, agricultural products, timber, ceramics, handicrafts – converted raw materials into goods for further trade and export on hundreds of ships, controlled by the Crown, which ventured to markets as far afield as Egypt and Crete, and perhaps beyond. Two recent excavations of ships from the 14th and 13th centuries BC off the south coast of Turkey (at Kaş and at Cape Gelidonya) illustrate the variety of goods carried: copper, tin, tools, chemicals, glass ingots, faience and amber beads, ceramics (Canaanite, Cypriot and Mycenaean), ivory, jewellery, semi-precious stones, timber and foodstuff. Merchants also carried weights reflecting standards in different areas, personal seals, and equipment for manufacturing metal goods en route.

Goods were exchanged by barter but the values were calculated by the equivalent value of silver. Tin, essential in the production of bronze, was trans-shipped from Ugarit in ingot form. Ships also transported livestock and, occasionally, more exotic animals. Ugarit was a cosmopolitan city formed by diverse ethnic and linguistic groups. There were ten different languages in five different scripts, one of which, alphabetic cuneiform, was probably developed in the local scribal academy. Through international treaties and via a sophisticated legal system the merchants were assured safety and correct dealings. The political skills of Ugarit's rulers allowed the kingdom to participate in international trade by walking a tightrope between the two major powers of the era, Hatti and Egypt, although bound to the former by vassal treaty for much of the period.

1/ UGARIT'S TRADE AND INFLUENCE

▼	find of Ugaritic text
△	find of cuneiform text
→	trade route

DURING the Amarna Age (c 1400-1350 BC) Egyptian control over Canaan became less intense because Egypt was at peace with the Mitanni to the north. An archive of clay tablets found at El-Amarna dates from the period and includes letters from Canaanite rulers describing the turbulent local situation in Palestine. The tablets are also important because they name places in Canaan at a time when the Bible is silent.

The archive of about 380 texts and fragments from the ruins of El-Amarna (the official modern name of Akhetaten) in Egypt records the first great international period in ancient history. The documents are written in the cuneiform script and, except for one in Hittite and one in Hurrian, they are all in various dialects of the Akkadian language, the tongue of Mesopotamia. This language was commonly used for international correspondence. The texts from Canaan, however, contain examples of local inflection and syntax. The documents are mostly letters written to or by Pharaohs Amenophis III (1417-1379), Amenophis IV (better known as Akhenaten) (1379-62) and Tutankhamun (1361-52). Those addressed to the first were brought to the new capital city of Akhetaten when Amenophis IV moved the foreign office there in about the sixth year of his reign. All of the tablets were discarded when the city was abandoned around 1358.

The Amarna letters provide a good picture of Canaan at this time. The area of direct Egyptian control conformed more or less to the borders of the land of Canaan (NUM 34.1-12) with the addition of the states of Qatna, Qadesh (on the Orontes) and Amurru (on both sides of the Nahr el-Kebir, the classical Eleutherus). International recognition of Canaan as a legal-political entity is confirmed by a document from Ugarit in which the 'sons [citizens] of Canaan' had to pay an indemnity to the 'sons [citizens] of Ugarit'. The Egyptians maintained several centres for administrative purposes in Canaan; their commissioners were posted at

Gaza, Sumur (Simyra) and Kumidi. They also had a supply base governed by a commissioner at Yarimuta (unidentified) and a major quartermaster and ordnance base at Joppa. The troops posted at Beth-shean manned the garrison for the Egyptian authorities; their main task was watching over the caravan route which crossed the Jordan on the way to Damascus. Other contingents of support or garrison troops were posted at some of the city states, such as Jerusalem. Those units were recruited from Nubian (Cushite) and other subject peoples. Renegades ('apiru) were recruited in Canaan for service in Nubia.

The commissioners and other officials were actively involved in the affairs of the various city states, frequently carrying out instructions from the pharaoh himself. Amenophis IV did not neglect his empire, as has been sometimes assumed, but kept himself well informed on matters of state and issued directives for dealing with troublemakers.

Canaanite society consisted of small city-states with one town at the centre, often with subordinate neighbouring towns around it. All the villages nearby were subject to the overlordship of the local king and his noblemen. The council of these oligarchs supported the king and advised him on policy. On occasion they even ousted one ruler in favour of another. The land was cultivated by tenant farmers working for the nobles; they also served as infantry. Every city-state was subject to tribute payments and its fighting men were subject to call-up whenever the Egyptian king required them to march with his army.

Two additional groups appear in the Amarna texts, the bedouin Sutu (Shasu) and the outlaws/renegades ('apiru). They served as 'legionnaires' under Egyptian representatives but often were found acting independently, creating a threat to the city-state populations. The 'apiru were runaways who, for various reasons, had to flee from their home countries (city-states). They tended to band together in isolated places like the forested hillsides of the Lebanon, the sparsely settled hill country around Shechem, or on the ridges of Upper Galilee. Whenever they appear in the Amarna letters they are portrayed as engaged in violent or subversive activity on behalf of one or other of the city-state rulers. They had a major role in founding the dynastic state of Amurru on the northern border of Canaan.

In c1318BC Pharaoh Sethos I, one of the pharaohs of the new 19th dynasty in Egypt, campaigned to reassert Egyptian control over an area in which Egyptian prestige had fallen considerably during the Amarna period. At the end of May in his first regnal year, perhaps as little as three months after he had ascended the throne as sole ruler, Sethos received intelligence that the headman of Hammath, in concert with the town of Pella, was harassing the towns of Beth-shean and Rehob. Perhaps simultaneously word was

1/ **map below** Clay tablets from El-Amarna name places in Canaan thus proving their existence in the 14th century BC. The map also shows Sethos I's campaigns to restore Egyptian authority.
2/ The chiefs of Lebanon cutting down cedars for the 'great barque upon the river ... as well as for the great flagpoles of Amon'. Relief on the exterior of the north wall of the great hall at Karnak.
3/ Wall painting of Pharaoh Sethos I before the goddess Isis, on a pillar of a doorway in the 4th corridor of the tomb of Sethos at Thebes.
4/ Stela of Sethos I from the first year of his reign, found at Beth-shean, recounting the pharaoh's success in overthrowing Asiatic princes. In the text appears: 'The wretched foe, who is in the town of Hammath is gathering to himself many people, while he is seizing the town of Beth-shean'. At the top of the stela the king makes an offering before Re-Har-akhti who holds a sceptre in his right hand and the ankh emblem in the left. Between the two figures is an altar stand holding a libation pot and a lotus. Height c 8ft.

3

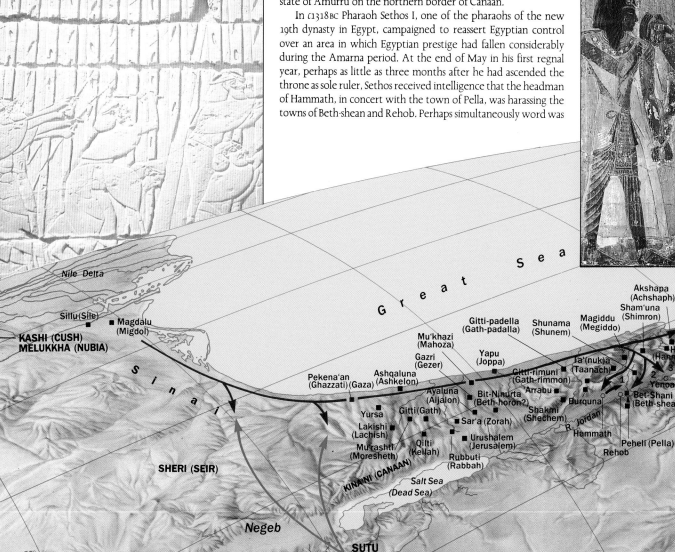

5 and 6/ below right Two clay tablets from El-Amarna. These clay tablets have proved to be an important source of information not only about Egyptian affairs, but also about those of Egypt's near neighbours, such as Canaan. The translation is by Dr I. Finkel of the British Museum.

brought that the bedouin Sutu (*Shasu*), a large settlement of whom was located in southern Transjordan, had irrupted into the Negeb and north Sinai, thus posing a threat to Egypt's land-route to Asia. These minor incidents were probably used by Sethos as an excuse to attack the Hittites under the guise of local punitive action. The army, which was quickly mustered, easily defeated the *Sutu*, took Gaza, and moved up the coast probably to Acco where Sethos despatched three divisions to successfully quell the disturbance Hammath had fomented.

From here details of the campaign become more doubtful. The Karnak reliefs depict the felling of timber in the Lebanon by Canaanite chiefs, while the place-name lists mention a sequence of places along the Phoenician coast (Tyre, Uzu and Ullaza being the best known), and it is not unreasonable to assume that these mark the main itinerary of the expedition (a *stela* of Sethos was, in fact, recovered from Tyre.) Reference to Takhsi, Tunip, Qadesh and Hazor may belong to a subsequent campaign, when Sethos had decided to re-open the old Egypto-Hittite conflict.

4

THE AMARNA TABLETS

The following text is a translation of (5) the Amarna tablet below. Yahtiri, governor of Gaza and Joppa, *c* 1400 BC, writes to the Pharaoh for permission to come to Egypt to serve in his army:

'To the king my lord, my pantheon and my Sun-god I speak: thus says Yahtiri, your servant, the dust of your feet. At the feet of the king my lord, my pantheon and my Sun-god, seven and seven times I fell. Moreover, I am a faithful servant of the king my lord. I looked here and I looked there, but there was no light; I look to the king my lord and there is light. And even though one brick might move from beneath its neighbour, I will not move from beneath the feet of the king my lord. And let the king my lord ask Yanhamu, his deputy! When I was young he brought me to Egypt, and I served the king my lord, and I stood in the gate of the king my lord. And let the king my lord ask his deputy whether I guard the gate of Azzati and the gate of Yapu. And I, with the troops of the king my lord will go wherever they go. And now indeed have I set the front of the king's yoke upon my neck, and I will bear it'.

The tablet below right (6) was written in *c* 1375 BC by Tushratta, King of Mitanni, complaining about the detention of his envoys in Egypt:

'To Naphuririya [Amenophis IV] king of Egypt, my brother, my son-in-law, who loves me and whom I love, I speak: thus says Tushratta King of Mitanni, your father-in-law, who loves you, your brother. I am well. May it be well with you! May it be exceedingly well with your estates, with Teye, your mother, the queen of the land of Egypt, Taduhepa, my daughter, your wife, the remainder of your wives, your sons, your houses, your chariots, your soldiers, your country, and whatever is yours.

Pirizzi and Tulupri, my messengers, have I sent to my brother as express messengers, and ordered them to hurry exceedingly. Indeed I sent them off with [only] a small party. Earlier I said to my brother "I shall detain Mane, my brother's messenger, until my brother releases my messengers, and they come back."

And now my brother will by no means release them so that they can return, but has detained them exceedingly! Why? Are my messengers not birds, that fly away and come back? Why does my brother agonize so over the messengers? Why should the one not... in the presence of the other, and that one not hear the greeting of the other? Every day we ought to be exceedingly happy! Let my brother speedily release my messenger so that I may hear my brother's greeting and rejoice!

Indeed I do love my brother, and I will despatch my messenger to my brother for good things; meanwhile let me hear good things for my brother! For my brother is good, and my brother will do what I wish, and not make my heart grieve.

And all the words which I spoke to your father, Teye your mother knows them all. No other person knows them, and you might ask Teye your mother all about them.

5

6

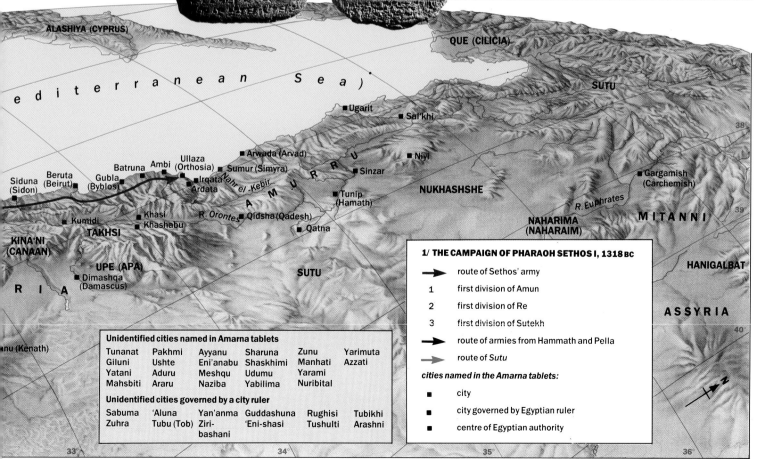

ALASHIYA (CYPRUS)

QUE (CILICIA)

e d i t e r r a n e a n   S e a)

SUTU

■ Ugarit

■ Sal'khi

38

■ Arwada (Arvad)   ■ Niyi

Ullaza   ■ Sumur (Simyra)

Batruna   (Orthosia)   ■ Sinzar   ■ Gargamish

Ambi   ■ Irqata   ■ Tunip   NUKHASHSHE   (Carchemish)

Siduna   Beruta   Gubla   ■ Ardata   (Hamath)   R. Euphrates

(Sidon)   (Beirut)   (Byblos)   *Nahr el-Kebir*   ■ Qidsha (Qadesh)   39

■ Kumidi   ■ Khasi   *R. Orontes*   ■ Qatna   NAHARIMA   MITANNI

KINA'NI   ■ Khashabu   (NAHARAIM)

(CANAAN)   TAKHSI

UPE (APA)   SUTU   HANIGALBAT

R   I   A   ■ Dimashqa
(Damascus)

ASSYRIA

40

1/ THE CAMPAIGN OF PHARAOH SETHOS I, 1318 BC

➤	route of Sethos' army
1	first division of Amun
2	first division of Re
3	first division of Sutekh
➤	route of armies from Hammath and Pella
➤	route of *Sutu*

cities named in the Amarna tablets:

■　city

■　city governed by Egyptian ruler

■　centre of Egyptian authority

nu (Kenath)

Unidentified cities named in Amarna tablets

Tunanat	Pakhmi	Ayyanu	Sharuna	Zunu	Yarimuta
Giluni	Ushte	Eni'anabu	Shaskhimi	Manhati	Azzati
Yatani	Aduru	Meshqu	Udumu	Yarami	
Mahsbiti	Araru	Naziba	Yabilima	Nuribital	

Unidentified cities governed by a city ruler

Sabuma	'Aluna	Yan'anma	Guddashuna	Rughisi	Tubikhi
Zuhra	Tubu (Tob)	Ziri-bashani	'Eni-shasi	Tushulti	Arashni

33°   34°   35°   36°

IN THE early part of the 13th century BC the Egyptians and the Hittites, two major world powers, were engaged in a struggle for the control of the Syro-Palestinian area. Ramesses II left a record of no less than six campaigns northward into the Levant as well as a detailed description of the battle of Qadesh in texts and pictures in bas-reliefs on the Ramesseum at Thebes. Not only is there data on the geography of contemporary Canaan but information about contemporary military tactics. Such strategies as espionage, surprise attacks, and skilful military manoeuvres were later to be used by the Israelites in their war against the Canaanites as told in the Book of Joshua.

Pharaoh Ramesses II spent a decade at least, trying to recapture Egypt's Syrian possessions. In his fourth year (1300 BC), he swept north through the Egyptian province of Canaan and along the Lebanese coast through Tyre and Byblos. Ramesses then struck a surprise attack on Amurru itself, forcing its ruler to acknowledge Egyptian overlordship. So successful had the first campaign been that the pharaoh launched a second campaign the following year to conquer Qadesh. At Gaza Ramesses II divided his force into two unequal parts. A trusted elite corps was sent up the coast to rendezvous with Ramesses himself. The pharaoh then led the main force into the Beqa'a Valley to Kumidi and on north to the Qadesh ridge from which he could see the city. There he met two bedouin who had been planted by the Hittite king to lull the pharaoh into a false sense of security. The trick worked. Unaware that his foe was camped just east of Qadesh, Ramesses crossed the south Orontes ford with his personal retainers and the division of Amun, to begin setting up camp (Phase I). However, as the division of Re approached across the plain he was aware of his predicament and aides were sent to hasten the arrival of the divisions of Ptah and Seth.

At that moment the Hittite chariot-force swept west over the Orontes and scattered the 2nd Egyptian division of Re on the march and attacked the Amun division still setting up camp (Phase II). With the arrival of the elite force of the Ne'arim the Hittite chariotry wavered and then broke (Phase III). The Hittites were driven back pell-mell to the River Orontes. Then Ramesses and the Ne'arim elite pushed the Hittites in a mad scramble across the Orontes (Phase IV). The following day, Ramesses launched his own counter-attack, but the stolid Hittite infantry stood their

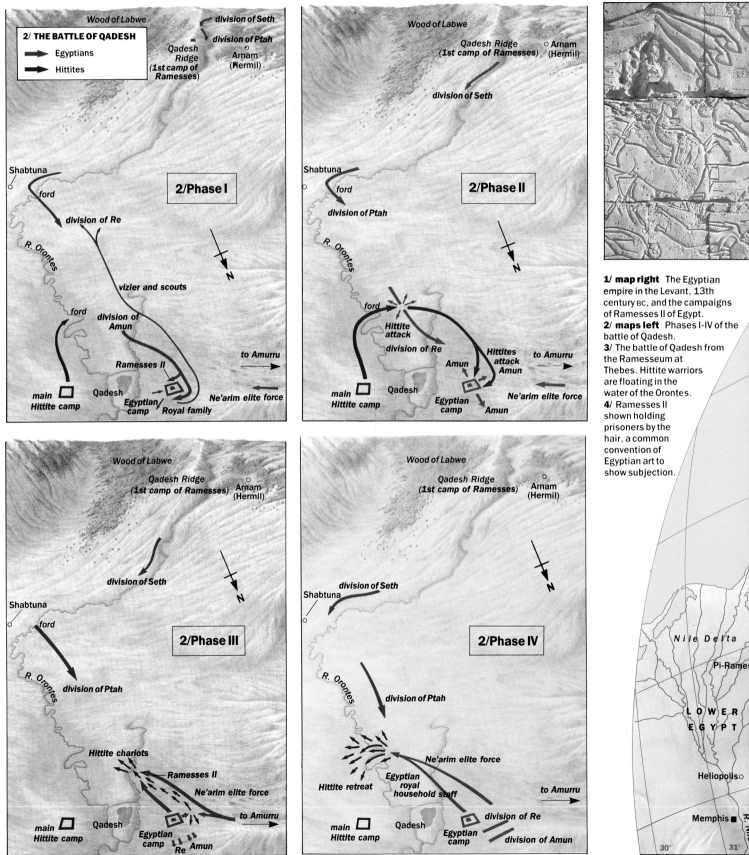

2/ THE BATTLE OF QADESH
→ Egyptians
→ Hittites

2/Phase I

2/Phase II

2/Phase III

2/Phase IV

1/ map right The Egyptian empire in the Levant, 13th century BC, and the campaigns of Ramesses II of Egypt.
2/ maps left Phases I-IV of the battle of Qadesh.
3/ The battle of Qadesh from the Ramesseum at Thebes. Hittite warriors are floating in the water of the Orontes.
4/ Ramesses II shown holding prisoners by the hair, a common convention of Egyptian art to show subjection.

ground. The Hittite king, Muwatallis, proposed the renewal of peace; as before, Amurru and Qadesh would remain Hittite, while Egypt retained the coastland up to Simyra. When Ramesses returned to Egypt Muwatallis reclaimed Amurru and Qadesh and even proceeded to invade the Egyptian province of Upe (including Damascus).

With a refurbished army, in Year 8 of his reign (1296 BC), Ramesses marched back into Canaan. First, he had to crush unrest in Galilee and probably in Transjordan, before going on to recover the province of Upe and to strengthen his hold on the Phoenician coastlands. No sooner was Ramesses back home than Dapur rebelled. By Year 10, he was back north again, and personally led another attack on Dapur. So long as the powerful Hittite centres at Aleppo and Carchem-

ish remained untouched, raids on lesser city-states like Dapur were doomed to failure.

There had been no aggressive Hittite attacks on North Syria. Muwatallis was followed by his son Mursil III who, after seven years of insecure reign, was ejected from office by his uncle who took power as Hattusil III. The dethroned king eventually fled to Egypt for refuge. When extradition was refused Hattusil threatened war and Ramesses II made an expedition northward as far as Beth-shean in Year 18, 1286 BC. Hattusil

opened negotiations and in Year 21 (1283 BC) a treaty of peace and alliance was drawn up. Subsequently Egypto-Hittite relations became so close that Hattusil III married off two of his daughters to the pharaoh.

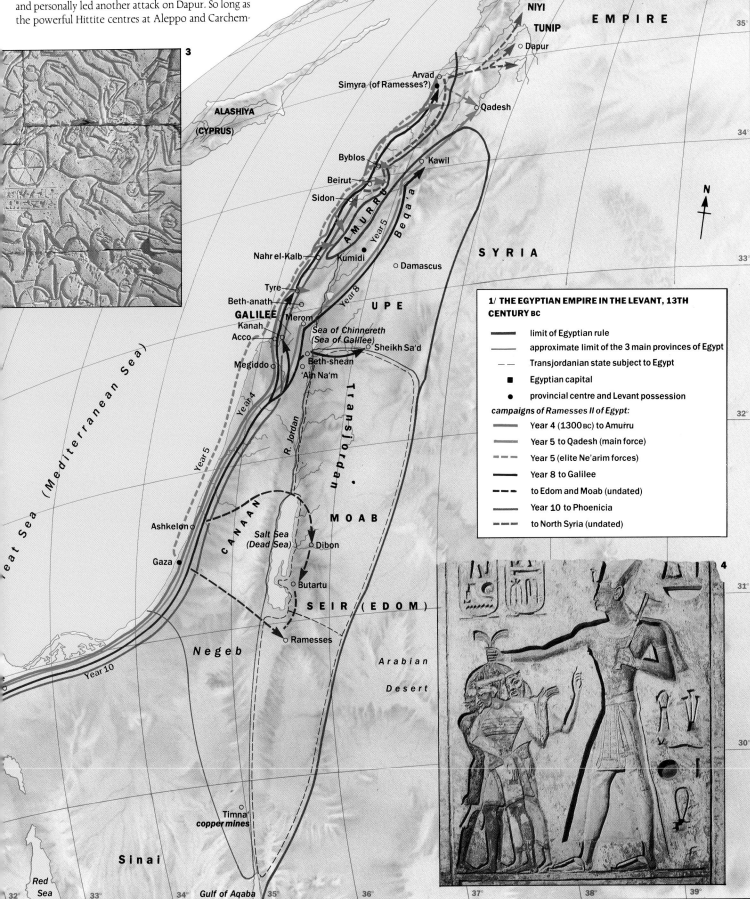

1/ THE EGYPTIAN EMPIRE IN THE LEVANT, 13TH CENTURY BC

——	limit of Egyptian rule
——	approximate limit of the 3 main provinces of Egypt
– – –	Transjordanian state subject to Egypt
■	Egyptian capital
●	provincial centre and Levant possession

campaigns of Ramesses II of Egypt:

——	Year 4 (1300 BC) to Amurru
——	Year 5 to Qadesh (main force)
– – –	Year 5 (elite Ne'arim forces)
——	Year 8 to Galilee
– – –	to Edom and Moab (undated)
——	Year 10 to Phoenicia
– – –	to North Syria (undated)

MANY centuries before the age of Ramesses II and Merneptah, Egyptian scribes had used irony and humour to proclaim the advantages and superior career-prospects open to those who trained diligently to become skilled scribes (as opposed to all 'lesser' callings). Under the Empire, with wider administrative horizons reaching far into the Levant, the scribal curriculum was duly extended and modernized to match. Within the two centuries from Tuthmosis III to Ramesses II, the Egyptian civil administration would have built up a considerable body of knowledge – travel information – concerning the principal routes through Canaan and Syria to other kingdoms, stopping points, obstacles and lengths of time needed, for royal envoys abroad and armies in the field.

Composed under Ramesses II and still popular under Merneptah and his successors, the satirical letter was designed to give instruction in various subjects to budding scribal administrators – constructing building ramps, transporting obelisks, erecting a colossal statue, organizing supplies for a military expedition abroad, and finally a sampling of the geography and routes in Syro-Palestine.

Such a document was found in the 19th century by a Greek merchant, Anastasi, who lived in Alexandria. The document is in the form of a letter from one scribe (Hori) to another (Amenemope), in which Hori turns his sarcastic wit to showing up the ignorance and incompetence of his colleague in the matters covering the section on Syrian geography. Hori depicts his correspondent as an envoy who falls prey to various misadventures. The portion on geography can be viewed in seven segments and is important for its description of Syria and Canaan.

Unlike the pompous accounts of victories so characteristic of the pharaohs, this source of geographic information is often humorous and informative about other matters of human interest. In the sixth section the scribe pictures his rival penetrating the rocky ravine (through the Carmel ridge) on his way to Joppa: 'The narrow ravine is infested with bedouin hiding in the bushes, men seven or nine feet tall from head to toe, ferocious and merciless, heedless of pleas. You're on your own, no one to help you.... Your path is strewn with boulders and pebbles, overgrown... the abyss yawns on one side, and the mountain towers up on the other... You think the enemy is after you, and you panic! You reach Joppa, finding the meadows in full bloom, you push into one, and find the pretty girl looking after the gardens. She makes up to you, and gives you a sample of her embrace – but you are found out, must confess, and are judged as a chariot-warrior, and sell your best shirt to pay the fine!'

The seventh and final section on geography is a gazetteer of twelve principal forts and wells along the Sinai coastal road from Sile on the Egyptian border to Gaza in Canaan.

1/ map right The author of the 'Satirical Letter' picks out the main coast-roads from Phoenicia to Egypt.
2/ below Papyrus Anastasi I, provides much of the information about the training and work of Egyptian scribes, as well as the geography of the Levant during the 2nd millennium BC. Papyrus, an early form of paper, was made from the pith of a reed.

UPON the death of Ramesses II in his sixty-seventh year of sole reign, the throne passed to his thirteenth son Merneptah in 1236 BC (scholars suggest dates as varied as 1238/1224/1213 BC for this event), a man already turned 60 at least. Almost half a century of peace had elapsed since the famous Hittite treaty (page 26) without Egyptian military activity in Canaan. In order to check any dissident activity that might arise from the accession of a new pharaoh, the elderly Merneptah dispatched a punitive expedition to Canaan in his first or second regnal year, possibly led by the Crown Prince Sethos (later Sethos II). The blows fell on the towns of Ashkelon, Gezer and Yenoam and defeat was inflicted on a 'new' people, Israel, still settling in the hill-country, as the hieroglyphic writing clearly implies. This allusion in a triumphal hymn of Merneptah (the so-called 'Israel' *stela*) of his fifth year, is the earliest mention of Israel in ancient documents. It sets that people's initial entry into Canaan at an undetermined date prior to the first five years of Merneptah's reign, ie. before 1236 BC, or other dates adopted for his accession.

By Year 3 of the pharaoh, a postal register shows the frequent arrivals and departures of royal messengers based at the Delta capital of Pi-Ramesse and travelling via the border-port of Sile. Besides the expected links with Gaza, a letter goes to the Prince of Tyre, and three centres of royal rule are mentioned. The 'Wells of Merneptah' (doubtless with a fort) were probably the (Me-)Nephtoah of JOSH 15.9 and 18.15, being 'on the (mountain) ridge',

3/ map far right Pharaoh Merneptah quickly crushed any signs of revolt in Canaan after his father's death. His forces struck successively at Ashkelon, Gezer and Yenoam, engaging also with elements from the people of Israel, then settling in the hill-country of Canaan.

4 and 4a/ right The black, basalt 'Israel' stela, inscribed with a triumphal hymn to the victory of Pharaoh Merneptah over Canaan, 13th century BC. It names places in Canaan, and it specifically mentions the word 'Israel' (**4a**), evidence of a people settling in Canaan at this time.
5/ far right The mummified body of Pharaoh Merneptah was discovered by the French archaeologist Loret in 1898. The body had been placed in the tomb of Pharaoh Amenophis II (page 21) in the Valley of the Kings. Merneptah, coming to the throne at 60, ruled for only ten years and left no important buildings as monuments to his reign. His funerary temple at Thebes was built, in part, from stone taken from the temple of Amenophis III.

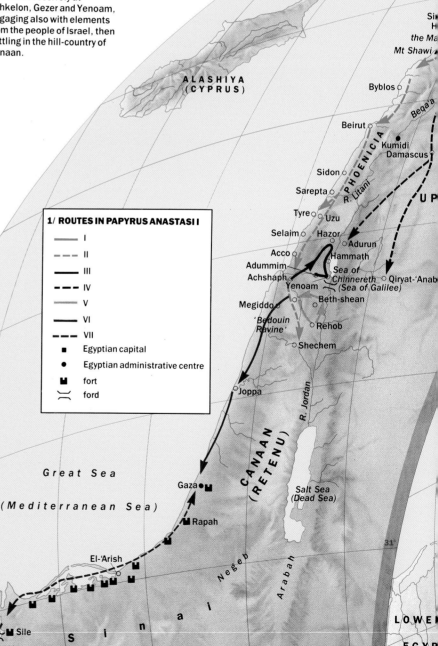

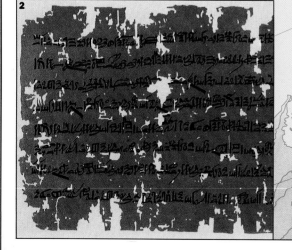

1/ ROUTES IN PAPYRUS ANASTASI I

———	I
- - - -	II
▬▬▬	III
- ▬ - ▬	IV
———	V
▬▬▬	VI
- ▬ - ▬	VII
■	Egyptian capital
●	Egyptian administrative centre
⬕	fort
⊃⊂	ford

and located at Lifta, just north-west of Jerusalem. Such a strongpoint would have enabled Merneptah's agents to keep an eye on the growing conflicts between the Canaanite vassals and their new Israelite neighbours. A second centre of rule was the Castle of Merneptah near Selalim (a slip for Selaim?), probably a new fort to guard the coastal pass at Ras en-Nakura just south of Tyre. A third centre, 'the Town of Merneptah in the district of Pi-Aram', is most likely the Beqa'a centre Kumidi, renamed from its former epithet 'Town of Ramesses II in the Cedar Valley'. The picture of the peaceful links of Egypt with her satellites in Canaan, Upe and the Phoenician coastlands is further reinforced by evidence of Merneptah's rule from Lachish in south Canaan, in Year 4. In the end, Merneptah was able to leave an outwardly intact realm to his successors.

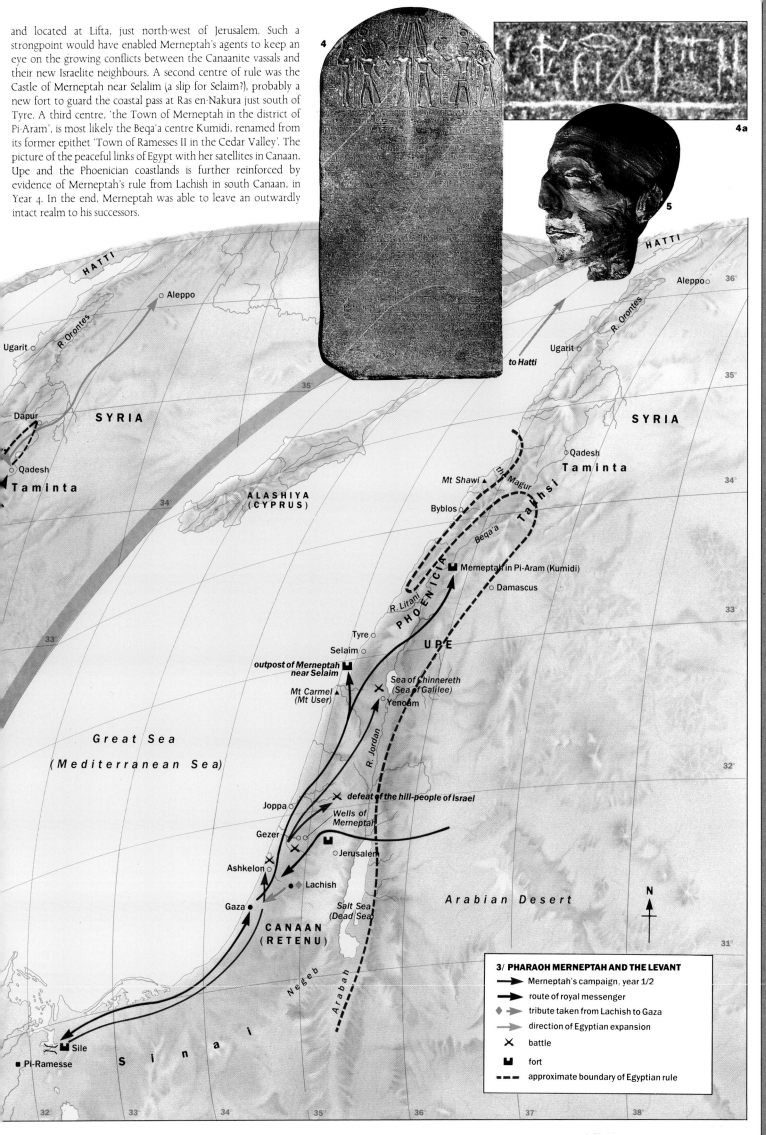

4

4a

5

HATTI

Aleppo○   36°

Ugarit○

R. Orontes

SYRIA

35°

Dapur●

Qadesh○

Taminta

ALASHIYA
(CYPRUS)

to Hatti

HATTI

Aleppo○   36°

Ugarit○

R. Orontes

SYRIA

Qadesh○   Taminta   35°

Mt Shawi▲   the Magur   Tachsi   34°

Byblos○

Beqa'a

Merneptah in Pi-Aram (Kumidi)

Damascus○   33°

R. Litani

PHOENICIA   UPE

Tyre○

Selaim○

**outpost of Merneptah
near Selaim**

Mt Carmel▲
(Mt User)

Sea of Chinnereth
(Sea of Galilee)

Yenoam

R. Jordan

Great Sea
(Mediterranean Sea)

defeat of the hill-people of Israel

Joppa○

Wells of
Merneptah

Gezer○

○Jerusalem   Arabian Desert

Ashkelon○

Lachish●◆

Gaza●   Salt Sea
(Dead Sea)   31°

CANAAN
(RETENU)

Negeb

Arabah

N

Sinai

⚓ Sile
■ Pi-Ramesse

	3/ PHARAOH MERNEPTAH AND THE LEVANT
➤	Merneptah's campaign, year 1/2
➤	route of royal messenger
◆--➤	tribute taken from Lachish to Gaza
➤	direction of Egyptian expansion
✕	battle
⚒	fort
---	approximate boundary of Egyptian rule

THE era before the coming of the Israelites was marked by a cosmopolitan culture in Canaan. Evidence for international trade with Minoan and Mycenaean centres has been found in quantities of a distinctive imported pottery in the Late Bronze Age settlements and tombs. From these archaeological discoveries in Syria and Palestine it is possible to chart the routes from ports to inland cities and to date more precisely the layers of debris by the types of imported pottery found within them.

Mycenaean pottery is found at about 100 excavated sites in the Levant and Egypt. The distinctive wheel-made pots are usually found with large deposits of Cypriot hand-made wares, illustrating international commerce in goods, people and ideas in the Late Bronze Age.

Towards the end of the Aegean Early Bronze II or during Early Bronze Age III (c 2300-2000 BC) many settlements in mainland Greece were destroyed, probably by invaders from Anatolia, speaking a language which eventually became Greek. A reduced, impoverished and ethnically mixed population survived. In Crete the first palaces were built about 1930 BC in direct development from earlier Minoan society, enlivened by contacts with the Levant and Egypt. Minoan trading, and occasionally settlement, reached Sicily, western Anatolia, the Levant and Egypt.

By the end of the Middle Bronze Age (c 2100-c 1600 BC) the Mycenaeans were prosperous and powerful, commanding a fertile plain in southern Greece, acquainted with but not riding the horse, and trading with the Cyclades and Crete.

In the Middle Minoan II or beginning of III (c 1700 BC), the Cretan palaces were rebuilt after destruction by earthquake. The effect on Minoan Crete of the eruption of Thera in Late Minoan IA is still a debatable question, but it may have accelerated a new relationship with the Mycenaeans. Joint enterprise can be traced at the Minoan settlement Ialysos (Trianda) in Rhodes, as well as Cyprus, the Levant and Egypt. Scenes in the chapel of Rekhmire, the last vizier of Tuthmosis III and first official of his successor Amenophis II reflect and help to date the Mycenaean takeover at Knossos at the end of Late Minoan IB, and the shift of influence from Crete to the mainland and Mycenae.

Archaeological research shows that military force helped to achieve and maintain Mycenaean supremacy, stimulated the need for improved defences and weapons, and sustained efforts to obtain copper from Cyprus, and tin and luxuries from further east. Mycenaean (and a few Minoan) goods, were perhaps distributed through the international market of Ugarit (pages 22-23), where palace archives list commodities of likely Aegean origin, but Cyprus was always the prime target. The vast amount of Mycenaean pottery found in Cyprus is proof of trade which included perishables, domestic and perfumed oil, wine, herbs, wool, leather. Exported Mycenaean pottery travelled far beyond Cyprus as part of shipments of Cypriot hand-made base ring and white slip wares (base ring juglets may have been containers for opium). Since Mycenaeans needed the oriental trade it is likely that Aegean ships carried the metals home, together with exotic goods, known from excavation at Aegina, Athens, Mycenae, Gournia and Kommos in Crete.

The excavation of a Late Bronze Age shipwreck off Kaş, in south-west Turkey (now called the Ulu Burun wreck) was begun by George Bass in 1984. Its international cargo included copper, tin and glass ingots; Syro-Palestinian amphorae, one packed with Cypriot pottery, others with traces of grapes, olives, unidentified seeds; Mycenaean and Syrian pottery; artefacts and ornaments in faïence, amber, gold and silver; bronze weapons and tools.

Except at El-Amarna, the capital of Egypt under Akhenaten, and at Deir el-Medina, the artisan village at Thebes, no varied or large deposits of Mycenaean pottery have been found in Egypt, perhaps because it was at the end of the trade route, or because few Egyptian cities have been excavated. The stirrup jar, however, was copied in clay, faïence and calcite.

In the cities of the Levant, menaced by hostility among Hittites and Egyptians, by internal faction and external attack, Aegean imports were comforting luxuries which gave social status in life and death.

DECLINE AND END OF MYCENAEAN TRADE

In the 19th dynasty of Egypt, the trade between Mycenae and the Levant declined. Fine exports were replaced by local imitations and derivatives. In Cyprus wheel-made pottery replaced hand-made wares. Aegean society became unstable, perhaps because of disastrous harvests, earthquake, local warfare or social discontent. People began to leave the Mycenaean centres, and soon were arriving in Cyprus in mixed groups, seeking new homes. Some established precarious footholds at Maa-Palaiokastro, and Pyla-Kokkinokremmos. Others reached the Levant coast. Those who succeeded in settling in Cyprus adapted their culture to a new environment, and maintained tenuous contact with their homelands. The international network pioneered by Minoan seafarers was broken by the Sea Peoples (see pages 32-33).

MYCENAEAN POTTERY

Mycenaean pottery was a highly organized industry combining Helladic ceramic tradition with Cycladic and Minoan inventiveness. Pots were usually thrown, but some special shapes and most figurines were hand-made. All Mycenaean pottery was unglazed and porous, and although burnishing before firing could reduce porosity, containers used for long-term storage or transport had to be lined with resin, easily

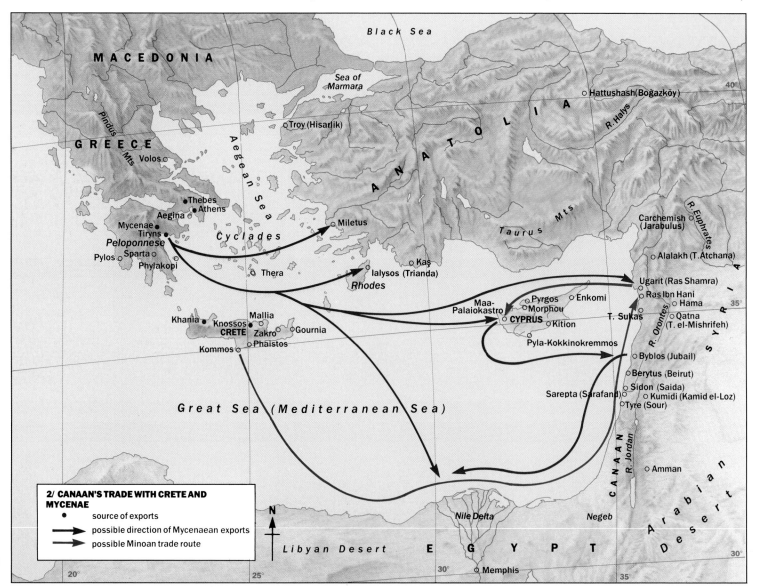

2/ CANAAN'S TRADE WITH CRETE AND MYCENAE

- ● source of exports
- → possible direction of Mycenaean exports
- → possible Minoan trade route

obtainable in the Aegean. Colour variation in body and decoration show that kilns were vertical, like the Late Bronze Age kilns excavated at Sarafand in Lebanon or like simple modern kilns in the Mediterranean. The stirrup or false-necked jar, Minoan in origin, was designed for liquids, with a narrow pouring spout, and handle across the top like an inverted stirrup. This popular shape was a hall-mark of Mycenaean activity, and survived after the Mycenaeans were forgotten. Some pottery was custom-made for the export market, particularly the Mycenaean version of the eastern 'pilgrim flask' and the amphoroid krater. The krater seems too big to drink from, too small to use for burial. Its decoration often celebrates a social, religious or official event, in which chariots and horses are prominent. Their humorous pictures give an endearing insight into Mycenaean life, and are worthy ancestors of the masterpieces of Classical Greece.

1/ map right Late Bronze Age sites with imported Minoan, Mycenaean or Cypriot pottery.
2/ map left Trade routes for importing pottery from Crete and Greece.
3/ Mycenaean stirrup jar, with false neck and spout, from Tell el-'Ajjul.
4/ Mycenaean, wheelmade flask from Gezer, LBIIIA.
5/ Cypriot base ring jug, from Gezer, LBIIA.

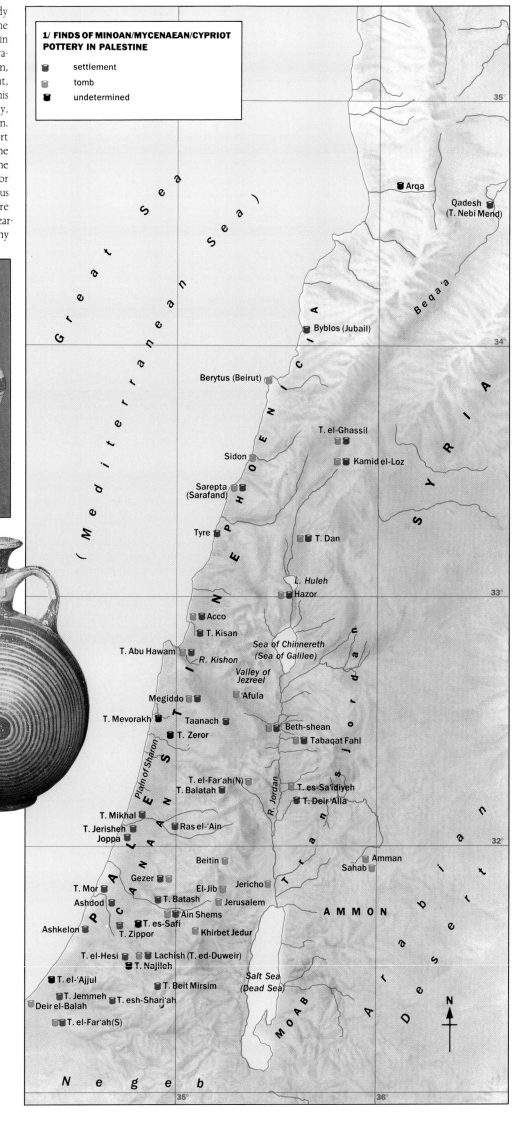

1/ FINDS OF MINOAN/MYCENAEAN/CYPRIOT POTTERY IN PALESTINE
- settlement
- tomb
- undetermined

Great Sea
(Mediterranean Sea)

Arqa
Qadesh (T. Nebi Mend)

Byblos (Jubail)

Berytus (Beirut)

T. el-Ghassil
Sidon
Kamid el-Loz

Sarepta (Sarafand)

Tyre
T. Dan

L. Huleh
Hazor

Acco
T. Kisan
Sea of Chinnereth (Sea of Galilee)
T. Abu Hawam
R. Kishon
Valley of Jezreel
Megiddo
'Afula
T. Mevorakh
Taanach
T. Zeror
Beth-shean
Tabaqat Fahl

T. el-Far'ah(N)
T. Balatah
T. es-Sa'idiyeh
T. Deir 'Alla
T. Mikhal
R. Jordan
T. Jerisheh
Ras el-'Ain
Joppa

Beitin
Amman
Sahab
Gezer
Jericho
T. Mor
El-Jib
Ashdod
T. Batash
Jerusalem
'Ain Shems
AMMON
Ashkelon
T. es-Safi
Khirbet Jedur
T. Zippor

T. el-Hesi
Lachish (T. ed-Duweir)
T. Najileh
T. el-'Ajjul
T. Beit Mirsim
Salt Sea (Dead Sea)
T. Jemmeh
T. esh-Shari'ah
Deir el-Balah
T. el-Far'ah(S)

MOAB
Arabia
Desert

N e g e b

PHOENICIA
SYRIA
Beqa'a
CANAAN
PALESTINE
Plain of Sharon
Transjordan

35°
34°
33°
32°
35°
36°

N

ISRAEL at the end of the Late Bronze Age (c1200 BC), according to the traditions preserved in its own history, was securing a foothold in Canaan (pages 38-41). Although aware of the surrounding world (pages 58-59), little is said in the Bible of the movement of people and tribes in other parts of the eastern Mediterranean. The Philistines (pages 42-43), one of the Sea Peoples, appear as a major contestant for the fertile lands on the coastal plains. The name of the major power to the north, the Hittites, occurs occasionally to identify a foreigner, such as Uriah, the husband of Bathsheba, or Ephron, from whom Abraham bought a field in which later both he and his wife Sarah were buried. These are exceptions; Israel in its early days was interested in its own problems. There is reason to believe, however, that in the eastern Mediterranean, the end of the Late Bronze Age was a time of mass movement of peoples and consequent warfare.

THE 'SEA PEOPLES'

Texts from Boğazköy (Hattushash, the Hittite capital) and Ras Shamra (ancient Ugarit) make it clear that, in the 12th century BC, invaders came into the area of the eastern Mediterranean by sea, supporting the traditional designation of these invaders as Peoples of the Sea. There is even an account of three sea battles fought by Suppiluliumas II, the last known Hittite king, against the 'enemy ships from the land of Alashiya' (Cyprus). Many place-names in the Mediterranean owe their origins to the Sea Peoples: Sardinia (from the Sherden), Sicily (the Sheklesh), Palestine (the Philistines or Peleset), Achaia (the Akwash or Akaiwasa) and Lycia (the Lukka).

Earlier texts from the reign of Suppiluliumas II, as well as those of his immediate predecessors, established that Cyprus was a vassal, paying tribute to its Hittite overlord. Consequently the enemy ships that fought the Hittites in what were the only recorded sea battles in Hittite history, were probably those of Sea Peoples using the island as a base for operations against the surrounding coastal areas.

Shortly after this the Hittite empire must have fallen to the invaders. The Hittite capital of Hattushash was burned to the ground in a massive conflagration, and destruction levels are recorded at a series of sites on Cyprus and along the Levantine coast. At Meskene (ancient Emar) this destruction was associated with a legal text dated to the second year of the reign of the Babylonian king Meli-Shipak (1187 BC). This date is in close agreement with the Egyptian evidence, which puts the great raid by the Sea Peoples in the 8th year of the reign of Ramesses III (1190 BC).

However, a closer look at the dating of these destructions reveals many problems. It is difficult to find any evidence for Hittite overlords or for resident Sea Peoples on Cyprus. Nor were the massive fortifications of the inland fortress of Hattushash likely to have fallen to a band of sea raiders. Egyptian reliefs at Medinet Habu, in Upper Egypt, depict whole families on the move, travelling by ox-cart, but these representations seem to show the contingent which travelled along the coastal strip; warriors operated from ships that carried only fighting men.

There is further evidence that during the 12th century BC there were extensive migrations of peoples not only in the Levant but in the Aegean as well, and for any explanation of the forces behind these movements one must go beyond Cyprus and the Levant. The traditional dates for the Trojan War (1193-1184 BC) would have the Mycenaean Greeks at Troy at the same time that the Sea Peoples were ravaging sites of the eastern Mediterranean. According to archaeologists, Troy VIIa, the Homeric Troy, fell at a time when Mycenaean IIIB pottery was being replaced by the new IIIC style (page 30). This transition has come to be dated to c1190 BC. This ceramic clue is also associated with the destructions at Enkomi and Kition on Cyprus and other cities along the Levantine coast. Moreover, the same type of pottery is associated with destructions in Greece itself at Mycenae, Tiryns, Pylos,

Gla, Thebes and Orchomenus. At the site of Teichos Dymeion a wall seems to have been built to hold back the invader, and a similar construction has been identified at the Isthmus of Corinth.

On the Greek mainland these destructions have been attributed to invaders from the north. In Cyprus and along the Levantine coast these destructions are seen as the work of the Sea Peoples. In Palestine, on the other hand, destructions which can be assigned to the same period have been seen as archaeological evidence for the conquest of Canaan by the Israelites in some areas and by the Philistines in others.

THE NEO-HITTITES

Archaeology provides no clues to the identity of those responsible for the destruction of the Hittite capital at Hattushash. However, it is evident that, following the destruction, the main centres of power moved from central Anatolia, at Boğazköy, Alaca Hüyük and Maşat, to the south-east, to the areas surrounding Melitene (Malatya), Carchemish and Aleppo. It is there that the post-1200 BC development of the so-called Neo-Hittite (or Syro-Hittite) civilization took place, maintaining certain cultural connections with its Late Bronze Age predecessor, but using a different language (Luvian rather than Hittite) and script (hieroglyphic instead of cuneiform). The situation is complicated because Luvian language and hieroglyphic writing also appear at the Late Bronze Age sites of central Anatolia.

These Neo-Hittites are almost certainly the Hittites of the Bible who figure in the stories connected with David and the beautiful Bathsheba, whose husband, Uriah the Hittite, David put in the front ranks of the army to increase his chances of getting killed in battle (II SAM 11), or with Solomon the horse-trader, who brought horses from Que (Cilicia) and chariots from Egypt and sold them to 'all the kings of the Hittites and to the kings of Syria.' (I KINGS 10. 28-29). The geographical and political terminology of these stories is in keeping with their Iron Age background, for Que was known to the Bronze Age Hittites as Kizzuwadna and the kings of Aram ruled over an Aramaean state that only developed after 1200 BC.

THE END OF THE MYCENAEAN CIVILIZATION

In the Aegean new elements can be detected at the end of the 13th century BC: bronze weapons and a hitherto unknown type of crude, handmade pottery suggest the appearance of the northern invaders who put an end to Mycenaean civilization. With the introduction of new weapons went corresponding changes in defensive body armour. Bronze helmets,

corselets and greaves became more popular than they had been in Mycenaean times. Greaves were of special importance, offering protection against the new cut-and-thrust sword. For the biblical scholar the most interesting aspect is the remarkable parallel between these new weapons and armour and the new style of fighting they must have entailed. Certain details in the story of David and Goliath, as recorded in I SAM 17 (page 49) may reflect these developments. The account of the arming of Goliath (I SAM 17.5-7) emphasizes his bronze armour fitting the description of the 'northern' warriors, whose path across the eastern Mediterranean seems to coincide with the destruction of all the major Late Bronze Age sites in the area.

In the search for explanations of events that brought the Late Bronze Age to an end in the eastern Mediterranean, it seems that every trail leads back to Anatolia and Cyprus. How events in the Aegean, Anatolia, Cyprus and the northern Levant relate to the end of the Late Bronze Age in Palestine remains to be worked out in detail.

1/ map right Trade routes of the 13th and 12th centuries BC, some utilized by the Mycenaeans (map 2, page 30) and others followed by the Sea Peoples later.

2/ A beardless Hittite prisoner with a rope around his neck; on the wall of the great temple at Abu Simbel in Upper Egypt.

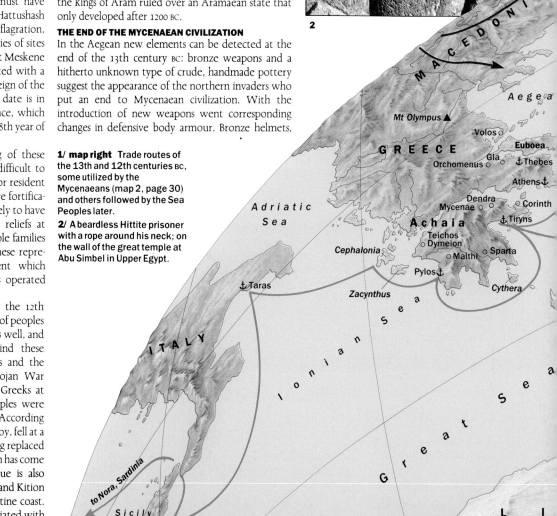

2

MACEDONIA

Aegea[n]

Mt Olympus ▲

Volos

GREECE

Euboea

Orchomenus ○   Gla   ⚓Thebes

Athens⚓

Dendra

Adriatic Sea   Mycenae ○   ○ Corinth

Achaia   ⚓Tiryns

Teichos   Cephalonia   ○ Dymeion   ○ Sparta

○ Malthi

Pylos⚓

⚓Taras   Zacynthus   Cythera

I T A L Y

Ionian Sea

to Nora, Sardinia   Great   Sea

Sicily   L I

○ Thapsus   15   20

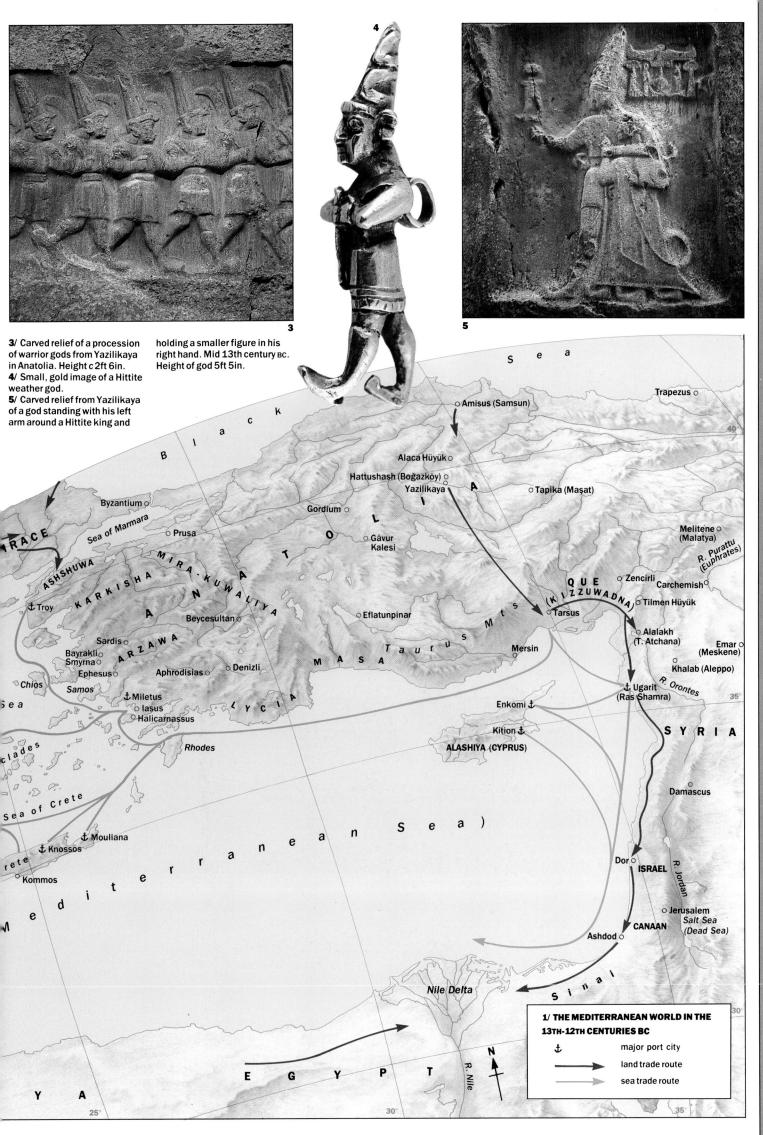

3/ Carved relief of a procession of warrior gods from Yazilikaya in Anatolia. Height *c* 2ft 6in.

4/ Small, gold image of a Hittite weather god.

5/ Carved relief from Yazilikaya of a god standing with his left arm around a Hittite king and holding a smaller figure in his right hand. Mid 13th century BC. Height of god 5ft 5in.

1/ THE MEDITERRANEAN WORLD IN THE 13TH-12TH CENTURIES BC

⚓   major port city

→   land trade route

→   sea trade route

THE Exodus was to the Israelites the most important event in their history. The story of the oppression in Egypt, the choice of Moses as deliverer, the difficulties of the escape and the dangers of the journey to the Promised Land were central not only to Israelite history but also to the Passover festival in the Jewish calendar. Yet in spite of the importance of these events in Israel's tradition, controversy surrounds the biblical accounts of this period. The Bible contains insufficient information to allow a precise dating of these events. Biblical chronology (I KINGS 6.1) places the Exodus 480 years before Solomon

began to build the temple, about 1440 BC. This figure conflicts with other data in the Bible and from archaeology and has generally been regarded as too early. The events in Egypt just before the Exodus have been placed in the 13th century BC, when the use of foreign labour is well attested and the city of Rameses (EX 1.11) is often mentioned in Egyptian sources. Since the Merneptah *stela* (c 1230 BC) mentions Israel among various names in Canaan, it seems that Israelites had settled there by then and the Exodus must fall in the earlier part of the century. How much earlier it is impossible to say. There is no reference to it in

Egyptian records, which is hardly surprising when the number of participants must have been far fewer than is indicated in some Old Testament passages which are known to have been written much later than the events described (EX 12.37; compare with NUM 1.46 and 26.51). These state that the Israelites who left Egypt numbered some 600,000 male adults. Allowing for women and children the total company would have been two million or more, a group that would have been larger than the barren area of Sinai could possibly have supported for long. The high numbers appearing in the biblical references may be ascribed to the

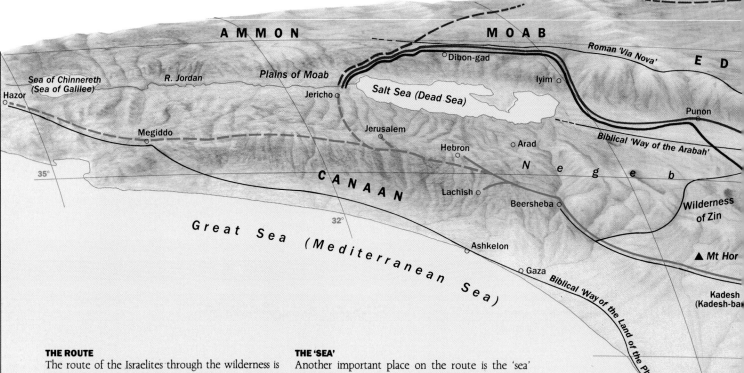

THE ROUTE

The route of the Israelites through the wilderness is described in a series of itinerary notes scattered through the books of Exodus, Numbers and Judges (for example EX 12.37, 13.20 – compare also 13.17-18) and again more compactly in NUM 33.1-49. It is likely that this latter passage supplied many of the details of the main narrative. Certain sections of the journey are described in other books of the OT (DEUT 1.19-3.29; JUDG 11.16-22). The result of this is to show that the earliest accounts contain very little geographical information, only references to key points such as the Red Sea, Mount Sinai/Horeb, Kadesh and the crossing of the River Jordan, and actually laid very little stress on movement from place to place at all. The notion of an Exodus route is due chiefly to NUM 33. 1-49, an itinerary composed on the pattern of similar documents known from other parts of the ancient Near East. It is probable that in NUM 33 the references to Kadesh and Mount Hor originally preceded the mention of Ezion-geber, as is still the case with Kadesh in DEUT 1-2. The idea that the Israelites passed through the wilderness east of Moab and Edom is not present in NUM 33 and is to be traced to editing in the historical books during the Babylonian exile (NUM 21.11-13; DEUT 2.8, JUDG 11.18).

MOUNT SINAI

The location of Mount Sinai (or Mount Horeb as it is known in some texts) is a particular problem and over a dozen sites have been proposed for it. Much of the evidence which has been used in this discussion is insufficiently precise for the purpose and some of it perhaps relates to a distinct 'mountain of God' (EX 3.1, 4.27, 18.5) rather than to Sinai. The clearest evidence is found in DEUT 1.2: 'It is eleven days' journey from Horeb by way of Mount Seir to Kadesh-barnea'. This points to the south of the Sinai peninsula, in the region which Christian, Jewish and the oldest Arabic tradition favours, or perhaps less likely to a mountain east of the Gulf of 'Aqaba.

THE 'SEA'

Another important place on the route is the 'sea' where the Israelites were saved from the pursuing Egyptians (EX 14-15). This is sometimes referred to in the Bible as *yam suf*, traditionally equated with the Red Sea (or more exactly the Gulf of Suez). The Hebrew term has often been thought to mean 'the sea of reeds' and a location for it has consequently been sought in a fresh-water lake in north-eastern Egypt. This later view cannot be sustained in the face of passages like I KINGS 9.26, which uses *yam suf* to refer to the Red Sea (in fact the Gulf of 'Aqaba), and those texts which place the deliverance at *yam suf* must be presumed to be referring to the Gulf of Suez (which may have extended further to the north in antiquity). Thus the case for the so-called 'northern route' for the Exodus is considerably weakened. This view, upheld by several distinguished students of the problem, relies on the identification of Migdol and Baal-zephon in EX 14.2 with places near the Mediterranean coast and locates the 'sea' at Lake Bardawil, where catastrophes of a comparable kind have occurred. These names are, however, attested elsewhere in eastern Egypt, and EX 13.17 states explicitly that the Israelites did not leave by the coast road, 'the way of the land of the Philistines'.

A southerly direction is therefore to be preferred for the initial stages of the itinerary. The route suggested is a plausible one for traders and mining expeditions, from whose experience it was probably derived. There is evidence of a connection between southern Sinai and Arad already in the Early Bronze Age, and the recent discoveries at Kuntillet 'Ajrud attest the use of 'the way of the Red Sea' in the period of the Israelite kingdoms. Some deviation from the most direct route was required by the traditional belief that the Children of Israel were detained in the wilderness by God as a punishment for their disobedience, followng a loss of confidence after a preliminary exploration of the land (NUM 13-14; DEUT 1-2).

tendency of later OT writers to inflate population statistics (compare I CHRON 21.5 with II SAM 24.9) coupled perhaps with a reading back into the Exodus period of the total population of Israel at some later time. It may well be that certain of the Israelite tribal groups were in Egypt, but attempts to identify, date or number them have produced little agreement among scholars. Whether there was a single historical journey through the wilderness must remain doubtful – those who experienced the deliverance from Egypt may have made their way to Canaan by separate routes in small groups – but geographical study can seek to

determine the route described in NUM 33 and so discover how later generations of Israelites believed that their forefathers had travelled from Egypt to Canaan. However, Arabic names provide less help than usual in desert areas and very few of the traditional locations are attested earlier than the 4th century AD. Research has to proceed on the basis of the limited number of places whose identification is relatively certain and choose between various routes linking them which are known from other sources.

The difficulties in charting the route taken by the Israelites on their journey from Egypt to Canaan are

also encountered in any attempt to be precise about the route taken by the spies sent by Moses to report on the land to be occupied by the Israelite tribes. Two versions of the story of their mission appear, one in NUM 13-14, and another in DEUT 1.19-46. Both list Kadesh, or the more general Wilderness of Zin, as the point of departure for their expedition. The DEUTER-ONOMY account implies that they explored the region of Hebron only. However, NUM 13.21 tells of a journey through the land of Canaan from the Wilderness of Zin to Rehob of Lebo-hamath, used elsewhere (I KINGS 8.65) to define the northern part of the land.

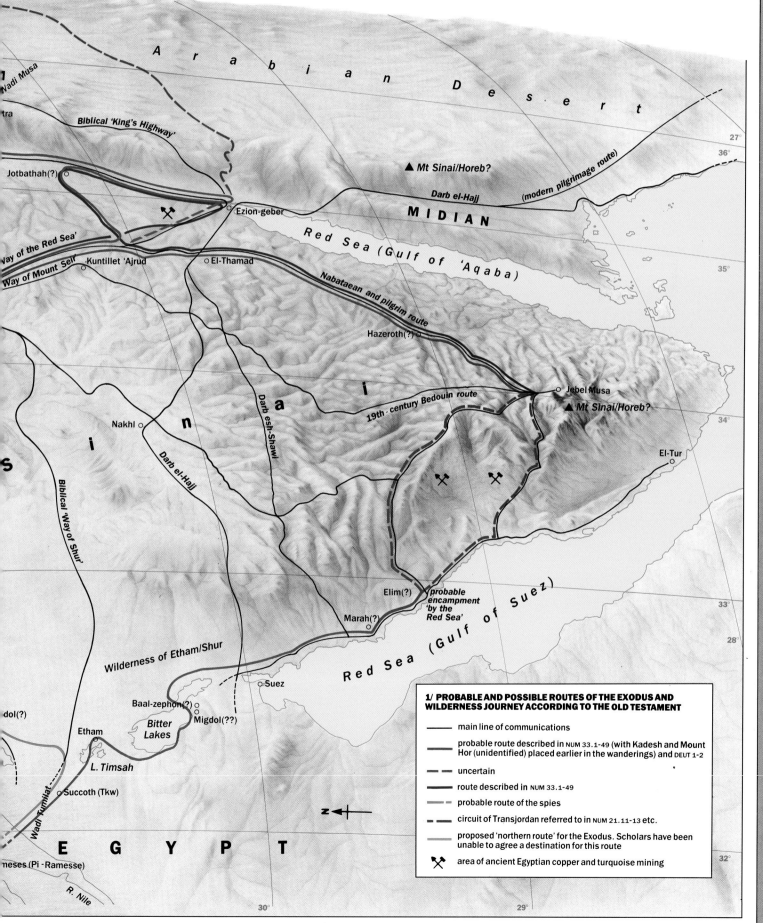

1/ PROBABLE AND POSSIBLE ROUTES OF THE EXODUS AND WILDERNESS JOURNEY ACCORDING TO THE OLD TESTAMENT

—————— main line of communications

—————— probable route described in NUM 33.1-49 (with Kadesh and Mount Hor (unidentified) placed earlier in the wanderings) and DEUT 1-2

– – – uncertain

—————— route described in NUM 33.1-49

– · – · – probable route of the spies

– – – circuit of Transjordan referred to in NUM 21.11-13 etc.

—————— proposed 'northern route' for the Exodus. Scholars have been unable to agree a destination for this route

⚒ area of ancient Egyptian copper and turquoise mining

BECAUSE of its geographical location Palestine has served as a bridge between the continents of Asia and Africa and, in historic times, as an important passageway between the two centres of ancient civilization: Mesopotamia and Egypt. The land has a basic relief of rounded mountains and incised valleys which have determined the pattern of major roads. Seen from the west, Palestine consists of a coastal plain, a lowland and two lines of mountains, divided by the great rift which can be traced from Syria southward to the source of the African River Zambezi. The River Jordan is the most conspicuous feature of the Palestinian section of this rift.

Palestine is located in a subtropical zone, having a short rainy season in winter and a long dry summer. Precipitation varies greatly. The northern mountains of Carmel, Upper Galilee and northern Samaria were once covered with dense woodland sustained by the fair amount of rain. Now, however, only a narrow strip along the Mediterranean enjoys a relatively large amount of rainfall. The desert surrounds Palestine on the south and east.

The geological foundations of the land have had an influence on human activities. The hard limestone in the hills of Palestine have weathered into a rich red-brown soil called *terra rossa*, favourable to farming. The soft limestones (the intermediate Senonian rock) tends to erode into a grey infertile soil. Blocks of building stone were quarried from the limestone rocks of Cenomanian, Turanian and Eocene formations. Quarries have been found at Megiddo, Samaria and Ramat Rahel in Iron Age contexts. Basalt exists in eastern Galilee and in the Golan; since prehistoric times it has been the basic material for making querns and mortars. Palestine is not very rich in mineral resources. A thick layer of red Nubian sandstone, containing deposits of copper, is known from southern Transjordan and around the River Jabbok; iron is mined in the mountains of Transjordan. Salt is obtained from the Mediterranean or from the Dead Sea.

AGRICULTURE

The economy of Palestine has generally been pastoral-agrarian in character. Some plant species have migrated from as far away as Western Europe, Inner Asia and Central Africa. Agriculture has traditionally been based on grain, wine and olive oil. Barley was usually grown in areas of poor soil and limited precipitation. Supplementing these were the fig, pomegranate, the date and the almond. Terraces were frequently built in serried fashion on the slopes of hills for farming. Easy access between fields and the market places was vital and in many areas of Palestine a complex network of regional and rural roads was established.

The great variety of soil and rainfall makes for a diversity of flora. In the narrow belt of land known as the Mediterranean zone, the climate is characterized by a short and wet winter with an annual total rainfall of between 15.5 and 47.25 in. The zone originally supported evergreen woodlands and high maquis vegetation, but this has now been destroyed. The typical trees are the Aleppo pine, the common oak, the Palestine terebinth, the laurel, the carob and the mastic terebinth.

Loess or thin calcareous soils exist in the Irano-Turanian zone. The climate is characterized by a low rainfall with an annual total ranging between 7.5 and 11.5 in. Since this is the absolute limit for dry-farming, only sparse trees and shrubs are to be found, notably the lotus jujube and the Atlantic terebinth.

The Saharo-Arabian zone has the poorest flora in the Levant. The rainfall does not exceed 7.5 in and can be much less. The soils are not conducive to plant growth, but thorny acacias of African savannah origin grow in the wadi beds and survive on the water of the occasional flash flood.

FAUNÂ

A great variety of animals are known from the Levant, including over 100 species of mammals and almost 500 species of birds. The Bible refers to numerous kinds of wild and domesticated animals but many have become extinct as a result of intensive hunting. Among those mentioned are the lion, tiger, bear, antelope, wild ox, the Mesopotamian fallow deer, ostrich, crocodile and hippopotamus. The lion can no longer be found in the Levant: a good representation, however, appears on an 8th-century BC seal found at Megiddo (page 75). Five ostrich eggs have been found near T. Mikhal dating to the Chalcolithic period. At the turn of the century the crocodile, which originally inhabited the River Jordan, could still be seen in Nahal Tanninim ('the crocodile river') in the coastal plain of Palestine. The ibex, mentioned in PS 104.18 as living in the high hills, exists today in a number of rocky locations in Sinai, Negeb and at En-gedi near the Dead Sea. In nearby Nahal Mishmar, objects decorated with ibex horns were found in the bronze hoard (page 10) dating back to the Chalcolithic period. The Sinai leopard referred to in a number of biblical passages was thought to have become extinct, but it was identified in 1974 in the cliffs at En-gedi. Ancient representations of the leopard have come to light on a Neolithic wall painting at Çatal Hüyük in Anatolia, in stone constructions in the desert floor next to a structure of the late 6th millennium BC at Biq'at 'Uvda in southern Palestine, and in ancient wall carvings in Sinai (Wadi Abu-Jada).

Domesticated animals are also mentioned in the Bible. Among them are the horse, donkey, goat, sheep and cattle. Insects too, such as fleas, mosquitoes and locusts are sometimes referred to in biblical passages. As in the case of plants, animals found, in each of the phytogeographic regions of Palestine, a habitat suitable to their respective needs.

1/ map left The geography of the country is directly related to the quality of its soil. Palestine's most fertile soil derives from Cenomanian limestone, which with adequate rainfall breaks down into the rich *terra rossa*. The Senonian chalk is easly eroded and is infertile. Numbers indicate elevations in feet.
2/ map right Map of major climatic and floral zones in Palestine. Lines show average yearly rainfall in inches.

5

3/ map far right The contours of the land obviously had their effect on travel. The map shows the major lines of communication in biblical times, the biblical names for the major highways and the position of the passes through high ground. These roads were important both for troop movements and for trade and commerce.
4/ Dog attacking a lion marked with a star on the shoulder. On a *stela* of c1400BC from Beth-shean.
5/ Ivory comb carved on both sides with scenes of an ibex being attacked by a dog. From Megiddo, c1350BC.
6/ Two camels with their drivers bearing tribute from Musir to Shalmaneser III of Assyria. The inscription reads 'Camels whose backs are doubled'. From the black obelisk found at Nimrud in 1846 and now in the British Museum.

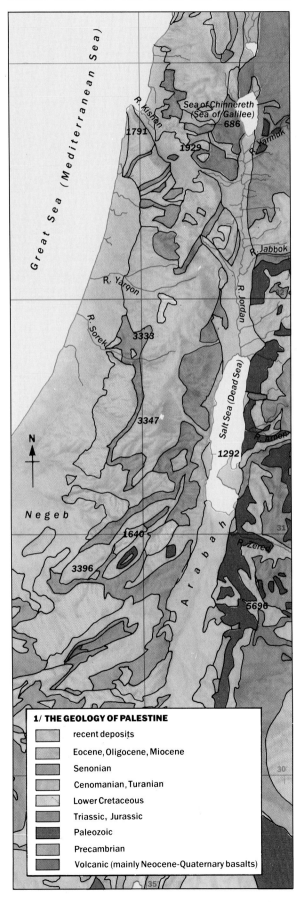

1/ THE GEOLOGY OF PALESTINE
- recent deposits
- Eocene, Oligocene, Miocene
- Senonian
- Cenomanian, Turanian
- Lower Cretaceous
- Triassic, Jurassic
- Paleozoic
- Precambrian
- Volcanic (mainly Neocene-Quaternary basalts)

6

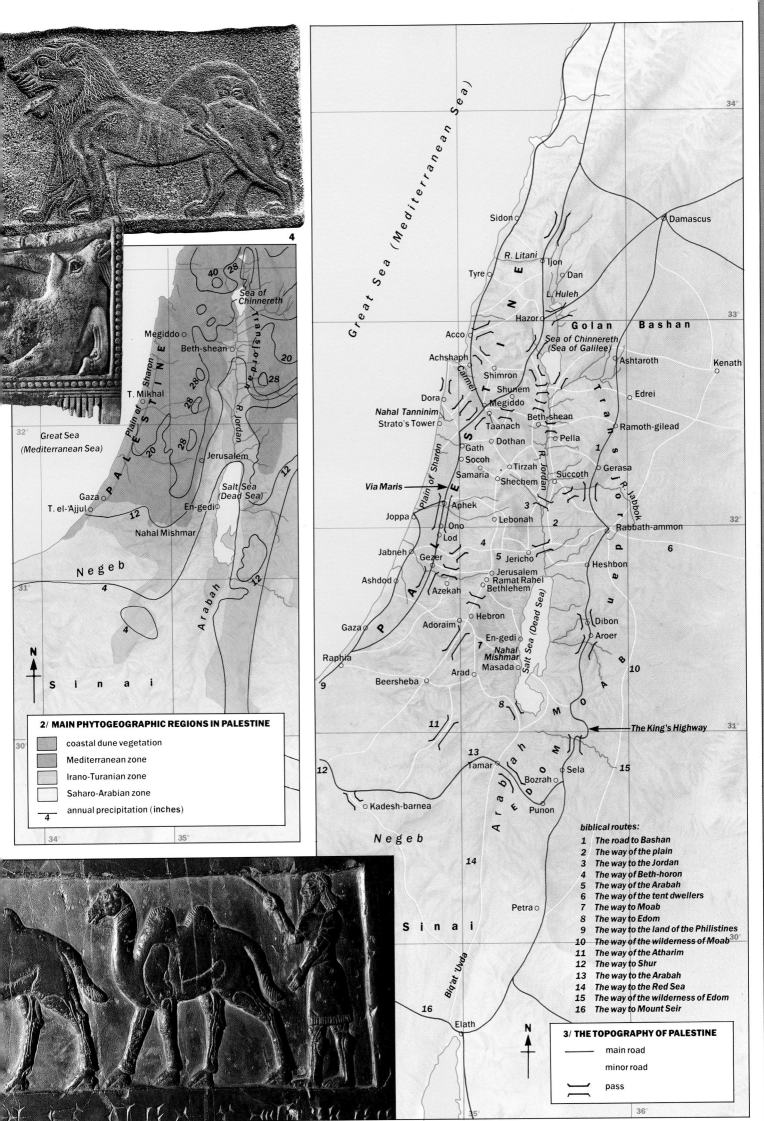

2/ MAIN PHYTOGEOGRAPHIC REGIONS IN PALESTINE

- coastal dune vegetation
- Mediterranean zone
- Irano-Turanian zone
- Saharo-Arabian zone
- 4 annual precipitation (inches)

Map 2 labels:

Sea of Chinnereth
Megiddo
Beth-shean
T. Mikhal
Plain of Sharon
T R A N S J O R D A N
R. Jordan
P A L E S T I N E
Great Sea (Mediterranean Sea)
Jerusalem
Gaza
T. el-'Ajjul
En-gedi
Salt Sea (Dead Sea)
Nahal Mishmar
N e g e b
A r a b a h
S i n a i
N

Map 3 labels:

Great Sea (Mediterranean Sea)
Sidon
Damascus
R. Litani
Ijon
Tyre
Dan
L. Huleh
P H O E N I C I A
Hazor
Golan
Bashan
Acco
Sea of Chinnereth (Sea of Galilee)
Ashtaroth
Kenath
Achshaph
Shimron
Shunem
Edrei
Dora
Megiddo
Nahal Tanninim
Beth-shean
Ramoth-gilead
Strato's Tower
Taanach
Pella
Gath
Dothan
Socoh
Tirzah
Succoth
Gerasa
Samaria
Shechem
Via Maris
Aphek
Lebonah
Rabbath-ammon
Joppa
Ono
Lod
Jabneh
Gezer
Jericho
Heshbon
Ashdod
Jerusalem
Ramat Rahel
Bethlehem
Azekah
Hebron
Dibon
Gaza
Adoraim
Aroer
En-gedi
Nahal Mishmar
Raphia
Arad
Masada
Beersheba
The King's Highway
Tamar
Bozrah
Sela
Kadesh-barnea
Punon
E D O M
M O A B
A r a b a h
N e g e b
Petra
S i n a i
Biqat 'Uvda
Elath
R. Jabbok
R. Jordan
P A L E S T I N E
Carmel
Plain of Sharon

biblical routes:

1   The road to Bashan
2   The way of the plain
3   The way to the Jordan
4   The way of Beth-horon
5   The way of the Arabah
6   The way of the tent dwellers
7   The way to Moab
8   The way to Edom
9   The way to the land of the Philistines
10 The way of the wilderness of Moab
11 The way of the Atharim
12 The way to Shur
13 The way to the Arabah
14 The way to the Red Sea
15 The way of the wilderness of Edom
16 The way to Mount Seir

3/ THE TOPOGRAPHY OF PALESTINE

- main road
- minor road
- pass

N

ACCORDING to the Book of Joshua, the Israelites under the leadership of Joshua, the successor to Moses, invaded Canaan from Transjordan. After crossing the Jordan the twelve tribes quickly took the whole country, which had been promised to them, in three campaigns. The most spectacular battles were those at Jericho, Ai and Gibeon, cities located in the central part of the land (JOSH 6-9); other campaigns were in the south (JOSH 10.16-42) and in north Canaan (JOSH 11.1-15). The conquest is summarized succinctly in JOSH 10.40: 'So Joshua smote all the land, the hill-country, and the South, and the Lowland, and the slopes, and all their kings; he left none remaining; but he utterly destroyed all that breathed...' Later he assigned the tribes to their inheritances and set borders for each.

A more careful reading of the biblical traditions about the entry into the land presents a different picture of the concept. It is apparent that the vivid accounts of victories found in the first half of the book of Joshua, stories filled with details about spies, the collapse of a city wall at a shout and the sun standing still, related to the conquest of Benjamin, a relatively small part of Canaan. JUDG 1.27-30 (as well as scattered references in Joshua) lists cities not taken in the conquest: Beth-shean, Taanach, Dor, Ibleam, Megiddo, Gezer, Acco, Achzib, Aphek and Beth-shemesh. According to this report the major cities were not taken. The Canaanites were not driven out but the Israelites are said to have dwelt in peace with them. This informa-

tion concurs with the fact that long after Solomon many Canaanites still lived unhindered in the land. Apparently the original inhabitants were later incorporated into Israel.

The problems arising from the very complex picture of the Israelite conquest presented in biblical traditions have prompted theories about how the land was actually occupied.

One theory of Israel's settlement in Canaan is that this must have occurred through 'gradual infiltration' of semi-nomads from desert areas into the less populated regions of Palestine. This process could have extended over a long period of time. Certainly there are references in the OT to groups of people coming to Canaan from elsewhere and in all probability from two different directions: one from Kadesh-barnea towards the south and one via Transjordan moving toward the centre of the land and perhaps northwards. No evidence, according to this view, points toward a violent invasion on a large scale. More probably, apart from the two groups just mentioned, other groups entered Canaan from time to time, but it is impossible to say from the preserved record how the process of settlement was actually accomplished. It seems practically certain that, with the exception of some local conflicts, the process was fairly pacific. In the era of the patriarchs the Israelites lived mostly in harmony with the local population. In the family of Judah there was marriage with Canaanite women (cf GEN 38). Furthermore, references to attacks on Canaanite cities are very limited, while the city-states continued to exist

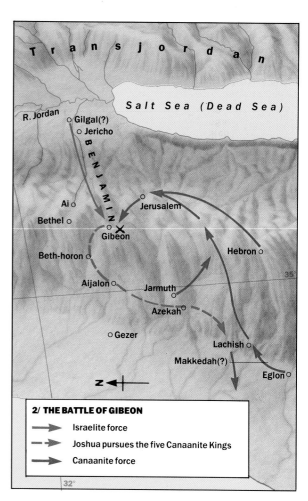

2/ THE BATTLE OF GIBEON

→ Israelite force

→ Joshua pursues the five Canaanite Kings

→ Canaanite force

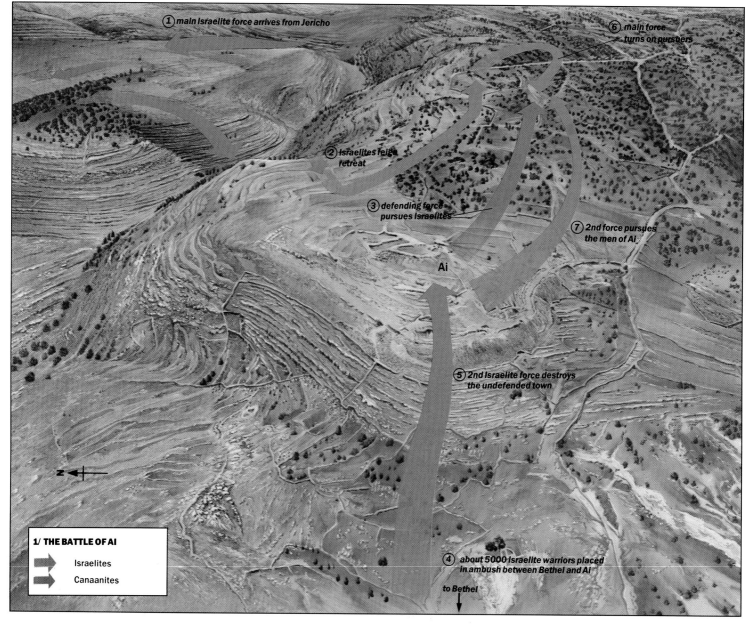

① main Israelite force arrives from Jericho

⑥ main force turns on pursuers

② Israelites feign retreat

③ defending force pursues Israelites

⑦ 2nd force pursues the men of Ai

Ai

⑤ 2nd Israelite force destroys the undefended town

④ about 5000 Israelite warriors placed in ambush between Bethel and Ai

to Bethel

1/ THE BATTLE OF AI

⇒ Israelites

⇒ Canaanites

1/ map below left Having been defeated at Ai, Joshua decided to launch a full-scale attack on the city. This battle is described in great detail in JOSH 8.10-29. This large-scale map shows the remains of Ai, located in hill-country ten miles north of Jerusalem. Excavation of the remains has thrown up some conflicting evidence. For example, the town may have covered an area of about six acres and thus could have held a maximum of 1000 people. JOSH 8, however, speaks of 12,000 inhabitants defeated by 30,000 Israelites.

2/ map left In JOSH 10.1-13 a league of Canaanite kings attacked Gibeon. In answer to the Gibeonites' plea for help, Joshua came up from Gilgal and defeated the Canaanites.

3/ map right After the battle of Gibeon, Joshua pursued the five Canaanite kings into southern Canaan (JOSH 10.16-39). The decline of the Egyptian 19th dynasty had left this area unprotected and it fell easily to Israelite conquest.

4/ map below Joshua defeated the Canaanite kings of the North at Merom, and then destroyed their stronghold at Hazor (JOSH 11.1-15).

5/ map below right JOSH 12.9-24 lists 31 royal Canaanite cities west of the Jordan Israelites. Not all the sites can be identified.

3/ THE CONQUEST OF THE SHEPHELAH AND THE SOUTH
→ Israelite force
➤ Canaanite auxiliary force under Horam

for a considerable period of time, indeed throughout the patriarchal period. In JOSH 24 there are also references to an agreement between the different tribes, some of whom had always lived in Canaan or had been settled there for so long that those coming later considered them to be indigenous.

A third recently proposed explanation of the settlement is the so-called 'peasant uprising', put forth by G. Mendenhall and later enlarged upon by N. K. Gottwald. According to this theory the group which later became known as Israel was not composed entirely of immigrants, but was created out of a variety of elements. Among them were Canaanites who had rebelled against their overlords. These were joined by the 'apiru (cf page 24) and by a group of Israelites who came into Canaan from Egypt. The emphasis

which this latter group placed upon liberation from slavery and the exodus from Egypt made a deep impression upon the other two groups. The 'Conquest' was a socio-political revolution of the oppressed against exploitation. The struggle mentioned in the OT concerns local battles in which only the rulers in a particular area were driven out. Obviously this theory has certain elements in common with the other two. There are references to a conquest and gradual penetration, but according to this view they take place harmoniously, and with a certain amount of co-operation from a section of the Canaanite people.

These three settlement theories show that from the partial record of this crucial event in Israel's history it is impossible to determine exactly what is meant by the term 'Conquest'.

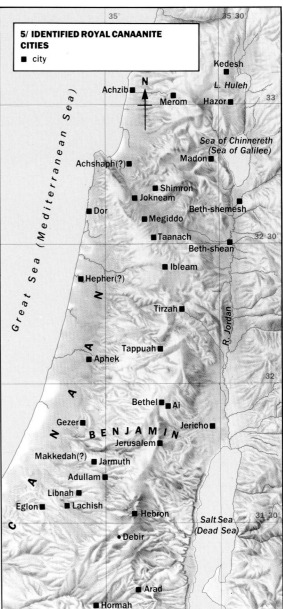

5/ IDENTIFIED ROYAL CANAANITE CITIES
■ city

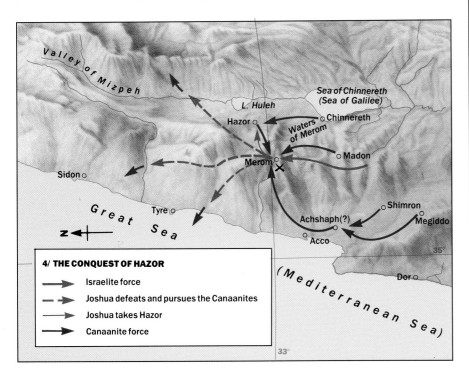

4/ THE CONQUEST OF HAZOR
→ Israelite force
⇢ Joshua defeats and pursues the Canaanites
→ Joshua takes Hazor
➤ Canaanite force

ISRAEL'S entry into the land of Canaan as described in JOSH 1-12 was clearly a 'conquest' (see pages 62-63). Beginning with a series of victories at Jericho, Ai – Gibeon escaped by deceit – Joshua defeated the five Amorite kings and proceeded southward to 'utterly destroy all that breathed'. He is said to have taken all these kings and their lands 'at one time' (JOSH 10.42). After a thrust northward there appears the tally: slain were 31 kings (JOSH 12.24).

Now that the land had been conquered it must be occupied. In JOSH 13-19 territories are assigned by clearly defined borders and the cities within them to the nine and one-half tribes (two and one-half tribes had already been allotted by Moses). Now that the opposition had been eliminated the settlement took place easily.

However, in JOSH 13-17 (and in JUDG 1 and 2), some exceptions appear. Over 20 unconquered cities are named. They lay in the area west of the Jordan; in the northern Shephelah, the north of the Plain of Sharon, in the Plain of Jezreel, in the northern coastal plain, in Upper Galilee and one (Jerusalem) in the central hills. Among them are some of the oldest and most important centres of

population (see pages 46-47). The settlement was gradual and certainly partial.

This impression gained from reading the biblical account in the second half of JOSHUA is strengthened by the evidence for new settlements in the hill regions. These were areas which had until the beginning of the Iron Age I been neither inhabited nor cultivated. There is a remark in JOSH 17.16-18 that the tribes of Manasseh and Ephraim were instructed by Joshua to fell forests in the hill country in order to establish new settlements. Most of these Israelite settlements were in the beginning small and were more like unfortified villages. Little archaeological research has been carried out in such small areas. Only in a few cases, with the larger settlements, is it possible to locate them with more precision.

A characteristic feature of Early Iron Age settlements is the distinctive architectural plan of the pillared house. The most popular of the so-called 'four-room' house was one with two rooms subdivided by rows of pillars. The origins of the pillared house plan are obscure and the four-room house appears in a fully developed form at the very beginning of the Iron Age without any apparent antecedents. It does not seem to have any forerunners in the Canaanite architectural tradition of a central courtyard surrounded by rooms on all sides. It has been suggested that the four-room house plan developed out of a more simple type (for example building no.90 at T. Esdar) which, in turn, was derived from a nomadic tent used by the Israelites. It is generally agreed that the homeland of the

four-room pillared house, and its variants was in the central hill country. Those who adhere to this view maintain that the pillared four-room house plan was a local invention, around 1200 BC, which was the result of rapid Israelite adaptation to the available resources and to a new rural way of life in the hilly regions. Examples of this plan dating to the Early Iron Age have been found in the central hill country at Ai, Shiloh, Kh. Raddana, and Giloh.

During the course of the 11th century BC, the four-room house plan rapidly spread to other regions of the country, such as Philistia, (T. Qasila Strata X-IX and T. Sera' Stratum VIII), to the Jezreel Valley (T. Megiddo Stratum VIB) and to Transjordan (Sahab near Amman and Kh. el-Medeiyineh). The four-room house plan was also adopted during the 11th century BC at Israelite settlements in the Negeb Desert. Numerous pillared houses have been unearthed at T. Masos in the Beersheba region. They were built out of mud-brick on stone foundations and the pillars were constructed out of stone segments. The four-room house plan remained a dominant characteristic of Israelite dwellings throughout the Iron Age and down to the early 6th century BC.

Although frequent attempts have been made in the earlier days of excavations to equate a layer of destruction at a site with a biblical reference to the 'conquest', it has become patent that cities were destroyed by such causes as accidental fire, wars with neighbouring cities or other causes. A more valid evidence for an occupation of a site by a new people is a change in the material culture. Unfortunately discontinuity between the material culture of the Late Bronze Age and that of the Early Iron Age is slight. But the change in architectural style from the courtyard plan to the four-room house seems to have occurred at about the time of Israel's gradual settlement in the land as it is described in the second half of JOSHUA and chapters 1 and 2 of JUDGES.

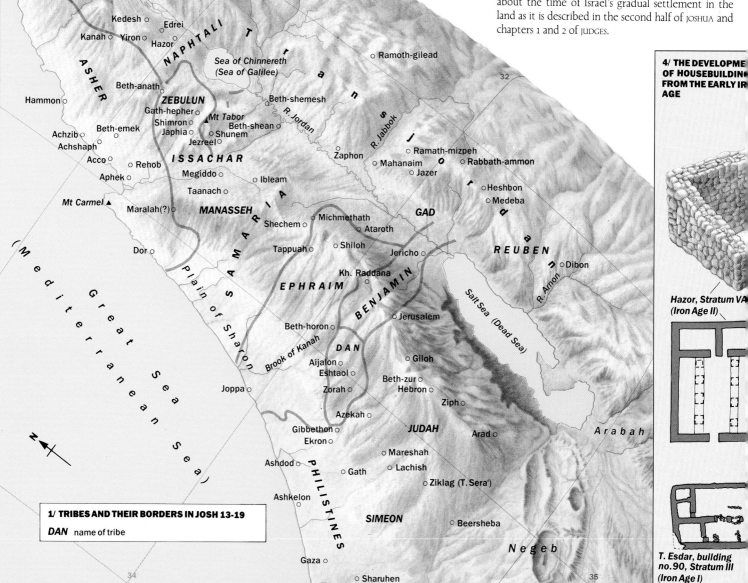

1/ TRIBES AND THEIR BORDERS IN JOSH 13-19

DAN name of tribe

4/ THE DEVELOPMENT OF HOUSEBUILDING FROM THE EARLY IRON AGE

Hazor, Stratum VA (Iron Age II)

T. Esdar, building no.90, Stratum III (Iron Age I)

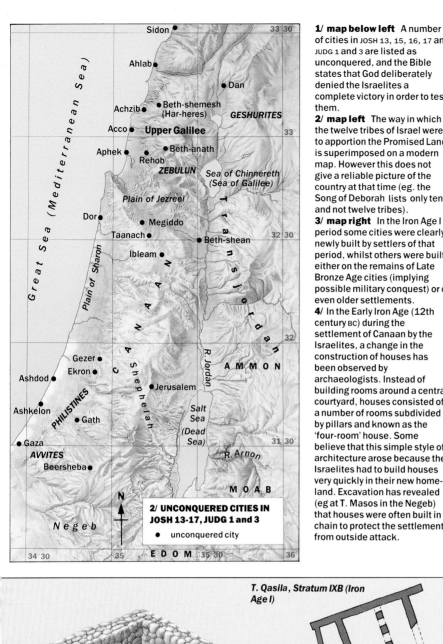

2/ UNCONQUERED CITIES IN JOSH 13-17, JUDG 1 and 3
- unconquered city

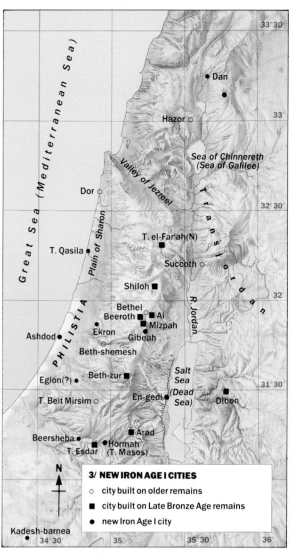

3/ NEW IRON AGE I CITIES
- ○ city built on older remains
- ■ city built on Late Bronze Age remains
- ● new Iron Age I city

1/ map below left A number of cities in JOSH 13, 15, 16, 17 and JUDG 1 and 3 are listed as unconquered, and the Bible states that God deliberately denied the Israelites a complete victory in order to test them.

2/ map left The way in which the twelve tribes of Israel were to apportion the Promised Land is superimposed on a modern map. However this does not give a reliable picture of the country at that time (eg. the Song of Deborah lists only ten and not twelve tribes).

3/ map right In the Iron Age I period some cities were clearly newly built by settlers of that period, whilst others were built either on the remains of Late Bronze Age cities (implying possible military conquest) or of even older settlements.

4/ In the Early Iron Age (12th century BC) during the settlement of Canaan by the Israelites, a change in the construction of houses has been observed by archaeologists. Instead of building rooms around a central courtyard, houses consisted of a number of rooms subdivided by pillars and known as the 'four-room' house. Some believe that this simple style of architecture arose because the Israelites had to build houses very quickly in their new homeland. Excavation has revealed (eg at T. Masos in the Negeb) that houses were often built in a chain to protect the settlement from outside attack.

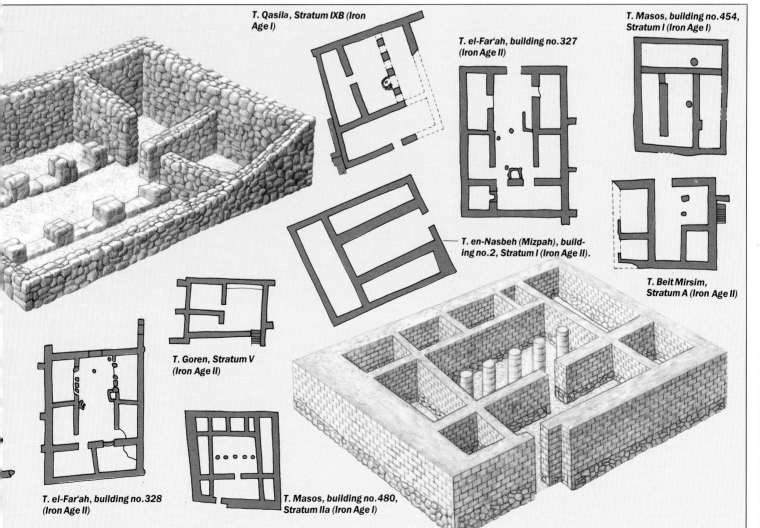

T. Qasila, Stratum IXB (Iron Age I)

T. el-Far'ah, building no.327 (Iron Age II)

T. Masos, building no.454, Stratum I (Iron Age I)

T. en-Nasbeh (Mizpah), building no.2, Stratum I (Iron Age II).

T. Beit Mirsim, Stratum A (Iron Age II)

T. Goren, Stratum V (Iron Age II)

T. el-Far'ah, building no.328 (Iron Age II)

T. Masos, building no.480, Stratum IIa (Iron Age I)

SHORTLY after Israel's entry into Canaan (generally placed in the 13th century BC), the Philistines became a major threat to its settlement. Samson, the hero of the tribe of Dan, engaged in skirmishes with the Philistines and eventually the entire tribe was forced to migrate to a new home in the north (page 46). The major battles with the Philistines were those fought by Saul (page 46) and David for the possession of strategic and fertile areas. Yet never did the Philistines exercise permanent control over more than the limited area occupied by their five-city league of Gaza, Ashkelon, Ashdod, Ekron and Gath. In addition to the wealth of information about the Philistines found in the Books of JUDGES and SAMUEL, there are Egyptian accounts of an invasion in the 12th century BC of 'Sea Peoples' (page 32), one of which was the Philistines (Peleset). Settlements of these people have been attested at a number of archaeological sites.

In the fifth year of Pharaoh Merneptah (1236-1223 BC) groups of Sea Peoples allied themselves with the Libyans in an attempt to invade Egypt. The peoples named are the Sherden, Sheklesh, Lukka, Tursha and Akawasha (Achaeans). However, the Philistines themselves, and the groups closely associated with them are not mentioned until the reign of Pharaoh Ramesses III (1198-1166).

The Tale of Wen-amon (mid-11th century BC) vividly illustrates the chaos existing in the Levant and the lack of Egyptian control over peoples ostensibly under their domination. The story is told by a priest of the god Amon who is sent to Byblos to purchase lumber for the sacred barge of the god. The priest is treated with little respect by the rulers of the cities he visits. He is robbed during his stay at Dor, a city belonging to the Tjekker and

nominally under Egyptian control. He then has to flee and is pursued by the Tjekker in their fleet of eleven ships as far as Cyprus. This story is of great importance because of its reference to the Tjekker, one of the Sea Peoples closely allied to the Philistines, and to their city of Dor, in the northern coastal plain, just north of the Philistine settlement area.

The 12th-century BC reliefs and inscriptions of the mortuary temple of Ramesses III, at Medinet Habu in Upper Egypt, are the most important records of the arrival of the Sea Peoples. The inscriptions record the destruction of the Hittite empire and the attempts by the Sea Peoples to invade Egypt. The reliefs depict and

1/ map below The route of Wen-amon and the migration of the tribe of Dan.
2/ map right Sites yielding Philistine artefacts and those where iron has been found.
3/ Scene from the temple of Ramasses III at Medinet Habu, showing a ship engaged in battle with the Philistines and other Sea Peoples who wear feather crowns.

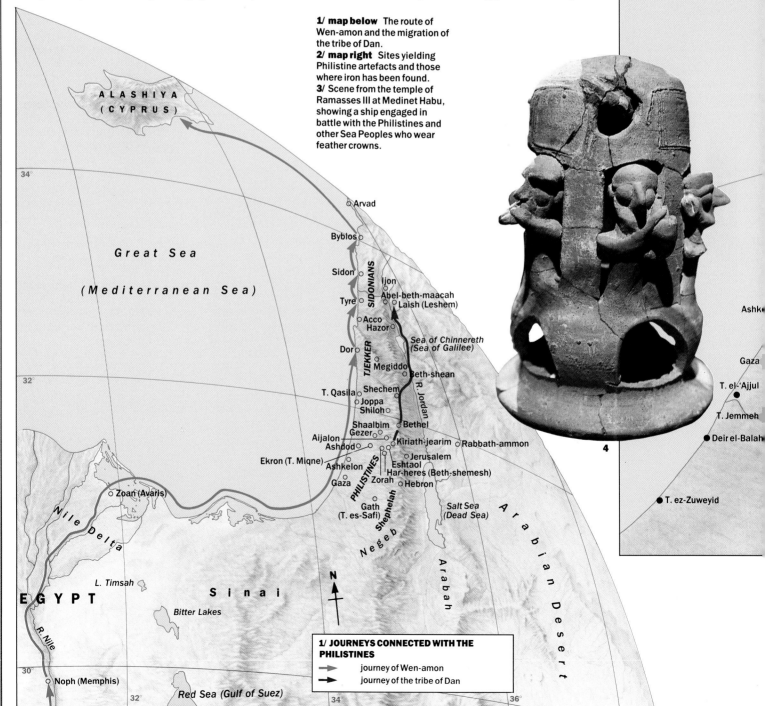

1/ JOURNEYS CONNECTED WITH THE PHILISTINES

→ journey of Wen-amon
→ journey of the tribe of Dan

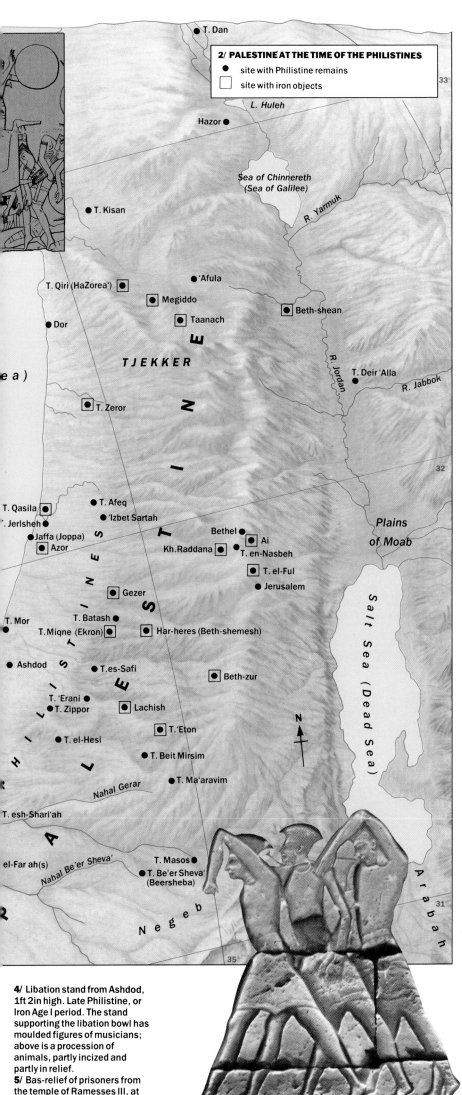

2/ PALESTINE AT THE TIME OF THE PHILISTINES

● site with Philistine remains

□ site with iron objects

describe two great battles with the Sea Peoples, one on land, fought in Phoenicia or Syria, and the other on the sea, probably fought in the Nile Delta.

In the land battle the Sea Peoples are shown fighting in chariots; their families travel with them in ox-drawn carts with solid wheels, similar to a type of cart still used in parts of Anatolia. Three groups are distinguishable by their headdresses: the Philistines, Tjekker and Denyen (Danuna) wear high 'feathered' headdresses; the Sherden, who in this battle are fighting for the Egyptians, wear horned helmets, and the Sheklesh have fillet headbands.

In the great naval battle, the Sea Peoples are shown in their fighting ships, with duck-shaped prow and stern, powered only by sail. Here the Sherden are shown fighting with the other Sea Peoples against the Egyptians. Both groups carry round shields and wield long broadswords. They wear panelled kilts with tassels and corselets, reminiscent in design of Mycenaean armour.

The evidence of these reliefs makes it clear that one group of Sea Peoples fought the Egyptians in a great land battle but were not decisively defeated. They were strong enough to attempt to invade Egypt by sea, this time in alliance with another of the Sea Peoples, the Sherden, when they were defeated and eventually settled permanently in Palestine. This group included the Philistines, Tjekker and Denyen or Danuna. The latter group may have some connection with the tribe of Dan who, according to the biblical account (JUDG 18) did not succeed in taking possession of the area allocated to them and had to migrate from the Shephelah to the Canaanite city of Laish in the north.

The arrival of a new cultural element was reflected in the style of architecture, burial customs and religious cults. At Tel Qasila, the first unmistakable Philistine temples were found, often containing cult vessels and even a socketed bronze double axe, which has Aegean connections. No exact parallels for the temples' architecture have been found in Palestine though some features show Canaanite influence. However, small sanctuaries excavated at Mycenae, Cyprus, and the island of Melos in the Aegean, resemble the Qasila temples in a number of ways.

The cult vessels excavated at Philistine sites include ring *kernoi* (libation vessels), animal, bird and human-shaped vessels, *rhyta* (one-handled cups with a bottom often in the form of a lion's head), storage jars with cup holders and terracotta figurines. The terracotta female figurines are clearly derived from Mycenaean prototypes not previously known in Canaan. A unique example from Ashdod, of the 12th century BC, has the body merging into a chair or couch and almost certainly represents a goddess (see page 44). It is not known what gods the Philistines worshipped when they arrived in Canaan but their deities of later times, Dagon, Ashtoreth and Beelzebub, are of Canaanite origin.

Philistine pottery is a large, homogeneous group, locally made, painted in black and red, usually on a white-slipped background. It appears in levels dated to the first half of the 12th and the 11th century BC and continues until the 10th century BC when the Philistines were assimilated into the local culture.

The decoration of the pottery is mainly derived from Mycenaean prototypes and is varied and colourful, with a highly developed artistic sense. Birds are a common motif, but the most striking and readily recognizable feature is the many types of geometric and linear designs, such as spirals, semi-circles, chevrons, zig-zags and lozenges. Animals and humans are rarely portrayed but are not unknown. Cult vessels show similar decoration but have different shapes.

It has been generally accepted that the Philistines introduced iron into Palestine and that their control of the metal industry was one of the factors that enabled them to achieve military superiority over the rest of the population (I SAM 13.19-21). Most iron tools and weapons of the Iron I Age come from sites showing Philistine occupation or influence. Very few iron products, and even fewer bronze objects, have been found at Canaanite or Israelite sites.

Although the Philistines ceased to be a threat to Israel after the time of David, they maintained their identity for centuries in their traditional homeland. Assyria extracted tribute and their cities often played a role in the political conflicts involving Assyria, Egypt and Judah down until the time of the Babylonian exile. The Greeks and the Romans, who approached the Levant from the west, made use of the term 'land of the Philistines' (Palaestina) as a designation for the entire land extending as far east as the River Jordan. It is ironical that Israel's land should for centuries be called by the name of its most bitter and persistent enemy.

4/ Libation stand from Ashdod, 1ft 2in high. Late Philistine, or Iron Age I period. The stand supporting the libation bowl has moulded figures of musicians; above is a procession of animals, partly incized and partly in relief.

5/ Bas-relief of prisoners from the temple of Ramesses III, at Medinet Habu. Height c 3ft, 12th century BC.

THE heroes who emerged among the individual tribes, who became known as 'judges', were very different from the national figures of Moses and Joshua. They were chosen to lead in times of emergency, sometimes obtained the help of other tribes, and when the crisis was over seemed to lapse into obscurity. In this respect they differed too from the kings, who were later chosen and anointed to rule for life over all Israel. These tribal figures such as Jephthah, Barak, Gideon, Ehud and Samson distinguished themselves by bravery, daring, cleverness and physical strength as they repulsed assaults upon the individual tribes. The punitive raids of Ammonites, the Canaanites from the north, Midianites, Moabites and Philistines threatened the security of settlers. Then 'Yahweh raised them up a saviour'.

Colourful stories of these heroes are preserved in the Book of Judges, even though they were later edited to support a theological pattern prominent in the development of Israel's religion. Conspicuously absent in these accounts are the Canaanite city-states which dominate the accounts of both the Egyptian conquerors and the accounts of the conquest of the land by Joshua. Rather the occasion generally for the appearance of a judge 'to save Israel' was a tribal invasion into the territory of one of the tribes. The stories of the judges are vignettes or 'snapshots', storylike fragments which are difficult to date. However, the traditions preserved in the Book of Judges afford a glimpse of some aspects of the experience of pre-monarchal Israel as she attempted to consolidate a hold on the land. The tribes and clans rarely acted together. Ehud's battle against the Moabites at most involved the tribes of Benjamin and Ephraim. Gideon's repulsion of the Midianites probably involved only his own clan of Abiezrites, together, perhaps, with the tribe of Ephraim. Jephthah led Gilead to victory over the Ammonites. Samson was likewise a local hero of the tribe of Dan who skirmished with the Philistines. The extent of Israel's lack of effective unity at this time is well illustrated by these stories, and by JUDG 4, which records a significant victory of a relatively wide tribal alliance led by Deborah and Barak over the Canaanites, to which, however, so many tribes failed to contribute (JUDG 5.16-17).

The period of the Judges marked a transition in the social history of Palestine. The stage when the land was under control of a number of Canaanite city-states (page 24) which from time to time were subject to Egyptian control, was followed by a weakening of Egyptian dominance and by the rise of serious economic problems at home. The Canaanite city-state system broke down and in its place there developed the decentralized tribal society which is reflected in the Book of Judges. Eventually this relatively weak system of social control was to be succeeded by a monarchy, which, in some respects, reintroduced some

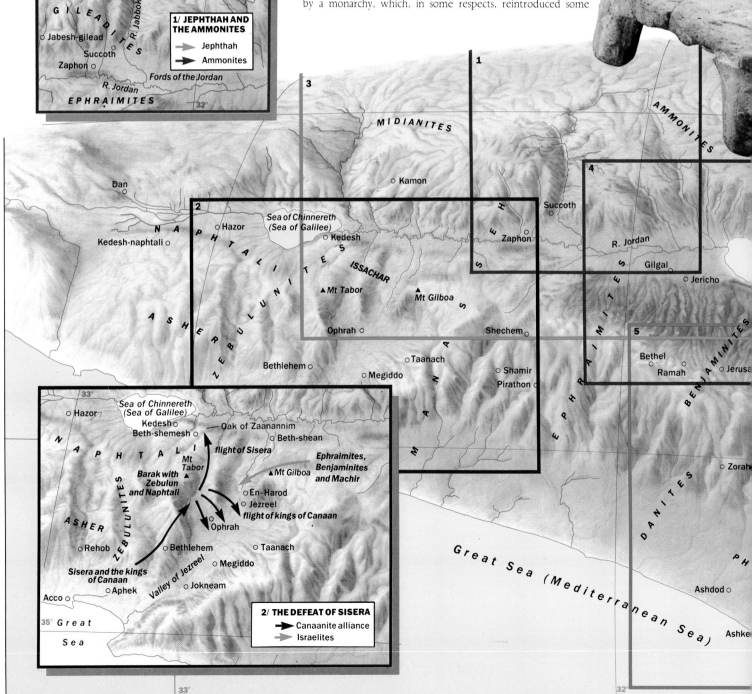

LAND OF TOB
○ Ramoth-gilead

AMMONITES

○ Rabbath-ammon

Mizpeh-gilead ○

Abel-keramim ○

GILEADITES

R. Jabbok

○ Jabesh-gilead

Succoth

Zaphon ○

R. Jordan

Fords of the Jordan

EPHRAIMITES

1/ JEPHTHAH AND THE AMMONITES
→ Jephthah
→ Ammonites

MIDIANITES

AMMONITES

Dan ○

○ Kamon

Hazor ○

Sea of Chinnereth (Sea of Galilee)

Kedesh-naphtali ○

NAPHTALI

○ Kedesh

Succoth ○

Zaphon ○

R. Jordan

Gilgal ○

○ Jericho

ISSACHAR

MANASSEH

▲ Mt Tabor

ZEBULUNITES

ASHER

▲ Mt Gilboa

Ophrah ○

Shechem ○

Bethel ○

Ramah ○

Jerusa...

Bethlehem ○

○ Taanach

○ Shamir
Pirathon ○

BENJAMINITES

○ Megiddo

EPHRAIM

MANASSEH

○ Zora...

DANITES

2/ THE DEFEAT OF SISERA

Sea of Chinnereth (Sea of Galilee)

Hazor ○

Kedesh ○

Beth-shemesh ○ — Oak of Zaanannim

NAPHTALI

○ Beth-shean

flight of Sisera

Mt Tabor ▲

Barak with Zebulun and Naphtali

▲ Mt Gilboa

Ephraimites, Benjaminites and Machir

ZEBULUNITES

○ En-Harod

○ Jezreel

ASHER

flight of kings of Canaan

○ Ophrah

○ Rehob

○ Bethlehem

○ Taanach

Sisera and the kings of Canaan

Valley of Jezreel

○ Megiddo

○ Aphek

○ Jokneam

Acco ○

Great Sea

→ Canaanite alliance
→ Israelites

Great Sea (Mediterranean Sea)

Ashdod ○

Ashke...

Maps 1-6 below

1/ Jephthah leads the Gileadites in resisting the Ammonite expansion (JUDG 11.1-12.7).

2/ Sisera is defeated by forces of Barak and Deborah in a decisive battle at Taanach (JUDG 5.19). Sisera is slain by Jael at the 'Oak of Zaanannim' (JUDG 4-5).

3/ Gideon and his clan of Abiezer mount a surprise attack on Midianite raiders and expel them from Israelite territory (JUDG 6-8).

4/ Ehud of Benjamin kills Eglon the Moabite king and inflicts a decisive defeat on the Moabites (JUDG 3.12-30).

5/ Samson of Dan kills Philistines with his own strength, destroys their fields until, betrayed by Delilah, he meets his death at the Philistine temple at Gaza (JUDG 13-16).

6/ Background map showing the tribal areas of settlement.

7/ left Figurine from Ashdod in the form of both a woman and a bed (c 12th century BC).

aspects of the old city-state system of government.

The society of the Canaanite city-states was marked by a sharp distinction between ruler and ruled, rich and poor, and by the separation of workers into guilds, such as those of weavers, masons, chariot-makers and others. In contrast Israelite tribalism, as found in the Book of Judges, was an egalitarianism based on a pastoral-agricultural economy. The Gideon story tells of Midianite raids on Israel's fields, their destruction and looting of crops and animals (JUDG 6.1-6). The growing of wheat and barley, the tending of sheep, goats and cattle, and the cultivation and pruning of vineyards, were fundamental to tribal life. Outside this agricultural-pastoral work there seems to have been no other significant contribution to the tribal economy. The Book of Judges occasionally mentions cities, but these were probably unfortified settlements inhabited by agricultural workers.

In Israelite tribal society the fundamental social and economic unit was the extended family. This was a largely self-sufficient unit, owning property and having few occupations apart from tending of livestock and the growing of crops. The wider association to which the family belonged was the clan, which functioned as the social context within which the families intermarried and found material aid and protection. The tribe was a much more fluid and changeable entity. It was both a social and a territorial unit and as such it was subject to continual change in the internal clan membership and indeed in its very existence.

The social structure encouraged independence on the part of clans and families. Trade was probably non-existent, external pressure was occasional and usually involved only isolated groups; thus, there was little need for the creation of more comprehensive social structures. It was the clan or family rather than Israel which was of primary importance to the Israelites.

Occasional unified leadership was afforded in times of emergency by charismatic leaders who came forward to deal with just those situations. The elders exercised a representative function, but with no real power; effective decision-making was done by general assemblies of the 'men of the city'. Defence was the responsibility of all those capable of bearing arms rather than of a professional army. Disputes were settled either by the elders or by judges. Some cultic associations may have existed in Israel for the maintenance of sanctuaries, but society in general was decentralized, and leagues of any nature were exceptional.

Israelite tribalism emerged primarily in the mountain areas of Palestine, while the Canaanite city-state system continued to dominate the plains (JUDG 1.27-35). With the significant exception of JUDG 4, the events of the period of the judges took place in those less accessible districts lying largely outside the city-state range of control. The victory over Sisera (JUDG 4) marks the first appearance of Israelite tribes in the plains, and a significant stage in the development by which Israel under the monarchy came, though not without setbacks, to dominate Palestine.

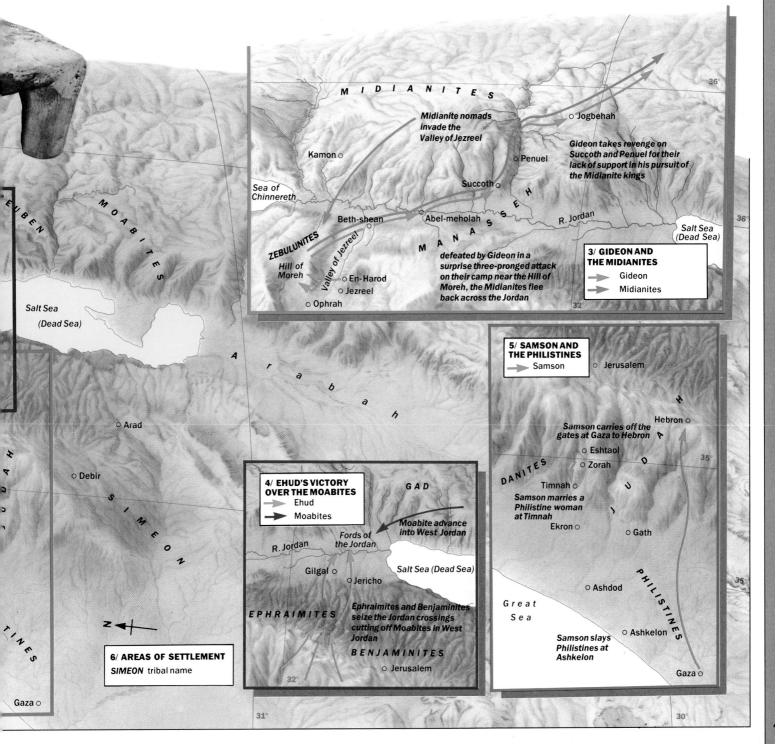

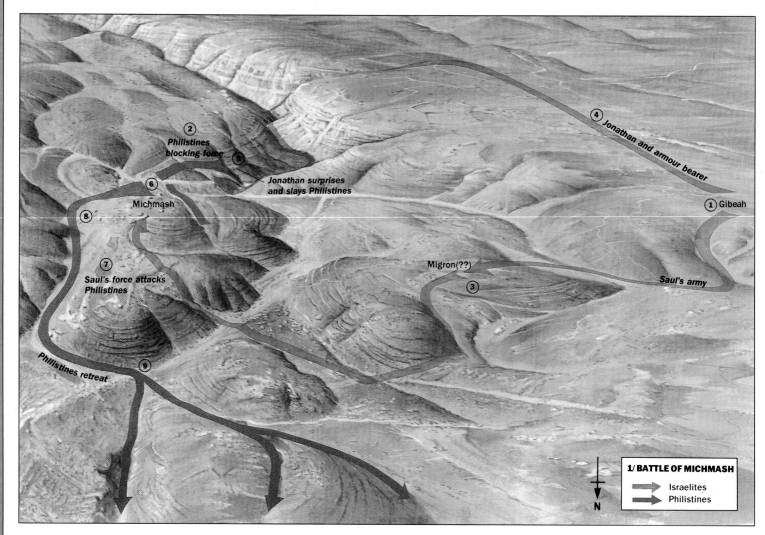

Map labels:
- ② Philistines blocking force
- ⑤ Jonathan surprises and slays Philistines
- ④ Jonathan and armour bearer
- ① Gibeah
- ⑥ Michmash
- ⑧
- ⑦ Saul's force attacks Philistines
- Migron(??) ③
- Saul's army
- ⑨ Philistines retreat

1/ BATTLE OF MICHMASH
→ Israelites
→ Philistines

N

BY proclaiming Saul as their king, the Israelites entered a new phase of their history. Traditional segmented society gave way to centralized political power.

Saul lived *c*1000 BC and belonged to the small Israelite tribe of Benjamin which was overshadowed by (if not a sub-branch of) the neighbouring tribe of Ephraim. Both tribes were settled in the hill country north of Jerusalem, along with various other population elements such as Hivites and Arkites. Jerusalem was not yet a city of prominence and the villagers of the hill country were vulnerable to oppression from all sides. Thus Saul emerged as a local military hero who led the Benjaminite-Ephraimite resistance against surrounding enemies, especially the Philistines. Pro-

claimed king by his countrymen in response to his early victories, Saul spent the remainder of his career, a reign of unknown duration, defending what thus became the fledgling kingdom of Israel. His public career ended the same way it had begun, in battle. Both Saul and his son Jonathan were killed while fighting the Philistines on the slopes of Mt Gilboa.

Saul accomplished two major victories early in his career, one against the Philistines in his own Benjaminite neighbourhood, at the strategic crossing of a steep valley which separated Gibeah and Michmash (I SAM 13.2-14.40); and one against the Ammonites who were attacking the city of Jabesh in Gilead (I SAM 11). Although the defeat of the Ammonites is reported first in the Bible, it is doubtful that Saul could have

collected an army and undertaken a military campaign so far afield as Gilead unless he had already expelled the Philistines from his own home area. It is more likely therefore, that Saul's first military venture was the surprise seizure of Gibeah which controlled the southern end of the crossing and may have had a small fortification. When Philistine reinforcements arrived, they camped at Michmash on the opposite (northern) side of the crossing and began to raid the countryside (see especially I SAM 13.16-18). The turning point in the struggle occurred, according to the biblical narrative, when Jonathan made a surprise raid on the Philistine camp. The Philistines were routed and fled the hill country (map 1) leaving Saul to establish his residence at Gibeah.

Map labels:
- ⑤ En-dor Saul consults witch
- Hill of Moreh
- Valley of Jezreel

The biblical account of the Jabesh-gilead victory in I SAM 11 begins, therefore, with Saul residing at Gibeah (map 2). The Ammonites attacked Jabesh, a Gileadite city with Israelite tribal connections, and when the Jabesites appealed for a peace settlement the Ammonite king offered impossible terms. 'On this condition I will make a treaty with you, that I gouge out all your right eyes, and thus put disgrace upon all Israel' (I SAM 11.2). Thereupon the Jabesites, having heard no doubt of Saul's recent victory over the Philistines, sent to Gibeah for help. Saul hurriedly mustered an army, marched to Jabesh, and saved the day.

Two other military campaigns, recorded in I SAM 15.1-9 and 31.3-7 respectively, give some impression of the extent of Saul's domain by the end of his career. The first describes a raid conducted by Saul against the Amalekites, a semi-nomadic people who roamed the Negeb and often raided the villages of the hill country south of Jerusalem (for example I SAM 39.2-3). Saul defeated the Amalekites and then set up a victory monument at Carmel, a town south-east of Hebron. This was possibly to signify his claim to political authority over the area. That he exercised some degree of political authority in the southern hill country is suggested also by the fact that Saul was able to move more freely in that region in pursuit of David while the local people are pictured reporting to Saul from time to time on David's whereabouts (I SAM 23.6-14; 24.2, 26.1).

The second military action, recorded in I SAM 31.1-7, is the final battle with the Philistines in which he and Jonathan met their deaths (map 3). The Philistines camped at Aphek on the eve of the battle, which itself was fought on the slopes of Mt Gilboa at the south-eastern end of the Jezreel Valley. Presumably Saul controlled the central hill country as far north as the Jezreel, therefore, and possibly an attempt on his part to secure control of the valley itself was what occasioned the battle. By the same measure, his kingdom obviously did not include Galilee.

Saul's kingdom did not have a highly organized administration or precisely defined boundaries. In peripheral areas the degree of Saul's authority will have varied from time to time, depending on whether his troops were present or whether the local people needed his protection against other threats. But even in the Benjamin-Ephraim-Gilead zone, the core of his territorial domain, some cities may have remained independent. Certainly Jerusalem was never incorporated into his kingdom (II SAM 5.6-8).

Very few details are known about Saul's reign, other than the military actions mentioned above and his dealings with David. Moreover, there are conflict-

1/ map left I SAM 14 describes a battle between the Israelites (led by Saul and Jonathan) and the Philistines at Michmash.
① Saul is at Gibeah-Geba with 600 men.
② The Philistines had blocked the passage of Michmash.
③ Saul moves to Migron.
④ Jonathan and his armour bearer carry out a raid.
⑤ In a surprise attack Jonathan kills some Philistines.
⑥ There is panic in the Philistine camp at Michmash.
⑦ A frontal assault by Saul's force adds to the Philistines' confusion.
⑧ The Philistines are defeated.
⑨ They retreat north and west.

2/ map right According to SAM 11 Saul was sent for by the Jabesites when they were attacked by Ammonites. He came up from Gibeah and scattered the Ammonite army.

3/ map below Saul's final battle on Mt Gilboa (I SAM 28-31).
① The Philistines are at Aphek.
② They advance along the Via Maris to Shunem.
③ Saul's army is on Mt Gilboa.
④ Saul encamps at Jezreel.
⑤ Saul sought the outlawed witch of Endor to call up Samuel who predicted defeat (I SAM 28.6-25).
⑥ In the ensuing battle Saul and his three sons are killed.
⑦ Their bodies are taken to Beth-shean.
⑧ The Israelites flee to Gilboa.
⑨ Saul is finally buried at Jabesh.

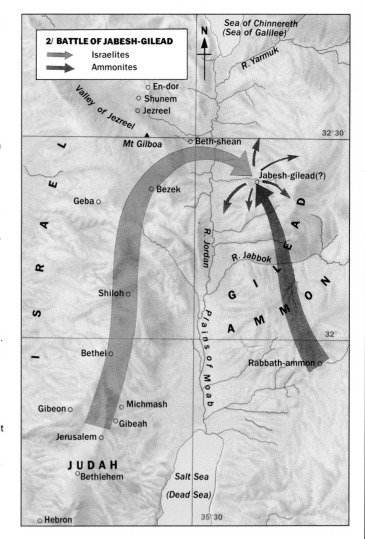

ing reports on how it happened that David, from the tribe of Judah and the village of Bethlehem, came to join Saul's court. Whatever the circumstances, David quickly gained a reputation as a daring and successful Philistine fighter, became close friends with Jonathan, and married Michal, Saul's daughter. Eventually, and probably with good reason as it turned out, Saul began to regard David as a threat even to his own position as king, and also to Jonathan's chances of ascending the throne. Thus Saul sought to kill David, who escaped to the vicinity of Adullam, south-west of Jerusalem. There David was joined by others who opposed Saul for one reason or another. When Saul learned of David's whereabouts in the Adullam vicinity, David and his men transferred to the 'wilderness' area

south-east of Hebron, where Saul, with support from the local people, continued to search and pursue. Finally, still on the run from Saul, David joined the Philistines and placed his army in their service. Specifically, he allied himself with Achish, the Philistine ruler of Gath, who in turn, as a mark of favour, assigned to David the city of Ziklag.

David and his men were thus allied with the Philistines at the time of the battle of Mt Gilboa in which Saul and Jonathan were killed, and actually marched with the Philistines to Aphek on the eve of the battle. The Philistines, however, fearing that David might switch sides during the fighting, sent him and his troops back to Ziklag (I SAM 29). The battle was a disaster for Israel, with Saul's kingdom left in shambles.

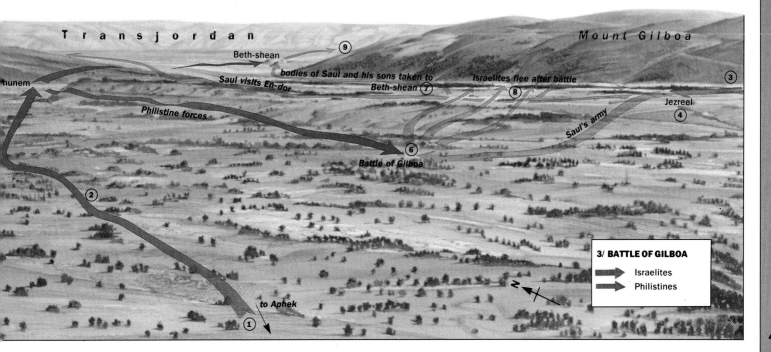

ISHBOSHETH (or Eshbaal as the name is sometimes written), one of Saul's sons, was recognized as Saul's successor – apparently without opposition, but without much enthusiastic support either. As it turned out, Ishbosheth was an exceedingly weak king who attempted to rule from the safety of a Transjordanian city, Mahanaim. David, in the meantime, perhaps still regarded by the Philistines as a vassal acting on their behalf, occupied Hebron with his soldiers and was crowned king there by the elders of the tribe of Judah.

Three military incidents illustrating his rapidly expanding influence are reported for the next stage of David's career. II SAM 2.12-32 describes the first of these: a skirmish between David's and Ishbosheth's soldiers which erupted 'by the pool' at Gibeon and ended with David's men victorious (map 1). Gibeon, situated at modern El-Jib, eight miles north-west of Jerusalem and bordering Benjaminite territory, played an important role in Israel's early history. Joshua is said to have made a treaty with the Gibeonites, for example, and Saul seems to have offended the people of the city in some way. The offence was so serious that he was forced to give seven of his sons to the Gibeonites to be hanged before Yahweh on the mountain (II SAM 21.1-6). The fact that David's and Ishbosheth's men met at Gibeon suggests that David was the aggressor, encroaching on the edge of Benjaminite territory.

The second incident, and perhaps the most important of David's career, was his conquest of Jerusalem described in II SAM 5.6-10 (map 2). Jerusalem was held at the time by the Jebusites, one of the population groups living in the hill country along with the Israelites, Hivites, Judaeans and others. Heretofore it had not been a city of particular importance and still was a relatively small place compared to its size in later periods. Probably the city which David conquered was confined to Ophel, the knoll immediately south of what is known today as the 'Temple Mount' or 'Haram esh-Sharif'. Yet for David's purposes, Jerusalem was an ideal capital, and no doubt it had already begun to expand during his reign. Besides offering a defendable position with a good spring for water, Jerusalem represented neutral ground between the Israelites and Judaeans. As a city of the Jebusites it had no strong tribal or family ties with either the Israelite tribes to the north or the tribes of Judah. Also later on, as David's kingdom expanded beyond the hill country into the lowlands and Transjordan, Jerusalem's location, in a central position, continued to serve him well for administrative purposes.

Naturally, as David assumed his role of king and protector of the Israelite and Judaean villages, the vassal relationship which had existed between him and the Philistines turned to enmity. After all, it was primarily the Philistines against whom the hill country villages needed protection. Thus II SAM 5.17 reports that 'when the Philistines heard that David had been anointed king over Israel, all the Philistines went up in search of David'. The following verses (17b-25) report two Philistine raids. In both cases they are said to have 'spread out in the valley of Rephaim'; both times David is reported to have defeated them.

David's monarchy is understood to have been a direct continuation of Saul's Israelite kingdom. Indeed David himself may have intentionally emphasized the continuity – by bringing the Ark to Jerusalem, for example, and by using the name 'Israel' for his realm. Yet a close reading of the biblical materials indicates that the 'Israelites' and 'Judaeans' were distinct groups, neither of which had prior connections with Jerusalem. Moreover, it is clear that once David had established himself in Jerusalem it became the real administrative, military and cult centre of a state which eventually extended well beyond the range of Israelite and Judaean settlement and depended heavily on foreign mercenaries (including Philistines) for internal and external security. Thus, while the Israelites and Judaeans remained important constituents of David's kingdom, under his rule it was essentially a Jerusalem-based monarchy with a far more pluralistic constituency than Saul's Israel. It is not surprising, therefore, that at some point after establishing himself in Jerusalem David had to crush two rebellions. One of these was led by Absalom his son, apparently the crown prince; the other by Sheba, a Benjaminite.

Appealing to popular grievances, and drawing support from both Israelites and Judaeans, Absalom had himself crowned king in Hebron and then marched on Jerusalem. David evacuated the city and fled to Mahanaim in Transjordan followed by a core of loyalists. Thus Absalom actually ruled in Jerusalem for a short time, and had he moved quickly against David's fleeing army, the course of history may have turned out quite differently. Absalom delayed, however, until he had lost the tactical advantage, and

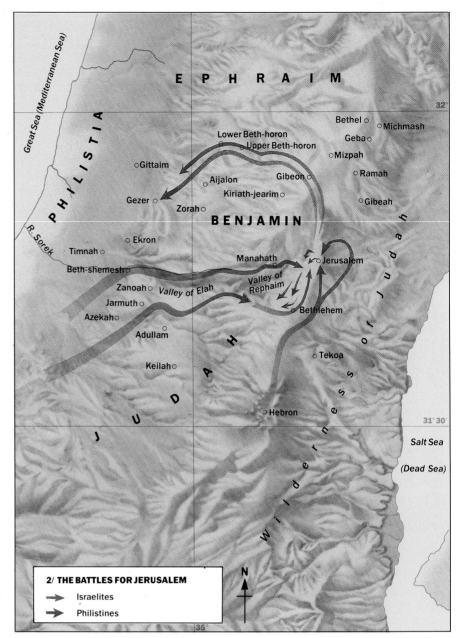

2/ THE BATTLES FOR JERUSALEM
→ Israelites
→ Philistines

N

Great Sea (Mediterranean Sea)
EPHRAIM
PHILISTIA
BENJAMIN
JUDAH
WILDERNESS OF JUDAH
Salt Sea (Dead Sea)

Bethel · Michmash
Geba · Mizpah · Ramah
Lower Beth-horon / Upper Beth-horon
Gibeah
Gittaim · Aijalon · Gibeon · Kiriath-jearim
Gezer · Zorah
Ekron
Timnah · Beth-shemesh · Manahath · Jerusalem
Zanoah · Valley of Elah · Valley of Rephaim
Jarmuth · Bethlehem
Azekah
Adullam · Tekoa
Keilah
Hebron
R. Sorek

then, when he did pursue, was himself killed in the resulting battle. II SAM 18.9-15 describes how Joab executed him when the long hair for which he was famous became entangled in the branches of a tree.

In the narrative of events following the death of Absalom, an episode appears which, if objectively reported, as it seems to have been, displays an emotional side of David's character that may account for the failures of the latter part of his reign (II SAM 19.1-8). Upon receiving the news of the death of Absalom, who had not only usurped the throne of his father but had pursued him and his army, David withdrew into seclusion and refused to take any responsibility for his army. It was only after the strong rebuke of Joab for this indulgence in personal grief that he arose to participate in the celebration of the victory.

The second rebellion was initiated by Sheba, a Benjaminite, and seems to have received less widespread support. It was quickly crushed, in any case, and Sheba himself beheaded, having fled to Abel-beth-maacah. Since Sheba was from the same tribe as Saul, and his call was directed specifically to the Israelites exhorting them to reject David's rule, the possibility must be considered that he hoped to revive the Saulide kingdom and place one of Saul's descendants on its throne. Immediately following the account of Sheba's rebellion appears the report of the execution of Saul's descendants at Gibeon (II SAM 21.1-14), possibly an added precaution against future attempts to revive the dynasty of Saul.

An enduring tribute to David is the association of his name with an anthology of religious poems from various centuries, 'The Psalms of David'. The superscriptions of 73 psalms carry his name and 13 of these connect the poem with particular incidents in his career. Jerusalem, the small Jebusite city, which he took and made his capital, has endured for three millennia as the 'City of David' (II SAM 5.7).

Bethel

Gibeon

battle between young men of and Abner

1/ map bottom II SAM 2.12-32 describes the battle between the twelve men of Joab and the twelve men of Abner at the pool of Gibeon. The map shows the pursuit of Abner's men by Joab's force and the death of Asahel by the hand of Abner.

2/ map left David's capture of Jerusalem from the Jebusites gave him the capital city he needed. He twice defended it from Philistine attacks in the Valley of Rephaim (II SAM 5.17-25). After the second attack he pursued the Philistines as far as Gezer.

3/ below Cross section of Jerusalem showing a tunnel and a shaft cut through the rock beneath the walled city to provide access to the Gihon spring from inside the fortified

city in time of siege. From the text of II SAM 5.6-9 it seems probable that David's men took the city by first discovering an outside entrance to the spring, entering the tunnel and climbing up the shaft leading to the city within the walls.

4/ map right The most widely known account of David's introduction to King Saul is that in I SAM 17, which tells of the dramatic victory of David, the shepherd boy, over Goliath, the giant Philistine. Although II SAM 21.19 reports that 'Elhanan the son of Jaare-Oregim the Bethlehemite slew Goliath' the geographical setting of the battle in the Valley of Elah and location of the cities mentioned seem to fit the topography of the area.

Kidron Valley

Jebusite Wall

Gihon Spring

3

Judaean Hills

○ Socoh

○ Azekah

Valley of Elah

Ekron ○

rout of Philistines

Gath ○

4/ BATTLE OF THE VALLEY OF ELAH
➤ Israelites
➤ Philistines

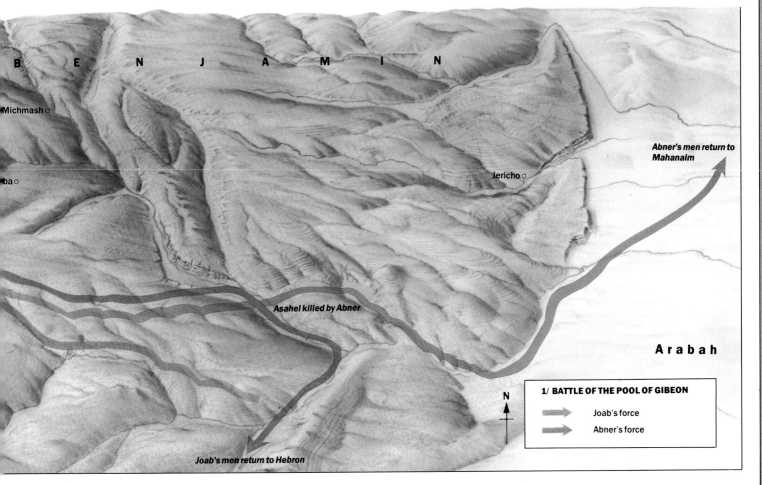

B E N J A M I N

Michmash ○

ba ○

Jericho ○

Abner's men return to Mahanaim

Asahel killed by Abner

A r a b a h

1/ BATTLE OF THE POOL OF GIBEON
N
➤ Joab's force
➤ Abner's force

Joab's men return to Hebron

THE most important areas of territorial expansion in David's reign were: firstly the Jezreel Valley and Galilee, which were taken largely at the expense of Hadadezer, the Aramaean king of Zobah, in the Beqa'a Valley; secondly the Transjordan, perhaps also from Hadadezer, but encroaching as well on traditional Ammonite and Moabite territory; and finally the Negeb, where David encountered Edomite resistance. Early in his reign David formed an alliance with Nahash, king of the Ammonites, which apparently remained in effect until Nahash died. Then hostilities erupted, with the result that David sent troops commanded by Joab to attack Rabbah, the chief Ammonite city. Eventually the city fell and the prisoners were put to forced labour (II SAM 10-12). It was during the Ammonite war that David came into conflict with Hadadezer. It was also at this time that David had the affair with Bathsheba.

Circumstances surrounding the Aramaean wars seem to have been as follows: the Ammonites, with their city under siege by David's troops, appealed to Hadadezer, who represented a major power in southern Aram. He dominated Damascus and probably considered Galilee and northern Transjordan as belonging to his realm as well. Hadadezer responded with troops from various Aramaean cities under his influence, but was defeated by David's army at Rabbah and at Helam, somewhere in Transjordan. He also lost control of Damascus to a marauding band led by Rezon. Thus, David expanded his domain, presumably to include some of the area between Damascus and Gilead. Toi of Hamath, a long-standing enemy of Hadadezer, sent his son to David with congratulations and gifts (II SAM 8.9-10). Whether David invaded the heartland of Hadadezer's realm depends on the interpretation of II SAM 8.7-8. 'And David took the shields of gold which were carried by the servants of Hadadezer and brought them to Jerusalem. And from Betah and Berothai, cities of Hadadezer, King David took very much bronze.' Does this passage mean that he actually took Betah and Berothai? And where were these cities located? David is reported to have defeated the Moabites as well and to have executed two-thirds of the prisoners taken (II SAM 8.2). It is significant to note that his census officials began at the River Arnon (page 100). Even if David conducted military campaigns into Moab proper, the geographical isolation of that region would have rendered impractical any sort of permanent rule from Jerusalem. David also made war with the Edomites. The one battle reported took place 'in the Valley of Salt', probably between the Dead Sea and Beersheba. Presumably, therefore, it was Edomite-related tribal groups along the southern frontier that David defeated and garrisoned.

Two city lists, while not specifically associated with David, may pertain to his reign. One is the list of 'unconquered cities' in JUDG 1.21; 27-36 (page 41). Saul may have annexed some of them, but it was David probably that brought most of them under control. The other list is that of the Levitical cities (JOSH 21.8-42, I CHRON 6.54-81). Although schematic in its present form – four cities listed for each of the twelve tribes – it may be regarded as dating to the time of the monarchy.

In summary, the area under David's direct control must have included most of western Palestine (excluding Philistia and some Phoenician presence along the coast north of Mt Carmel) and a large portion of Transjordan extending from the River Arnon to Damascus. David's kingdom has often been depicted as including much more territory. I KINGS 4.24 reports, for example, that Solomon, David's successor, 'had dominion over all the region west of the Euphrates from Tiphsah to Gaza, over all the kings west of the Euphrates'. Since no wars of conquest are reported for Solomon, it is assumed that he must have inherited this mini-empire from David. However, this does not take into account the editorial hyperbole so characteristic of the biblical account of Solomon's reign. Embedded in the sweeping claims for the wealth and wisdom of Solomon are occasional details that suggest a territorial domain no larger than that described above for David.

1/ map below The cities of David's time are attested by the description of his census of the kingdom which was carried out by Joab and some of the army commanders (II SAM 24.1-9) and from the lists of Levitical cities (JOSH 21, I CHRON 6).

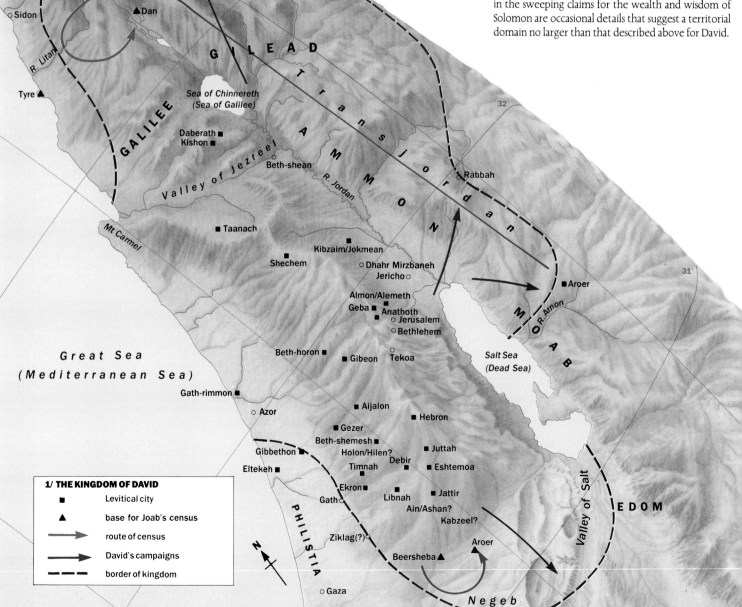

1/ THE KINGDOM OF DAVID

■   Levitical city

▲   base for Joab's census

→   route of census

→   David's campaigns

- - -   border of kingdom

BURIAL practices in Palestine are abundantly documented by graves which have been discovered dating from prehistoric times down to the end of the biblical period. Throughout this long span care was taken to preserve human remains properly and to provide the dead with gifts, whether in tribute or for use in an afterlife. Yet the manner of interment varied widely through the centuries, as did undoubtedly the beliefs about life after death.

In the later Neolithic Age the usual method of burial in Palestine was 'inhumation'. The body was laid in a shallow hole dug into the ground, often beneath the house floor. A few objects were sometimes buried with the body – a jar or two, simple items of adornment and occasionally a cult object. In the Chalcolithic period the practice began of burying the bones in a house-shaped ossuary, which was placed in a cave-tomb. During the Early Bronze Age (3150-2200 BC) the practice of cremation arose, attested by charnel houses found at Bab edh-Dhra'.

From about 2100 BC until the end of the Iron Age (c600 BC) the dominant kind of tomb was a low chamber cut from the rock, approached by a shaft closed with a single stone or a pile of rubble. These tombs served as burial vaults primarily for families. They could be enlarged and used repeatedly. As previously, weapons and foodstuff were provided, apparently in expectation of an afterlife. At the height of the Canaanite culture in the Middle Bronze Age, around the 18th-17th centuries BC, not only food

offerings and personal items were left in the tombs but also beds, tables, stools, baskets, gameboards and other objects of everyday life.

Many of the same practices continued during the early centuries of the Israelite period, the Iron Age (c1200-600 BC). Although the most frequent form of burial was that in which the body was laid on its back in a rock-cut chamber, the position of the bodies varied considerably. Sometimes large quantities of bones were piled up in a tomb, those from earlier burials having been pushed into a heap when there was need for new interments. Large quantities of funerary objects often accumulated in tombs, particularly those containing many burials. Jars continued to be used occasionally for the interment of infants and cremation was still practiced by some.

Toward the end of the Iron Age single-grave burials began appearing, and by the Persian period they were frequent. Fewer food offerings were

deposited and proportionately larger numbers of small, varied objects were interred, such as mirrors, cosmetic implements, jewellery, amulets, and weapons. During the Hellenistic period (332-37 BC) tombs began to change both in form and contents. Rock-cut tombs became more uniform in plan and were provided with narrow loculi (burial slots) radiating out from a central chamber, and tomb walls began to be painted. Multiple chambers became frequent. Hellenistic influences continued into Early Roman times, when ordinary tombs regularly had a small, almost square, central chamber and numerous loculi. Occasionally a tomb of the Roman period had a rounded stone fitted into a slot in front of the entrance to serve as a rolling door. A typical group of funerary gifts of this period included perfume and unguent bottles, lamps, sometimes a few coins, and a relatively small number of practical funerary gifts such as water-jars or plates of food.

Throughout the many changes in funerary practices the economic status of the deceased and his family is clearly reflected. Death came to the rich and to the poor, and the distinction between the two is readily apparent in the grave.

1/ Four jars from a Middle Bronze Age tomb at Dhahr Mirzbaneh.

2/ Ossuary from Azor, used in the Chalcolithic period.

3/ Multiple burial tomb of MBII at Jericho with furniture, bowls and jars.

4/ A rolling stone door of the family tomb of the Herods in Jerusalem, and sketch (below) of such a tomb.

5/ Anthropoid sarcophagus from Beth-shean, Philistine jug with a strainer spout and a lentoid 'pilgrim flask'.

SITUATED athwart the old north-south trade routes – the 'Way of the Sea' and the Transjordanian King's Highway (page 14) – the kingdom of David and Solomon was well placed to intercept and benefit from the trade which passed between Egypt and Syria. The Bible speaks of Solomon trading with Egypt, Africa, Arabia, Phoenicia and the Lebanon.

Of all Israel's great men it was Solomon who was most famous for his wealth and for the extravagance of his court. I KINGS 10.7 reports of the amazement of the Queen of Sheba, itself a wealthy kingdom of Arabia. Upon being shown Solomon's resources she exclaimed: 'I believed not the words until I came and mine eyes had seen it. The half was not told me; thy wisdom and prosperity exceed the fame which I heard'. After almost a millennium the proverbial association was alluded to, 'Solomon in all his glory' (MT 6.29). Yet allowing for the expansion of hyperbole which attaches itself to famous men there are clues within the relatively small amount of biblical material about Solomon that he was unusually successful in trade and commerce. Freed from the necessity of making war he was able to devote himself to building a strong economy and to engage in foreign trade to a degree never before seen in Israel's history. It must be borne in mind, however, that while it has been observed by archaeologists that there can be seen in the Solomonic period a rise in the general standard of living, and progress in technical matters, there are as yet no collaborative sources for Solomon's prosperity. Records about him do not exist apart from those within the Bible.

Solomon, who came to the throne of Israel in c.965 BC, was in a position to be the middle-man in the important trade in horses and chariots between Asia Minor and Egypt (I KINGS 10.28-29). It appears that Solomon's tradesmen were importing horses from the horse-rearing country of Cappadocia via the kingdom of Que, along the coastal region of Cilicia, and were supplying them to Egypt as well as to some of the Syrian kingdoms located to the west of the R. Euphrates. I KINGS 10.29 would seem to indicate that Solomon was obtaining wooden chariots from Egypt. Biblical sources also credit Solomon with maritime operations on the Red Sea and with expeditions of Phoenician-built ships sailing from Ezion-geber to Ophir (I KINGS 9.26-28; 10.22-12). During Solomonic times, the Gulf of 'Aqaba was probably referred to as Ezion-geber.

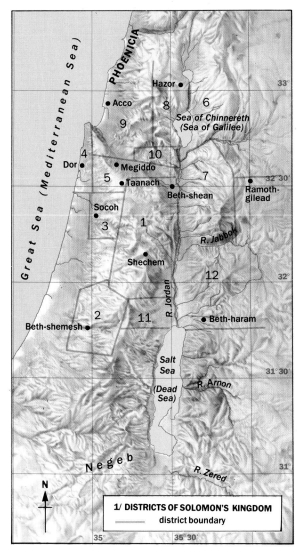

1/ DISTRICTS OF SOLOMON'S KINGDOM
district boundary

1/ map left The list of Solomon's twelve tax collectors responsible for providing food for the king and his household is given in I KINGS 4.7-19, along with several cities to identify each of the twelve districts. The area of Judah is conspicuously missing from the administrative districts, thus indicating the tacit recognition of the division between the two kingdoms. This omission of Judah in the list is perhaps a harbinger of the subsequent division of the United Kingdom into Israel and Judah upon the death of Solomon. Although the list of the twelve officials is complete, the areas are poorly designated. Some of the districts coincide with the old tribal areas, while others are defined only by the names of the cities found within them.

2/ below left Two lists of provisions: Solomon's requirements for one day (I KINGS 4.22-23) and a list of food and drink for a banquet given by King Ashurnasirpal II of Assyria for over 69,000 guests at the inauguration of the palace at Calah, in northern Mesopotamia. It is impossible, obviously, to compare the quantities of food needed by Solomon and his relatively small tribal household with those required by more than 69,000 guests. The two lists are, however, revealing for the variety of foodstuff mentioned.

2

SOLOMON'S BANQUET

'Solomon's provision for one day was thirty cors of fine flour, and sixty cors of meal, ten fat oxen, and twenty pasture-fed cattle, a hundred sheep, besides harts, gazelles, roebucks and fatted fowl.' (I KINGS 4.22)

ASHURNASIRPAL'S BANQUET

'When Ashurnasirpal, king of Assyria, inaugurated the palace in Calah, a palace of joy and (erected with) great ingenuity, he invited into it Ashur, the great lord and the gods of his entire country, (he prepared a banquet of) 1,000 fattened head of cattle, 1,000 calves, 10,000 stable sheep, 15,000 lambs – for my lady Ishtar (alone) 200 head of cattle and 1,000 *sihhu*-sheep – 1,000 spring lambs, 500 stags, 500 gazelles, 1,000 ducks, 500 geese, 500 *kurkū*-geese, 1,000 *mesuku*-birds, 1,000 *qāribu*-birds, 10,000 doves, 10,000 *sukanūnu*-doves, 10,000 other (assorted) small birds, 10,000 (assorted) fish, 10,000 jerboa, 10,000 (assorted) eggs; 10,000 loaves of bread, 10,000 (jars of) beer, 10,000 skins with wine, 10,000 pointed bottom vessels with *šu'u*-seeds in sesame oil, 10,000 small pots with *sarhu*-condiment, 1,000 wooden crates with vegetables, 300 (containers with) oil, 300 (containers with) salted seeds, 300 (containers with) mixed *raqqūte*-plants, 100 with *kudimmu*-spice, 100 (containers with) ..., 100 (containers with) parched barley, 100 (containers with) green *abahšinnu*-stalks, 100 (containers with) fine mixed beer, 100 pomegranates, 100 bunches of grapes, 100 mixed *zamru*-fruits, 100 pistachio cones, 100 with the fruits of the *šūsi*-tree, 100 with garlic, 100 with onions, 100 with *kuniphu* (seeds), 100 with the ... of turnips, 100 with *hinhinni*-spice, 100 with *budū*-spice, 100 with honey, 100 with rendered butter, 100 with roasted ... barley, 100 with roasted *šu'u*-seeds, 100 with *karkartu*-plants, 100 with fruits of the *ti'atu*-tree, 100 with *kasū*-plants, 100 with milk, 100 with cheese, 100 jars with "mixture", 100 with pickled *arsuppu*-grain, ten homer of shelled *luddu*-nuts, ten homer of shelled pistachio nuts, ten homer of fruits of the *šušu*-tree, ten homer of fruits of the *habbaqūqu*-tree, ten homer of dates, ten homer of the fruits of the *titip*-tree, ten homer of cumin, ten homer of *sahhunu*, ten homer of *uriāna*, ten homer of *andahšu*-bulbs, ten homer of *šišanibbe*-plants, ten homer of the fruits of the *simbūru*-tree, ten homer of thyme, ten homer of perfumed oil, ten homer of sweet smelling matters, ten homer of ..., ten homer of the fruits of the *nasubu*-tree, ten homer of *zimzimmu*-onions, ten homer of olives.

When I inaugurated the palace at Calah I treated for ten days with food and drink 47,074 persons, men and women, who were bid to come from across my entire country (also) 5,000 important persons, delegates from the country Suhu, from Hindana, Hattina, Hatti, Tyre, Sidon, Gurguma, Malida, Hubushka, Gilzana, Kuma (and) Musasir, (also) 16,000 inhabitants of Calah from all ways of life, 1,500 officials of all my palaces, altogether 69,574 invited guests from all the (mentioned) countries including the people of Calah; I (furthermore) provided them with the means to clean and anoint themselves. I did them due honors and sent them back, healthy and happy, to their own countries.'

From the Palace of Ashurnasirpal II at Calah

Ophir is usually identified with the land of 'Punt' along the eastern coast of Africa. Gold appears to have been the major import from Ophir and an ostracon found at Tel Qasila had a Hebrew inscription referring to 'Gold [from] Ophir [belonging] to Beth-haram'. The Israelites also traded at this time with Phoenicia and the Lebanese mountain communities for timber (I KINGS 5.10-11). According to the biblical text, Hiram from Tyre gave Solomon timber of cedar and fir in exchange for large quantities of wheat and olive oil. The most significant factor in the panorama of Mediterranean trade (pages 56-57), certainly from the 9th century BC, and possibly already in the 10th, was the unrivalled maritime commerce of the Phoenician cities. The Phoenician traders had complete access to Eygptian ports with the result that, not only did items of Egyptian manufacture pass by way of Tyre and Byblos to the rest of the Near East, but in addition decorative and artistic motifs of Nilotic origin became familiar around the Mediterranean in Phoenician 'guise'. The most travelled routes for Phoenician merchantmen were those which led to Cyprus, the Aegean, North Africa and the western Mediterranean. To all the communities alongside the Mediterranean shore the resourceful merchants peddled their timber, cloth, purple dye, metalwork and grain, in return for the products of North Africa, the silver and iron of Spain, the slaves and manufactures of the Aegean, and possibly the opium of Cyprus.

Among the more specific pieces of information about the economy of Solomon is the list of tax collectors for each of the twelve districts of his kingdom. Each of the collectors (two of them were sons-in-law of Solomon) was responsible for the provisions needed for the king and his household for one month of the year. To judge from the list of provisions for one day given in I KINGS 4.22-23 the tax liability for one month would have been quite considerable. The panel *left* gives a comparison between Solomon's provisions for a day and the food and drink served at the gargantuan inaugural banquet given by King Ashurnasirpal II of Assyria (883-859 BC).

The reputation which Solomon enjoyed for his wisdom (I KINGS 4.30) and the ascription of authorship to him (PROV 1.1 and SONG 1.1) was a fitting accolade for the king who brought Israel to its peak of prosperity at home and involvement in affairs abroad.

TEMPLES are as old as man's first permanent settlements. The very first cult places were outside, perhaps by a sacred tree or spring. They were eventually enclosed, though much of the ritual continued to be conducted in the open air of a walled courtyard. The earliest Palestinian temples were based on the broadroom plan but later other designs developed. The most famous temple of all, that of Solomon in Jerusalem, was a longroom structure.

One of the best preserved early temples is that found at En-gedi, dating from the Chalcolithic period. It consists of a broadroom entered from one of the long sides, together with an annex, a walled courtyard with a basin in the centre, and a gatehouse as part of the enclosure wall. Similar temples have been found from this period at Ai, Teleilat el-Ghassul, Megiddo, and Arad.

A well-preserved example of the distinctive Canaanite broadroom temple, which became popular in the Early Bronze period, is the EBA III temple at Megiddo. It has a broadroom with a roof that was supported by two columns, open porch and a court. Against the wall facing the entrance was an altar with four steps. Just south of the building was an open-air altar, 25ft wide and 5ft high with steps leading to the top, which when excavated was covered with soot from fires. A similar broadroom temple with circular altar has since been discovered at Khirbet ez-Zeragon, north-east of Beth-arbel in Gilead.

In the Middle Bronze period there appears what is called the 'Migdal' (or fortress) temple at Shechem with its thick walls and towerlike entrance. Similar structures have been found at Megiddo and Hazor. In the Late Bronze period there is a decided break in tradition. The earlier broadroom plan developed into the Canaanite and Israelite tripartite structure with its porch and main room with cult niche or Holy of Holies. Typical is the temple from Stratum II at Hazor. There were two courtyards, an outer and an inner. The former was entered through a propylaeum or gateway. Benches lined the walls and on both sides of the entrance were tables (cf EZEK 40.39-43). Among the finds of the inner court, where the main feature was an altar, were fragments of clay liver models used for divination, including one with an Akkadian inscription. In the main room of the latest temple at Hazor built on this general plan several cult objects were found, as well as libation tables, incense altars, seals and bronze figurines. In addition two columns, one on each side of the temple entrance, are reminiscent of the position of the pillars Jachin and Boaz in the Temple of Jerusalem (I KINGS 7.21).

Connected with the Hazor temples is a basalt statue of a deity which originally stood on a bull; on its breast was a four-pointed star within a circle. The same emblem has also been found on an incense altar and on one of the seven *stelae* discovered in the vicinity. This emblem and the basalt bull suggest that the temple was dedicated to the Canaanite weather god, Baal.

At Beth-shean the Late Bronze Age temples show strong Egyptian influence and one of them, like the Mekal temple which continued to be used into the Iron Age, seems to have been part of a palace-temple complex. A temple complex, occupying the entire mound, has been found at Tel Mevorakh. Among the finds was a coiled bronze snake.

At the end of the Bronze Age many cities throughout Palestine were destroyed and their temples with them. Only two Iron Age sites have so far produced buildings correctly identified as temples: a series of superimposed Philistine temples found at Tel Qasila and an Israelite temple which has been found at Arad.

The temple at Arad was in use from c 700-600 BC. It is the earliest Israelite, as opposed to Canaanite, temple to be discovered. It was built in the north-west corner of the citadel, with an eastward orientation. The temple consisted of a main room with a raised cult niche and a courtyard. Benches lined the walls of the main room. In the cult room was found a *massabah* (standing stone). Two incense altars were found on the steps of the niche. The courtyard was divided into two parts and in the larger outer area was found an altar built of unworked stones, conforming to the regulations laid down in EX 20.25. Two column bases were found, one on each side of the entrance to the main room, recalling the pillars in Solomon's temple. An inscription on pottery referring to 'the House of Yayweh' shows unmistakably that there was an Israelite temple at Arad.

In addition to the characteristic buildings, with their distinctive features of altars, pillars, courtyards and benches, used in the practice of religion, there exists a great variety of associated paraphernalia of the cult as well as an extensive iconography (pages 68-69).

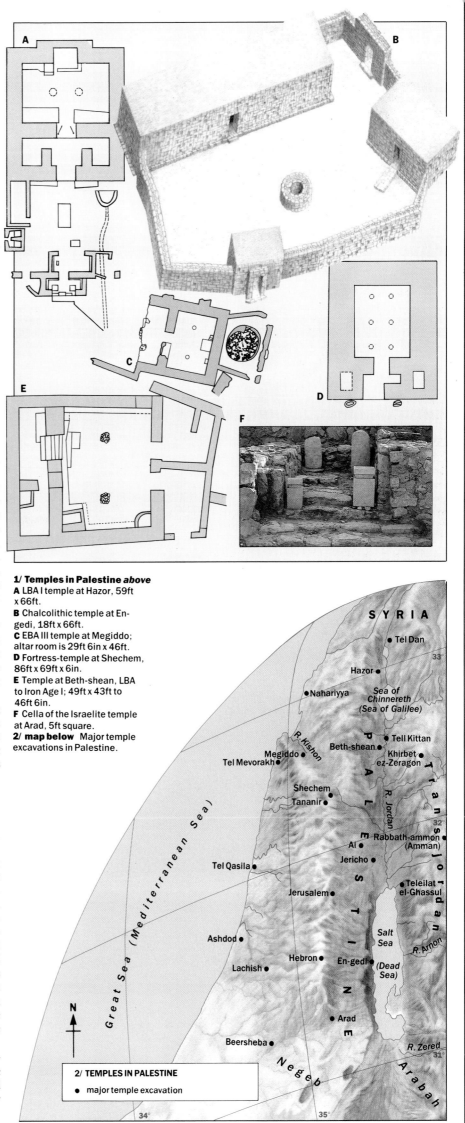

1/ Temples in Palestine *above*
A LBA I temple at Hazor, 59ft x 66ft.
B Chalcolithic temple at En-gedi, 18ft x 66ft.
C EBA III temple at Megiddo; altar room is 29ft 6in x 46ft.
D Fortress-temple at Shechem, 86ft x 69ft x 6in.
E Temple at Beth-shean, LBA to Iron Age I; 49ft x 43ft to 46ft 6in.
F Cella of the Israelite temple at Arad, 5ft square.
2/ map below Major temple excavations in Palestine.

2/ TEMPLES IN PALESTINE
● major temple excavation

FOR the first time in Israel's history, the development of international trade and the establishment of a strong central government by Solomon, made possible a public building programme not only in Jerusalem but throughout the kingdom. The construction of fortified cities with massive walls and citadels displays a new scale of grandeur, and the appearance of ashlar masonry (hewn stone blocks) in public buildings is one of the major advances in technology which emerged in the Solomonic Age.

The Israeli archaeologist Yigael Yadin was the first to observe the remarkable similarity in plan and measurements between the city gates of Gezer, Hazor and Megiddo. This observation was of particular interest since I KINGS 9.15 attributes the building of these three cities to King Solomon. These city gates, as well as similar structures found at Lachish and Ashdod, have three large gate chambers or rooms on each side of the passageway leading to the city. The outer doorway could be closed by wooden gates and the rooms could be used by the defence forces in times of attack; in times of peace these chambers could serve civic or administrative purposes.

THE SOLOMONIC CITY OF JERUSALEM

Solomon was responsible for converting the embryonic city, which David had captured, into a royal capital by adding to it the Temple Mount and turning it into a monumental acropolis. The main architectural feature of the city is a stepped structure about 50 feet high, which is thought to have served as a retaining wall for the southern end of the raised platform on which Solomon's royal city was built. If this structure is to be identified with the Millo ('the fill'), as has been proposed, then the building activities in I KINGS 9.15 proceeded in geographical order from north to south: the house of the Lord, the house of the King, the Millo and the city wall.

The purpose of the Millo was twofold: to make a sharper topographical distinction between the lower city which the commoner occupied and the upper precinct, and at the same time to expand the area devoted to public buildings from about 10-12 acres to 20-35 acres (partially at the expense of the area for private houses). This expansion of the city, however, was not accompanied by a corresponding increase in the total population which is unlikely to have exceeded 1500 during Solomon's reign.

The temple and its courtyards covered a consider-

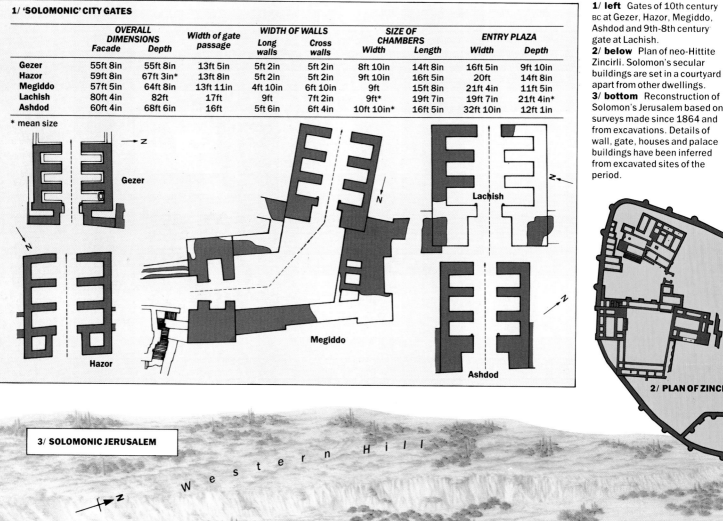

1/ 'SOLOMONIC' CITY GATES

	OVERALL DIMENSIONS		Width of gate passage	WIDTH OF WALLS		SIZE OF CHAMBERS		ENTRY PLAZA	
	Facade	Depth		Long walls	Cross walls	Width	Length	Width	Depth
Gezer	55ft 8in	55ft 8in	13ft 5in	5ft 2in	5ft 2in	8ft 10in	14ft 8in	16ft 5in	9ft 10in
Hazor	59ft 8in	67ft 3in*	13ft 8in	5ft 2in	5ft 2in	9ft 10in	16ft 5in	20ft	14ft 8in
Megiddo	57ft 5in	64ft 8in	13ft 11in	4ft 10in	6ft 10in	9ft	15ft 8in	21ft 4in	11ft 5in
Lachish	80ft 4in	82ft	17ft	9ft	7ft 2in	9ft*	19ft 7in	19ft 7in	21ft 4in*
Ashdod	60ft 4in	68ft 6in	16ft	5ft 6in	6ft 4in	10ft 10in*	16ft 5in	32ft 10in	12ft 1in

* mean size

Gezer

Hazor

Megiddo

Lachish

Ashdod

2/ PLAN OF ZINCIRLI

3/ SOLOMONIC JERUSALEM

Western Hill

Tyropoeon Valley

city wall

1/ **left** Gates of 10th century BC at Gezer, Hazor, Megiddo, Ashdod and 9th-8th century gate at Lachish.
2/ **below** Plan of neo-Hittite Zincirli. Solomon's secular buildings are set in a courtyard apart from other dwellings.
3/ **bottom** Reconstruction of Solomon's Jerusalem based on surveys made since 1864 and from excavations. Details of wall, gate, houses and palace buildings have been inferred from excavated sites of the period.

able area, most probably at the highest and north-ernmost end of the city. The plan of the king's palace is not clear. While it has been suggested that all the palace units were incorporated within a single building of the *bit hilani* type (distinctive plan of north Syrian palaces with a portico), it is more likely that there was a cluster of palaces, possibly arranged around a common courtyard, similar to the plan of the acropolis at Zincirli (ancient Sam'al) of the 9th-8th centuries BC.

SOLOMON'S TEMPLE

The description of the Temple appears in I KINGS 6-8; II CHRON 3-5 and in Ezekiel's vision described in EZEK 40-42. Since any actual remains of Solomon's Temple are yet to be discovered from archaeological work, these passages have for generations been subject to detailed scrutiny. T. A. Busink, who has recently made an exhaustive study of the biblical material, suggests that the tripartite division of the Temple in *ulam* (porch or vestibule), *hekal* (nave or temple) and *debir* (inner sanctuary) applies more to the ceremonial significance of these units than to their structural arrangement. The term used for the main unit, which includes the *hekal* and *debir*, is the 'house' (I KINGS 6.2-3, 17, etc). The *debir* was most probably a large cabinet made of cedar beams at the rear of the *hekal*, while the *ulam* was evidently an unroofed passage open at the front and protected by two side walls.

The 'house' measured 60 x 20 cubits (about 90 x 30ft), surrounded by lower storerooms (*yasia'*) on three sides. Two ceremonial copper pillars, called Jachin and Boaz, stood before the Temple, apparently between the walls of the *ulam*. The plan follows the tradition of the longroom temple type (megaron) excavated at several Middle and Late Bronze Age sites in northern Syria. The sacrificial altar, the molten sea (bronze basin) and the ten stands for lavers of bronze (*mekonot*) stood in the courtyard in front of the Temple (I KINGS 7.23-39). The ten lampstands of pure gold, the golden altar, table and utensils (I KINGS 7.48-49) were inside the *hekal*. The cherubim of olivewood overlaid with gold (I KINGS 6.23-28) were in the *debir* alongside the Ark of the Covenant with the two tables of stone (I KINGS 8.9). The entire Temple was panelled with precious cedar wood and inlaid with gold.

Of such extravagance was the Temple of Solomon as biblical tradition has described it. Unfortunately archaeology has as yet little to add to these descriptions of the most important building in ancient Israel.

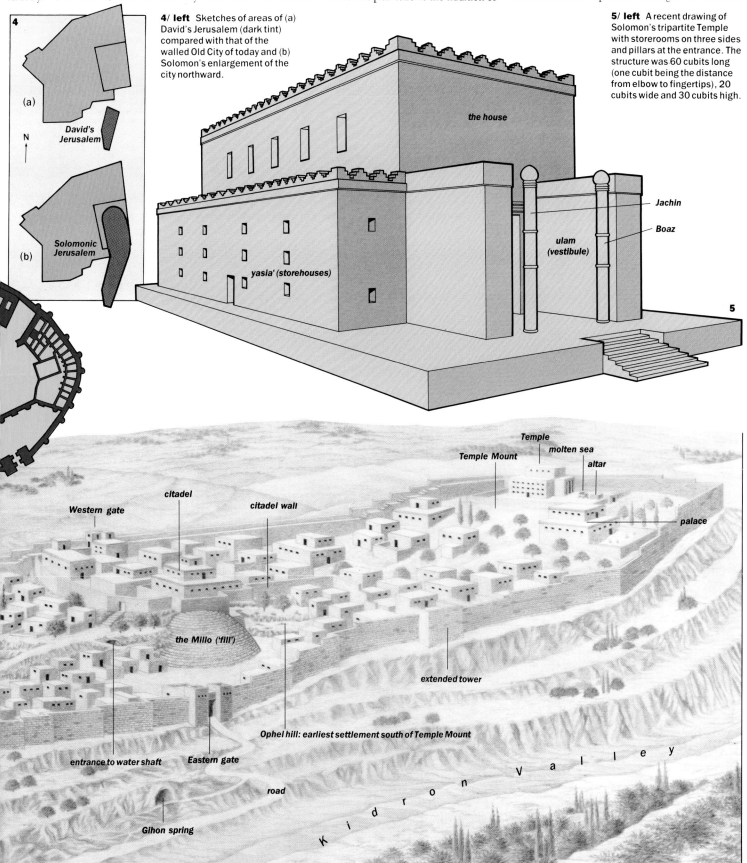

4/ left Sketches of areas of (a) David's Jerusalem (dark tint) compared with that of the walled Old City of today and (b) Solomon's enlargement of the city northward.

5/ left A recent drawing of Solomon's tripartite Temple with storerooms on three sides and pillars at the entrance. The structure was 60 cubits long (one cubit being the distance from elbow to fingertips), 20 cubits wide and 30 cubits high.

(a)

N

David's Jerusalem

(b) Solomonic Jerusalem

the house

Jachin

Boaz

ulam (vestibule)

yasia' (storehouses)

5

Temple

Temple Mount

molten sea

altar

palace

citadel

Western gate

citadel wall

the Millo ('fill')

extended tower

Ophel hill: earliest settlement south of Temple Mount

entrance to water shaft   Eastern gate

road

Gihon spring

Kidron valley

WHEN the Levant recovered from the chaotic events which caused the collapse of the Bronze Age empires in the 11th century BC, both Israel and its Phoenician neighbours developed into important regional entities. They inherited much from their Canaanite past, including closely related languages, but with significant differences. Remaining divided into city-state kingdoms, the Phoenicians were heirs and developers of Canaanite tradition in culture, religion and political organization.

Geographical conditions were one reason for the development of the two peoples in different directions. While the Israelite kingdom was mainly agricultural, the fertile but narrow coastal plain encouraged the Phoenicians to look outwards. There were natural resources available: timber (especially cedar), fish and the murex shell from which a highly prized purple dye was extracted. However, like their Canaanite ancestors, the Phoenicians were sailors, traders and craftsmen, producing and selling luxury goods of the highest quality, especially in bronze, ivory, precious metals and textiles.

They traded in the Levant and sailing all over the Mediterranean and beyond, the Phoenicians developed markets and acquired raw materials from places hitherto unknown to the Near East. Their ships (the 'ships of Tarshish' as they are known in the Bible) sailed as far as the Straits of Gibraltar and beyond into the Atlantic. Gold, ivory and slaves, along with other exotic goods, came from Africa; metals, especially silver and tin, came from Spain, and copper from Cyprus. Foreign products such as faïence and glass were imported and redistributed abroad and were later imitated and produced locally.

Claims by classical writers that Gades (modern Cádiz, on Spain's Atlantic coast) and Utica and Lixus in North Africa were founded about 1100 BC cannot be verified. The earliest Phoenician material so far found in the west has been tentatively dated to the 9th century BC, not without dispute. By the 8th century BC, however, Phoenician settlements were flourishing in many places. Traders were active in Spain, particularly in the south and around the Guadalquivir basin (known as Tartessos to the Greeks and sometimes proposed as the biblical Tarshish) where there were rich metal deposits. In Cyprus Phoenician influence is discernible from the 11th century BC, and by the 9th century the Tyrians had established a large settlement at Kition (Larnaca).

According to classical tradition the greatest of all Phoenician colonies, Carthage, was founded in 814/3 BC at the height of Tyrian expansion in the Mediterranean, though the earliest material so far found there seems to date from the 8th century BC.

The riches which flowed into the Phoenician city-states, of which Sidon and Tyre were the most powerful, rendered them much sought after as partners in political and commercial alliances. Phoenician deities were often worshipped abroad – the ruler of Damascus set up a stela to the Tyrian god Melqart, the same deity worshipped by Jezebel, the Sidonian wife of king Ahab, in Israel.

The alphabet, probably the most important legacy of the Phoenicians, was generally adopted and passed on by the Greeks to the western world.

Collaboration between the Phoenicians and Israel obviously made economic sense: Israel controlled important sections of international trade routes (for example, to the Red Sea and South Arabia) and could supply agricultural products such as corn, wine, oil and balsam (EZEK 27.17). A cuneiform tablet of the 7th century BC refers to Phoenician grain merchants in Assyria using a Judaean grain measure. In return the Phoenicians provided craftsmen of great skill and fine luxury goods for sale, both of which were highly prized in Israel. Alliances established by David and Solomon and renewed by the House of Omri were strengthened by the dynastic marriages of Jezebel and Athaliah into the royal families of Israel and Judah.

The Phoenicians were closely involved with Solomon's building programme (II CHRON 2) and a joint venture to Ophir along the Red Sea coast. Though perhaps not purely Phoenician in style and craftsmanship, Solomonic and later royal buildings in places such as Jerusalem, Megiddo and Samaria show the collaboration between Phoenician and Israelite workmen referred to in the biblical account of Solomon's building programme (I KINGS 5.18; II CHRON 2.13-14).

Inscriptions reveal that the Phoenicians were widely present in Israel and Judah, not only in Galilee and the coastal plain but also inland, even in places as remote as Kuntillet 'Ajrud, in the Negeb Desert. Phoenician carved ivory has been found in quantity at Samaria and metal bowls, apparently of Judaean origin but Phoenician in style, have been found at Nimrud in Mesopotamia.

EZEK 27 gives a vivid description of Tyrian trade. Yet the Phoenicians had, for a century and a half, suffered the economic consequences of first Assyrian and then Babylonian pressure, involving tribute, deportations, sieges and destructions. However, under the Persians better days were to dawn. The Phoenicians became favoured members of the Persian empire. Both Sidon and Tyre regained their original trading importance and established harbours and territory along the Palestinian coast, on the sea route to Egypt.

The relationship of peace and economic cooperation which prevailed between the Phoenician city-states and Israel was unique. Even though the religious practices of Tyre and Sidon were a threat at times to the monotheistic faith of Israel (as evidenced by the contest between Elijah and the prophets of Baal on Mt Carmel – I KINGS 18.16-40) there was never armed conflict between these two adjacent powers.

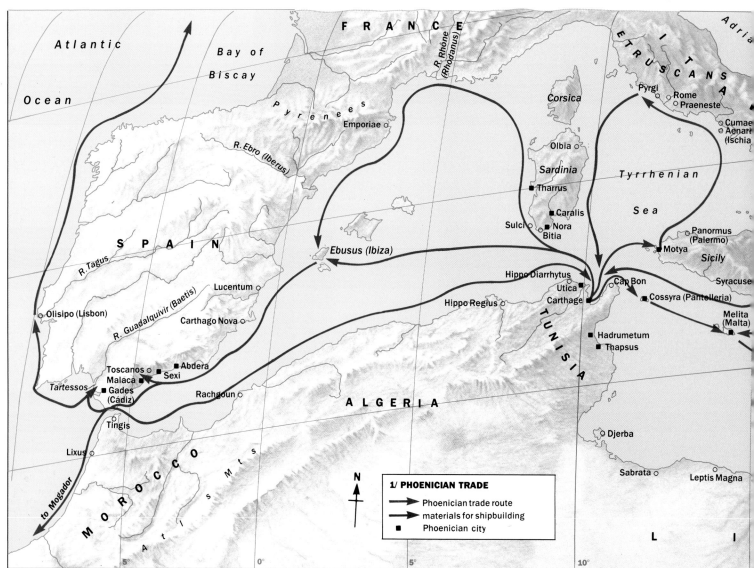

1/ PHOENICIAN TRADE
→ Phoenician trade route
→ materials for shipbuilding
■ Phoenician city

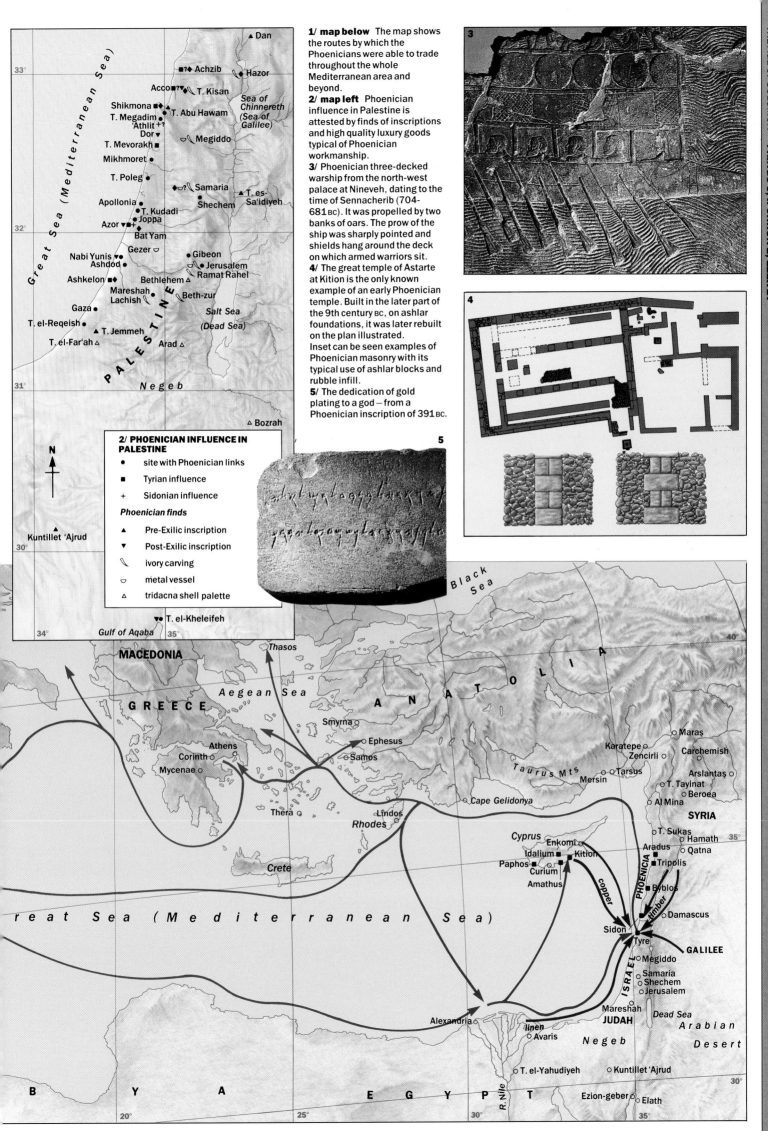

1/ map below The map shows the routes by which the Phoenicians were able to trade throughout the whole Mediterranean area and beyond.

2/ map left Phoenician influence in Palestine is attested by finds of inscriptions and high quality luxury goods typical of Phoenician workmanship.

3/ Phoenician three-decked warship from the north-west palace at Nineveh, dating to the time of Sennacherib (704-681 BC). It was propelled by two banks of oars. The prow of the ship was sharply pointed and shields hang around the deck on which armed warriors sit.

4/ The great temple of Astarte at Kition is the only known example of an early Phoenician temple. Built in the later part of the 9th century BC, on ashlar foundations, it was later rebuilt on the plan illustrated.
Inset can be seen examples of Phoenician masonry with its typical use of ashlar blocks and rubble infill.

5/ The dedication of gold plating to a god — from a Phoenician inscription of 391 BC.

2/ PHOENICIAN INFLUENCE IN PALESTINE
- • site with Phoenician links
- ■ Tyrian influence
- + Sidonian influence

Phoenician finds
- ▲ Pre-Exilic inscription
- ▼ Post-Exilic inscription
- ✎ ivory carving
- ▽ metal vessel
- △ tridacna shell palette

THE ancient Hebrews' world was as widely diversified as our own and, due to their widespread trading contacts they were in touch with countries from Greece and Lydia in the west to Persia in the east, from the Caucasus in the north to Sudan and southern Arabia in the south. In their society kinship played an important role, and it was possible to build up a picture in which the relationships between peoples could be expressed as family relationships.

Before the rise of Greek scholarship there was no science of geography in the ancient world. Some maps were religious and cosmological, but most were for practical purposes such as trade, taxation and welfare. There was neither systematic surveying nor cartography according to precise measurements and uniform scale. Not all maps were necessarily drawn on two-dimensional planes; some were linear, consisting of individual roads (later known as *itinerae*) which provided information useful to a traveller.

GEN 10 is yet another kind of map: it contains information which can be superimposed on a modern map. The chapter gives, in the briefest fashion, an ethnographic lineage of the peoples of the Earth, who are said to have descended from Noah and his three sons, Ham, Shem and Japheth. Within the context of the patriarchal narrative in Genesis such descent was inevitable, in as much as all other males are said to have perished in the Flood. Two broad streams of tradition can be seen in this larger narrative; an early epic story which existed in its essential form by the time of the Hebrew United Monarchy in the 10th century BC, and priestly traditions that were added to the older narrative as late as the 7th-6th centuries BC, the latter often systematizing and embellishing the earlier material in ways which reflected the knowledge and theological views of the later period. Because they lived at a time when tribal relationships were still a major concern in Hebrew religious thought, the authors of the old patriarchal epic in Genesis tended to see the world from an ethnic perspective. People are categorized not by their geographical locations or their linguistic affinities but by their ethnic origins. Furthermore, each ethnic group is represented eponymously, that is, by a single person who bears the name of the group and is said to be that group's ancestor. The use of eponymous figures led easily to the arrangements of the persons into a single, comprehensive lineage. This method was not unique to the Hebrews; it had been employed, with variations, in epic narratives and priestly records throughout the ancient Near East.

The Hebrew priests of the 7th and 6th centuries BC who edited the earlier epic tradition retained the essentially ethnographic

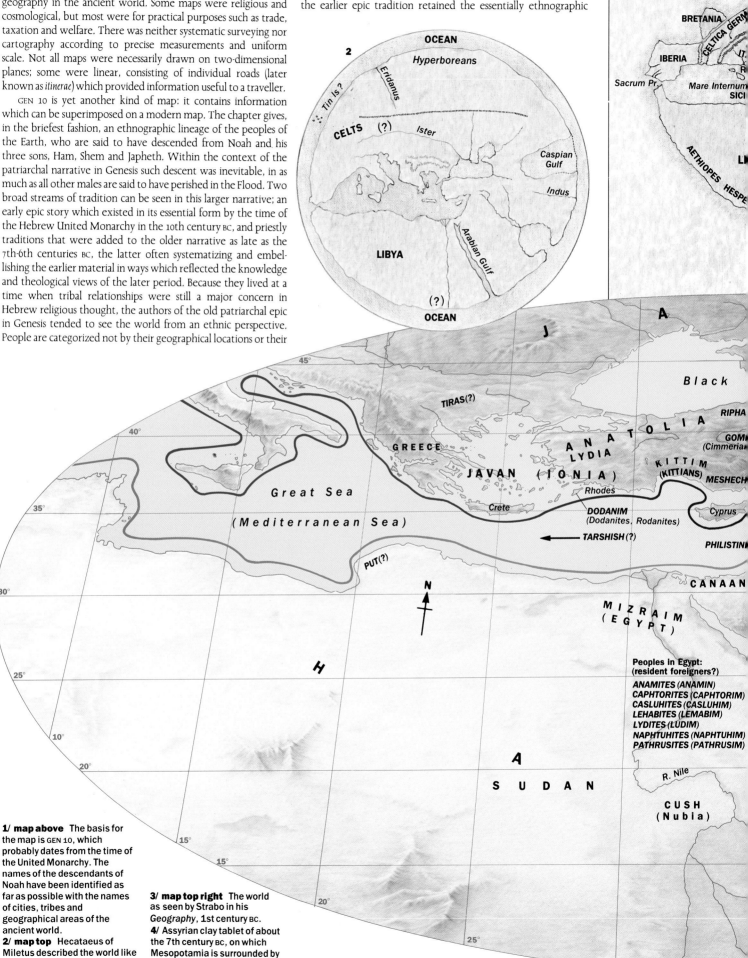

1/ **map above** The basis for the map is GEN 10, which probably dates from the time of the United Monarchy. The names of the descendants of Noah have been identified as far as possible with the names of cities, tribes and geographical areas of the ancient world.

2/ **map top** Hecataeus of Miletus described the world like this in his *Periodos* (c 520 BC).

3/ **map top right** The world as seen by Strabo in his *Geography*, 1st century BC.

4/ Assyrian clay tablet of about the 7th century BC, on which Mesopotamia is surrounded by a broad ring, the cosmic ocean.

structure of GEN 10, but added to the earliest list some names which reflected their awareness of the larger world – peoples of Anatolia to the north, Media and Elam to the east, and Cush to the south. Although they seem to have had some interest in geography in its own right, their concerns were heavily theological. The centre of the world was, as in the epic narrative, Canaan, the land which the Israelites had taken as their home. The extent of the inhabited Earth known to priestly editors was not more than 1500 miles in any direction from the hub of Canaan/Palestine, less than one-twentieth of the Earth's actual surface.

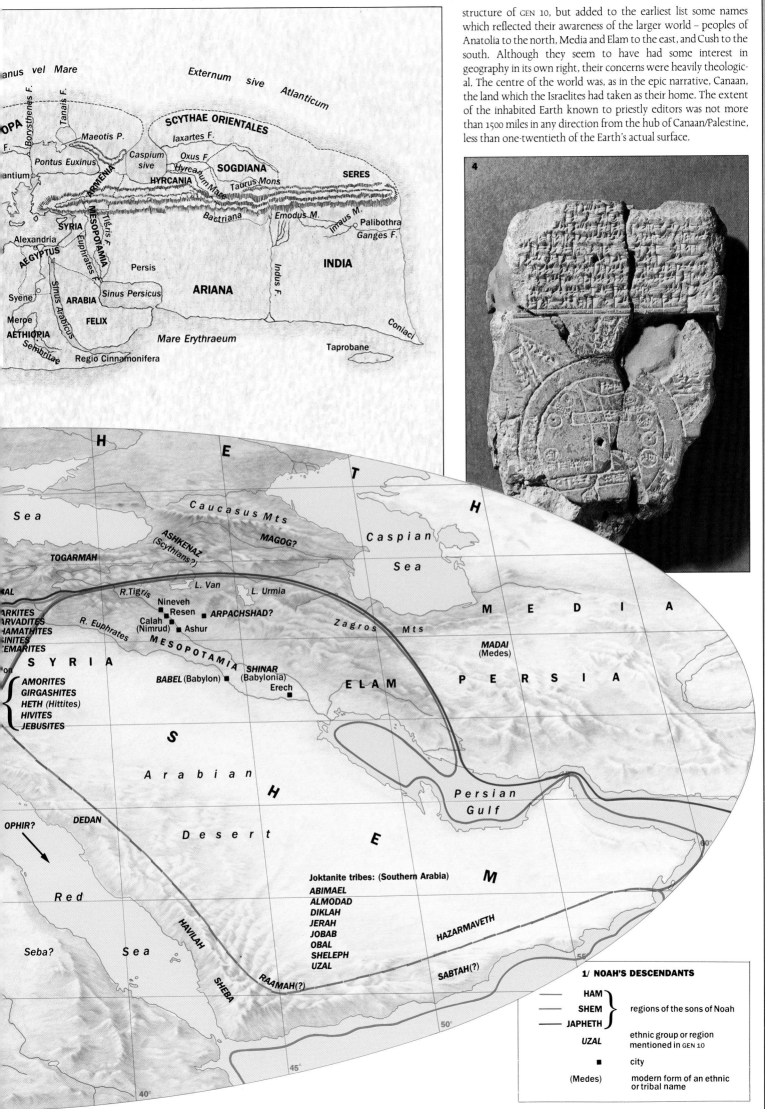

Map labels (upper map):

Oceanus vel Mare
Externum sive Atlanticum
SCYTHAE ORIENTALES
Borysthenes F.
Tanais F.
Maeotis P.
Pontus Euxinus
Iaxartes F.
Caspium sive Hyrcanium Mare
Oxus F.
SOGDIANA
SERES
ARMENIA
HYRCANIA
Taurus Mons
SYRIA
MESOPOTAMIA
Tigris F.
Bactriana
Emodus M.
Imaus M.
Palibothra
Alexandria
Euphrates F.
Ganges F.
AEGYPTUS
Persis
INDIA
Syene
Sinus Persicus
ARIANA
Indus F.
ARABIA
Meroe
AETHIOPIA
FELIX
Mare Erythraeum
Coniaci
Sembritae
Regio Cinnamonifera
Taprobane

Map labels (lower map – 1/ NOAH'S DESCENDANTS):

H E T H
Sea
Caucasus Mts
ASHKENAZ (Scythians?)
MAGOG?
Caspian Sea
TOGARMAH
MEDIA
L. Van
L. Urmia
R. Tigris
Nineveh
Resen
ARPACHSHAD?
ARKITES
ARVADITES
HAMATHITES
SINITES
ZEMARITES
Calah (Nimrud)
Ashur
R. Euphrates
Zagros Mts
MADAI (Medes)
MESOPOTAMIA
SHINAR (Babylonia)
PERSIA
SYRIA
BABEL (Babylon)
Erech
ELAM
AMORITES
GIRGASHITES
HETH (Hittites)
HIVITES
JEBUSITES
S
Arabian
H
Persian Gulf
OPHIR?
DEDAN
Desert
E
M
Red
Joktanite tribes: (Southern Arabia)
ABIMAEL
ALMODAD
DIKLAH
JERAH
JOBAB
OBAL
SHELEPH
UZAL
HAZARMAVETH
SABTAH(?)
Seba?
Sea
HAVILAH
RAAMAH(?)
SHEBA

Legend:

1/ NOAH'S DESCENDANTS

HAM
SHEM } regions of the sons of Noah
JAPHETH

UZAL ethnic group or region mentioned in GEN 10

■ city

(Medes) modern form of an ethnic or tribal name

SOME ancient systems of writing have been kept alive – Hebrew and Greek for example – but many more have been forgotten. Decipherment of forgotten scripts of the ancient Near East only began in the 1750s, when Phoenician was first read: the Rosetta stone provided Champollion with the key to Egyptian hieroglyphs in about 1821; Assyrian cuneiform was fairly well understood by 1857 and Ugaritic was read in 1930, just a year and a half after the first tablet was found. Thus, only recently have the increasing number of known ancient texts been able to speak of life in the ancient Near East.

The survival of examples of ancient writing depends on the durability of the medium to which the writing was committed. Most literate societies of the ancient Near East have left commemorative inscriptions on stone, or sometimes on metal. These monumental texts, however, were limited as to their subject matter, usually to proclaim the greatness of a king, record his victories, entreat the favour of a god, or to display the laws of the land.

Other documents were written on less permanent material. In Egypt, and in places under its influence, writing was normally on papyrus or wood. Neither of these media survive well enough to preserve a full library or archive, though fragmentary hoards are sometimes sufficient to imply the existence of a larger collection (pages 18 and 28).

The clay tablet, which originated in Mesopotamia, is a medium uniquely suitable for survival. It is easily produced and an inexpensive object that has filled the great library and archival collections of the ancient Near East. The languages written in cuneiform signs on these unimpressive tablets of clay are principally Sumerian and Akkadian, but due to the borrowing of the script and the medium, Hittite and some other languages appear. Although 15 libraries can be listed (far right), there are some important centres which must have had huge archives that have simply never been discovered, for example, Carchemish and Aleppo. Here, a distinction should be made between libraries and archives. The latter are essentially practical collections of law, diplomacy and economics. The documents in general relate strictly to their own generation. Libraries, on the other hand, are collections of documents for which a greater permanence was required. Among these are literary texts, epics, poetry and 'wisdom'. The last group would include texts on religion, mythology, rituals, festivals and incantations; also 'scientific' and scholastic texts dealing with medicine, mathematics, astrology and the vocabularies and syllabaries required to maintain the writing system itself.

1/ map right Transmission of languages and scripts.
Ancient scripts in Syro-Palestine, *above right*
A/ Ugaritic cuneiform alphabet.
B/ Akkadian cuneiform, c1400 BC, from Kumidi.
C/ Hittite hieroglyphic seal, from Ugarit.
D/ Sinaitic alphabet, c1500 BC.
E/ Proto-Canaanite alphabet, c1150 BC.

F/ Phoenician, on statue of Osorkon, 914-874 BC.
G/ Ivory pen-case fragment with hieroglyphs of Ramesses III.
H/ Hebrew on Gezer calendar, c900 BC.
I/ Aramaic, c635 BC.

1/ THE SPREAD OF WRITING
→ Mesopotamian cuneiform
→ Egyptian hieroglyphic
→ Alphabetic script

solid arrows indicate definite transmission
dashed arrows indicate possible transmission

MESOPOTAMIAN CUNEIFORM

(1) The earliest writing consists of pictographic signs on clay tablets from Uruk, from the 'Protoliterate' period (c3200-2800 BC). These should probably be read as Sumerian, implying that the Sumerians invented the script, but definite proof is lacking.

(2) In the Early Dynastic period (c2800-2400 BC) archaic inscriptions certainly in Sumerian are found on many sites, including Ur and Lagash. The script has developed from pictographic to 'Cuneiform': ie, the signs are made up of wedge (Latin *cuneus*)-shaped strokes.

(3) A late Early Dynastic palace archive has been discovered at Ebla (c2500-2300 BC) containing some 15,000 tablets, written in Sumerian Cuneiform but also 'Eblaite', a Semitic language.

(4) The Semitic Dynasty of Akkad (c2400-2250 BC), borrowed Cuneiform for its inscriptions. Akkadian, known in two dialects, Babylonian and Assyrian, replaced Sumerian as the spoken language of Mesopotamia. Sumerian was retained as a learned language. Cuneiform always remained primarily a script for clay tablets but was also carved on stone objects.

(5) At Susa a large group of tablets contemporary with the later Protoliterate was found, inscribed in an undeciphered pictographic script different from that of Mesopotamia, but apparently modelled on it. These 'Proto-Elamite' tablets are still being found at several sites across Iran.

(6) After 2000 BC Cuneiform Akkadian on clay tablets was widely used as an international means of communication. Other peoples borrowed the script and the tablet for writing their own languages: the Elamites (c2250-350 BC); the Hurrians (c2200-1300 BC); the Hittites (c1650-1200 BC); and latest, the Urartians (c8500-600 BC).

(7) The Indus valley cities have produced many short undeciphered inscriptions on seals, etc, c2500-1800 BC. Links with Mesopotamia by sea or overland may have spread the idea of writing and led to the local invention of the script.

(8) In the Persian Empire c550-330 BC, a 'Cuneiform' script was used to write the language Old Persian on monumental stone inscriptions. This script is Cuneiform only in appearance; actually it was modelled on the Aramaic alphabet with influence from the Akkadian syllabary.

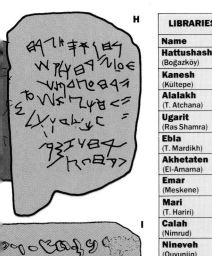

LIBRARIES OF THE ANCIENT NEAR EAST

Name	Excavation	No. of texts	Dates	Language	Document type	Comments
Hattushash (Boğazköy)	since 1906	thousands	c 1650-1200 BC	principally Hittite, Akkadian	royal library and archives	Hittite imperial capital, temples and citadel.
Kanesh (Kültepe)	since 1925, 1948	thousands	c 2000-1800 BC	Old Assyrian	merchant colony archives	Assyrian merchant colony in Anatolian city-state.
Alalakh (T. Atchana)	1936-1949	hundreds	c 1700-1400 BC	Akkadian	letters, administrative texts	Small palace of vassal kingdom of Aleppo.
Ugarit (Ras Shamra)	since 1929	thousands	1400-1200 BC	Akkadian, Ugaritic	libraries and archives	Phoenician kingdom, vassal of Hittite Empire.
Ebla (T. Mardikh)	since 1964	thousands	2500-2300 BC	Sumerian, 'Eblaite'	palace archives	Very early Syrian palace, archive remarkably intact.
Akhetaten (El-Amarna)	since 1887	hundreds	c 1417-1362 BC	Akkadian	royal correspondence	Egyptian chancery for relations with Levant.
Emar (Meskene)	1972-1976	thousands	c 1400-1200 BC	Akkadian, Hurrian	palace archives	Hurrian/Semitic vassal kingdom of Hittite Empire.
Mari (T. Hariri)	since 1933	thousands	c 1830-1760 BC	Akkadian	palace archives	Amorite kingdom between Syria and Mesopotamia.
Calah (Nimrud)	since c 1850	more than 1000	c 860-612 BC	Assyrian	palace and temple library and archives	One time capital of Assyria.
Nineveh (Quyunjiq)	since c 1850	thousands	c 700-612 BC	Assyrian	palace library and archives	Last, greatest capital of Assyria.
Ashur (Qal'at Sharqat)	since 1903-1914	thousands	c 1400-612 BC	Assyrian	libraries and archives	Original centre of Assyria.
Nuzi (Yorghan Tepe)	1925-1931	thousands	c 1550-1450 BC	Akkadian	private contracts and letters	Small Hurrian vassal kingdom.
Huzirina (Sultan Tepe)	1950s	hundreds	7th century BC	Assyrian	provincial library	Assyrian provincial city.
Susa (Shush)	c 1897-1939	thousands	2800-? BC	Akkadian, Elamite	various	Great Elamite capital city.
Babylonian cities	since c 1850	many thousands	3000-300 BC	Sumerian, Akkadian	various	Centre of Sumero-Akkadian civilizations.

THE ALPHABET

16. N. and S. Arabian scripts appear at an uncertain date, c 500 BC, and the latter gave rise to Ethiopic. These scripts may have split off the developing alphabetic tradition as early as the Proto-Canaanite stage, ie, before 1000 BC.

17. Scattered graffiti in a linear pictographic script on various objects dating to c 1500-1100 BC come from Canaan. Termed Proto-Canaanite, the signs are found arranged in alphabetic order c 1150 BC. A system of writing for papyrus or skin may be inferred from the cursive letters.

18. In Ugarit a 'cuneiform alphabet' was used c 1400-1200 BC to write the local language, and this is also found in Canaan. Signs were arranged in alphabetic order, linking the script closely to the Proto-Canaanite linear alphabet.

19. From Byblos an undeciphered 'Pseudo-Hieroglyphic' script on stone and metal, dated uncertainly c 2000-1000 BC, occurs. More significant, the earliest readable inscriptions in the true Alphabet are found here in a group of Phoenician inscriptions on sculpture.

20. The Hebrews adopted the Alphabet c 1150-1050 BC, and would have written mostly on papyrus, of which almost none survives. Preserved contemporary documents from the Hebrew kingdoms c 620-595 BC are sparse: ostraca, seals, and very few stone inscriptions.

21. The Aramaeans adopted the Phoenician-Hebrew Alphabet after 900 BC, and established their script and language in Mesopotamia. Aramaic became the administrative language of the Persian Empire, c 500-330 BC, thereby disseminating their Alphabet widely from Anatolia to India.

22. Phoenician colonization c 1000-700 BC took them to the west, to Carthage, Malta, Sardinia and Spain, and their language and script went with them. As usual, survivals are mostly stone inscriptions, not very representative of their general literacy.

23. By c 800 BC, the Greeks had adopted the Phoenician Alphabet and remodelled it for their language. At first many different forms of the Alphabet are attested, but by 400 BC the Ionic Alphabet had been adopted as the common script.

24. In Anatolia several peoples adopted a variant of the Alphabet and left stone inscriptions, etc; Phrygian (from c 750 BC), Lydian, Carian (from c 600), Lycian (from c 500). These Anatolian writings continued until Alexander's conquest, when they were superseded by Greek.

25. Greek colonization of the west, Sicily, S. Italy and S. France in the period c 800-500 BC effectively Hellenized the coastal areas, and established the Greek language and script. Each colony used its own variant of the Alphabet.

26. The Etruscans began writing after 700 BC. Earliest attested inscriptions are from c 650 BC. Their Alphabet was probably the Euboean variant borrowed from Cumae. They maintained their script and their still largely undeciphered language until the 1st century AD.

27. Early Rome was under strong Etruscan influence, and borrowed much, including the Alphabet. Most of the letters of the alphabet passed directly from the Greek through the Etruscan (A B E H I K M N O Q T) though some in variant forms (D L P R S V). Three acquired new values (C, F and X), and three were later additions (G, Y, Z), as were the Mediaeval J, V, W.

HIEROGLYPHIC

9. The earliest writing in Egypt is on stone monuments c 3100 BC, where the signs already show the characteristic monumental ('Hieroglyphic') forms. Since the period shows Mesopotamian cultural influences, it is thought that the knowledge of Mesopotamian writing inspired the invention of an original system.

10. The use of Hieroglyphic expanded in the Early Dynastic period (c 3100-2900 BC), surviving largely as tomb inscriptions on stone, wood and ivory, also sealings. It was certainly also written on papyrus, but none survives until c 2600-2500 BC.

11. The script, besides its monumental Hieroglyphic form, developed cursive hand-written forms for papyrus, Hieratic and later Demotic. Unlike Cuneiform, Hieroglyphic was never borrowed directly for writing any other language than its original, Egyptian.

12. In Crete, under Egyptian influence c 2000 BC a native 'Hieroglyphic' script begins to appear on seals and clay dockets. This developed into two linear scripts, A and B. Linear B (c 1400-1200 BC) has been deciphered and shown to write Mycenaean Greek.

13. Cyprus has two indigenous scripts, the undeciphered Cypro-Minoan written on clay (c 1500-1200 BC), and the Cypriot syllabary (c 750-300 BC), descended from the earlier script and used for writing monumental inscriptions in Greek and an unknown language.

14. The Hittites employed a Hieroglyphic script for seals and monumental inscriptions, c 1500-700 BC, but the language written was Luvian not Hittite. Probably the Luvians constructed their own script with a knowledge of the Aegean and perhaps also the Egyptian scripts.

15. Many Egyptian Hieroglyphic inscriptions dated c 2700-1000 BC were discovered at the Egyptian mines in Sinai. Beside these there is a small group of linear pictographic inscriptions, 'Proto-Sinaitic', connected both with Hieroglyphic and with the Proto-Canaanite alphabet.

H I N D I A

R. Indus

Himalayas

Mohenjo-Daro

Thar Desert   Lothal

PERSIA

Shahr-i-Sokhta

Tepe Yahya

Persepolis
Malyan

Arabian Sea

spian Sea

alk

sa

Failaka

Persian Gulf

Bahrain

MER

A R A B I A

SOUTH ARABIA

ETHIOPIA

THE occasion for the separation of Israel from Judah was the accession of Solomon's son Rehoboam to the throne of his father. When confronted by an assembly at Shechem which was critical of Solomon's oppressive policies, Rehoboam chose a hard line: 'My father', he said, 'made your yoke heavy, but I will add to your yoke; my father chastened you with whips, but I will chastise you with scorpions' (I KINGS 12.14). This policy, according to the colourful account in I KINGS 12, was the occasion for the split that was to last for more than three centuries.

Rehoboam's accession to the throne in Jerusalem was automatic: the dynastic principle was favoured in the south and his acceptance as Solomon's heir was unquestioned. In the north, however, charismatic leadership was customary and the choice of Rehoboam was not a foregone conclusion. Also, the rift between north and south had widened since Saul's death. His son, Eshbaal, or Ish-bosheth, had been murdered by David's supporters – obviously to insure David the Judaean kingship – and further northern resentment had been engendered when David placed the re-captured Ark of the Covenant in Jerusalem (page 48). The northern tribes had been bound into the United Kingdom by treaty rather than by any inherent concept of unity. Thus, following his accession in Jerusalem it was necessary for Rehoboam to travel to Shechem to renew the covenant. At the meeting was Jeroboam ben-Nabat, who, for dissident activities, had been banished by Solomon and had taken refuge with Pharaoh Shoshenq I (known in the Bible as Shishak). At the assembly the northerners appeared willing to accept Rehoboam's kingship, but only under certain conditions, chiefly a reduction in taxation and of the forced labour which had been imposed by Solomon. Rehoboam requested three days to consult his advisers; then he refused. The reaction was swift: Rehoboam's chief of forced labour was murdered and Jeroboam was proclaimed king of Israel. Rehoboam returned to Jerusalem and launched a campaign against the north.

After the assembly at Shechem there would seem to have been continuous war between Israel and Judah. Most disputed was the territory of Benjamin, and the border between the two kingdoms was not fixed for several generations. Initially it seems to have run south of Bethel, and on the west and east it ran north of Aijalon and south of Jericho respectively. The period of conflict between the rival states allowed the areas conquered under the United Monarchy to break away. The situation in Transjordan is unclear but, since, according to the Mesha *stela*, Omri re-conquered Moab, it must be assumed that it had gained independence. That Israel maintained control over at least part of Ammon is clear from Jeroboam's claim to have 'built' Penuel, a site on the Wadi Zerqa. This may have been one of Jeroboam's capitals in the new state. He also enlarged Shechem (T. Balatah) and Tirzah (T. el-Far'ah(N)) for use as royal residences.

Shishak, founder of the 22nd (Libyan) dynasty, became Pharaoh during Solomon's reign. Relations between Egypt and Israel were probably peaceful, although Shishak did offer refuge to Jeroboam, Solomon's enemy. With the division of the kingdom it is likely that relations between Egypt and Israel remained initially cordial, and possibly for this reason Rehoboam, fearing that the 'special relationship' between Shishak and Jeroboam might develop into an alliance, built fortified cities in the Judaean hills extending south and west from Jerusalem possibly in preparation for an Egyptian invasion (page 78).

There are two principal sources for the invasion of Shishak. That found in the Bible is limited to two brief accounts. The first is in I KINGS 14.25-26, and records only Shishak's plunder of the Jerusalem Temple and the royal palace in the fifth year of Rehoboam: 'Shishak king of Egypt came up against Jerusalem; and he took away the treasures of the house of the Lord, and the treasures of the king's house', specifically, 'all the

shields of gold which Solomon had made'. A longer account in II CHRON 12.2-9 contains essentially the same information, but adds that Shishak 'took the fortified cities which pertained to Judah' and added an explanation for the disaster spoken by the prophet Shemaiah: Rehoboam and the princes had been unfaithful to the Lord. It was the repentance of the king and the princes that had spared the city of Jerusalem from attack.

The second source for the campaign is that of the Pharaoh himself. Among the relatively few independent sources which provide links with the Bible (page 71) is the long inscription of Shishak carved on a wall of the Amon temple at Karnak. It is a topographical list of cities conquered by Shishak. The order of the cities in the list as it stands is such that it has long been impossible to trace a route of march; it seemed that the arrangement is haphazard. However, in 1957 Benjamin Mazar suggested that the text was written in boustrophedon order (like oxen ploughing), that is, one line from left to right and the following from right to left and so on. According to Mazar's suggestion it would be possible to establish a plausible line of advance from one city to another. Shishak's campaigns would appear to have been principally in Israel to the north and in the Negeb; the territory of Judah would seem to have escaped.

Yet another piece of evidence for Shishak's campaign is a fragment of a *stela* of victory containing the cartouche of the Pharaoh found at Megiddo, a city which appears in the list at Karnak. The absence of Jerusalem in the Shishak list presents a problem in the light of the explicit statement in I KINGS 14.25 about the Pharaoh's visit to Jerusalem. One suggestion for resolving this discrepancy is that Rehoboam negotiated for the payment of gold shields at some nearby city, possibly Gibeon, and that Shishak agreed to bypass Jerusalem and then proceeded northward to attack the cities of Israel.

Although the campaign route is still disputed the main force probably followed a line through Gaza in Philistia to Gezer and the Judaean hills. Having received the tribute of Rehoboam the army advanced into Israel, probably taking Shechem and then Tirzah. The Egyptians appear to have turned eastwards, crossing the Jordan opposite Adam (T. ed-Damiyeh). This foray into Transjordan may have been to capture Jeroboam's residence at Penuel and the cities of Succoth (T. Deir 'Alla) and Zaphon (possibly T. es-Sa'idiyeh). Afterwards, Shishak re-crossed the river and went to Beth-shean and the Plain of Esdraelon. The Egyptians may have set up a base at Megiddo and then returned home via the Plain of Sharon and the Via Maris; the exact itinerary cannot be reconstructed further, as the Karnak inscription breaks off here.

In addition to the main campaign route the Karnak list shows that an army detachment was sent to Gaza to attack settlements in the Negeb. Sharuhen (T. el-Far'ah(S) and Arad (T. Arad) are mentioned and destruction levels at Beersheba and Ezion-geber (T. el-Kheleifeh) may reasonably be attributed to the activities of Shishak.

Despite the biblical, Egyptian and archaeological data available for the invasion of Palestine by Shishak in 924BC, much remains obscure and uncertain. There seems to have been no intention to establish permanent control over Israel and it has even been conjectured that this extensive campaign was carried out for the purpose of showing Egyptian strength in the time of weakness occasioned by the division of the kingdom of David and Solomon. Nevertheless, the list of cities conquered provides a unique source of topographical information about the occupation of the land at the end of the 10th century BC.

Rehoboam's 18-year reign was not a happy one. At the beginning the northern tribes were lost; he was invaded by Shishak; and insecurity within may have necessitated the 'cities of defence'. The unity of Solomon's kingdom was short-lived.

1/ **map right** Shishak's route in the invasion of 924 BC reconstructed from the topographical list of conquered cities on the Temple of Amon at Karnak.
2/ **map below** The division of Solomon's kingdom in 931BC into Israel and Judah and the excavated sites with Iron Age II remains.
3/ Fragment of an Egyptian victory *stela* found at Megiddo with the name Shishak. *Right* drawing the fragment.
4/ A pair of golden bracelets made for Shishak's son, Nimlot.
5/ Drawing of four cartouches with name conquered cities (Taa Shunem, Beth-shean, Rehob – right to left) f the Karnak list of Shish

2/ MAJOR EXCAVATED SITES IN ISRAEL

▲ site with Iron Age II remains

— state boundary

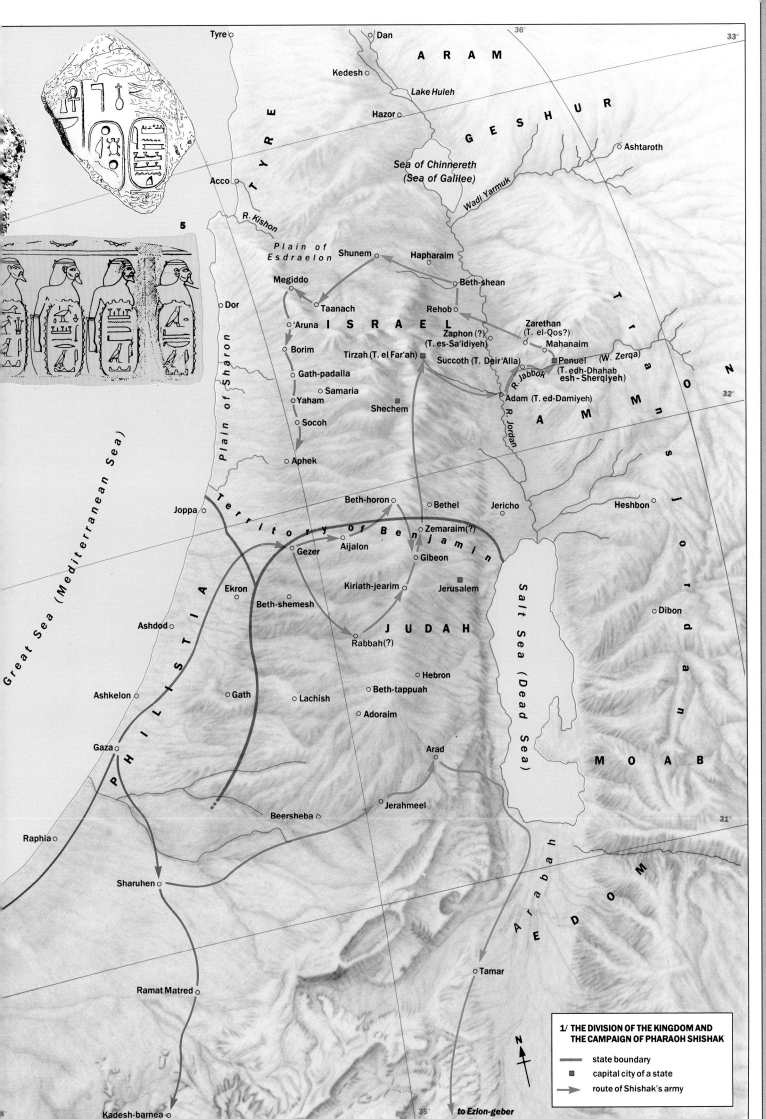

Tyre
Dan
A R A M
Kedesh
Lake Huleh
G E S H U R
Hazor
Ashtaroth
Acco
Sea of Chinnereth
(Sea of Galilee)
Wadi Yarmuk
R. Kishon
5
Plain of
Esdraelon
Shunem
Hapharaim
Megiddo
Beth-shean
Dor
Taanach
Rehob
'Aruna
I S R A E L
Zarethan
(T. el-Qos?)
Borim
Zaphon (?)
(T. es-Sa'idiyeh)
Mahanaim
Tirzah (T. el Far'ah)
Succoth (T. Deir 'Alla)
Penuel
(W. Zerqa)
Gath-padalla
(T. edh-Dhahab
esh – Sherqiyeh)
Samaria
R. Jabbok
Yaham
Adam (T. ed-Damiyeh)
Shechem
Socoh
A M M O N
Aphek
Great Sea (Mediterranean Sea)
Plain of Sharon
Territory of Benjamin
Beth-horon
Bethel
Jericho
Heshbon
Joppa
Zemaraim(?)
Gezer
Aijalon
Gibeon
Kiriath-jearim
Jerusalem
P H I L I S T I A
Ekron
J U D A H
Dibon
Beth-shemesh
Ashdod
Rabbah(?)
Salt Sea (Dead Sea)
Hebron
Ashkelon
Gath
Beth-tappuah
Lachish
Adoraim
Gaza
Arad
M O A B
Jerahmeel
Beersheba
E D O M
Raphia
Arabah
Sharuhen
Tamar
Ramat Matred
Kadesh-barnea
to Ezion-geber

**1/ THE DIVISION OF THE KINGDOM AND
THE CAMPAIGN OF PHARAOH SHISHAK**

state boundary
capital city of a state
route of Shishak's army

N

36°   33°

32°

31°

35°

OMRI (885-874 BC) did not acquire the kingship of Israel by normal succession or easily. Yet he founded a dynasty that ruled over Israel for forty eventful years and chose the site for and built a new capital, Samaria, which was to become both religiously significant and internationally important in the ancient Near East. He first appears in the Bible as commander-in-chief of the army at Gibbethon during a campaign against the Philistines in 885 BC (I KINGS 16.15-18). During the campaign another army commander, Zimri, murdered Elah, the King of Israel (886-5 BC), at Tirzah, the capital city, and made himself king. Omri's army then proclaimed him king in the field and Omri marched against his rival at Tirzah. After a siege of seven days Zimri burnt the royal palace and perished in the flames. The kingdom was in such turmoil during this period that even this event did not give Omri sole control; another group was supporting an alternative ruler, Tibni, whose claim to the throne was probably as legitimate as that of Omri. This rivalry continued until the death of Tibni in 880 BC.

At the beginning of his reign Omri retained Tirzah as his royal residence and capital city. It had already been used, on occasion, by Jeroboam I, Israel's first king (931-910 BC) (I KINGS 14.17), and had been the permanent capital of King Baasha (909-886 BC). Excavations at T. el-Far'ah (N), a large mound located near two springs at the head of a fertile valley (modern Nahal Tirza), have revealed several well-built but apparently unfinished buildings which are thought to represent the building activity of Omri at Tirzah, with which the site has been identified.

Another building project achieved during the dynasty of Omri was the construction of Samaria. It was a large, unoccupied site lying some nine miles to the south-west of Tirzah and a little over seven miles to the north-west of Shechem, an important shrine of early Israel. The site was the property of a private citizen named Shemer, and was purchased for two talents of silver (I KINGS 16.23-24) as the site for his new capital city. However, it was not until Tibni had been successfully eliminated in 880 BC that Omri made the move and named his new capital Samaria (today Sebastiyeh) after its former owner Shemer (I KINGS 16.24).

By acquiring a new site, Omri, like David before him, established a capital city with no earlier associations or loyalties to previous kings. The move to Samaria, with its westward orientation, may also have reflected a growing association with Solomon's old ally, Phoenicia, or the Sidonians (I KINGS 16.31), ruled at this time by Ethbaal I of Tyre. Indeed there is abundant evidence for close links between Israel and the Phoenicians during the time of Omri's son and successor Ahab (874-853 BC). Ahab married the daughter of Ethbaal (or Ittobaal), Jezebel, who brought her cult with her to the Israelite kingdom. Phoenician influence is also evident in the architectural remains of the period found at Samaria.

Excavations on the citadel at Samaria have shown two early building phases which are ascribed to Omri and Ahab respectively. Omri only lived for six years after moving to Samaria, so his building projects had to be completed by his son, Ahab. The work attributed to Omri includes the construction of a large terrace, about 583 by 291 ft in size, enclosed by a massive wall some 5 ft thick and built of large well-dressed masonry blocks with smaller blocks in the upper courses. In the second phase, attributed to Ahab, outer defensive casemate (chambered) walls were built, having a thickness of 32 ft on the north side and 16 ft on the west. These were connected to a western extension of the area. It seems, from what remains, that there were substantial rectangular buildings on the extension aligned with the retaining walls. Comparisons of the fine masonry of Samaria with Phoenician work at Tyre and elsewhere suggests that Omri and Ahab may have enlisted the aid of Ethbaal to supply Phoenician craftsmen for this work.

An increasing threat to the Israelite kingdom and its neighbours during the 9th century BC was the growing power of Assyria. A coalition of states which included Damascus, Hamath, Arvad and Ammon, as well as Israel, under Ahab, assembled in northern Syria in 853 BC in an attempt to halt the advance of the Assyrian king, Shalmaneser III (858-824 BC), and his armies. A major battle was fought at Qarqar (page 72) in which, though Shalmaneser was not defeated, the Assyrian advance was stopped. Soon after, Ahab was killed during a battle against the Aramaeans at Ramoth-gilead and was succeeded by his son Ahaziah (853-852 BC). Ahaziah had close links with Jehoshaphat, King of Judah; they were both involved in an unsuccessful attempt to revive sea trade down the Red Sea from Ezion-geber. Ahaziah was succeeded by another son of Ahab, Joram (or Jehoram) (852-841 BC). During the short reign of Ahaziah and Joram, increasingly close links developed with the kingdom of Judah, expressed by dynastic marriages and joint ventures.

Control of the kingdom was also hampered by the religious fervour of the prophets Elijah and Elisha.

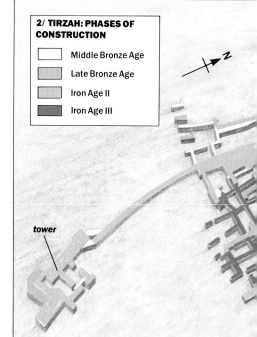

2/ TIRZAH: PHASES OF CONSTRUCTION

☐ Middle Bronze Age
▨ Late Bronze Age
▨ Iron Age II
▨ Iron Age III

tower

3

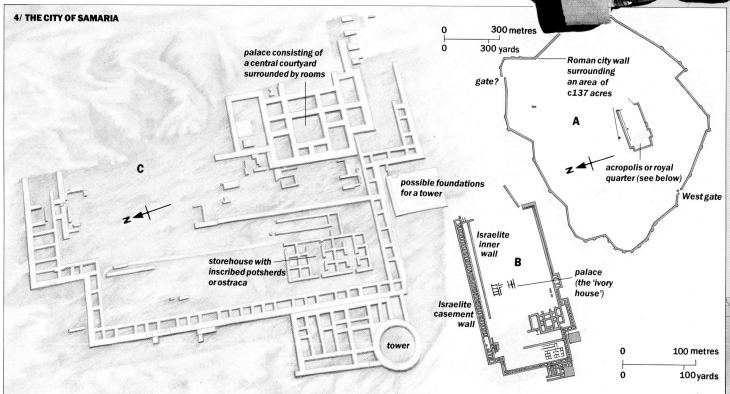

4/ THE CITY OF SAMARIA

palace consisting of a central courtyard surrounded by rooms

C

possible foundations for a tower

storehouse with inscribed potsherds or ostraca

tower

0 —— 300 metres
0 —— 300 yards

gate?

Roman city wall surrounding an area of c137 acres

A

acropolis or royal quarter (see below)

West gate

Israelite inner wall

B

palace (the 'ivory house')

Israelite casement wall

0 —— 100 metres
0 —— 100 yards

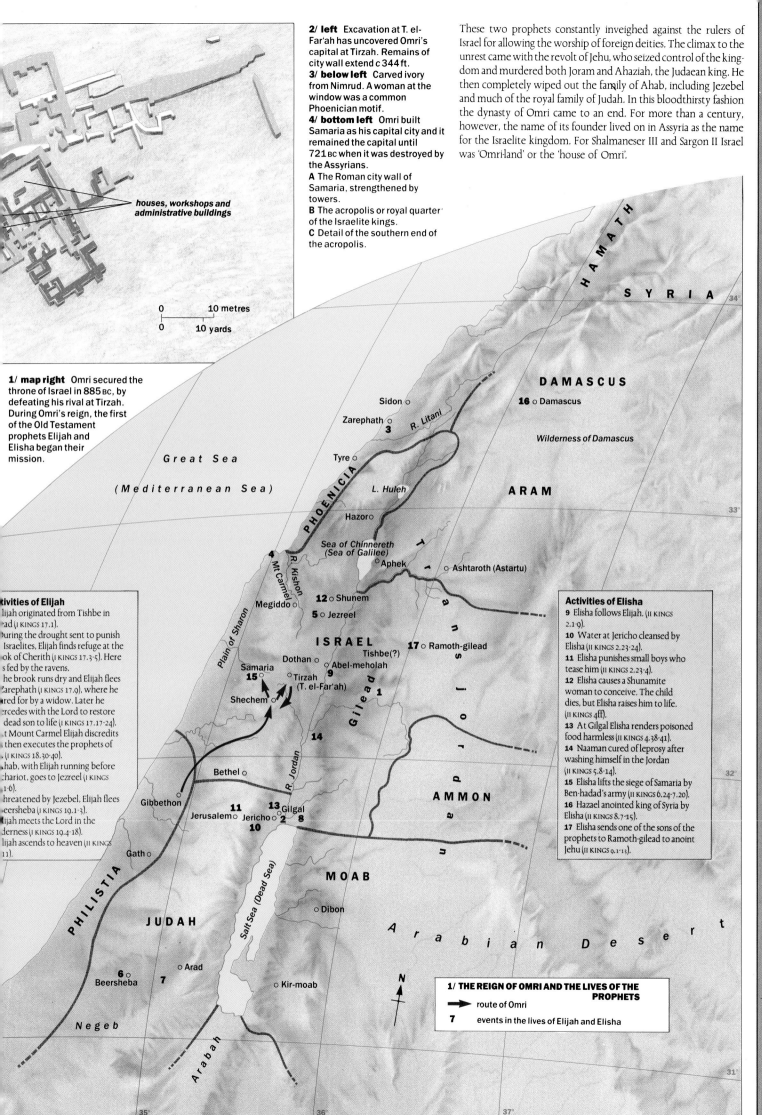

2/ left Excavation at T. el-Far'ah has uncovered Omri's capital at Tirzah. Remains of city wall extend c 344 ft.

3/ below left Carved ivory from Nimrud. A woman at the window was a common Phoenician motif.

4/ bottom left Omri built Samaria as his capital city and it remained the capital until 721 BC when it was destroyed by the Assyrians.

A The Roman city wall of Samaria, strengthened by towers.

B The acropolis or royal quarter of the Israelite kings.

C Detail of the southern end of the acropolis.

These two prophets constantly inveighed against the rulers of Israel for allowing the worship of foreign deities. The climax to the unrest came with the revolt of Jehu, who seized control of the kingdom and murdered both Joram and Ahaziah, the Judaean king. He then completely wiped out the family of Ahab, including Jezebel and much of the royal family of Judah. In this bloodthirsty fashion the dynasty of Omri came to an end. For more than a century, however, the name of its founder lived on in Assyria as the name for the Israelite kingdom. For Shalmaneser III and Sargon II Israel was 'Omri-land' or the 'house of Omri'.

houses, workshops and administrative buildings

0   10 metres
0   10 yards

1/ map right Omri secured the throne of Israel in 885 BC, by defeating his rival at Tirzah. During Omri's reign, the first of the Old Testament prophets Elijah and Elisha began their mission.

Activities of Elijah
Elijah originated from Tishbe in Gilead (I KINGS 17.1).
During the drought sent to punish the Israelites, Elijah finds refuge at the brook of Cherith (I KINGS 17.3-5). Here he is fed by the ravens.
The brook runs dry and Elijah flees to Zarephath (I KINGS 17.9), where he is cared for by a widow. Later he intercedes with the Lord to restore her dead son to life (I KINGS 17.17-24).
At Mount Carmel Elijah discredits and then executes the prophets of Baal (I KINGS 18.30-40).
Ahab, with Elijah running before his chariot, goes to Jezreel (I KINGS 18.1-6).
Threatened by Jezebel, Elijah flees to Beersheba (I KINGS 19.1-3).
Elijah meets the Lord in the wilderness (I KINGS 19.4-18).
Elijah ascends to heaven (II KINGS 2.11).

Activities of Elisha
9 Elisha follows Elijah. (II KINGS 2.1-9).
10 Water at Jericho cleansed by Elisha (II KINGS 2.23-24).
11 Elisha punishes small boys who tease him (II KINGS 2.23-4).
12 Elisha causes a Shunamite woman to conceive. The child dies, but Elisha raises him to life. (II KINGS 4ff).
13 At Gilgal Elisha renders poisoned food harmless (II KINGS 4.38-41).
14 Naaman cured of leprosy after washing himself in the Jordan (II KINGS 5.8-14).
15 Elisha lifts the siege of Samaria by Ben-hadad's army (II KINGS 6.24-7.20).
16 Hazael anointed king of Syria by Elisha (II KINGS 8.7-15).
17 Elisha sends one of the sons of the prophets to Ramoth-gilead to anoint Jehu (II KINGS 9.1-13).

1/ THE REIGN OF OMRI AND THE LIVES OF THE PROPHETS
→ route of Omri
7 events in the lives of Elijah and Elisha

THE land of Moab was a strip of arable land lying between the Dead Sea and the desert to the east. The Book of Ruth, set shortly before the time of the Monarchy, describes a family of Bethlehem which went to live in 'the field of Moab' in a time of famine (RUTH 1.1-2). Ruth distinguished herself by her loyalty to Naomi, her widowed mother-in-law. They returned to her native Bethlehem, where Ruth married Boaz and eventually became the great-grandmother of King David. Moab and Israel shared a common material culture, spoke closely-related languages, but had distinctive religions. The northern region of Moab, separated from Moab proper by the River Arnon (Wadi el-Mujib), was disputed territory between the Israelites, Ammonites and Moabites for centuries. The Book of Joshua (13) claims for Israel the cities north of the Arnon; David, Solomon and Omri dominated that area, but were probably unable to exercise any permanent control over the more isolated cities lying between the Wadi el-Mujib and the Wadi Hasa at the southern end of the Dead Sea.

The relations between Israel and Moab are more fully documented during the reign of King Mesha over Moab. In addition to the information which has been preserved in II KINGS 1.1 and 3.4-27, there is a detailed account of Mesha's wars and building accomplishments engraved on a *stela* discovered near Dibon in 1868. This inscription mentions Omri, King of Israel, Yahweh, god of Israel, Moab's national god Ashtar-Chemosh (I KINGS 11.7) and some ten of the Moabite cities found in the Old Testament text.

It was Omri (885-874 BC) who extended Israelite control over northern Moab and extracted payments of tribute from its cities. Ahab (874-853 BC) continued his father's policy. Mesha probably did not challenge Israel's authority in Moab until Ahab died (I KINGS 1.1; 3.4), and his challenge at that time consisted of refusing to deliver the annual tribute, seizing control of northern Moab, and making preparations to defend his country against Israel's retaliatory attack which he assumed would occur as soon as a new king was established in Samaria. The expected attack only came after Ahaziah had died and was succeeded by Jehoram (Joram). After collecting the King of Judah in Jerusalem, Jehoram marched 'by the way of the wilderness to Edom.' Thus they approached Moab from the south-west where the terrain is extremely rugged. This surprise approach to the heartland of Moab by a route that led up the steep north bank of the Wadi Hasa proved successful. The invaders devastated Moab until only Kir-hareseth was left standing and the King of Moab had taken refuge behind its walls.

The Mesha *stela* was probably erected in connection with the dedication of a sanctuary to Chemosh at a place called Qarhoh. Presumably Dibon served as Moab's capital during Mesha's reign and Qarhoh was some sort of suburb or royal quarter of Dibon. Surrounded by rolling agricultural land, Medeba was the key city of northern Moab, as it is today. Lines 9-21 of the inscription recount Mesha's key moves in his recovery of the land of Medeba from Israel. Specifically, he attacked, massacred, and looted two Israelite settlements in northern Moab (Ataroth and Nebo); fortified two other sites, Beth-baal-meon and Qaryaten (probably biblical Kiriathaim), and placed his own loyalists in Jahaz which had been built (or fortified) by the Israelites to serve as a military and administrative base during their occupation of northern Moab.

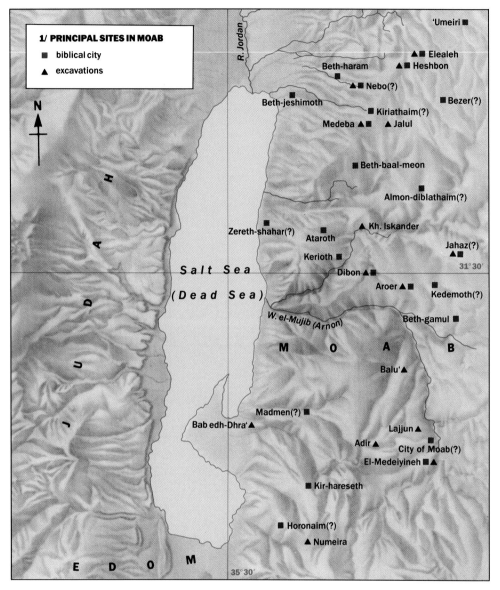

1/ PRINCIPAL SITES IN MOAB
■ biblical city
▲ excavations

N

R. Jordan

'Umeiri ■
▲■ Elealeh
Beth-haram ■   ▲■ Heshbon
■ ▲■ Nebo(?)
Beth-jeshimoth ■   ■ Bezer(?)
■ Kiriathaim(?)
Medeba ▲■   ▲ Jalul
■ Beth-baal-meon
■ Almon-diblathaim(?)
Zereth-shahar(?) ■   ▲ Kh. Iskander
Ataroth ■
Kerioth ■   Jahaz(?) ▲■
Dibon ▲■   31°30'
Aroer ▲■   ■ Kedemoth(?)
W. el-Mujib (Arnon)   ■ Beth-gamul
Salt Sea
(Dead Sea)
M O A B
Balu'▲
Madmen(?) ■   Lajjun ▲
Bab edh-Dhra'▲   Adir ▲   City of Moab(?)
El-Medeiyineh ■▲
■ Kir-hareseth
■ Horonaim(?)
▲ Numeira
E D O M
35°30'

1/ map left Biblical cities and major excavations in Moab.
2/ below left Copy of the Mesha *stela*, inscribed c 830 BC, made before the *stela* was broken by vandals. With English translation.
3/ below The restored black basalt Moabite *stela* as it now stands in the Louvre.

2

by local bedouin tribesmen, and in 1873 it was taken to the Louvre.

The date of the Mesha Stela is roughly fixed by the reference to Mesha, king of Moab in II KINGS 3.4 as about the mid-9th century BC.

The following is a translation of the stela:

I (am) Mesha, son of Chemosh-[...], king of Moab, the Dibonite – my father (had) reigned over Moab thirty years, and I reigned after my father, – (who) made this high place for Chemosh in Qarhoh [...] because he saved me from all the kings and caused me to triumph over all my adversaries. As for Omri (5) king of Israel, he humbled Moab many years (lit., days), for Chemosh was angry at his land. And his son followed him and he also said, "I will humble Moab". In my time he spoke (thus), but I have triumphed over him and over his house, while Israel hath perished for ever! (Now) Omri had occupied the land of Medeba, and (Israel) had dwelt there in his time and half the time of his son (Ahab), forty years; but Chemosh dwelt there in my time.

And I built Baal-meon, making a reservoir in it, and I built (10) Qaryaten. Now the men of Gad had always dwelt in the land of Ataroth, and the king of Israel had built Ataroth for them; but I fought against the town and took it and slew all the people of the town as satiation (intoxication) for Chemosh and Moab. And I brought back from there Arel (or Oriel), its chieftain, dragging him before Chemosh in Kerioth, and I settled there men of Sharon and men of Maharith. And Chemosh said to me, "Go, take Nebo from Israel!" (15) So I went by night and fought against it from the break of dawn until noon, taking it and slaying all, seven thousand men, boys, women, girls and maidservants, for I had devoted them to destruction for (the god) Ashtar-Chemosh. And I took from there the [...] of the Lord, dragging them before Chemosh. And the king of Israel had built Jahaz, and he dwelt there while he was fighting against me, but Chemosh drove him out before me. And (20) I took from Moab two hundred men, all first class (warriors), and set them against

Jahaz and took it in order to attach it to (the district of) Dibon.

It was I (who) built Qarhoh, the wall of the forests and the wall of the citadel; I also built its gates and I built its towers and I built the king's house, and I made both of its reservoirs for water inside the town. And there was no cistern inside the town at Qarhoh, so I said to all the people, "Let each of you make (25) a cistern for himself in his house!" And I cut beams for Qarhoh with Israelite captives. I built Aroer, and I made the highway in the Arnon (valley) I built Beth-bamoth, for it had been destroyed; I built Bezer – for it lay in ruins – with fifty men of Dibon, for all Dibon is (my) loyal dependency.

And I reigned (in peace) over the hundred towns which I had added to the land. And I built (30) [...] Medeba and Beth-diblathen and Beth-baal-meon, and I set there the [...] of the land. And as for Hauronen, there dwelt in it [...And] Chemosh said to me, "Go down, fight against Hauronen. And I went down [and I fought against the town and I took it], and Chemosh dwelt in my time....

THE MOABITE STONE
This important inscription was discovered intact in 1868; it was subsequently broken, presumably

3

THE poetry of the Bible, especially the prophetic oracles, frequently refers to crafts and industries in simile and metaphor. Bas-reliefs from ancient Egypt and Mesopotamia, as well as the artefacts from excavations, record technologies which have been superseded or confined to the more primitive, isolated areas of the world. These are a means for understanding analogies that were obvious to the ancient reader.

WINE-MAKING

Wine-making was a relatively simple process in which grapes were pressed by treading them in a rock-cut basin. The juice was collected in a basin, also cut from the rock, and then stored in jars for fermentation. Eventually they were stored in rock-cut cellars where the temperature was constant. An alternative method of pressing was applying pressure to a porous bag by means of two levers attached to the ends of the bag. In the Israelite period, labels giving the name of the town and the name of the producer were engraved on the handles of the wine jar (numerous examples have been found at El-Jib, ancient Gibeon).

POTTERY

Pottery makes its appearance in Palestine in the Late Neolithic period (c 6000-5000 BC), with vessels first fashioned by hand or shaped on a slowly turning base, often painted or incised, and fired in a closed kiln. In time techniques were improved and ceramic containers for storage, cooking and serving food became an important part of material culture.

Clay was dug, weathered in the potter's workshop and mixed (by treading, ISA 41.25) with a 'temper' of crushed stone and organic matter such as chopped straw. It was then moulded by hand, or built up with coils or slabs of clay. In later times the vessel was 'thrown' on a fast wheel. After it had been dried to a leather hardness it was fired in a kiln heated by brush and wood. The changing styles in shape and decoration of pottery serve as a basis for identifying the succession of cultures that flourished in Palestine, from the Neolithic down to modern times.

METALLURGY

Metals were expensive because their sources were often distant and techniques for producing them complicated. Copper was first smelted and cast sometime around 4000 BC. Major sources of ore were Sinai and the southern part of the Wadi 'Araba. After it had been crushed, copper ore was placed in a furnace on a bed of charcoal. By using bellows or *tuyères*, it was possible to attain a temperature high enough to produce molten copper. When the ingot was hammered out, the metal was reheated and cast in a mould to form a tool or weapon. Bronze, a harder alloy, was produced by the addition of arsenic or more commonly tin (c 3000 BC).

The production of iron was a more complex procedure. Smelting required a temperature of several hundred degrees more than copper. The resulting spongy mass had to be hammered to free the iron of impurities and carbon had to be added to harden it (as in the production of steel).

Craftsmen were often organized in hereditary guilds, living and working together. The metalworking guilds probably made seasonal expeditions to the mining areas, and worked up the ingots into finished products in the neighbourhood of their home cities during the rest of the year.

SPINNING AND WEAVING

On account of the damp climate of Palestine, very few examples of ancient textiles have survived. Recently, however, a number of pieces of cloth have been found, dating to around 7000 BC, in a cave at Nahal Hemar near the Dead Sea. Flax (grown in Palestine since the Early Bronze Age) and wool have been widely used in making textiles. A stone relief from Susa illustrates the common method of spinning fibres into thread, using only the most basic equipment; numerous examples of spindle whorls, made of stone, bone or faience, have come from excavations throughout Palestine, documenting the use there of the same

1/ Wall painting showing traditional brickmaking. From the tomb of Rekh-mi-Re and Nakht, Thebes, Egypt, 15th century BC.
2/ Stone relief from Susa showing a noblewoman spinning. She is seated cross-legged on a stool and her servant stands behind her with a fan. Early 1st millennium BC.

3/ Wall painting showing grape-gathering from an arbor, treading, and the storage of wine in jars with stoppers. From the tomb of Rekh-mi-Re and Nakht, Thebes, Egypt, 15th century BC.
4/ One of 22 pottery kilns in the industrial area of Sarepta, Lebanon (Zarephath, visited by the prophet Elijah). Preserved is the oval firing chamber, measuring inside 6ft 7in by 7ft 8in, and flues which conducted the heat to a chamber above. The kiln's doorway to the left could be closed with a temporary wall to control the heat.

method of spinning as that used in Susa.

Three types of loom were used in the ancient Near East. The vertical loom with the warp beam at the top and the cloth beam at the bottom; the welt was beaten downward. The second was reversed, with the cloth beam at the top and the warp weighted at the bottom by clay weights, many of which have been found in excavations; here the weft was beaten upward. A third type was the horizontal loom held in place by pegs which secured the two beams to which the threads of the warp were attached.

In the nomadic societies weaving was done in the household by the women. In the sedentary societies it was, to some extent, done by the women in the home, especially in Egypt, but there were also professional weavers, most of whom were men.

67

HEBREW monotheism was constantly struggling to resist Canaanite polytheism and its practices which had survived from the Late Bronze Age. How diverse were religious allegiances as late as the 9th and 8th centuries is evident from recent discoveries at Kuntillet 'Ajrud to the south of Kadesh-barnea. Inscriptions record the names of Baal, Asherah and El, as well as Yahweh 'and his consort'. The popular cults did not die easily.

The custom of setting up a stone for religious purposes reaches back to Neolithic times, as evidenced by the basalt upright stone found at Jericho. Basalt *stelae* were found within the Late Bronze Age at Hazor. Biblical accounts of memorial stones are many: to mark Jacob's covenant with Laban (GEN 31.45); a cult object at Bethel (GEN 28.18-19). The altar was for slaughtering animals and burning offerings. They were of mud brick or unquarried stone (EX 20.24-26; DEUT 27.5) and examples have been found at Megiddo and Lachish. Altars from the Iron Age have also been found, that from Beersheba having 'horns' at the four corners and a snake engraved on one side.

Cylinder seals of the Late Bronze Age often show a worshipper standing in front of a tree; other seals dating from the 10th to the 8th centuries depicting a tree flanked by worshippers have come from T. Halif, Lachish, Beth-shemesh, Gibeon, Samaria and elsewhere. Gold pendants from T. el-'Ajjul and Ugarit display trees growing out of the navel or the pudenda of a stylized goddess. According to HOS 4.13-14, sexual intercourse took place under holy trees and was considered a part of the sacrifice to the goddess. Numerous Canaanite bronzes of a young man with his right hand raised in a gesture of victory are thought to represent Baal (page 19). Jeroboam is said to have violated the Law by setting up images of golden calves in the temples at Dan and Bethel (1 KINGS 12.28-30). Bronze bulls, possibly representing Baal, are known from Hazor, Ugarit and Samaria.

The female deity is referred to as the consort of Baal (JUDG 3.7; II KINGS 23.4), and Astarte is often described as a fertility goddess. Numerous clay figurines, found in great numbers from the 10th-6th centuries BC, have generally been taken to be symbols of eroticism rather than representations of the 'nourishing goddess'. Maternal traits were usually expressed in animal rather than human form. The cow suckling her calf, which is familiar from Phoenician ivories, can be regarded as the counter-part of the god in the form of a bull.

The small bronze snakes found in the Late Bronze Age temples at Hazor, Megiddo, T. Mevorakh, Gezer, and in the Early Iron Age shrine at Timna' may have been votive offerings to a goddess, since a figurine of a female has been found holding a serpent in her hands. This same image, or one like it, was probably worshipped as Nehustan by the Israelites (II KINGS 18.4).

Within the various religions, naturalistic symbols such as standing stones, trees, the bull, cow, serpent, played an important role. The pantheon was large and varied as the natural world, including deities for such awe-inspiring phenomena as sky, sun, moon, storm with its thunder and lightning, the sea as well as the more abstract war, love, healing, wisdom and writing. These systems of belief reflected much of the prevailing personal, social and family relationships.

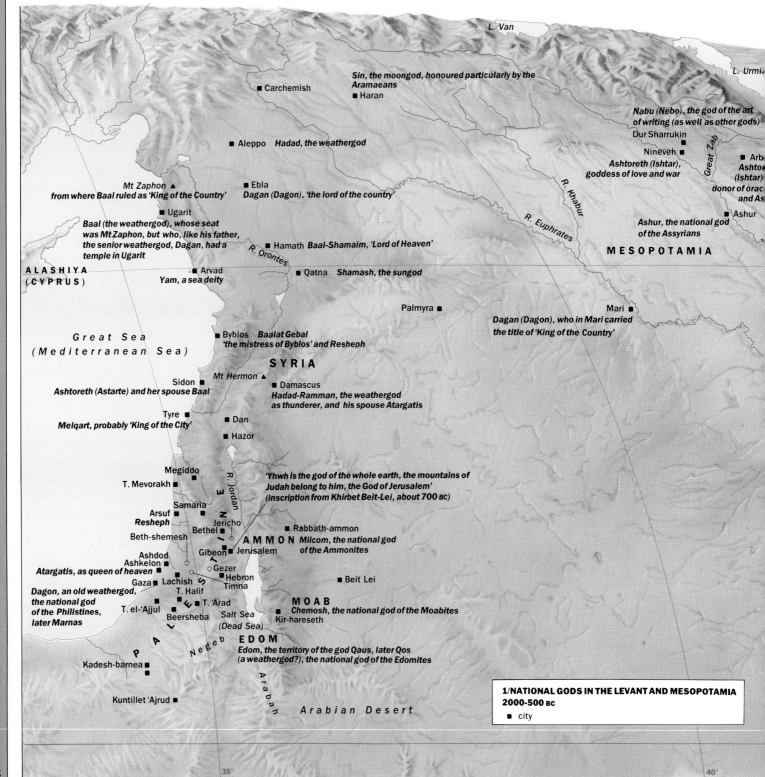

L. Van

L. Urmi.

■ Carchemish

Sin, the moongod, honoured particularly by the Aramaeans
■ Haran

Nabu (Nebo), the god of the art of writing (as well as other gods)
Dur Sharrukin ■
■ Aleppo **Hadad, the weathergod**
Nineveh ■
Ashtoreth (Ishtar), goddess of love and war
■ Arb
Ashto
(Ishtar)
donor of orac
and As

Mt Zaphon ▲
from where Baal ruled as 'King of the Country'
■ Ebla
Dagan (Dagon), 'the lord of the country'
■ Ashur
Ashur, the national god of the Assyrians

■ Ugarit
Baal (the weathergod), whose seat was Mt Zaphon, but who, like his father, the senior weathergod, Dagan, had a temple in Ugarit
R. Khabur
R. Euphrates
M E S O P O T A M I A
Great Zab

R. Orontes
■ Hamath **Baal-Shamaim, 'Lord of Heaven'**

A L A S H I Y A (C Y P R U S)
■ Arvad
Yam, a sea deity
■ Qatna **Shamash, the sungod**

Palmyra ■
Mari ■
Dagan (Dagon), who in Mari carried the title of 'King of the Country'

G r e a t   S e a (M e d i t e r r a n e a n   S e a)
■ Byblos **Baalat Gebal 'the mistress of Byblos' and Resheph**

S Y R I A

Sidon ■ Mt Hermon ▲
Ashtoreth (Astarte) and her spouse Baal
■ Damascus
Hadad-Ramman, the weathergod as thunderer, and his spouse Atargatis

Tyre ■   ■ Dan
Melqart, probably 'King of the City'
■ Hazor

Megiddo ■
T. Mevorakh ■
R. Jordan
'Yhwh is the god of the whole earth, the mountains of Judah belong to him, the God of Jerusalem' (inscription from Khirbet Beit-Lei, about 700 BC)

Samaria ■
Arsuf ■
Resheph
Bethel ■ Jericho ○
Beth-shemesh ■
Gibeon ■ ■ Jerusalem
■ Rabbath-ammon
AMMON Milcom, the national god of the Ammonites

Ashdod ■
Ashkelon ■
Atargatis, as queen of heaven
■ Gezer
Hebron ■
Gaza ■ Lachish ■ Timna
■ Beit Lei
Dagon, an old weathergod, the national god of the Philistines, later Marnas
T. Halif ■
T. 'Arad ■
T. el-'Ajjul ■ Beersheba ■
Salt Sea
(Dead Sea)
M O A B Chemosh, the national god of the Moabites
Kir-hareseth ■

P A L
Negeb
E D O M
Edom, the territory of the god Qaus, later Qos (a weathergod?), the national god of the Edomites

Kadesh-barnea ■

Arabah

Kuntillet 'Ajrud ■

Arabian Desert

1/NATIONAL GODS IN THE LEVANT AND MESOPOTAMIA 2000-500 BC
■ city

35°   40°

1/ map below The distribution of religious cults throughout Palestine, Phoenicia, Syria and Mesopotamia.

2/ Egyptian *stela* showing the Canaanite Qudshu ('holiness') between the ithyphallic Min on the left and the warlike Reshef on the right. 13th century BC.

3/ Phoenician ivory carving of a cow suckling her calf. Often seen as the female counterpart of the god Baal in his manifestation as a bull. The idea of a goddess providing nourishment was often conveyed by animal, rather than human, imagery.

4/ Gold pendant from T. el-'Ajjul showing a tree growing out of the stylized navel of a goddess. Late Bronze Age.

5/ Seal cylinder showing a worshipper standing before a sacred tree. Holy trees, symbols of life force, were often associated with Canaanite cults. Late Bronze Age.

6/ Bronze bull from Samaria associated with the worship of Baal ('master'), one of the major gods of the Canaanite cult. c.12th century BC.

7/ Fertility figurine from Palestine. The trunk-like body and extended breasts of the 'nourishing goddess' contrast with the carefully moulded face. These figurines date from the Iron Age and are never discovered intact, which suggests they were broken intentionally

Caspian Sea

ASSYRIA

R. Tigris

R. Diyala

Z a g r o s   M t s

Sippar   *Utu (Shamash) (the sungod) and his spouse Shenirda- Aja*

■ Cuthah   *Nergal (the god of the Underworld) and his spouse Ereshkigal*

Babylon
Marduk (Merodach), combative god of creation, national god of Babylonia and his spouse Sarpanitum   ■ Adab   *Ninhursag, the great, old mother goddess*

Borsippa ■

...bu (Nebo), god of the art of writing and wisdom; ...ether with Marduk (Merodach) the ...tional god of Babylonia   ■ Nippur
Enlil ('Lord Breath of Wind'), the main god of the Sumerians, Lord of Destiny and his spouse Ninlil

BABYLONIA

■ Kish   *Zababa, a wargod who had equal status with Ningirsu and his spouse Inanna (as warrior)*

■ Lagash   *Ningirsu (Ninurta), lord of farmland and war, and his spouse Baba, often identified with the goddess of healing, Gula*

E L A M

Erech ■
An (Anu), the god of heaven, and his daughter, Inanna (Ishtar), the goddess of love and war, who was later honoured as his spouse   ■ Larsa   *Utu (Shamash), the sungod, and his spouse Shenirda-Aja*

Nanna (Sin), the moongod and his spouse
■ Ur   *Ningal (Canaanite Nikkal)*

■ Eridu
Enki (Ea), god of the fresh water ocean and of wisdom, and his spouse Damkina (Damgalnunna)

N

55°
35°

30°

PERSIA   Persian Gulf

45°   50°

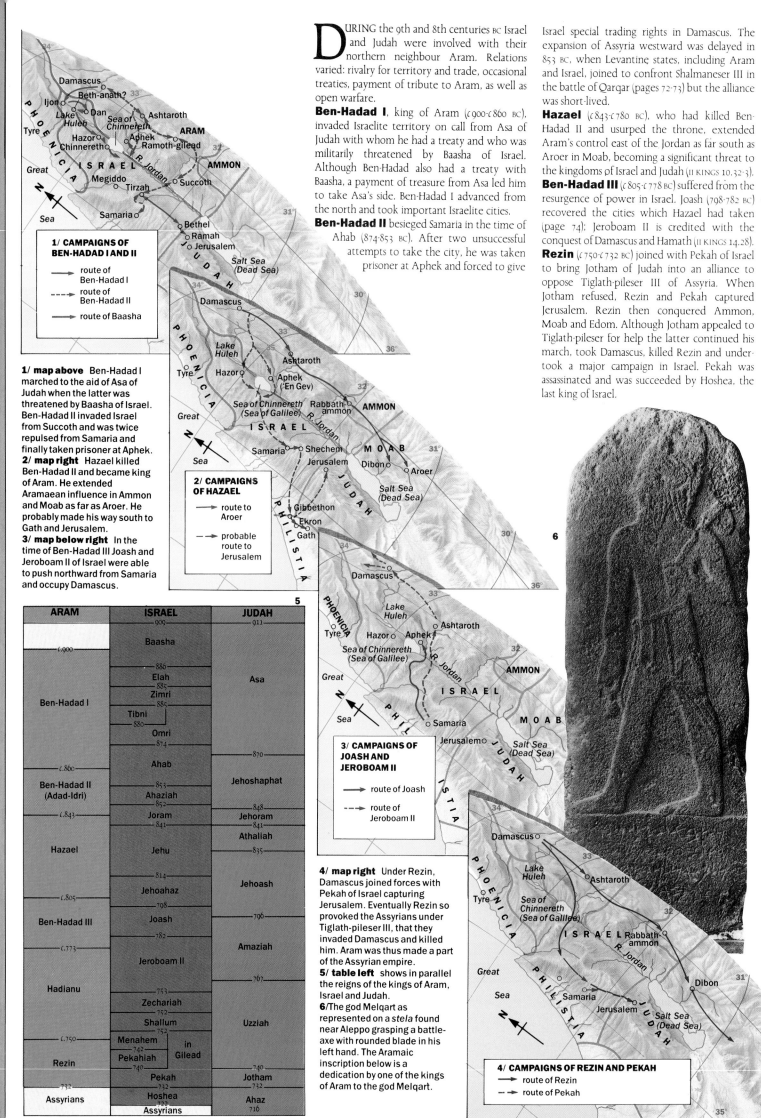

URING the 9th and 8th centuries BC Israel and Judah were involved with their northern neighbour Aram. Relations varied: rivalry for territory and trade, occasional treaties, payment of tribute to Aram, as well as open warfare.

Ben-Hadad I, king of Aram (c900-c860 BC), invaded Israelite territory on call from Asa of Judah with whom he had a treaty and who was militarily threatened by Baasha of Israel. Although Ben-Hadad also had a treaty with Baasha, a payment of treasure from Asa led him to take Asa's side. Ben-Hadad I advanced from the north and took important Israelite cities.

Ben-Hadad II besieged Samaria in the time of Ahab (874-853 BC). After two unsuccessful attempts to take the city, he was taken prisoner at Aphek and forced to give Israel special trading rights in Damascus. The expansion of Assyria westward was delayed in 853 BC, when Levantine states, including Aram and Israel, joined to confront Shalmaneser III in the battle of Qarqar (pages 72-73) but the alliance was short-lived.

Hazael (c843-c780 BC), who had killed Ben-Hadad II and usurped the throne, extended Aram's control east of the Jordan as far south as Aroer in Moab, becoming a significant threat to the kingdoms of Israel and Judah (II KINGS 10.32-3).

Ben-Hadad III (c805-c778 BC) suffered from the resurgence of power in Israel. Joash (798-782 BC) recovered the cities which Hazael had taken (page 74); Jeroboam II is credited with the conquest of Damascus and Hamath (II KINGS 14.28).

Rezin (c750-c732 BC) joined with Pekah of Israel to bring Jotham of Judah into an alliance to oppose Tiglath-pileser III of Assyria. When Jotham refused, Rezin and Pekah captured Jerusalem. Rezin then conquered Ammon, Moab and Edom. Although Jotham appealed to Tiglath-pileser for help the latter continued his march, took Damascus, killed Rezin and undertook a major campaign in Israel. Pekah was assassinated and was succeeded by Hoshea, the last king of Israel.

1/ CAMPAIGNS OF BEN-HADAD I AND II

→ route of Ben-Hadad I
⇢ route of Ben-Hadad II
→ route of Baasha

1/ map above Ben-Hadad I marched to the aid of Asa of Judah when the latter was threatened by Baasha of Israel. Ben-Hadad II invaded Israel from Succoth and was twice repulsed from Samaria and finally taken prisoner at Aphek.

2/ map right Hazael killed Ben-Hadad II and became king of Aram. He extended Aramaean influence in Ammon and Moab as far as Aroer. He probably made his way south to Gath and Jerusalem.

3/ map below right In the time of Ben-Hadad III Joash and Jeroboam II of Israel were able to push northward from Samaria and occupy Damascus.

2/ CAMPAIGNS OF HAZAEL

→ route to Aroer
⇢ probable route to Jerusalem

3/ CAMPAIGNS OF JOASH AND JEROBOAM II

→ route of Joash
⇢ route of Jeroboam II

4/ map right Under Rezin, Damascus joined forces with Pekah of Israel capturing Jerusalem. Eventually Rezin so provoked the Assyrians under Tiglath-pileser III, that they invaded Damascus and killed him. Aram was thus made a part of the Assyrian empire.

5/ table left shows in parallel the reigns of the kings of Aram, Israel and Judah.

6/ The god Melqart as represented on a *stela* found near Aleppo grasping a battle-axe with rounded blade in his left hand. The Aramaic inscription below is a dedication by one of the kings of Aram to the god Melqart.

4/ CAMPAIGNS OF REZIN AND PEKAH

→ route of Rezin
⇢ route of Pekah

ARAM	ISRAEL	JUDAH
	—900—	911—
	Baasha	
c.900		
	—886—	
	Elah —885—	Asa
	Zimri —885—	
Ben-Hadad I	Tibni —880—	
	Omri	
	—874—	
c.860	Ahab	—870—
Ben-Hadad II (Adad-Idri)	—853—	Jehoshaphat
	Ahaziah —852—	
c.843	Joram —841—	—848— Jehoram
		—841—
Hazael	Jehu	Athaliah —835—
	—814—	Jehoash
	Jehoahaz —798—	
c.805		—796—
Ben-Hadad III	Joash —782—	
c.773		Amaziah
	Jeroboam II	—767—
Hadianu	—753—	Uzziah
	Zechariah	
	Shallum —752—	
c.750	Menahem —742—	in Gilead
	Pekahiah —740—	
Rezin	Pekah	Jotham
—732—	—732—	—732—
Assyrians	Hoshea —722—	Ahaz 716
	Assyrians	

1
c924 BC
[Victories of Sheshonq I over the] Asiatics of distant foreign countries [with list of cities in Palestine and Syria].
AMON TEMPLE, KARNAK

In the fifth year of king Rehoboam, Shishak king of Egypt came up against Jerusalem…
I KINGS 14.25

2
853 BC
He brought along to help him… 200 chariots, 10,000 foot soldiers of Ahab the Israelite… I fought with them… I did inflict a defeat upon them… With their corpses I spanned the Orontes before there was a bridge.
SHALMANESER III, on monolith from Kurkh

No mention of this battle in the Bible.

3
c830 BC
As for Omri, king of Israel, he humbled Moab many years… And his son followed him… but I have triumphed over him… while Israel hath perished forever!
MESHA, king of Moab, on stela found at Dibon.

Now Mesha king of Moab was a sheep breeder; and he had to deliver annually to the king of Israel a hundred thousand lambs… But when Ahab died, the king of Moab rebelled against the king of Israel.
II KINGS 3.4-5

4
732 BC
They overthrew their king Pekah and I placed Hoshea as king over them.
TIGLATH-PILESER III, on inscription at Nimrud.

In the days of Pekah king of Israel Tiglath-pileser king of Assyria came… Then Hoshea… made a conspiracy against Pekah … and reigned in his stead…
II KINGS 15.29-30.

5
722 BC
I besieged and conquered Samaria, led away as booty 27,290 inhabitants of it.
SARGON II, on inscription at Khorsabad.

In the ninth year of Hoshea the king of Assyria captured Samaria, and he carried the Israelites away to Assyria…
II KINGS 17.6.

6
712 BC
Azuri, king of Ashdod, had schemed not to deliver tribute [any more]… I besieged and conquered the cities of Ashdod, Gath [and] Asdudimmu.
SARGON II, on inscription at Khorsabad.

In the year that the commander in chief, who was sent by Sargon the king of Assyria, came to Ashdod and fought against it and took it…
ISAIAH 20.1.

7
701 BC
As to Hezekiah, the Jew, he did not submit to my yoke, I laid siege to 46 of his strong cities… I drove out [of them] 200,150 people… Himself I made a prisoner in Jerusalem… like a bird in a cage… Hezekiah himself… did send me, later… 30 talents of gold, 800 talents of silver…
SENNACHERIB on a text from Nineveh.

And Hezekiah king of Judah sent to the king of Assyria at Lachish, saying, 'I have done wrong; withdraw from me; whatever you impose on me I will bear.' And the king of Assyria required of Hezekiah… three hundred talents of silver and thirty talents of gold.
II KINGS 18.14.

8
597 BC
The king of Akkad… laid siege to the city of Judah… and the king took the city… He appointed in it a [new] king of his liking, took heavy booty from it and brought it into Babylon.
NEBUCHADNEZZAR II on a tablet from Babylon.

And Nebuchadnezzar king of Babylon came to the city; and Jehoiachin the king of Judah gave himself up… The king of Babylon took him… and carried off all the treasures of the house of the Lord… made Mattaniah… king in his stead.
II KINGS 24.11-17.

IT is understandable that in the surviving literature of the great empires which surrounded ancient Israel there should be little mention of the characters and events of the Bible. Israel was small in comparison to such powers as Assyria and Egypt, and at most periods of its history played a minor role in the military and commercial affairs of the larger world. Patriarchs, judges, the three kings of the United Monarchy – Saul, David and Solomon – and the Hebrew prophets are known only from the pages of the Bible. Yet there are a few notable exceptions to this neglect of Israel's heroes. Over a span of two and a half centuries Assyrian kings took pains to enhance and preserve their fame by displaying, publicly, boastful accounts of their triumphs over their enemies, some of whom are the monarchs of Israel and Judah. With the discovery of the ancient palaces of the Assyrian kings at Khorsabad, Nineveh and Nimrud in the 19th century, details about ancient Israel came to light for the first time from sources outside the Bible.

The boxes shown to the left and below contain accounts of events which were written shortly after they occurred and have survived in the mounds of Assyria and Babylonia, on a *stela* found in Transjordan and on a temple wall at Karnak. Carved in stone or written on clay these documents have remained unchanged, a testimony contemporaneous with the campaigns, battles and conquests to which they bear witness. Whenever the Bible speaks of these events the appropriate quotation appears under the extra-biblical text.

It is of interest to note the points of agreement as well as the disagreements between the accounts. Some outside sources, like the inscription of Shalmaneser III mentioning Ahab, list events which are not referred to in the Bible.

Other Assyrian sources supplement the biblical account of events with specific details. Sargon II had engraved on the wall of his palace at Khorsabad that he had carried away 27,290 inhabitants of Samaria, and Sennacherib was specific in his boast of having taken 200,150 prisoners from 46 cities belonging to Hezekiah of Judah. Sheshonq I's (Shishak of the Bible) long list of cities conquered in Palestine not only confirms the account of the invasion found in the Bible but provides a valuable source for the geography of the 10th century BC. Mesha's *stela*, erected for all to read of the king's achievements, proclaims to his Moabite subjects that 'Israel has perished forever!' (pages 66 and 71). But even the wishful thinking of Israel's enemies serves to integrate events and kings – otherwise known only in the religious history of ancient Israel – with the history of the larger world.

The overlapping of Assyrian and biblical accounts of various events makes possible an absolute chronology for the kingdoms of Israel and Judah. Assyrian kings kept records of the years of their reigns and such lists have been found from the beginnings of the 9th through to the end of the 6th century BC. Among the important events recorded, according to the years of the various kings of this period, is a solar eclipse in a certain year of the reign of Ashur-Dan. With a high degree of certainty astronomical calculations fix this eclipse (as observed from Nineveh) at 763 BC. Thus this absolute date for a certain year in the reign of an Assyrian king makes possible the assignment of dates to the biblical kings whose history was interwoven with that of the kings of Assyria.

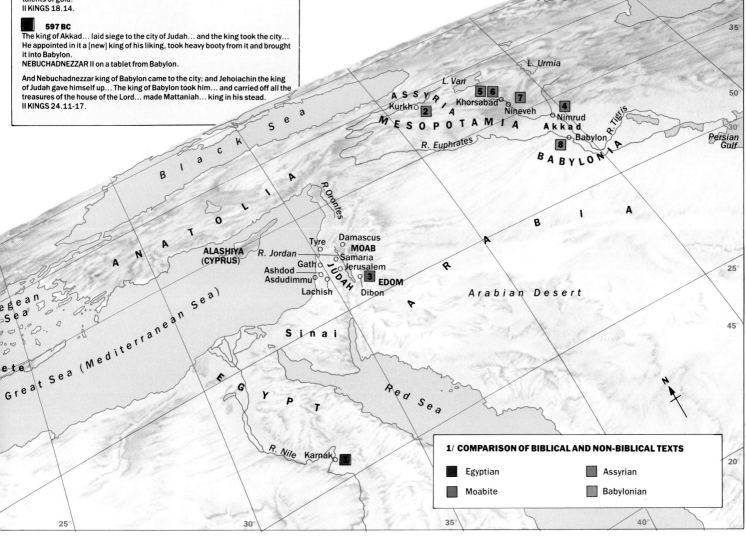

1/ COMPARISON OF BIBLICAL AND NON-BIBLICAL TEXTS

- Egyptian
- Moabite
- Assyrian
- Babylonian

IN order to secure his boundaries against raids by mountaineers to the east and north, King Ashurnasirpal II (883-859 BC), the founder of the Assyrian empire of the 1st millennium BC, began to conquer the foes of the national god Ashur and to impose tribute upon them. In pursuit of this goal he opened the way for an Assyrian advance to the Mediterranean, reached in c875 BC for the first time in two centuries.

By re-asserting Assyrian control over the Aramaean regions of the Middle Euphrates and the River Khabur Ashurnasirpal was able, in c875, to move from Carchemish into northern Syria, by a route skirting the powerful state of Hamath. After defeating the state of Patina, he went down the River Orontes as far as the Lebanon range and then to the Mediterranean. There he met no resistance, and the Phoenician states as far south as Tyre sent tribute.

Ashurnasirpal's son and successor Shalmaneser III (858-824 BC) made further penetration in the west. In 853, Shalmaneser moved south-westwards via Pethor (NUM 22.5) and Aleppo into the territory of Hamath. After taking several fortresses, he was met at Qarqar, east of the River Orontes, by a powerful coalition headed by Irhuleni of Hamath, Hadad-ezer of Damascus and Ahab of Israel, with supporting forces from several Phoenician city-states and from Egypt (probably the garrison in Byblos), as well as an Arab contingent mounted on camels. Shalmaneser claimed to have inflicted an enormous slaughter. This could be true, in view of the operational difficulties likely to have faced the coalition's rapidly assembled force of over 60,000 men under up to eleven commanders, unused to operating as a co-ordinated army. The coalition's resistance was, however, sufficient to check any further southward advance by Assyria for over a decade. The coalition eventually collapsed from internal problems, marked by the usurpation of Hazael in Damascus and Jehu in Israel (I KINGS 19.15-18; II KINGS 8.15, 9.14 etc.). These events enabled Shalmaneser to reach Damascus in 841 BC. From there he marched south to Khaurina and then through Israelite territory possibly to Mt Carmel; Jehu, Israel's king, is shown paying tribute on the black obelisk found at Nimrud.

After a setback in Syria, Shamshi-Adad V (823-811 BC) and Adad-nirari III (810-783 BC) reasserted Assyrian control between 805 and 796 BC. The latter conquered Damascus, which brought recognition of Assyrian suzerainty, marked by payment of tribute, by other

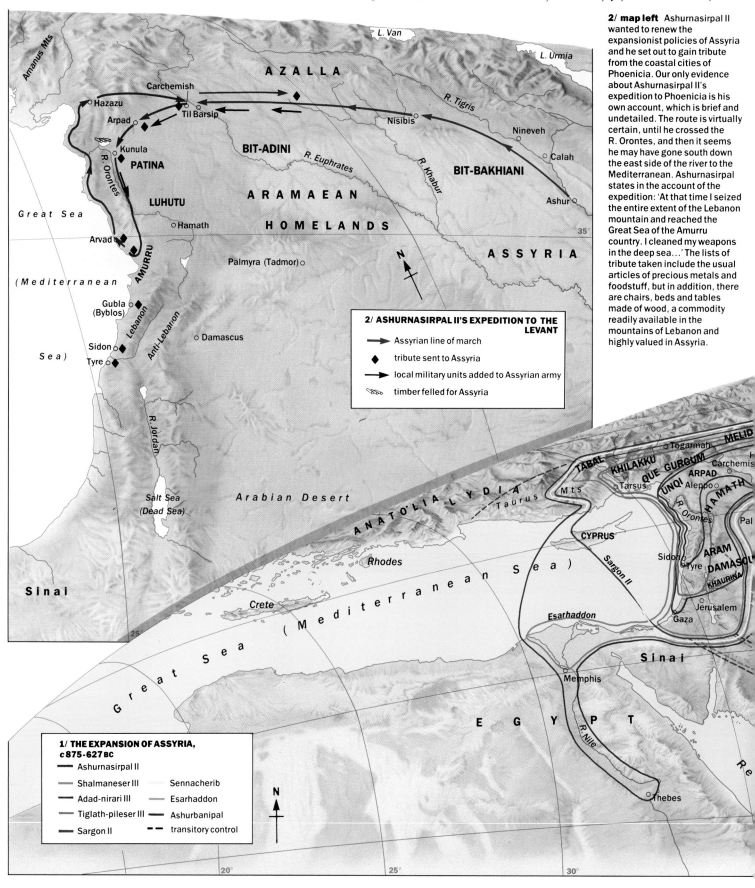

2/ map left Ashurnasirpal II wanted to renew the expansionist policies of Assyria and he set out to gain tribute from the coastal cities of Phoenicia. Our only evidence about Ashurnasirpal II's expedition to Phoenicia is his own account, which is brief and undetailed. The route is virtually certain, until he crossed the R. Orontes, and then it seems he may have gone south down the east side of the river to the Mediterranean. Ashurnasirpal states in the account of the expedition: 'At that time I seized the entire extent of the Lebanon mountain and reached the Great Sea of the Amurru country. I cleaned my weapons in the deep sea...' The lists of tribute taken include the usual articles of precious metals and foodstuff, but in addition, there are chairs, beds and tables made of wood, a commodity readily available in the mountains of Lebanon and highly valued in Assyria.

2/ ASHURNASIRPAL II'S EXPEDITION TO THE LEVANT
- → Assyrian line of march
- ◆ tribute sent to Assyria
- → local military units added to Assyrian army
- timber felled for Assyria

1/ THE EXPANSION OF ASSYRIA, c 875-627 BC
- —— Ashurnasirpal II
- —— Shalmaneser III
- —— Adad-nirari III
- ······ Tiglath-pileser III
- —— Sargon II
- —— Sennacherib
- —— Esarhaddon
- —— Ashurbanipal
- --- transitory control

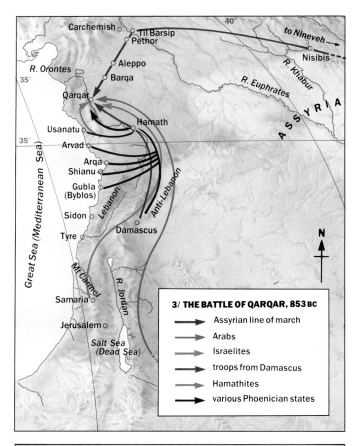

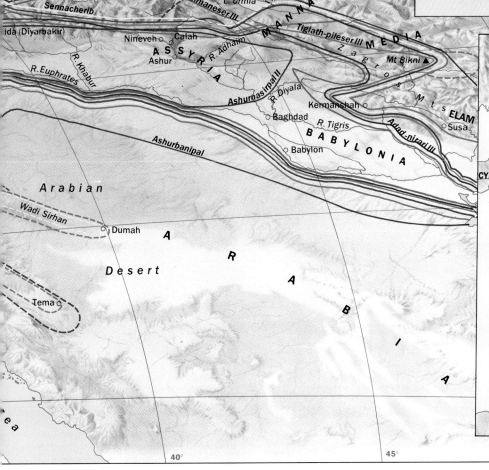

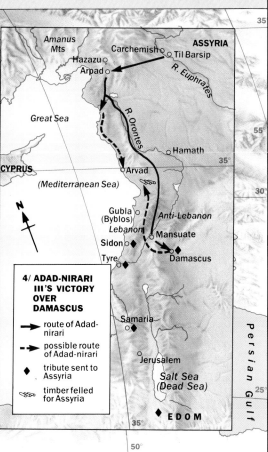

states including Sidon, Tyre, cities in Philistia and Israel under Joash. Beginning with attacks in 805 and 804 BC to subdue northern Syria, Adad-nirari III reached the Mediterranean in 803 BC, and may have continued down the coast in 802 BC to ensure the submission of the Phoenician cities. In 796 BC Adad-nirari mounted another Syrian campaign. He moved south to Mansuate (in the Beqa'a Valley), controlling the road to Damascus. With Damascus cut off from potential allies, Adad-nirari entered the city to receive the submission of its king, Ben-Hadad III.

A deteriorating situation in Assyria ended in rebellion, bringing to the throne Tiglath-pileser III (744-727 BC, called 'Pul' in II KINGS 15.19 etc), who treated conquered regions west of the Euphrates as tribute-paying vassals. Tiglath-pileser introduced the new strategy of establishing directly-ruled provinces in areas which proved troublesome. Vigorous military action pushed back Urartian influence in the west and north-west and established a chain of Assyrian provinces as far as Damascus, with Israel partly under provincial administration and partly tributary (page 76). Babylonia, unsettled by Chaldaean tribesmen, was taken under direct rule.

Tiglath-pileser's policy continued until the end of the empire, with ever-increasing territory, despite local setbacks. Shalmaneser V (726-722 BC) and Sargon II (721-705 BC) extended Assyrian control in Syria and Palestine (page 77), and Sennacherib attacked Judah (page 81). The developments under the last two major Assyrian kings are described on page 84.

From the time of the conquest of Canaan down to the Babylonian exile, Israel had many enemies varying from small tribal groups of raiders to the major world powers, but none can compare with Assyria for the destruction of property, the amount of tribute taken or captives carried away to foreign lands.

1/ map below Lacking natural boundaries and therefore physical defences from raiders, the Assyrians constantly needed to extend their kingdom in order to secure surrounding territories.
The maximum extent of the Assyrian kingdom was brought about by Ashurbanipal, and the boundaries shown combine maximum military penetration with the maximum area credibly claimed as paying tribute. The broken line indicates transitory control. Boundary lines have to be denoted by broad sweeps, which cannot claim accuracy at every point. Where there is a sudden change in the direction of a boundary, there is positive evidence either from inscriptional data combined with identified sites or from the demands of geography.
3/ map right At the battle of Qarqar, Shalmaneser III defeated a coalition of forces from Phoenicia, Egypt and Israel, and thus gained control over this area.
4/ map below right Adad-nirari III was able to take advantage of the Assyrian supremacy achieved by Shalmaneser III over Syria (map 3) and he received tribute from Damascus. A stone slab found at Calah boasts of his achievements.

3/ THE BATTLE OF QARQAR, 853 BC

→ Assyrian line of march
→ Arabs
→ Israelites
→ troops from Damascus
→ Hamathites
→ various Phoenician states

FORCES DEFEATED BY SHALMANESER III AT QARQAR

Damascus: infantry 20,000; cavalry 1200; chariots 1200
Hamath: infantry 10,000; cavalry 700; chariots 700
Israel: infantry 10,000; chariots 2000

Phoenician States:
Gubla (Gebal, Byblos): infantry 500
Egyptian garrison in Gubla: infantry 1000
Irqanata (Arqa): infantry 10,000; chariots 10

Arvad (of Arvadites of GEN 10.17): infantry 200
Usanatu: infantry 200
Shianu (cf Sinites of GEN 10.17): infantry 10,000; chariots 30

others:
Arabs: camels 1000
'Of Ruhubi of Amana' (= Rehob of II SAM 10.8. Amana was not Ammon in Transjordan but a region in the Anti-Lebanon, named in SONG 4.8): no details

4/ ADAD-NIRARI III'S VICTORY OVER DAMASCUS

→ route of Adad-nirari
--→ possible route of Adad-nirari
◆ tribute sent to Assyria
timber felled for Assyria

IN THE 8th century BC the kingdom of Israel reached a peak of political importance and prosperity under King Jeroboam II (782-753 BC). The Aramaean kingdom of Damascus, long Israel's rival to the north, had been weakened by Assyria's forays westward. King Adad-nirari III's successful campaigns of 805, 804 and 796 BC (page 72) against Damascus had removed an obstacle to Jeroboam's expansion northward. According to II KINGS 14.25 Israel's borders extended 'from Lebo-hamath until the sea of the Arabah' [Dead Sea]. Although little is said in II KINGS about Jeroboam (II KINGS 14.28 does credit him with the recovery of Damascus and Hamath) references in the book of AMOS and implications drawn from the Samaria ostraca combine to suggest that the time of Jeroboam II was a time of economic prosperity as well as one of geographical expansion.

Judah also saw a revival of political, military and economic power. The former clash between Israel and Judah which had resulted in Joash taking the silver and gold from the Jerusalem temple and the royal house to his capital at Samaria (II KINGS 14.8-14) was smoothed over ten years later with the death of Joash (782 BC) and the return of Amaziah to Jerusalem. The power of Judah was, however, in the hands of the co-regent, Azariah/Uzziah, who launched a campaign against the Philistines (II CHRON 26.6) and established strong points in the territory of Ashdod and elsewhere on the coastal plain. His control of the trade routes from Arabia and Sinai was secured by the restoration of Elath after his father died (II KINGS 14.22); thus he received tribute from the Arabs and also the Meunites (II CHRON 26.7).

The inland trade route across Transjordan was first controlled under Jeroboam II, who reorganized the Israelite tribes in this area by means of a census; but after his death, the initiative passed to Judah under Jotham (I CHRON 5.17).

THE SAMARIA OSTRACA

Among the discoveries of ancient Hebrew texts that contribute as independent sources to biblical geography and history, such as the Mesha *stela* (page 66) and the Siloam inscription engraved on the wall of a tunnel (page 83), the finding of a collection of potsherds at Samaria is one of the most important (page 64). Some 60 inscriptions were discovered in the Harvard University excavations of 1908-10 but were not published until 1924. Since then most scholars have agreed on the reading and translations of these brief texts, but the reason for writing them is widely debated.

These notations in Hebrew follow a general pattern: 1) a date [presumably the year of a reigning king], 2) 'from' a place name, 3) 'from' a clan name, 4) 'to' a personal name [the recipient(s)], 5) name of the sender(s), and 6) the commodity, generally a 'jar of aged wine' or 'jar of purified oil'. Several ostraca omit one or more of these elements, but the model remains fairly constant. It is generally agreed that these texts are dated notations of a transaction or shipment of oil or wine from a sender at a particular town and in a certain tribal district to a named recipient in another, presumably Samaria, where the inscriptions were eventually discovered.

One problem concerns the year numbers which begin the texts. The largest group of inscriptions are dated to the year 15; the remaining are from years 9 and 10 (plus one for year 17). If all these numbers refer to regnal years of a king who reigned over Israel during the first half of the 8th century BC, a period in which scholars would place the particular form of the Hebrew letters used, then the ostraca should be dated to Joash or Jeroboam II. But differences in the style of writing have been noted between those letters of 9 and 10 on the one hand, and those dated to year 15 on the other. This observation suggests that they are not from the reigns of Joash and Jeroboam.

The 18 places from which wine and oil were shipped (twelve also found in the Bible) are of geographical importance. The means for locating these names on an actual map is a familiar one, the assumption that names cling tenaciously to places over many centuries. From a survey of the towns and villages in the Samaria area no less than ten of the modern names are sufficiently similar in sound to places listed on the ostraca to postulate continuity. For example the ancient Geba is like the modern Jeba, four miles north of Samaria; Sepher, like Sepharim; Yashub, similar to Yasuf, etc. The Book of Joshua (13-19) gives long lists of borders and cities of the various tribes, yet, in the description of Manasseh (JOSH 17.1-13) borders are drawn, but the usual list of towns is omitted. The ostraca from Samaria remedies this ancient omission, at least to some extent.

The correspondence between the ostraca and the Bible becomes even more explicit when the names of tribes or clans listed in the texts are considered. In JOSH 17.2 the tribes ('children of') of Manasseh are listed as: Abiezer, Helek, Asriel, Shechem, Hepher, and Shemida. All but one (Hepher) of these names appear as clan names on the Samaria ostraca. This remarkable duplication provides evidence for the geographical reality underlying an otherwise obscure tribal list found in JOSH 17.2. By matching the clan with the town associated with it on the ostraca it has been possible to show the settlement pattern of the various clans of Manasseh.

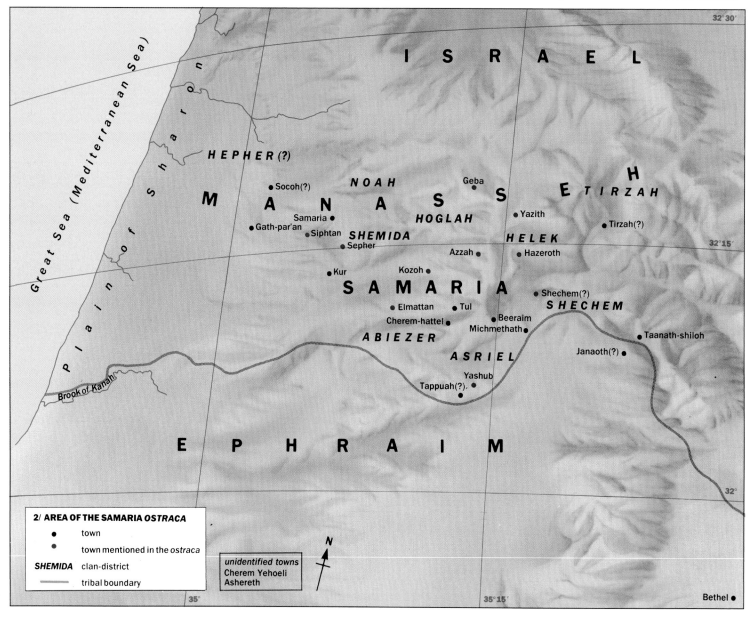

2/ AREA OF THE SAMARIA OSTRACA

- ● town
- • town mentioned in the *ostraca*
- **SHEMIDA** clan-district
- —— tribal boundary

unidentified towns
Cherem Yehoeli
Ashereth

N

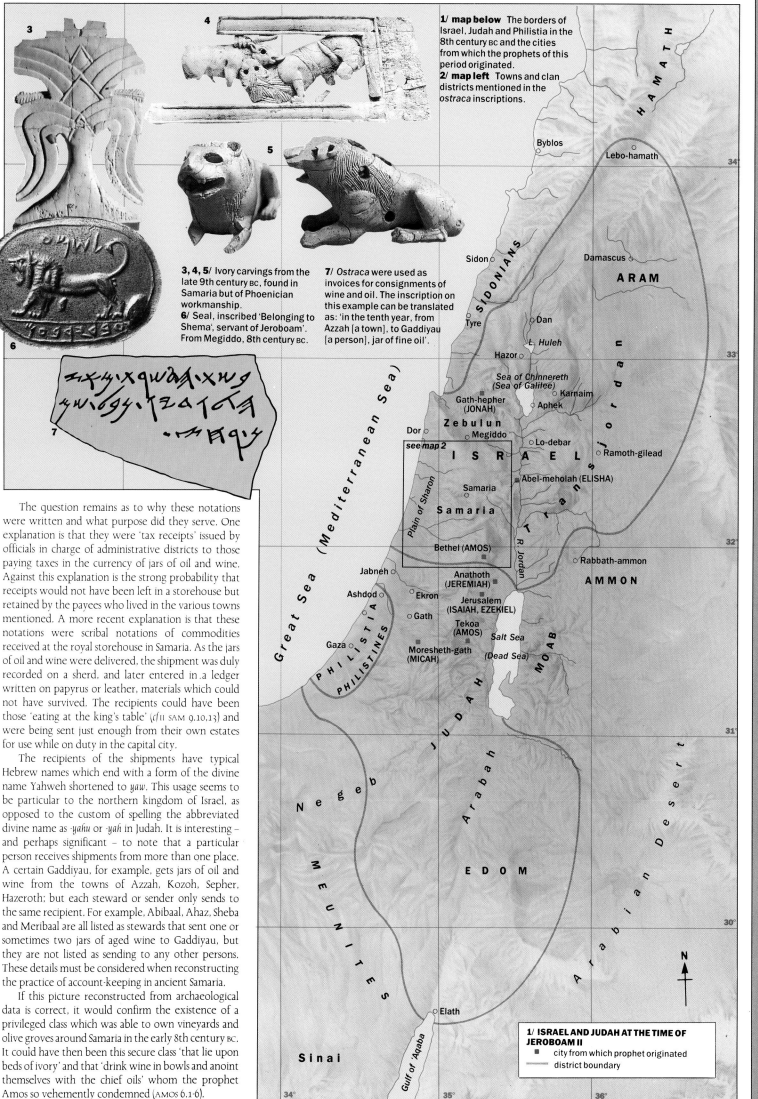

3, 4, 5/ Ivory carvings from the late 9th century BC, found in Samaria but of Phoenician workmanship.
6/ Seal, inscribed 'Belonging to Shema', servant of Jeroboam'. From Megiddo, 8th century BC.

7/ Ostraca were used as invoices for consignments of wine and oil. The inscription on this example can be translated as: 'in the tenth year, from Azzah [a town], to Gaddiyau [a person], jar of fine oil'.

1/ map below The borders of Israel, Judah and Philistia in the 8th century BC and the cities from which the prophets of this period originated.
2/ map left Towns and clan districts mentioned in the ostraca inscriptions.

The question remains as to why these notations were written and what purpose did they serve. One explanation is that they were 'tax receipts' issued by officials in charge of administrative districts to those paying taxes in the currency of jars of oil and wine. Against this explanation is the strong probability that receipts would not have been left in a storehouse but retained by the payees who lived in the various towns mentioned. A more recent explanation is that these notations were scribal notations of commodities received at the royal storehouse in Samaria. As the jars of oil and wine were delivered, the shipment was duly recorded on a sherd, and later entered in a ledger written on papyrus or leather, materials which could not have survived. The recipients could have been those 'eating at the king's table' (cf II SAM 9.10,13) and were being sent just enough from their own estates for use while on duty in the capital city.

The recipients of the shipments have typical Hebrew names which end with a form of the divine name Yahweh shortened to *yaw*. This usage seems to be particular to the northern kingdom of Israel, as opposed to the custom of spelling the abbreviated divine name as *-yahu* or *-yah* in Judah. It is interesting – and perhaps significant – to note that a particular person receives shipments from more than one place. A certain Gaddiyau, for example, gets jars of oil and wine from the towns of Azzah, Kozoh, Sepher, Hazeroth; but each steward or sender only sends to the same recipient. For example, Abibaal, Ahaz, Sheba and Meribaal are all listed as stewards that sent one or sometimes two jars of aged wine to Gaddiyau, but they are not listed as sending to any other persons. These details must be considered when reconstructing the practice of account-keeping in ancient Samaria.

If this picture reconstructed from archaeological data is correct, it would confirm the existence of a privileged class which was able to own vineyards and olive groves around Samaria in the early 8th century BC. It could have then been this secure class 'that lie upon beds of ivory' and that 'drink wine in bowls and anoint themselves with the chief oils' whom the prophet Amos so vehemently condemned (AMOS 6.1-6).

1/ ISRAEL AND JUDAH AT THE TIME OF JEROBOAM II
■ city from which prophet originated
district boundary

WHEN Tiglath-pileser III came to the throne of Assyria in 744 BC the kingdoms of Israel and Judah were soon caught up in world politics to a degree they had not known before. Four of their kings are mentioned by name in cuneiform texts at Nimrud, the distant Assyrian capital. Tiglath-pileser appears three times in the book of Kings. Deportation of Israelite captives to a foreign land was begun, a practice which was followed by the Babylonians with more far-reaching historical consequences.

Until the second half of the 8th century BC, Assyria had treated the River Euphrates as its western boundary. This changed when Tiglath-pileser made provinces out of areas formerly ruled by vassal native kings. A factor in this change of policy was the appearance of a threat to Assyria's major trade route. The kingdom of Urartu (the biblical Ararat), a region around Lake Van, had expanded westward and formed a coalition of north Syrian states extending from Melid to Arpad. Tiglath-pileser attacked this Urartian coalition in 743 BC and defeated it. Three years later Arpad, the main centre of resistance, fell and was made the capital of an Assyrian province. In short

order, other provinces were established. The capital of Unqi, Kullania, was taken in 738 BC and gave its name to a newly created province. Simirra and Khatarikka were made provinces in the same year, and tribute was paid by Rezin of Damascus, Menahem of Samaria, and the kings of Tyre, Byblos and Hamath. Tiglath-pileser lists a variety of loot taken: 'gold, silver, tin, iron, elephant-hides, ivory, linen garments with multicoloured trimmings, blue-dyed wool, purple-dyed wool, ebony-wood, boxwood-wood, whatever was precious (enough for a) royal treasure; also lambs whose stretched hides were dyed purple, (and) wild birds whose spread-out wings were dyed blue, (furthermore) horses, mules, large and small cattle, (male) camels, female camels with their foals'.

After two campaigns in the east and another against Urartu itself, Tiglath-pileser returned to the west in 734 to extend Assyrian control into Philistia. He took Gaza and reached the Brook of Egypt, subduing the nomadic tribes there. Recent changes of rulers in both Israel and Judah had brought new political alignments. Israel found itself opposed to Judah. Pekah of Israel had joined with Rezin of Damascus in an

anti-Assyrian coalition, which also included Tyre, Ashkelon and some Arab tribes of northern Arabia and Transjordan. The common concern was control of trade routes from southern Arabia. King Ahaz of Judah refused to join the coalition; rather he accepted Assyrian suzerainty and invoked assistance against attack (II KINGS 16.6-7). Upon the defeat of the leaders of the coalition, the coastal, northern and Transjordanian sectors of Israel were made into the Assyrian provinces of Dor, Megiddo and Gilead; Pekah was deposed, and what was left of the kingdom of Israel was placed under Hoshea as Tiglath-pileser's nominee and vassal. In II KINGS 15.29-30 the account of the royal succession mentions only that Hoshea made a conspiracy against Pekah and slew him. In Tiglath-pileser III's annals the Assyrian king takes credit for the placing of a new king on the throne: 'They overthrew their king Pekah and I placed Hoshea as king over them. I received from them 10 talents of gold, 1000(?) talents of silver as their tribute and brought them to Assyria'. The kingdom of Damascus was taken under direct Assyrian rule, divided into the three provinces of Damascus, Karnaim and Khaurina (perhaps Hauran). Following usual Assy-

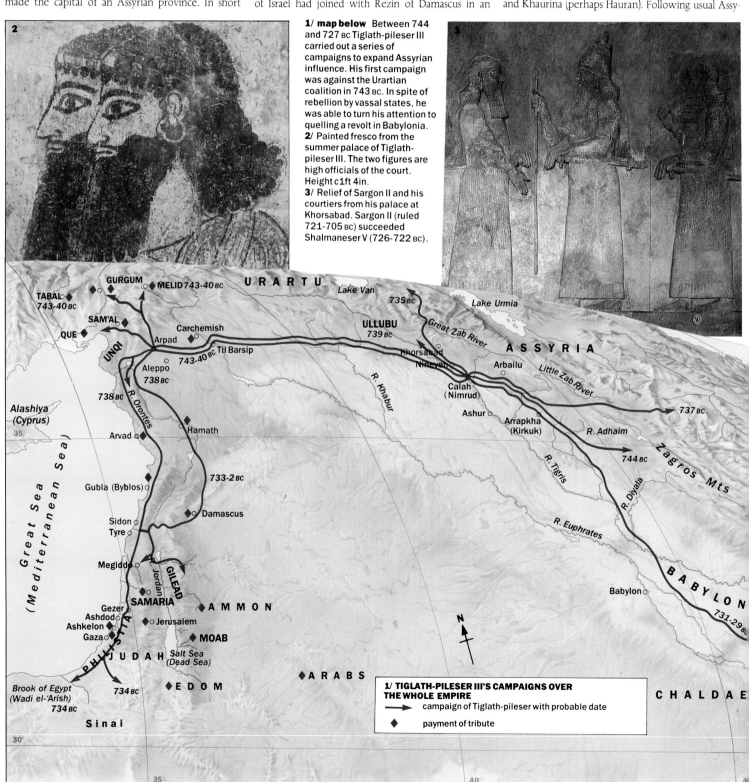

1/ map below Between 744 and 727 BC Tiglath-pileser III carried out a series of campaigns to expand Assyrian influence. His first campaign was against the Urartian coalition in 743 BC. In spite of rebellion by vassal states, he was able to turn his attention to quelling a revolt in Babylonia.
2/ Painted fresco from the summer palace of Tiglath-pileser III. The two figures are high officials of the court. Height c1ft 4in.
3/ Relief of Sargon II and his courtiers from his palace at Khorsabad. Sargon II (ruled 721-705 BC) succeeded Shalmaneser V (726-722 BC).

1/ TIGLATH-PILESER III'S CAMPAIGNS OVER THE WHOLE EMPIRE
→ campaign of Tiglath-pileser with probable date
◆ payment of tribute

rian policy, parts of the population of both kingdoms were deported and the area repopulated with conquered people from elsewhere. Ammon, Moab and Edom remained loosely under Assyrian control and paid tribute.

The main concern of the rest of Tiglath-pileser's reign was Babylonia, where a revolt broke out under a Chaldaean chieftain. When this had been quelled, Tiglath-pileser himself took the kingship of Babylon in person from 729 BC. His briefly reigning successor, Shalmaneser V (726-722 BC), clashed with vested interests in his capital Ashur. The resulting instability weakened Assyria's hold on the west, enabling Egypt to extend influence in Palestine. Hoshea, Assyria's appointee as king of Israel, transferred allegiance to Egypt. Assyria replied by sending an army against Samaria, which after a two-year siege was taken in late 722 BC. A display inscription on a stone slab on the wall at Khorsabad (Dur Sharrukin) gives the following Assyrian account of the fall of the capital of the northern kingdom of Israel: 'I besieged and conquered Samaria, led away as booty 27,290 inhabitants of it. I formed from among them a contingent of 50 chariots

and made remaining (inhabitants) assume their (social) positions. I installed over them an officer of mine and imposed upon them the tribute of the former king'. Although this inscription is that of Sargon II (721-705 BC) the successor of Shalmaneser V, this success is not mentioned in his earliest inscription dealing with the events of his campaigns in the west in 720 BC. The biblical implication in II KINGS 17.3-6 that the conquest of Samaria took place during the reign of Shalmaneser, can be reconciled with the Assyriological data by the assumption that Sargon boasted, in his later inscriptions, of the achievement of his immediate predecessor on the throne of Assyria. Israel was made into a province called Samerina, possibly incorporating the earlier Dor, although by the time of Esarhaddon's reign this was treated as an area of Philistia. Part of the population was subsequently deported to Assyria and then settled in Halah, on the River Khabur (Habor), and in the cities of the Medes (II KINGS 17.6).

Sargon's accession was linked to the opposition to Shalmaneser, but he quickly restored stability. He faced problems in three areas: Babylonia, where Chaldaean tribes supported by Elam were attempting

to oust Assyrian control; the far north, from south of Lake Urmia to Asia Minor, where Urartu was working to establish a chain of vassal states and allies; and Syria and Palestine, where a renascent Egypt was seeking to increase its influence. The most immediate problem was in Babylonia; although a military clash with Elam checked the threat from that quarter, Sargon was powerless against the Chaldaean leader Marduk-apil-iddina (Merodach-baladan of the Bible), who usurped the throne of Babylon and held it for a decade. In the west a widespread revolt broke out, headed by Hamath, with Arpad, Damascus, Samaria and parts of Phoenicia and Philistia implicated, and Egypt giving support (II KINGS 17.4). Sargon quelled the revolt in 720 BC; it was the major siege two years later, which allowed him in his records to claim credit for the original capture of the city.

In subsequent years Assyria had both military and diplomatic successes against Urartian influence in the north. A treaty was made with Urartu's former ally, Midas and Meshech, in Asia Minor – powerful from control of trade routes – and the Assyrians made a decisive invasion of Urartu itself in 714 BC.

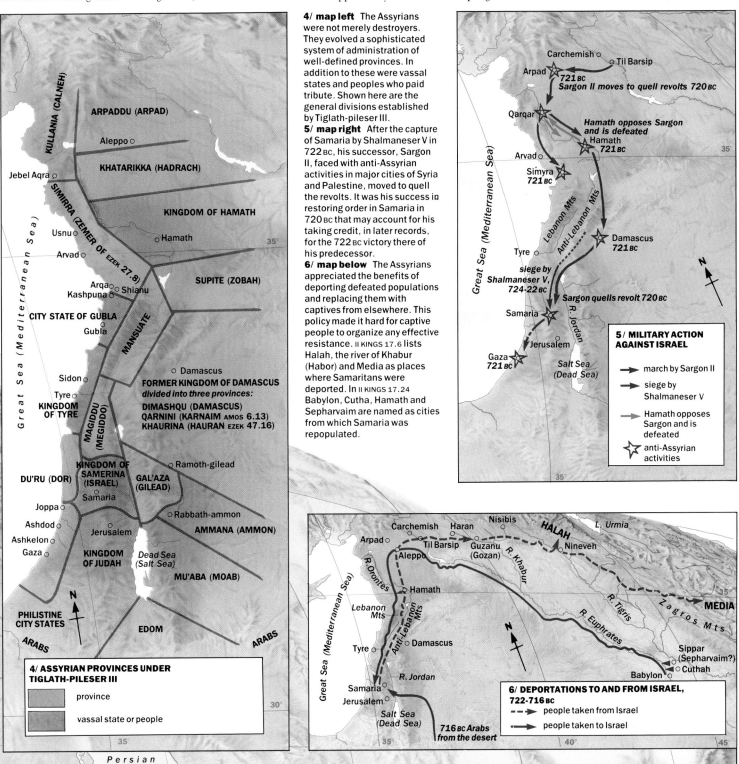

4/ map left The Assyrians were not merely destroyers. They evolved a sophisticated system of administration of well-defined provinces. In addition to these were vassal states and peoples who paid tribute. Shown here are the general divisions established by Tiglath-pileser III.

5/ map right After the capture of Samaria by Shalmaneser V in 722 BC, his successor, Sargon II, faced with anti-Assyrian activities in major cities of Syria and Palestine, moved to quell the revolts. It was his success in restoring order in Samaria in 720 BC that may account for his taking credit, in later records, for the 722 BC victory there of his predecessor.

6/ map below The Assyrians appreciated the benefits of deporting defeated populations and replacing them with captives from elsewhere. This policy made it hard for captive people to organize any effective resistance. II KINGS 17.6 lists Halah, the river of Khabur (Habor) and Media as places where Samaritans were deported. In II KINGS 17.24 Babylon, Cutha, Hamath and Sepharvaim are named as cities from which Samaria was repopulated.

4/ ASSYRIAN PROVINCES UNDER TIGLATH-PILESER III

- province
- vassal state or people

FORMER KINGDOM OF DAMASCUS *divided into three provinces:*
DIMASHQU (DAMASCUS)
QARNINI (KARNAIM AMOS 6.13)
KHAURINA (HAURAN EZEK 47.16)

5/ MILITARY ACTION AGAINST ISRAEL

- march by Sargon II
- siege by Shalmaneser V
- Hamath opposes Sargon and is defeated
- anti-Assyrian activities

Sargon II moves to quell revolts 720 BC
Hamath opposes Sargon and is defeated
siege by Shalmaneser V, 724-22 BC
Sargon quells revolt 720 BC

6/ DEPORTATIONS TO AND FROM ISRAEL, 722-716 BC

- people taken from Israel
- people taken to Israel

716 BC Arabs from the desert

THE division of the kingdom of David and Solomon into the two states of Israel and Judah brought about the collapse of the Empire. With the accession of Rehoboam, c931 BC, and his failure to achieve rule over the territory of Israel in the north, Judah emerged as a small and embattled state, greatly reduced both in area and prosperity. It was continuously at war with Israel throughout the reigns of Rehoboam and Abijah. The latter's successor, Asa, was faced with pressure from the north when the Israelite king, Baasha, took and fortified Ramah (I KINGS 15.17), a hill with a good view southwards. From it the Israelite king could control the route from the coastal plain in the south and also the main road north from Jerusalem which lay only some five miles away. By enlisting the aid of Syria, Asa was able to draw off this threat to Judah's lines of communication and to fortify the towns of Mizpah and Geba against his northern neighbour (I KINGS 15.22). Here the northern border of Judah remained, running through the middle of the territory of Benjamin.

The major sources for the history of this period are the biblical books of KINGS and CHRONICLES as well as a considerable amount of archaeological information. Because of its late origin and uncertainty about its sources, CHRONICLES presents problems for the historian. It frequently offers different information from that contained in KINGS, and its historical reliability is often disputed. If the Chronicler's information in II CHRON 11.6-10 on Rehoboam's system of fortresses may be taken as a historical record, they are a vivid reflection of Judah's threatened state. Whether built before, or to prevent a repetition of, the ravages of Shishak's campaign (page 62), the fortresses bear evidence of a concern to protect an area of the country which might be considered its heartland. The coastal plain and southern city of Beersheba lie outside the territory of the fortresses.

With the conclusion of hostilities between Judah and Israel under Asa's successor Jehoshaphat (870-848 BC), significant changes may be discerned within both states. The Judaean king entered an alliance with the dynasty of Omri in Israel to furnish troops for Israelite battles with Syria and Moab; the alliance was sealed by the marriage of his son Jehoram to the Omride princess Athaliah. Other information for the reigns of Jehoshaphat, Jehoram and Ahaziah is, however, scarce: Edom was at first subject to Judah but later broke free; Jehoshaphat attempted, though unsuccessfully, to revive trade on the Red Sea.

The Chronicler (II CHRON 17.2,12) affirms that Jehoshaphat 'placed forces in all the fortified cities of Judah and set garrisons in the land of Judah' and 'built in Judah fortressess and store cities'. This statement alone is an inadequate basis for crediting him with instituting a comprehensive administrative system for the kingdom. Yet, there is some probability that such a reform is to be dated to his reign. From the city list in JOSH 15.21-62; 18.21-28 it is possible to derive a series of twelve districts, defined by their cities, which as a whole, embrace the known territory of Judah. Some of the cities mentioned, such as Beth-haccherem, Jattir, Juttah and Eshtemoa, are known, from archaeological excavation and surveys, to have been founded in the Iron Age II period. The time of Jehoshaphat's reign is probably the earliest for placing the origin of the system represented by the list as a whole. Some scholars have proposed a later date, that of the reign of Uzziah or that of Josiah. If it is assumed that the list may reflect a continuing and developing situation, rather than a single act of administrative reform, it is probable that the organizational measures of a number of Judaean kings from Jehoshaphat to Josiah – a period of more than two centuries – are reflected in the city list.

Following the death of Ahaziah, in the course of the revolt of Jehu in Israel, and the six-year reign of Athaliah, the only non-Davidide to rule in Jerusalem, the line of David was represented once more by Joash. About his reign there is little information: he was forced to pay heavily to persuade the Aramaean king, Hazael, to withdraw from Jerusalem, and in the end he was assassinated. It was under his successor Amaziah that Judaean revival began again. He defeated the Edomites but was himself defeated by Israel in a battle, the background of which is obscure. Eventually he too was assassinated and was succeeded by his son Uzziah.

The book of KINGS mentions only a few details of Uzziah's (Azariah's) reign (II KINGS 15.1-7): he was sixteen years old when he began his fifty-two year reign; in his later years he was smitten with leprosy and was forced to live in a separate house. That he was credited with the building of Elath and restoring it to the Judaean kingdom presupposes considerable expansion of Judaean territory southward (II KINGS 14.22). The Chronicler's much fuller picture of Uzziah's military conquests in II CHRON 26.2-15 gives support to this brief but significant statement in KINGS. According to CHRONICLES Uzziah is said to have achieved a number of military victories: his forays into Philistine territory resulted in the breaching of the fortifications at Gath, Jabneh and Ashdod, and in building cities in the vicinity of Ashdod. He campaigned against the Arabs and Meunites, so that with the capture of the port of Elath at the head of the Red Sea, he controlled both the land and the sea routes to and from Arabia and the East. Tribute exacted from the Ammonites was also an economic asset for Uzziah's kingdom.

Domestic security was improved by the fortification of Jerusalem with towers at the city's gates containing equipment ('invented by skilful men') for shooting arrows and great stones. Noted too was his concern for armaments, such as shields, helmets, spears, coats of mail, bows and stones for slinging.

Uzziah was also interested in the agricultural development of his kingdom. He hewed out cisterns and he had herds of cattle; in the lowlands and plains he had farmers and vinedressers in the mountain region, 'for he loved husbandry' (II CHRON 26.10).

Fortresses which have been located or excavated in the south of Judah with foundations that can be dated to the 9th and 8th centuries BC, at Arad Rabbah,

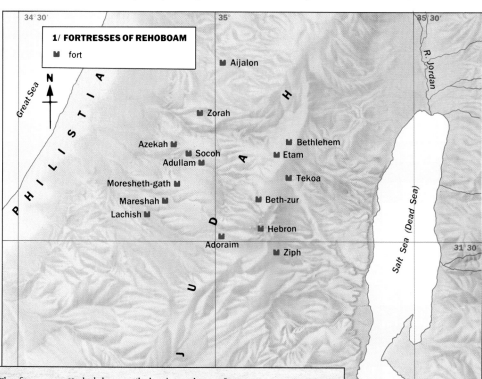

1/ FORTRESSES OF REHOBOAM
🏰 fort

N

Great Sea

PHILISTIA

Aijalon

Zorah

Azekah
Socoh
Adullam

Bethlehem
Etam

JUDAH

Moresheth-gath

Tekoa

Mareshah
Lachish

Beth-zur

Hebron

Adoraim

Ziph

R. Jordan

Salt Sea (Dead Sea)

34° 30'   35°   35° 30'

31° 30'

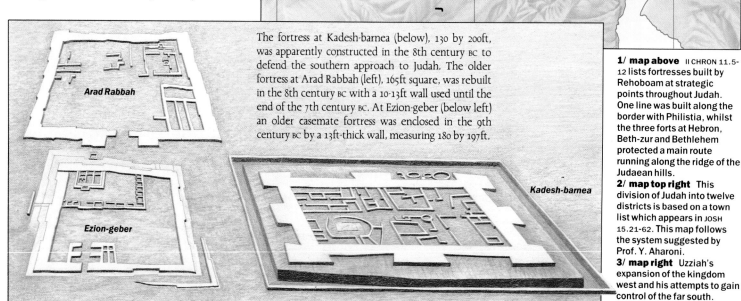

The fortress at Kadesh-barnea (below), 130 by 200ft, was apparently constructed in the 8th century BC to defend the southern approach to Judah. The older fortress at Arad Rabbah (left), 165ft square, was rebuilt in the 8th century BC with a 10-13ft wall used until the end of the 7th century BC. At Ezion-geber (below left) an older casemate fortress was enclosed in the 9th century BC by a 13ft-thick wall, measuring 180 by 197ft.

Arad Rabbah

Ezion-geber

Kadesh-barnea

1/ map above II CHRON 11.5-12 lists fortresses built by Rehoboam at strategic points throughout Judah. One line was built along the border with Philistia, whilst the three forts at Hebron, Beth-zur and Bethlehem protected a main route running along the ridge of the Judaean hills.

2/ map top right This division of Judah into twelve districts is based on a town list which appears in JOSH 15.21-62. This map follows the system suggested by Prof. Y. Aharoni.

3/ map right Uzziah's expansion of the kingdom west and his attempts to gain control of the far south.

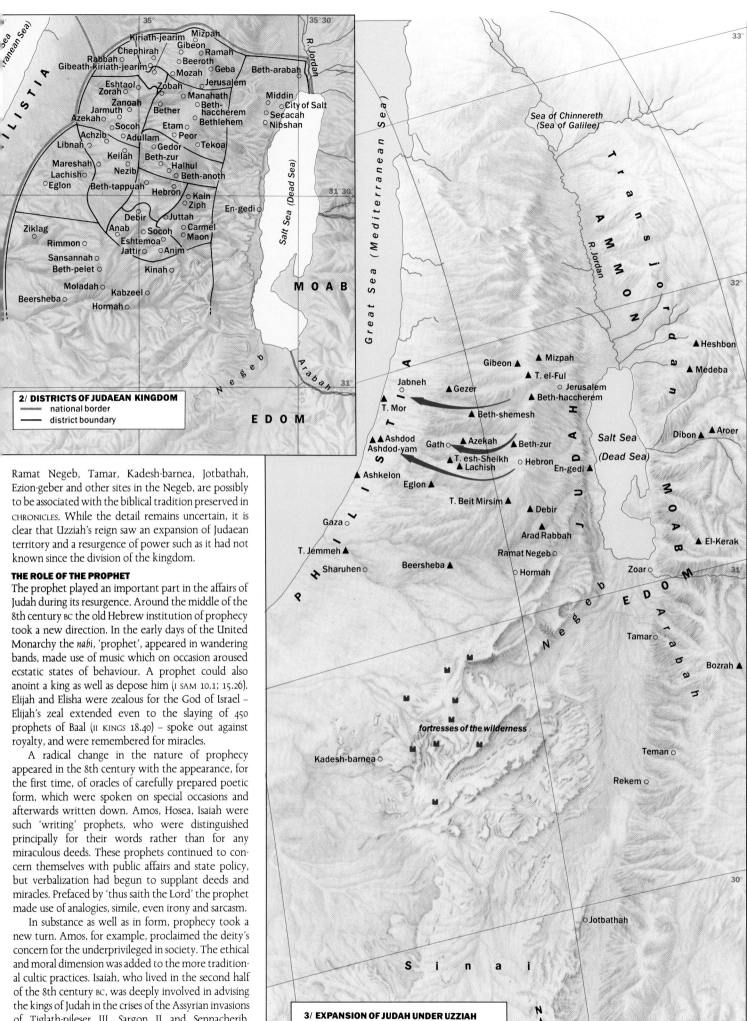

2/ DISTRICTS OF JUDAEAN KINGDOM
— national border
— district boundary

3/ EXPANSION OF JUDAH UNDER UZZIAH
→ route of Uzziah's army
▲ major excavated site of Iron Age II
🏰 fortress of the wilderness

fortresses of the wilderness

Ramat Negeb, Tamar, Kadesh-barnea, Jotbathah, Ezion-geber and other sites in the Negeb, are possibly to be associated with the biblical tradition preserved in CHRONICLES. While the detail remains uncertain, it is clear that Uzziah's reign saw an expansion of Judaean territory and a resurgence of power such as it had not known since the division of the kingdom.

THE ROLE OF THE PROPHET

The prophet played an important part in the affairs of Judah during its resurgence. Around the middle of the 8th century BC the old Hebrew institution of prophecy took a new direction. In the early days of the United Monarchy the *nabi*, 'prophet', appeared in wandering bands, made use of music which on occasion aroused ecstatic states of behaviour. A prophet could also anoint a king as well as depose him (I SAM 10.1; 15.26). Elijah and Elisha were zealous for the God of Israel – Elijah's zeal extended even to the slaying of 450 prophets of Baal (II KINGS 18.40) – spoke out against royalty, and were remembered for miracles.

A radical change in the nature of prophecy appeared in the 8th century with the appearance, for the first time, of oracles of carefully prepared poetic form, which were spoken on special occasions and afterwards written down. Amos, Hosea, Isaiah were such 'writing' prophets, who were distinguished principally for their words rather than for any miraculous deeds. These prophets continued to concern themselves with public affairs and state policy, but verbalization had begun to supplant deeds and miracles. Prefaced by 'thus saith the Lord' the prophet made use of analogies, simile, even irony and sarcasm.

In substance as well as in form, prophecy took a new turn. Amos, for example, proclaimed the deity's concern for the underprivileged in society. The ethical and moral dimension was added to the more traditional cultic practices. Isaiah, who lived in the second half of the 8th century BC, was deeply involved in advising the kings of Judah in the crises of the Assyrian invasions of Tiglath-pileser III, Sargon II and Sennacherib. Examples of his poetic genius are to be seen in the account of his call in ISA 6.1-12, the figure of the worthless vineyard in ISA 5.1-12 and the lament over the ruin of Judah in ISA 1.4-9. These and other passages indicate that the resurgence of power in Judah was matched, furthermore, by a flowering of its literature.

THE attempts of Sargon II and Sennacherib to control Philistia and Judah were a continuation of the policy of Tiglath-pileser III (page 76). Obviously the Assyrians were concerned with the taking of booty and the levying of tribute to be paid on a regular basis by subject peoples. Yet the cities of Philistia and Judah were poor in natural resources which could hardly have justified the expense and effort expended on campaigns from the distance of the Assyrian capitals. A more likely explanation for

Assyria's interest in the southern part of Palestine was the desire to control the trade routes along the eastern rim of the Mediterranean. Sargon II was successful in extending his hegemony to the very border of Egypt as well as his suzerainty over Cyprus.

Assyrian treatment of subject peoples varied. If payment of tribute was forthcoming the Assyrians could be accommodating. Yet determined resistance was met with force and even brutality. In times of crisis, Philistines and Judaeans often looked to Egypt

for help as well as to smaller states nearby. One method for quelling revolt against Assyria was the deportation of a local population to another land with foreigners brought in to replace it (II KINGS 17.6,24).

Upon the death of Shalmaneser V in 722 BC, Sargon II seized the throne of Assyria, taking the name of the famous Sargon who had ruled Akkad almost 2000 years earlier. In 720 BC he captured Qarqar and Hamath and put down a rebellion of Hanno of Gaza which had been aided by the Egyptians. By 716 BC Sargon had

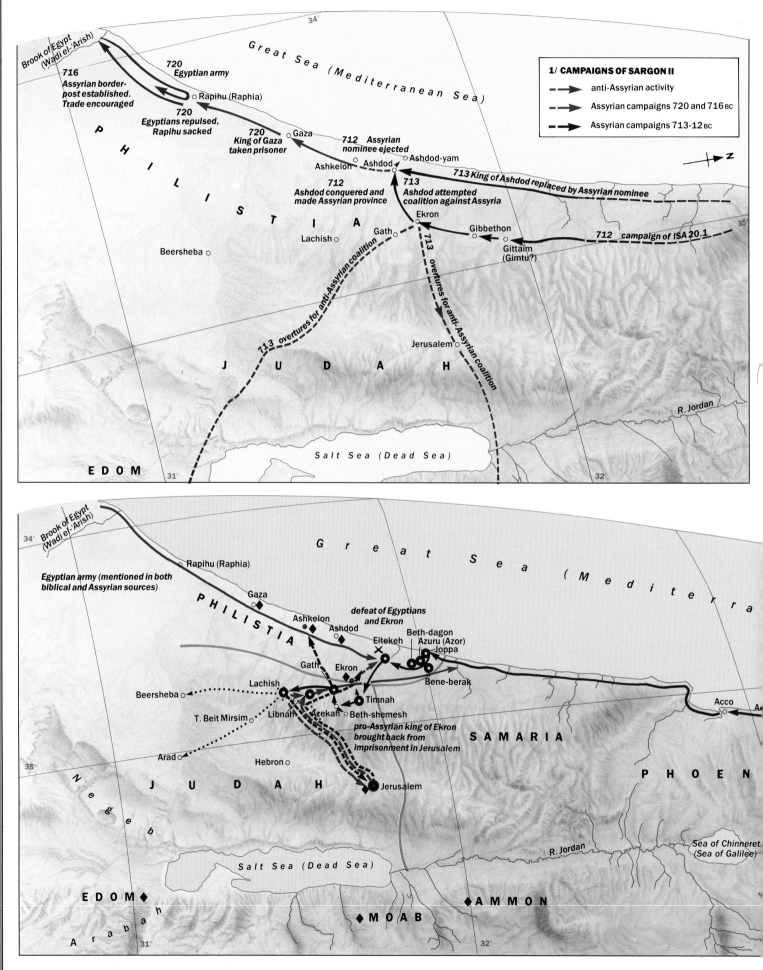

extended his boundary to the Brook of Egypt, where he established a colony and encouraged trade with Egypt. In his eleventh year, 712 BC, Sargon was faced with a rebellion on the part of Ashdod, which had attempted to involve other Philistine city-states, as well as Judah, Edom and Moab, in revolt against Assyrian rule. Sargon removed from the throne Azuri, king of Ashdod, because he had refused to send tribute, and placed on the throne his pro-Assyrian brother Ahimiti. After conquests in Syria, Palestine and Armenia, Sargon entered Babylon as a liberator. Mardukapaliddin (biblical Merodach-baladan) was defeated and Sargon proclaimed himself as governor of Babylon. During his reign Sargon extended the borders of Assyria from the Caucasus to Egypt and from Elam to Cyprus – the largest area of Assyrian domination until this time. Sargon died in 705 BC, probably in battle at Tabal in Asia Minor. This brought widespread revolt in which both Hezekiah of Judah and Merodach-baladan of Babylonia were involved (II KINGS 20,12 etc).

Sennacherib (704-681 BC), Sargon's son, soon found himself faced with trouble in Babylonia. Merodach-baladan had since regained the throne but Sennacherib decisively subdued the Babylonian insurrection and placed Bel-ibni upon the throne as vassal king. He then attended to rebellions in Syria and Palestine (701 BC). Luli, king of Sidon, fled overseas; Ethba'al was placed as king over the Phoenician cities, which submitted to Assyrian rule. Kings of Ashdod, Ammon, Moab and Edom hastened to send gifts of tribute. Sennacherib then moved southward, where he captured Ashkelon and surrounding cities. He set up a pro-Assyrian king and imposed tribute. At Eltekeh he met and defeated the Egyptians and Ethiopians who had been summoned by the revolutionists at Ekron. Padi, king of Ekron, had been put into fetters and given over to Hezekiah, king of Judah. After capturing Eltekeh, Timnah and Ekron, Sennacherib attacked Hezekiah in Jerusalem, released Padi and restored him to his throne. Assyrian officers (the Tartan, the Rabsaris and the Rabshakeh) went to Hezekiah (II KINGS 18,17) in Jerusalem to demand surrender of the city but Hezekiah refused. A second embassy from Sennacherib likewise failed. From the Assyrian account it is clear that Jerusalem was not captured.

In 681 BC Sennacherib was murdered by two of his sons (II KINGS 19,37), one of whom has been identified in a cuneiform source as Arad-mulishshi, whose name has been identified in the Bible as Adrammelech.

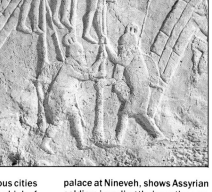

1/ map left Sargon II conquered Gaza in 720 BC after the revolt of 721. In 716 he extended his control to the Brook of Egypt (Wadi el-'Arish). In 712 he acted against Ashdod which had tried to form an anti-Assyrian coalition with other Philistine states plus Judah, Moab and Edom.

2/ map bottom Sennacherib's campaign of 701 BC was occasioned by rebellions in Syria, Philistia and Judah. He subdued the whole coast from Byblos to Ashdod, placed pro-Assyrian kings on the thrones of rebellious cities and imposed tribute. Hezekiah of Judah was forced to submit but Jerusalem itself was not captured.

3/ Relief from the palace at Nineveh, showing Sennacherib standing in a chariot drawn by a horse. The king is accompanied by a driver and an attendant.

4/ In 701 BC Sennacherib besieged and captured the city of Lachish (modern T. ed-Duweir) in Judah. This detail from a large relief depicting the attack upon the walled city, from the south-west palace at Nineveh, shows Assyrian soldiers impaling their captives on stakes. Two ramps of mud brick (running diagonally across the scene) had been constructed for siege engines that were rolled up to the city wall in order to make a breach in it.

5/ An Assyrian cart with spoked wheels, transporting women captives to a life of servitude in Assyria. Alabaster relief from the palace of Ashurbanipal at Nineveh.

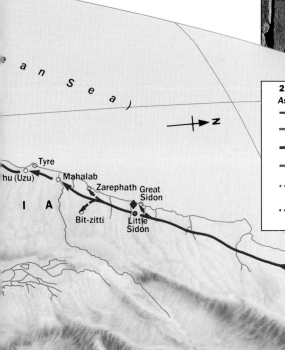

2/ SENNACHERIB'S INVASION OF JUDAH 701 BC

Assyrian routes:

→ major force from Assyriological data

→ major force from II KINGS 18-19; ISA 36, 37

⇢ detached or minor force

⇢ detached or minor force from II KINGS 18-19; ISA 36, 37

⋯⇢ detached or minor force from MIC 1.8-15

⋯⇢ route based on archaeological evidence

Egyptian routes:

→ major force

⇢ detached or minor force

◗ hostility to Assyria

◎ siege

◆ submission, marked by payment of tribute to Assyria

— approximate boundaries between Philistia, Judah and Samaria (formerly Israel)

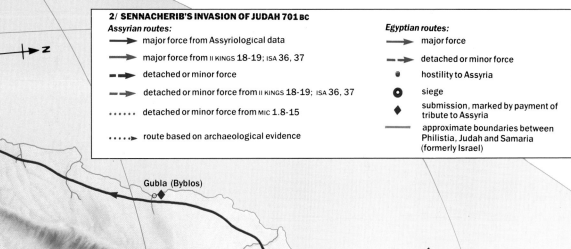

KING Hezekiah (716-687 BC) and his son Manasseh (687-643 BC), the two kings of Judah who reigned longer than any other two consecutive kings, lived under the shadow of Assyria's power. Over this span of 73 years, not only was Judah politically vulnerable but it was threatened by the growth of foreign cults. Manasseh went so far as to erect altars to foreign gods in the court of the Temple in Jerusalem, altars which were later destroyed by King Josiah.

The kingdom of Judah underwent its severest crisis at the end of the 8th century BC. King Hezekiah had come to the throne in 716BC and tried to unite 'all of Israel and Judah' in the worship at the Jerusalem Temple (II CHRON 30.1-5). He was thus trying to attract those Israelites who remained in the newly formed Assyrian provinces, such as Samaria, Megiddo and perhaps Gilead. When Sargon II of Assyria died in 605 BC Hezekiah followed the lead of many subject nations and raised the flag of revolt. The western league, of which he was a leader, included the Phoenicians, the Moabites, Ammonites, Edomites and especially some of the Philistine states. Ekron handed their quisling ruler over to Hezekiah and joined the rebels. Gaza remained loyal to Assyria and Hezekiah occupied some of its territory (II KINGS 18.8).

When the Assyrian army under Sennacherib appeared in Phoenicia, some of Hezekiah's allies rushed to surrender and pay their tribute leaving Judah and Ekron alone to face the Assyrian onslaught. Of the 46 Judaean cities captured, the foremost was Lachish (page 80). Though the capital at Jerusalem was not taken (II KINGS 18.13-19, 30), the kingdom was devastated and its Shephelah and Negeb districts largely transferred to Philistine control. Hezekiah found himself without direct access to the major trade routes, especially that from Elath to Gaza used by caravans.

On the eve of the Assyrian siege of Jerusalem, Hezekiah 'made a pool and a tunnel, and brought water into the city' (II KINGS 20.20). He also concentrated on the fortifications of the city. According to II CHRON 32.5, he 'built up all the wall that was broken down and raised it up to the towers, and another wall without, and repaired the Millo of the City of David'. The construction of 'another wall without' is probably

a reference to a new wall which was built around two residential and commercial quarters of the city: the second (*mishneh*) quarter (II KINGS 22.14) on the Western Hill and the Makhtesh quarter (ZEPH 1.10-11) in the Central Valley. A series of houses belonging to the *mishneh* quarter have recently been unearthed as well as the fortification wall, 23 feet wide, and part of a tower which may have belonged to a gateway (perhaps the 'Middle Gate' mentioned in JER 39.3). The population of the city at that time probably numbered about 20,000 individuals.

Large storage jars dating to Hezekiah's reign have been found in many Judaean excavations, bearing on their handles a royal seal impression with 'for the king' (*lamelech*) followed by one of four place names: Ziph, Socoh, Hebron and *mmst*. A similar handle also appears with the seal impression of a personal name; and at Ramat Rahel and Lachish, jars appear with impressions of both the royal seal and a personal name seal. Although the purpose of these impressions is debated by scholars the simplest explanation for the geographical names is that they designated the four centres where royal wineries were located and that the personal names may have been those of officials who inspected and certified the contents. On the map of Judah's districts, based on JOSH 15 (page 79), Socoh appears in the southern district, Ziph in the southeastern, Hebron in the central, and possibly *mmst* was located in the Bethlehem or Jerusalem district.

Manasseh was appointed co-regent by his father in 696 BC (II KINGS 21.1). By the time of Hezekiah's death in 686 BC, Manasseh had probably formulated his policy for Judah's survival. Trade routes were all in the hands of his neighbours; Sennacherib had reduced Judah to the area of the hill country and the wilderness. Manasseh elected to enter into diplomatic relations with the countries round about which were enjoying the benefits of Assyrian control of southern Levantine commerce. He invited embassies from Tyre and other adjacent countries and restored shrines to their

respective deities in Jerusalem for their use (II KINGS 21.3; 23.13). Thus, he sought to overcome the isolation in which Judah found itself after the crushing defeat at the hands of Sennacherib.

For half a century Judah was kept in this subservient position and Manasseh not only assisted in the corvée work of delivering timber to Assyria for Esarhaddon's palace, but also had to send troops to accompany the Assyrian army under Ashurbanipal in his campaign against Egypt (667/6 and 664/3 BC). However, a change in Judah's fortune eventually came about when, under pressure from Ashurbanipal (II CHRON 33.11-17), he renounced all his treaties with Tyre and the other neighbours (indicated by turning away from their gods) and was on good terms with the Assyrians. Permission was granted to rebuild the fortresses of Judah; this would indicate that Judah was once again being trusted with the supervision of the trade routes. Manasseh's new lease on life opened the way for a renaissance of Judaean power as the decline of the Assyrian empire allowed a degree of freedom to neighbouring states.

Manasseh, the longest reigning king of Judah, is described as the king who 'seduced' Judah 'to do that which is evil more than did the nations whom the Lord destroyed' (II KINGS 21.9). It was the introduction of foreign religious practices into the Jerusalem Temple by Manasseh that occasioned the reform of King Josiah for which he was famous (pages 86-87).

2

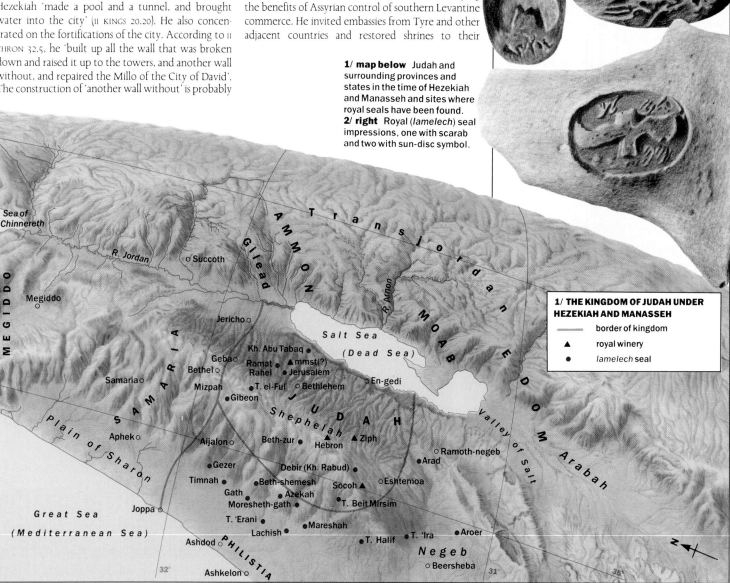

1/ **map below** Judah and surrounding provinces and states in the time of Hezekiah and Manasseh and sites where royal seals have been found.
2/ **right** Royal (*lamelech*) seal impressions, one with scarab and two with sun-disc symbol.

1/ **THE KINGDOM OF JUDAH UNDER HEZEKIAH AND MANASSEH**
———— border of kingdom
▲ royal winery
● *lamelech* seal

THE Bible is replete with accounts of battles and the instruments of war appear prominently in song and ritual: chariots and horses, the bow and arrow, the spear, the sword and armour. Although corrosion and decay have taken their toll of the weapons actually used, bas-reliefs in Egypt and Assyria have preserved a record of how war was waged in biblical times. City walls, city gates and tunnels which brought water to the defenders when enemies surrounded the city – these and other installations remain as reminders of the reality of warfare.

To judge from the scenes of fighting that have survived, hand-to-hand encounter with spear or sword seems to have prevailed widely. In the sea battle between the Egyptians and the Sea Peoples depicted on the wall of the temple of Ramesses III at Medinet Habu (page 42) the Sea Peoples made use of the long sword and round shields while defending themselves against the spears of the Egyptians in a sea battle. In the relief of Ashurbanipal from the south-west palace at Nineveh, the Assyrians, sometimes on horseback and sometimes on foot, wielded long spears and drew their bows at their Elamite enemies. The enemy is usually within easy reach and the battle is a scene of utter confusion. Arrows, bows, quivers, and discarded spears litter the ground. A large oblong shield, rounded at the top, appears as a defensive weapon and fragments of bronze and even iron armour have been found in excavations. Among the larger instruments of warfare was the battering ram, an excellent example of which is shown in the scene of Sennacherib's capture of Lachish (page 81/4 shows the brick ramps built for wheeling up the battering ram). This machine could be placed in position to knock down the wall at its weakest point, usually the gate. In the relief of Sennacherib the defenders of Lachish are shown hurling flaming torches, stones and arrows upon the siege engine. A soldier within, protected by a shield, pours water on the wooden structure and its ram to prevent them being set afire by the fagots hurled from the top of the wall.

FORTIFICATIONS
The prevalence of warfare and the fear of destruction of those who lived in the cities of Palestine during the Late Bronze and Iron Ages can be measured by the large expenditure of labour on civil defence. Throughout this span large cities were regularly enclosed by massive city walls built of stone and mud brick and equipped with entrances which were not only protected by towers but by a series of wooden gates, sometimes as many as three or four pairs (page 54). These walls were often strengthened by salients and recesses. Sometimes the fortification consisted of two strong walls (the casemate), strengthened by partitions at regular intervals between them. When the city was under siege means for obtaining water outside the city wall have been found at Megiddo, Hazor, Gibeon and at Jerusalem. At the latter, King Hezekiah diverted the flow of water from a protected spring, Gihon, by means of a tunnel cut through the bed rock to a pool (Siloam) which lay within the city wall (II CHRON 32.30).

CHARIOTS
The chariot was one of the most feared and effective weapons of ancient warfare. Over the flat terrain of Egypt and Mesopotamia and the deserts between, the chariot proved to be effective for speedy transportation and offensive attack for more than the millennium that extended from the Late Bronze Age through to the Iron Age. Assyrian chariots had crews of two

(driver and bowman) and three (an additional man with spear). Usually two horses were used, but heavier vehicles required three or even four. Although the chariot could not easily negotiate the hilly terrain of Palestine, mention is made in the Bible of its use from the time of David onward. For graphic representation of the design of the chariot used in Palestine the reliefs from upper Syria and Assyria must suffice.

CUSTOMS AND PRACTICES IN WAR
Certain customs and codes seem to have prevailed in warfare, to judge from Assyrian reliefs. Numerous examples of lines of shackled prisoners (usually naked) are shown being marched from the site of their capture, probably to the Assyrian capital. Such prisoners are shown on the bronze gates of Balawat from the time of Shalmaneser III. In the dramatic portrayal of Sennacherib's capture of Lachish (page 81/4) two helmeted soldiers are shown impaling three of the enemy, stripped bare of clothes, on poles. They

probably served to discourage resistance to the conqueror. That the Assyrians showed kindness to captive women may be deduced from a relief of Ashurbanipal's palace at Nineveh (page 81/5) which shows captive women being transported in a horse-drawn cart. However, less humane is the scene of counting heads of executed prisoners and an actual beheading of an Elamite by an Assyrian soldier, shown on reliefs from the south-west palace at Nineveh belonging to Sennacherib.

On occasion disputes between kingdoms were resolved by means other than military action. Treaties and covenants appear in foreign relations and prophetic oracles about the futility of war have been preserved. Most obvious is the apocalyptic vision of a world in which 'they shall beat their swords into plowshares and their spears into pruning-hooks; nation shall not lift up sword against nation, neither shall they learn war any more' (ISA 2.4).

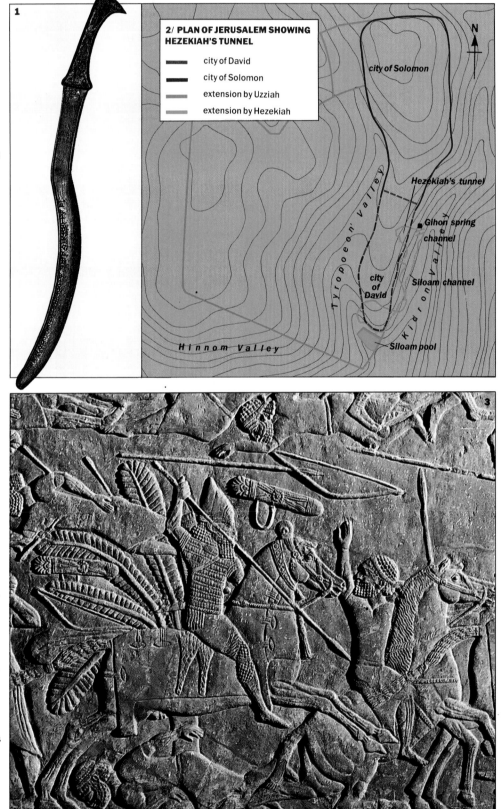

2/ PLAN OF JERUSALEM SHOWING HEZEKIAH'S TUNNEL

- city of David
- city of Solomon
- extension by Uzziah
- extension by Hezekiah

city of Solomon

Hezekiah's tunnel

Gihon spring channel

Tyropoeon Valley

city of David

Siloam channel

Kidron Valley

Hinnom Valley

Siloam pool

N

1/ above right Sickle sword belonging to Adad-nirari, King of Assyria (1310-1280 BC), for hand-to-hand fighting.
2/ above far right Hezekiah's tunnel cut to bring water from Gihon into the walled city of Jerusalem in time of siege.
3/ right Bas-relief from Nineveh showing Ashurbanipal defeating the King of Elam.

FOR more than a century (beginning with Tiglath-pileser III in 734BC) Assyria had come 'down like the wolf upon the fold', collecting tribute from the small states of Israel and Judah, destroying cities and taking captives away into exile. With the fall of Nineveh in 612BC, Assyrian might came to an end through a combination of factors. There was an internal struggle for the throne, foreign hordes from the north and the east invaded the homeland, and Babylon revolted. While it was Assyria that had so often threatened the peoples of Israel and Judah, it was left to Babylon to deal the final and heaviest blow

in the destruction of Jerusalem and the taking of its people into exile.

Esarhaddon (680-669BC), Sennacherib's son and successor, made major innovations in Assyrian imperial strategy. In Babylonia, he reversed his father's harsh policy, by rebuilding devastated Babylon with the help of vassals from the west and by appointing his son Shamash-shum-ukin to rule over Babylonia. He sought stability by making treaties with his more powerful vassals, notably the Medes, the kingdom of Tyre, the Scythian tribes in the north and the desert Arabs.

Esarhaddon's attitude toward Egypt represented a

radical change of policy. Since the reign of Tiglath-pileser III (page 76), the Brook of Egypt (Wadi el-'Arish) had been the south-western limit of Assyrian interests. However, Egypt had frequently supported anti-Assyrian movements in Palestine and Phoenicia, and in 669BC Esarhaddon sought to curb this policy by invasion through Sinai; an undertaking only made possible through friendship with the Arabs. His plan was to hold the Nile Delta area through native kings supervised by Assyrian officials.

At Esarhaddon's death, the senior heir, Ashurbanipal (668-627BC) of Assyria, continued his father's

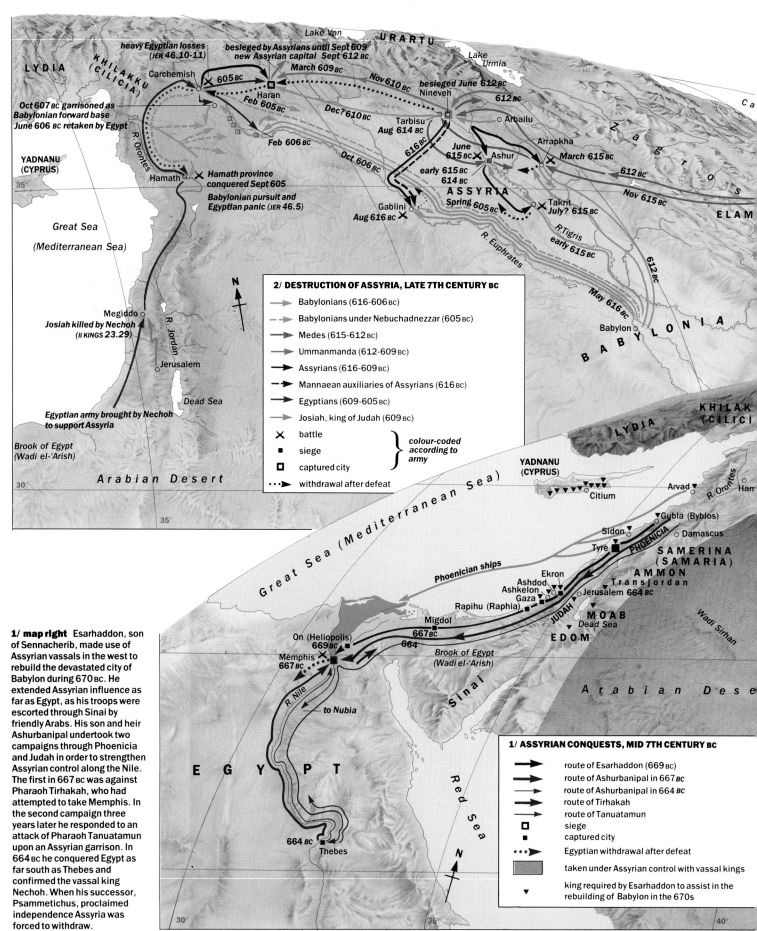

2/ DESTRUCTION OF ASSYRIA, LATE 7TH CENTURY BC

- → Babylonians (616-606 BC)
- ⇢ Babylonians under Nebuchadnezzar (605 BC)
- ⇛ Medes (615-612 BC)
- → Ummanmanda (612-609 BC)
- → Assyrians (616-609 BC)
- ⇢ Mannaean auxiliaries of Assyrians (616 BC)
- → Egyptians (609-605 BC)
- → Josiah, king of Judah (609 BC)
- ✕ battle
- ■ siege   } colour-coded according to army
- ▢ captured city
- ⋯▶ withdrawal after defeat

1/ map right Esarhaddon, son of Sennacherib, made use of Assyrian vassals in the west to rebuild the devastated city of Babylon during 670BC. He extended Assyrian influence as far as Egypt, as his troops were escorted through Sinai by friendly Arabs. His son and heir Ashurbanipal undertook two campaigns through Phoenicia and Judah in order to strengthen Assyrian control along the Nile. The first in 667BC was against Pharaoh Tirhakah, who had attempted to take Memphis. In the second campaign three years later he responded to an attack of Pharaoh Tanuatamun upon an Assyrian garrison. In 664BC he conquered Egypt as far south as Thebes and confirmed the vassal king Nechoh. When his successor, Psammetichus, proclaimed independence Assyria was forced to withdraw.

1/ ASSYRIAN CONQUESTS, MID 7TH CENTURY BC

- → route of Esarhaddon (669 BC)
- → route of Ashurbanipal in 667 BC
- → route of Ashurbanipal in 664 BC
- → route of Tirhakah
- → route of Tanuatamun
- ▢ siege
- ■ captured city
- ⋯▶ Egyptian withdrawal after defeat
- ▨ taken under Assyrian control with vassal kings
- ▼ king required by Esarhaddon to assist in the rebuilding of Babylon in the 670s

policy in Egypt. He undertook two major campaigns: the first in 667 BC to quell a rebellion in support of the former Egyptian king, Tirhakah, returning from his southern capital of Thebes to re-take Memphis; the second, in 664 BC, followed an attack on Assyrian garrisons by Tirhakah's Ethiopian successor Tanuata-mun. This time Ashurbanipal conquered Egypt as far south as Thebes, and confirmed one of the vassal kings, Nechoh of Sais, as paramount ruler. Ashurbanipal's control of Egypt, however, depended upon the loyalty of the vassal king, and when Nechoh's successor Psammetichus proclaimed independence, Assyrian

2/ map left After twelve years of attacks, Assyria finally succumbed to Babylon. In 616 BC the Babylonian king, Nabopolassar, moved into Assyrian territory. The Medes invaded Ashur in 615 BC, taking the old capital a year later. In 612 BC Nineveh, besieged by Babylonians, Medes and Ummanmanda hordes, fell quickly. The Assyrian army fled to Haran, then to Carchemish. Pharaoh Nechoh, while marching north to aid the Assyrians, was opposed by Josiah of Judah at Megiddo; Josiah was fatally wounded (page 87). Finally the Babylonian Crown Prince Nebuchadnezzar defeated the Egyptians at Carchemish in 605 BC.

withdrawal became inevitable.

Problems were developing elsewhere. Instability in Elam threatened Babylonia and required repeated Assyrian intervention from 667 BC onwards, producing tensions which led to civil war (652-648 BC) between Ashurbanipal and his brother Shamash-shum-ukin of Babylonia, ending in the latter's defeat and death. Ashurbanipal, in a series of campaigns, then devastated Elam. The death of Ashurbanipal in 627 BC unleashed many tensions inherent within the empire but the most significant development, which led to the fall of the empire, was the seizing of the kingship of Babylon by a Chaldaean chieftain, Nabopolassar, in 626 BC.

THE DOWNFALL OF ASSYRIA

Four particular factors contributed to the downfall of the Assyrian empire: a struggle for succession between two sons of Esarhaddon; the Chaldaean chieftain, Nabopolassar, who challenged Assyrian overlordship by assuming the kingship of Babylonia in 626 BC; the Medes, who under Cyaxares, attacked Assyria, and, lastly, tribal hordes from the north, known as Ummanmanda, mainly Cimmerians (biblical Gomer), who overran Assyrian territory. After several years of fighting to break the Assyrian hold on Babylonia, Nabopolassar moved against Assyria itself by 616 BC. In 615 BC the Medes invaded, and in 614 BC took the old capital Ashur. A formal alliance between Nabopolassar and Cyaxares followed this success. In 612 BC Nineveh itself fell, surprisingly quickly, to a combined siege by Babylonians, Medes and Ummanmanda. The Assyrian army withdrew first to Haran, and then to Carchemish where they called on Egypt for assistance. The Egyptians sent a large army northwards under Nechoh. Josiah of Judah, an ally of the Babylonians, attempted

to intercept the Egyptians at Megiddo and was killed (II KINGS 23.29). The Egyptians joined the Assyrian remnant at Carchemish. In 605 BC the Crown Prince Nebuchadnezzar, placed in charge of the Babylonian army, attacked the Egyptian army at Carchemish, with massive slaughter (JER 46.2-12).

THE RISE OF BABYLON

The pact between Nabopolassar and Cyaxares in 614 BC prepared the way for the orderly dismemberment of the Assyrian empire. The principal heir was Babylonia, with the Medes taking control of the most northerly areas in Asia Minor and the regions east of the Zagros Mountains. Parts of Syria and Palestine were still under Egyptian influence, and Nebuchadnezzar undertook several campaigns between 604 and 586 BC to establish his authority there. He also took action in Khilakku (Cilicia) and neighbouring areas in the north-west, a region in which Neriglissar (559-556 BC), the successor after Nebuchadnezzar's briefly reigning son Evil-merodach (II KINGS 25.27), had to undertake a further campaign to consolidate the Babylonian hold.

For the most part, the major powers of the 7th century BC, Assyria, Egypt and Babylonia, did not concern themselves with the relatively isolated kingdom of Judah. It survived, for more than a century, the conquest of the northern kingdom Israel, even to see the fall of the Assyrian empire. It was the campaign of Nebuchadnezzar of 587 BC against Judah which proved to be a turning point in the history of ancient Israel. He brought an end to the dynasty of David, which had lasted for more than three and a half centuries, and took Judaeans to Babylon, where they developed the practices of Judaism to replace the cult once performed in the Jerusalem Temple.

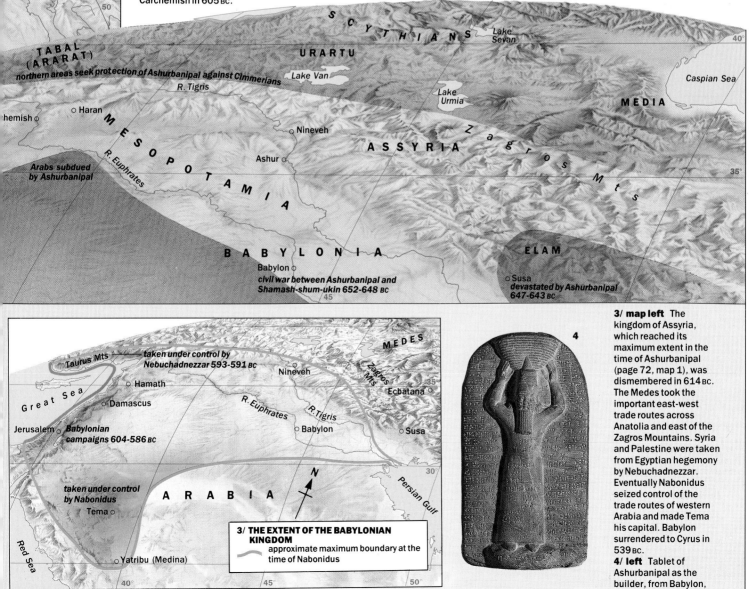

3/ map left The kingdom of Assyria, which reached its maximum extent in the time of Ashurbanipal (page 72, map 1), was dismembered in 614 BC. The Medes took the important east-west trade routes across Anatolia and east of the Zagros Mountains. Syria and Palestine were taken from Egyptian hegemony by Nebuchadnezzar. Eventually Nabonidus seized control of the trade routes of western Arabia and made Tema his capital. Babylon surrendered to Cyrus in 539 BC.

4/ left Tablet of Ashurbanipal as the builder, from Babylon, c 660 BC.

3/ THE EXTENT OF THE BABYLONIAN KINGDOM
approximate maximum boundary at the time of Nabonidus

JOSIAH came to the throne of Judah as a boy of eight years. He was put there by an assembly of common people at a time of national crisis. His father Amon had been murdered by his own palace servants in 641 BC. They, in turn, were put to death by a group called 'the people of the land', obviously not the wealthy landowners. These internal tensions and changes within the kingdom of Judah were followed by a weakening of the control which Assyria had long had over Palestine. Upon the death of Ashurbanipal of Assyria c627 BC, Judah was able to gain her independence and proceed with an expansion of her territory as well as with the religious reforms for which Josiah is most widely known (II KINGS 23.25).

Josiah's aim was to restore the area once held by the House of David and thus reunite the divided kingdom. From the places listed in connection with his religious reforms it seems that he quickly regained the land of Ephraim so that he could claim to rule from Beersheba to Geba (modern Jeba'). He controlled Bethel on the former Israel-Samaria border (II KINGS 17.28) and in the south he took Simeon territory back from Philistia. From archaeological evidence it is surmised that he fortified Arad and En-gedi, where he stationed Greek mercenaries in readiness against possible Egyptian reprisals. In the north he held sway as far as Naphtali, including the Valley of Jezreel and Galilee. Megiddo seems to have been reinforced with storage facilities for a large garrison. Since Josiah took a wife from Rumah (Khirbet er-Rumeh) he had access to, and even control of, the northern reaches.

This extension of political authority was accompanied by the most radical religious reforms in the history of Judah. According to the detailed account in II KINGS 22-23 reforms were underway by Josiah's 18th year. The repair of the Jerusalem temple revealed the 'book of the law' of Moses (II KINGS 22.8). Following this 'discovery', it is generally agreed that the Book of Deuteronomy, or a part of it, provided the legal basis for the religious reforms of King Josiah.

The reformation in the cult at Jerusalem and throughout the land was the most sweeping in all Israelite history. Symbols of Assyrian cults, which had made so evident the foreign domination of Judah's religious practices since the reigns of Manasseh and Ahaz, were quickly removed. Worship was concentrated in Jerusalem at the Temple of Yahweh, no longer seen as a mere royal chapel but as the sole place of worship for all the people. Priests from the abandoned rural shrines throughout Judah were brought in but not allowed to serve as temple officiants. The laws of Deuteronomy (DEUT 13), which made idolatry a capital offence, were enforced even in the areas of former Israelite territory as it was regained. False priests were slain and their altars desecrated. The male and female prostitutes employed in pagan ritual were removed. Even the decorative articles made for the divinities Baal and Asherah (the Canaanite mother goddess represented by a fertility pole and by statues elaborately dressed in fine garments) were destroyed. Special attention was paid to blotting out the old Canaanite worship of Molech (Moloch) which had been reintroduced by Ahaz. The rites involved passing children through the fire as a dedication to the god; some were even burned to death, though human sacrifice had been condemned in ancient law (LEV 18.21; 20.2-5). Later Punic inscriptions from c400-150 BC indicate that the term Molech eventually became a general term for sacrifice or votive offering. Josiah also stamped out solar and astral cults and divination, although pagan shrines at Arad and Lachish indicate some local resistance.

Jeremiah, the prophet, a contemporary of Josiah, was deeply involved in the life of the Judaean kingdom. Fortunately much is known about his political activity from the book which bears his name. During the 13th year of Josiah's reign (628 BC) Jeremiah began his important prophetic activity together with the religious reforms set in motion by Josiah. He gave counsel to monarchs up to and beyond the Babylonian capture of Jerusalem in 587 BC. He came from a priestly family from Anathoth in the territory of Benjamin and he prophesied during the reigns of Josiah, Jehoiakim and Zedekiah (JER 1.2-3). He had serious confrontations with the latter two kings, was imprisoned by Zedekiah and was rescued from death only through the good offices of an Ethiopian commander (JER 37-38). Despite his protestations that he and the remnant left in the land after the captivity by the Babylonians should remain in the land, Jeremiah was taken to Egypt by the refugees from Jerusalem (JER 42-43). It is possible that he died there in exile.

Jeremiah viewed political events in a context that extended beyond the narrow confines of the Judaean state. The rise and fall of empires, he believed, were controlled by a divine hand and the impending invasion by the Babylonians, 'the foe from the north', which he consistently predicted (JER 25, 28), was seen as a punishment for the moral corruption of the people and their failure to perform the ritualistic demands of their law. The unwelcome message which he brought to the rulers was to accommodate themselves to the Babylonians, and that those in exile should 'build houses, and live in them, plant gardens and eat their produce... and seek the welfare of the city' where they had been carried away captive (JER 29.5-7). This appeal was based on his conviction that the exiles would eventually return and the monarchy be restored in Judah (JER 30-33).

A valuable insight into the role of the prophet in Israelite society and the importance of the written as

2

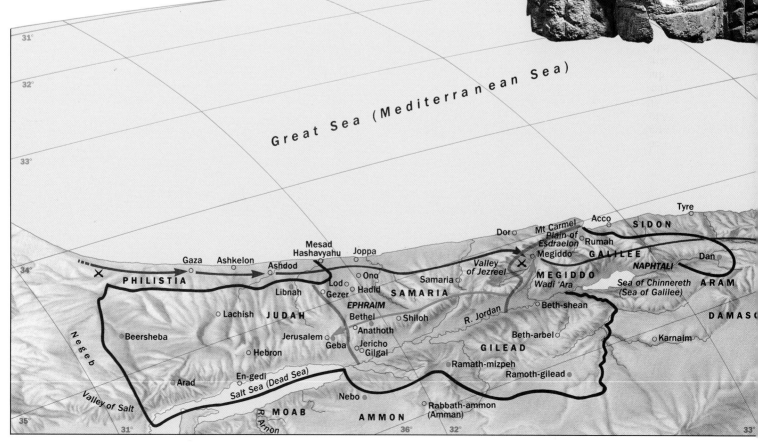

well as the spoken word is provided by the account of Jeremiah's relationship with Baruch, son of Neriah. He was the brother of Seraiah, a court minister, and a loyal friend of the prophet. A vivid account is given of how in the fourth year of Jehoiakim's reign (605 BC) Jeremiah dictated his prophecies to Baruch. Jeremiah commanded him to read them to the people in the temple, because the prophet was not able to go himself (JER 36.5). The court was informed and ordered Baruch to repeat the prophecies. The content was so inflammatory that the courtiers advised Baruch and Jeremiah to hide, while they took the scroll to Jehoiakim. It was read once again, but the king seized it before the reader had finished, cut it to pieces and threw it into the brazier (JER 36.23). When Jeremiah heard the news he dictated the prophecies again to Baruch and added more besides. It is very likely that large portions of the Book of Jeremiah, which recount details of the prophet's life in the third person, were added during the rewriting by Baruch.

Josiah's main concern was the expansion of Judah's territorial domain and the internal matters of religious reform. Eventually, however, he was faced with the development of international affairs. The Saitic kings of Egypt, being stronger than the pharaohs who preceded them, challenged the rising Babylonian power at the River Euphrates itself. Psammetichus I had sent the Egyptian army in 610 BC to help the Assyrians and their last ruler Ashur-uballit against the Babylonians and the Medes who captured Haran. In 611 BC the new Egyptian ruler Nechoh II (Nikku of the Babylonian Chronicle) tried to regain Haran but had once more to abandon the attempt on the approach of the Babylonians. To reach Haran on the River Balikh the Egyptians must have marched up by stages through Palestine via their garrison posts at Megiddo, Riblah and Carchemish.

Very little is known of the last decade of Josiah's reign until 609 BC. In that year Nechoh sent word to Josiah that he was not going to fight him but required passage to a garrison-post ('the house of my warfare', II CHRON 35.21) – presumably Megiddo or Carchemish.

This warning, given as Nechoh passed through Philistia, which Josiah dared not enter, alerted Judah to the threat that the Egyptians were supporting the Assyrians' cause against Babylon.

Josiah moved swiftly to Wadi 'Ara, opposite Megiddo, where the pass across Mt Carmel enters the Plain of Esdraelon. He clashed with the Egyptians in open warfare. The Egyptians had the superiority in that they were well equipped with chariots and archers. In the ensuing battle Josiah was badly wounded, taken to Jerusalem and died.

Josiah's 31-year reign was the last distinguished episode of Judaean history. Despite Josiah's tragic end, he was characterized in the Deuteronomic appraisal of the kings of Israel and Judah as having done what was 'right in the eyes of the Lord'. As for Nechoh, he was to fight one final battle against the Babylonians, at a point between Gaza and Pelusium (Lower Egypt) in 601 BC. The Egyptians, who from Canaanite times had made so many expeditions northward, were never again to enter Palestine in force.

1/ map below Extent of Josiah's kingdom with the routes of Josiah's and Nechoh's armies in 509 BC and sanctuaries abolished by Josiah in his reform.
2/ Carved head from Amman, resembling the Egyptian goddess Hathor. 7th century BC.

3/ Hebrew letter found at Mesad Hashavyahu, confirming the presence of an Israelite influence in the area.
4/ Tanit (or Tophet) sanctuary at Salambo, Carthage. Urns contained the charred remains of sacrificed children and animals.

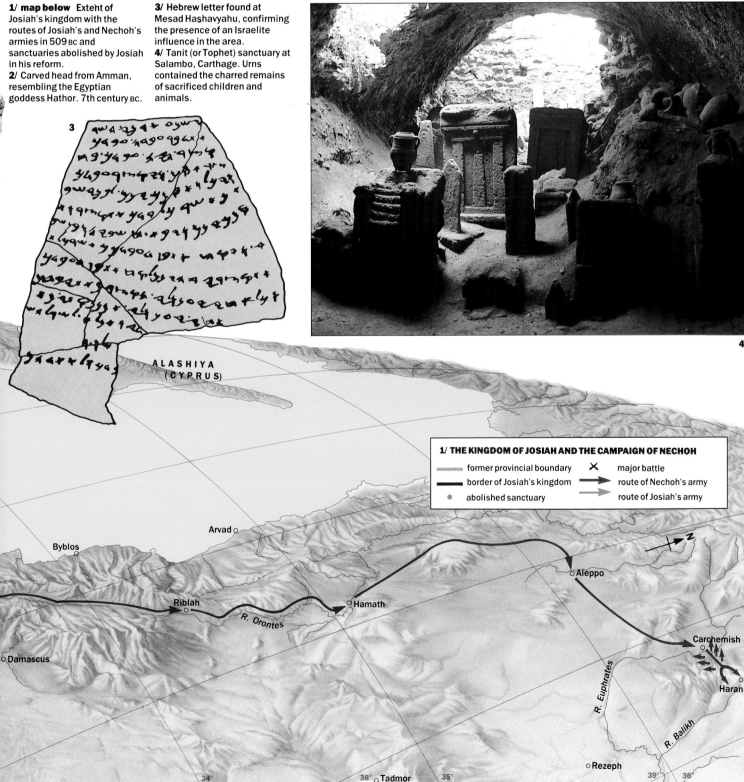

4

1/ THE KINGDOM OF JOSIAH AND THE CAMPAIGN OF NECHOH

- former provincial boundary
- border of Josiah's kingdom
- abolished sanctuary
- × major battle
- → route of Nechoh's army
- → route of Josiah's army

ALASHIYA (CYPRUS)

Arvad

Byblos

Aleppo

Riblah

Hamath

R. Orontes

Damascus

Carchemish

R. Euphrates

Haran

R. Balikh

Rezeph

Tadmor

THE Babylonian king Nebuchadnezzar II (605-562 BC) was the most powerful of the six kings that constituted the Chaldaean dynasty, a line whose rule extended over a period of 86 years (625-539 BC). During a reign which extended over more than half that period, Nebuchadnezzar was involved with the major world powers of the time and was responsible for the development of the city of Babylon both architecturally and artistically. In biblical history, however, his name is most widely known for the capture of Jerusalem and the exile of its inhabitants to Babylon. These events mark the end of a long period of Israelite history and the beginning for the religion of Judaism.

After Nabopolassar, king of Babylon and founder of the Chaldaean dynasty, had taken over former Assyrian territories in the upper region of the River Euphrates with the help of the Medes and Cimmerians, his son Nebuchadnezzar, the crown prince, proceeded to lead his own army against the hostile north-eastern hill tribes. The Egyptians established a garrison at the important city of Carchemish, forcing the Babylonians

at Quramati to retreat. Nebuchadnezzar, with the help of Greek mercenaries, then embarked on a reprisal raid. Moving up the east bank of the Euphrates he crossed to the west below Carchemish, surprised the enemy and captured the city in August 605 BC. The Egyptians who fled were cut off and the whole force destroyed so that, according to the Babylonian Chronicle, a reliable source, 'not a single Egyptian escaped home'. The whole region of Hamath was taken over, including Riblah, a former Egyptian stronghold dominating the road south and the routes to the Mediterranean coast. From here the Babylonians claimed sway over Palestine as far south as the Egyptian border at Wadi el 'Arish.

ASSUMPTION OF THE KINGSHIP

Following Nabopolassar's death in 605 BC, Nebuchadnezzar almost immediately claimed the throne as Nabu-kudurri-usur (Nebuchadnezzar). In 604 BC 'all the rulers of Hatti came before him and he received their heavy tribute'. Jehoiakim of Judah was among those submitting (II KINGS 24.1). Ashkelon refused to submit

and was captured with its king. At the end of 601 BC, there was a major battle with the Egyptians in which both sides suffered heavy losses, including chariots and cavalry. The clash could have taken place in the Gaza plain, through which the principal highway ran, for it effectively ended Egyptian control in Asia by land. Jehoiakim of Judah changed his allegiance to Egypt and the Babylonians now sought an opportunity for revenge.

CAPTURE OF JERUSALEM IN 597 BC

During 599-8 the Babylonians encouraged the Qedar Arabs, Moab and Ammon to invade Judah. Then 'on the second day of the month Addar in his seventh year [16 March 597] he captured the city of Judah [Jerusalem] which he had besieged. He seized its king and appointed there a king of his own choice. Taking heavy spoil he sent it to Babylon'. Thus the Babylonian Chronicle records the beginning of the Jewish exile.

Disturbances in the next year took Nebuchadnezzar as far north as Carchemish and down the Tigris against a raiding force from Elam (JER 49.34-39). Further

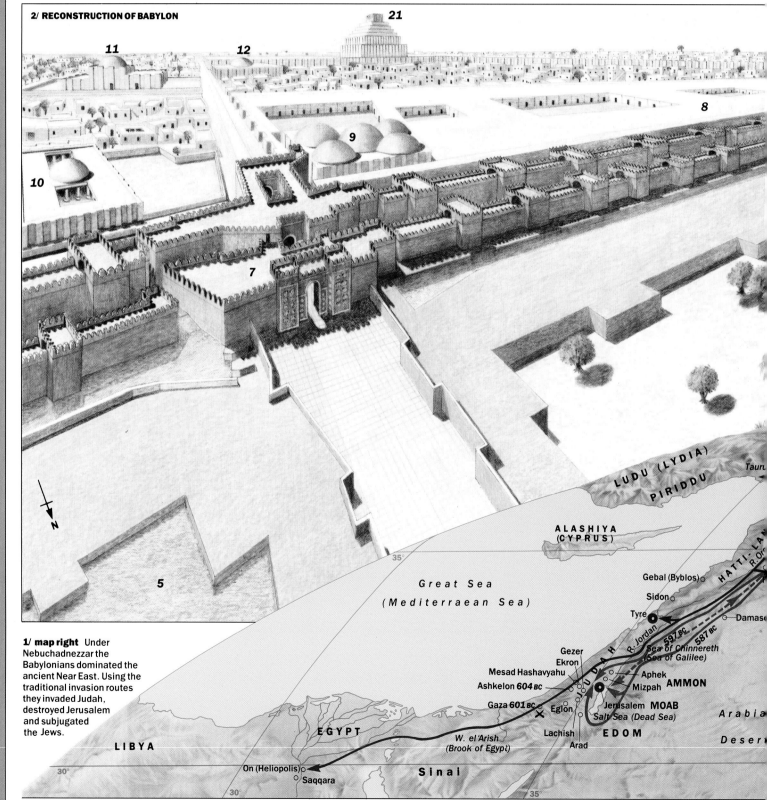

2/ RECONSTRUCTION OF BABYLON

1/ map right Under Nebuchadnezzar the Babylonians dominated the ancient Near East. Using the traditional invasion routes they invaded Judah, destroyed Jerusalem and subjugated the Jews.

unspecified operations in Syria were probably aimed against coastal cities such as Byblos or Tyre, the latter besieged by the Babylonians for 13 years between 596 and 563. His control extended as far as western Cilicia (Khume and Piriddu), where Nebuchadnezzar or his representative negotiated for the Medes against Lydia after the battle of the River Halys, dated 28 May 585 BC by the solar eclipse recorded then.

THE DESTRUCTION OF JERUSALEM

When King Zedekiah, placed on the throne by Nebuchadnezzar, planned an anti-Babylonian coalition with Edom, Moab, Ammon, Tyre and Sidon, contrary to the advice of Jeremiah (JER 27.1-11), Nebuchadnezzar was provoked to lay siege to Jerusalem again. After two years the Babylonians steadily closed in. Hill forts and watch-posts in the surrounding hills were taken and walls breached. The temple fell in August 587 BC (according to the Nisan calendar, or 586 by the Tishri new year reckoning) and the city fell a month later.

At the capture of Jerusalem the Babylonians took a major group of army and skilled Judaeans (10,000) off into exile, followed, at the fall of the city, by further bands totalling 3023, 832 and 745 prisoners (JER 52.28-30).

THE REIGN OF NABONIDUS

After the death of Nebuchadnezzar in 562 BC there were three kings of Babylon in seven years, only one of whom died a natural death. Eventually Nabonidus (555-539 BC) assumed the throne. Initiallly, he followed up the action of his predecessor Neriglissar, an official who had taken part in the sack of Jerusalem, and who had campaigned in Cilicia. From Hamath, Nabonidus then operated against the forces from Lydia which threatened the trade routes into western Anatolia. Afterwards he turned against the Ammananu (which was probably Edom). He claimed the control of Gaza, plus parts of Egypt and Syria. From these areas he called up work forces to engage in the restoration of his family-endowed shrines to the moon god Sin at Haran.

In 552 Nabonidus moved from Edom to adjacent north-western Arabia to win military control of an area around the oasis of Tema, which measures about 266 by 100 miles. He stayed there, in virtual voluntary exile, for ten years because of opposition from the Babylonians. This unpopularity had two causes: he had become increasingly eccentric, possibly due to some health problem, and he was suspected of harbouring unorthodox religious views. Nabonidus finally returned to Babylon (in 542 BC) where his son and co-regent Bel-sharra-usur (the biblical Belshazzar) had been left in charge.

By now the Babylonians had come under considerable pressure from the Medes and the Persians, and elaborate defences against any attack on the capital were prepared. The flood defences and the 'Median Wall' across the narrow land bridge between the Euphrates and Tigris south of Sippar and Opis became the scene of a pitched battle in which the Babylonians were defeated. The sudden fall of the city may have been in part due to a diversion of the river which subverted the defences. Belshazzar was killed and Nabonidus was captured. Cyrus entered Babylon on 30 October 539 BC, and brought Babylonian domination of the Near East to an end.

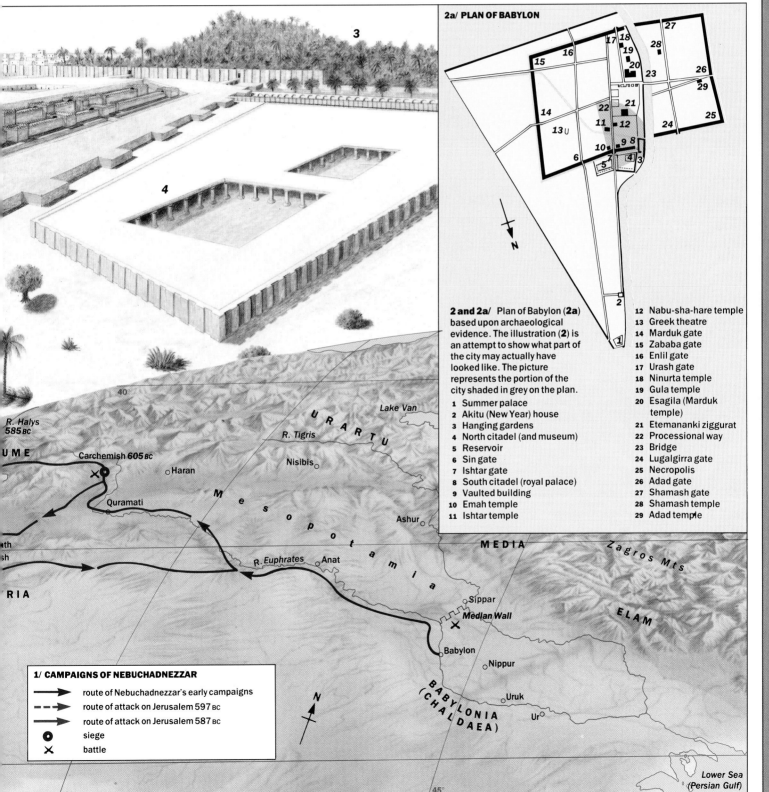

2a/ PLAN OF BABYLON

2 and 2a/ Plan of Babylon (**2a**) based upon archaeological evidence. The illustration (**2**) is an attempt to show what part of the city may actually have looked like. The picture represents the portion of the city shaded in grey on the plan.

1 Summer palace
2 Akitu (New Year) house
3 Hanging gardens
4 North citadel (and museum)
5 Reservoir
6 Sin gate
7 Ishtar gate
8 South citadel (royal palace)
9 Vaulted building
10 Emah temple
11 Ishtar temple

12 Nabu-sha-hare temple
13 Greek theatre
14 Marduk gate
15 Zababa gate
16 Enlil gate
17 Urash gate
18 Ninurta temple
19 Gula temple
20 Esagila (Marduk temple)
21 Etemananki ziggurat
22 Processional way
23 Bridge
24 Lugalgirra gate
25 Necropolis
26 Adad gate
27 Shamash gate
28 Shamash temple
29 Adad temple

1/ CAMPAIGNS OF NEBUCHADNEZZAR

→ route of Nebuchadnezzar's early campaigns
⇢ route of attack on Jerusalem 597 BC
→ route of attack on Jerusalem 587 BC
◉ siege
✕ battle

WHEN in 540 BC the Persian king, Cyrus the Great, captured the Lydian capital Sardis from Croesus and his troops looted the city, Croesus asked Cyrus, 'What are those men doing?' 'Plundering your city', replied Cyrus. 'Not my city, but yours', said Croesus. This event brought Persian rule to the Mediterranean seaboard, and it was not popular. In 498 BC Sardis was burnt again when the Ionians rebelled. The Athenians, anxious to keep the Persians out of the Aegean, supported the rebellion. This led to Persian invasions of Greece, and to the defeat of Darius' army at Marathon (490 BC) and Xerxes' fleet at Salamis (480 BC), and for the next two centuries Greeks and Persians eyed each other warily across the Aegean.

The Greek cities of Asia Minor were always unwilling Persian subjects, and the Persian satraps of these regions were frequently tempted to seek independence. In 401 BC some 13,000 Greek mercenaries marched from Sardis to help Cyrus depose his brother Artaxerxes II; defeated at Cunaxa near Babylon, 10,000 of them escaped north through Armenia to the Black Sea at Trapezus, led by Xenophon, who left a vivid account in his *Anabasis*. The event, however, demonstrated the potential of Greek mercenaries, and in the 350s the satraps of Anatolia, Phoenicia and Egypt, relying on mercenaries, all rebelled, but failed for lack of unity. Philip II of Macedon now prepared to take advantage of the weakened empire, and when his son Alexander crossed the Hellespont in 334 BC with 40,000 infantry and 7000 cavalry, the Persian opposition was composed mainly of Greek mercenaries.

PERSIA'S INTEREST IN EGYPT

The Persians coveted the wealth of Egypt. The gateway to Egypt was the satrapy of Abar Nahara, 'Beyond the River', in which lay the province of Phoenicia, with its ships, trade and timber, and the tiny province of Judah. When Cambyses invaded Egypt (525 BC), the Phoenicians supplied a supporting fleet, and the Arabs water for the desert route south of Gaza. Cambyses' successor Darius I colonized Egypt, opening a canal between the Nile and the Red Sea, encouraging building works, and codifying Egyptian law. The Arabian coast and the Indus were explored by Darius' admiral Skylax of Caryanda, who was later credited with the 4th-century BC description of the Mediterranean coast (Pseudo-Skylax). On Darius' death in 486 BC Egypt rebelled, but Xerxes swiftly restored order. The full-scale revolt of the 460s and 450s collapsed when a supporting Athenian fleet was trapped and destroyed. For the next 40 years Egypt was ruled by the satrap Arsames and her southern border was garrisoned by Jewish soldiers on the island of Elephantine (Yeb, near Aswan), who claimed to have settled there before Cambyses' time. Their archives, the Elephantine papyri, show that their garrison and temple suffered at local hands during renewed rebellion in c410-400 BC. Egypt remained independent until Artaxerxes recaptured it in 343 BC. But this Persian effort was too late. The Greeks had long coveted Egypt, and in 331 BC under Alexander they acquired her.

PALESTINE IN THE PERSIAN PERIOD

The province of Judah was subdivided into districts and half-districts (NEH 3). Palestine under the Persians was part of the satrapy called 'Beyond the River' (EZRA 4:10, 8:36; NEH. 2:7,9). The internal administrative divisions of the satrapy are not clearly evidenced, but it is generally agreed that the Persians inherited the divisions created under Assyrian and Babylonian rule. The Assyrians (733 BC) divided the land into the northern provinces of Megiddo, Dor and

Samaria, and the Transjordanian provinces of Hauran, Karnaim (biblical Bashan), and Gilead (page 77). The Babylonians annexed new provinces: Judah, Ashdod and Idumaea (the southern Judaean hills) in the west, and the Ammonite and Moabite regions in Transjordan. Some of these provinces may have been created only at the beginning of the Persian period. In the time of Ezra and Nehemiah, mention is made of the provinces of Samaria in the north, Ashdod in the west, and the Ammonites in the east; the southern region was occupied by Geshem the Arab. The existence of a province of Moab may be indicated by the reference to 'the sons of Pahath-Moab' (EZRA 2:6; NEH. 7:11). Contemporary evidence of the existence of the provinces of Samaria and Judah is found in the Elephantine papyri and in the documents from Wadi ed-Daliyeh.

Archaeological excavation has begun to throw light on this obscure period. By the beginning of the period, the country was culturally divided into two regions: the mountain region of Judah, Transjordan, Samaria to a lesser extent, and Galilee; and the coastal plain. The culture of the mountains was basically eastern, being composed of a continuing Israelite culture with cultural influence from Assyria, Babylonia and Egypt. The culture of the coast, in contrast, contained the essentially western East-Greek, Cypriot and Attic elements. The material culture of Greece thus appeared in Palestine much earlier than the Macedonian conquest. However, the products of the Greek culture were adapted to local traditions and customs and no longer possessed the same significance as in their country of origin. The chief carriers of this new Palestinian culture were apparently the Phoenicians, and only to a lesser extent Greek soldiers and colonists. Thus, the material culture of Palestine exhibits no influences of the ruling Persians, apart from some slight influence in the several pottery types, a few pieces of jewellery and metal-ware, which were also apparently produced by the Phoenicians.

Very little is known of the history of Judah under the Persians. The biblical writers remember it basically for three major events: the rebuilding of the temple in Jerusalem under the high priest Joshua and the governor Zerubbabel in 520-515 BC. (HAGGAI; ZECHARIAH chs. 1-8; EZRA chs. 1-6); the rebuilding of the walls of Jerusalem and the development of some limited autonomy for Judah under Nehemiah (444-432 BC) (NEH. chs. 1-13); and the establishment in Judah of the Jewish Law under Ezra (458 or perhaps 398 BC) (EZRA 7-10, NEH. 8-9). Persian culture and history thus left no lasting impression in Judah; Persia's destruction by Alexander the Great is vividly depicted in DAN 8.5-8.

Mediterranean Sea

Byblu
Berytu
Sidon
Sarepta
Tyre
Ecdippa
Acco
Megiddo
Mt. Carmel
'Athlit
Dor
Crocodilonpolis
Beth-shea
Samaria
Joppa
Lod
Mizpa
Gezer
Ashdod
Mozah
Ashkelon
Beth-zur
Gaza
Lachish
Hebron
T. Jemmeh
En-gedi
Beersheba
Arad
T. el-Far'ah(S)
Kadesh-barnea
Elath
34°   35°

4/ THE ROYAL PALACE AT PERSEPOLIS

phases of construction:
1 Principal stairway to terrace, gently graded to allow ascent on horseback.
2 Gate tower leading via processional way to Hall of 100 Columns (10) and to courtyard in front of the audience hall (4).
3 Eastern stairway to *apadana*, sides decorated with tribute reliefs.
4 Apadana principal audience hall of Darius I,

with open colonnades on three sides and a timber ceiling supported by 36 slender columns nearly 65.5ft tall.
5 Tripylon small central palace or vestibule.
6 Tachara or 'winter palace' of Darius I, notable for the use of Egyptian architectural features.
7 Hadish or palace of Xerxes, with reception hall and fine carvings.
8 Palace of Artaxerxes I.

9 Unfinished gate-tower leading to courtyard facing Hall of 100 Columns.
10 Hall of 100 Columns or 'throne hall'; larger in floor area but only half the height of the *apadana*.
11 Hall of 32 Columns small reception hall.
12 Royal stables and chariot-house.
13 Offices and storerooms of the Royal Treasury.

14 Additional treasury warehouses and storerooms.
15 Garrison quarters.
16 Remains of mud-b fortification wall with projecting towers.
17 Remains of mud-b fortification wall separating palace buildings from probab citadel area on higher ground to the east.

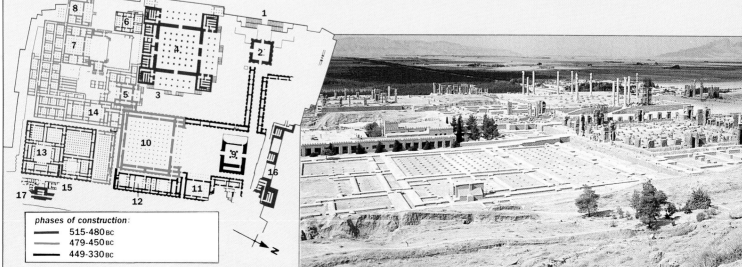

phases of construction:
515-480 BC
479-450 BC
449-330 BC

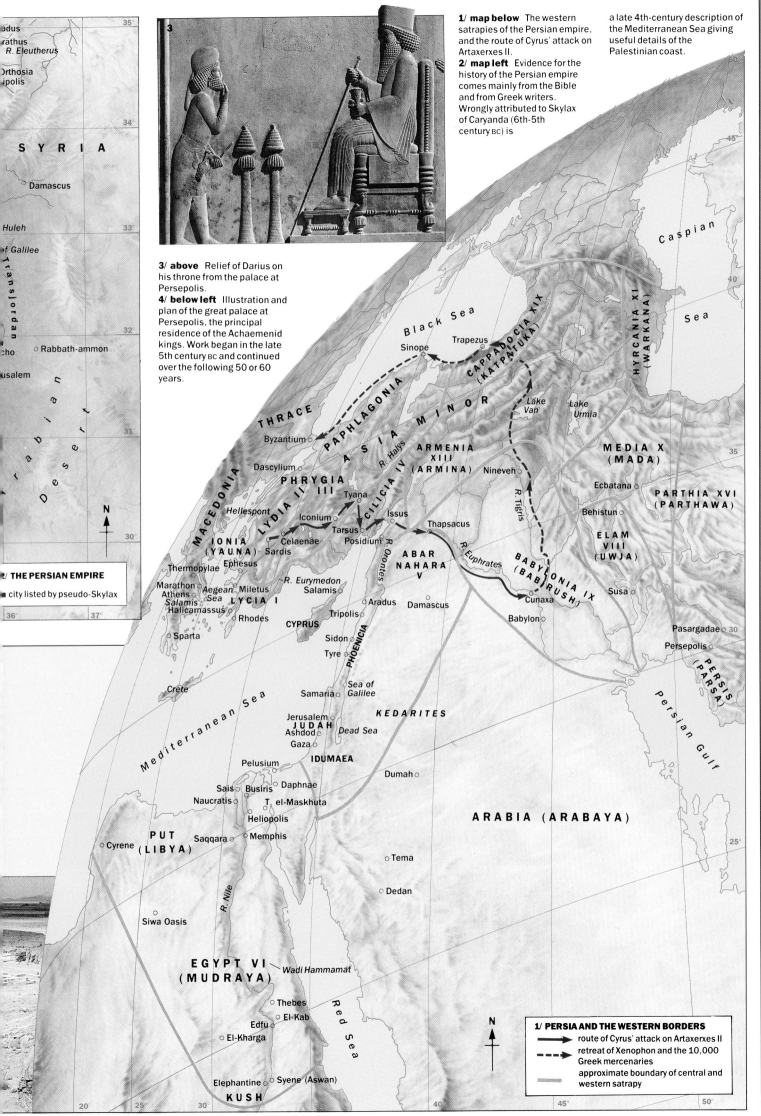

1/ map below The western satrapies of the Persian empire, and the route of Cyrus' attack on Artaxerxes II.
2/ map left Evidence for the history of the Persian empire comes mainly from the Bible and from Greek writers. Wrongly attributed to Skylax of Caryanda (6th-5th century BC) is a late 4th-century description of the Mediterranean Sea giving useful details of the Palestinian coast.

3/ above Relief of Darius on his throne from the palace at Persepolis.
4/ below left Illustration and plan of the great palace at Persepolis, the principal residence of the Achaemenid kings. Work began in the late 5th century BC and continued over the following 50 or 60 years.

SYRIA

Damascus

Huleh

f Galilee

(Transjordan

Rabbath-ammon

cho

usalem

2/ THE PERSIAN EMPIRE
■ city listed by pseudo-Skylax

Caspian Sea

Black Sea

Sinope   Trapezus

THRACE   PAPHLAGONIA   CAPPADOCIA XIX (KATPATUKA)   HYRCANIA XI (WARKANA)

Byzantium   ASIA MINOR   Lake Van   Lake Urmia

Dascylium   R. Halys   ARMENIA XIII (ARMINA)   Nineveh   MEDIA X (MADA)

PHRYGIA III   Tyana   CILICIA IV   Ecbatana   PARTHIA XVI (PARTHAWA)

Hellespont   Iconium   Tarsus   Issus   Thapsacus   Behistun   R. Tigris

LYDIA II   Celaenae   Posidium   R. Orontes   R. Euphrates   BABYLONIA IX (BAB RUSH)   ELAM VIII (UWJA)

MACEDONIA   IONIA (YAUNA)   Sardis   ABAR NAHARA V   Cunaxa   Susa

Thermopylae   Ephesus   R. Eurymedon   Salamis

Marathon   Aegean Miletus   Aradus   Damascus   Babylon

Athens   Salamis Sea   LYCIA I   Tripolis   Pasargadae

Halicarnassus   Rhodes   CYPRUS   Sidon   PHOENICIA   Persepolis   PERSIS (PARSA)

Sparta   Tyre

Crete   Samaria   Sea of Galilee

Mediterranean Sea   Jerusalem   KEDARITES   Persian Gulf

JUDAH   Dead Sea

Ashdod   Gaza   IDUMAEA

Pelusium   Dumah

Sais   Busiris   Daphnae

Naucratis   T. el-Maskhuta

Heliopolis   ARABIA (ARABAYA)

PUT (LIBYA)   Saqqara   Memphis

Cyrene   Tema

Dedan

R. Nile

Siwa Oasis

EGYPT VI (MUDRAYA)   Wadi Hammamat

Thebes   El-Kab

Edfu   Red Sea

El-Kharga

N

1/ PERSIA AND THE WESTERN BORDERS
→ route of Cyrus' attack on Artaxerxes II
- - → retreat of Xenophon and the 10,000 Greek mercenaries
━━━ approximate boundary of central and western satrapy

Elephantine   Syene (Aswan)

KUSH

THE Greeks were always fascinated by Persia and its wealth, though they affected to despise it. Many Greeks before Alexander went east, for example, Skylax, who explored the Indus and the Arabian coast for Darius, or Telephanes from Ionia who carved stone friezes at Persepolis. When the Athenians exiled their statesman Themistocles, who had saved them from the Persians in 480BC, he was welcomed to Persia and given an estate by Artaxerxes I. In the 4th century BC, many Greeks became Persian mercenaries, and throughout the Persian territory of coastal Asia Minor, cities were built or rebuilt in the Hellenistic grid-pattern invented by Hippodamus of Miletus. Hellenization was introduced to Caria by the independent-minded Persian satrap Mausolus; his tomb, the Mausoleum, was one of the seven wonders of the ancient world.

ALEXANDER AND THE EAST

Alexander's campaigns (334-323 BC), however, dramatically quickened the pace of Hellenization. In 334BC he crossed the Hellespont with approximately 35,000 men, against the Persians. Having defeated the Persians at the River Granicus in 334BC and at Gaugamela in 331BC, Alexander then continued north to the Caspian Gates and the Hindu Kush, in his unsuccessful search for the mythical river, which was thought to encircle the world. He was forced to return to Babylon from India when his troops refused to advance any further into the unknown.

Alexander laboured to unite Greeks and non-Greeks, encouraging intermarriage, founding Hellenistic cities, and settling Greek colonists. After his death in Babylon in 323 BC, his generals continued his policy in their new kingdoms: Cassander held Greece and Macedonia; Lysimachus, Thrace; Antigonus and his son, Demetrius Poliorcetes ('the Besieger'), Asia Minor; Seleucus, Babylon and Syria; and Ptolemy, Egypt. Further east arose the Indo-Greek kingdom of Bactria; its kings had Greek names – Euthydemus, Demetrius I and II, Eucratides and Menander – but they soon broke away from western loyalties, and shortly before 100 BC this kingdom developed overland links with China.

The east, however, was hardly flooded with Macedonian settlers (only 15,000 Macedonians campaigned with Alexander, and many returned, homesick for Greece). The Seleucid kings in particular founded new colonies to secure their communications with the east; sometimes merely renaming old towns with Greek dynastic names or granting Greek city status to such places for a fee. The Ptolemies similarly renamed cities (for example, Acco became Ptolemais, and Rabbath-ammon became Philadelphia). Both dynasties had large empires to control, and a strong, bureaucratic administration, conducted in Greek and conversant with the local Egyptian or Aramaic, served their need. The spread of Greek language and culture went hand-in-hand with the purposes of government.

HELLENISM IN JUDAH

Inevitably, Greek influence was felt in Judah also. In the late 7th century BC Greek mercenaries served the Egyptians on the Philistine coast; in the 5th century traders from Tyre (doubtless able to speak Greek) appeared at Nehemiah's Jerusalem. By the 4th century, Judah used coins bearing the Attic owl and the Greek helmet, and Attic red-figure ware was known at Ptolemais and Sebaste. Large quantities of Persian and Hellenistic period storage jars have been dredged up from the sea round Dora and Caesarea, Azotus and Ascalon, indicating regular trade through these ports; a Greek helmet of the same period was found off Azotus. Other evidence of imports includes a Ptolemaic faience bowl (c 200BC) from Alexandria, and perhaps a 4th-century BC palmette calyx from Boeotia. From a 3rd-century BC temple at Beersheba comes a terracotta figurine of Demeter and Persephone, closely paralleled by a similar object known from Larnaka in Cyprus. Jars from 3rd-2nd century BC Rhodes have been found at many sites.

Judah's interest in sea trade is evidenced by a graffito in Jason's Tomb (2nd century BC) in Jerusalem, showing a Greek monoreme (a galley with one bank of oars) chasing a cargo ship. One recalls that Simon the Maccabee decorated his family tomb at Modin, in sight of the sea, with ships (I MACC 13.29). The Maccabees were well aware of the Hellenistic Mediterranean world; Judas Maccabeus himself sent an embassy to Rome (I MACC 8.17), and Jonathan entertained diplomatic relationships with Sparta (I MACC 12.2), to which a few years earlier the ejected high priest Jason had tried to flee for exile (II MACC 5.9). Hellenistic life-style is illustrated by the town of Marisa, populated by colonists from the Phoenician town of Sidon, whose tombs contain Greek inscriptions and wall paintings of animals captioned with Greek names (for example, *rhinoceros, elephant*). Another important Hellenistic town of the 2nd-1st centuries BC has been excavated at Tell Anafa in Upper Galilee. Hellenistic administration is evidenced by a Greek inscription from Scythopolis (Beth-shean) dating from 195 BC, recording orders issued by Antiochus III and his son to Ptolemaios, the military governor of Coele-Syria and Phoenicia. A 2nd-century BC Greek tariff inscription refers to taxes on imported olive oil, and fees for money-changing and use of weighing facilities, all sure indications of international trade.

HELLENISTIC WRITERS AND THE JEWS

Greek writers naturally shared in the Hellenistic discovery of the east. Megasthenes of Ionia wrote on India (c 300 BC), and his contemporary Hecataeus of Abdera on Egypt; both included material about the Jews. Two of Aristotle's students, Theophrastus and Clearchus of Soli, also mentioned them. The general tendency was to present them as a race of philosophers. A less favourable picture of the Jews appears in the *Aegyptiaca*, a chronicle of Egyptian history to the time of Alexander the Great, by a 3rd-century BC Egyptian priest called Manetho from Sebennytus in the Delta.

1/ map right Alexander crossed the Hellespont in 334 BC with c 35,000 men, against the Persians. Having defeated them at the River Granicus in 334, he advanced into Syria and Egypt, and then moved into Armenia where he had a second decisive victory against the Persians at Gaugamela in 331. He then advanced through Media and Persia and north to the Caspian Gates and the Hindu Kush. Alexander wanted to find the mythical river, thought to encircle the world. In India, however, he had to turn back as his troops refused to advance any further into the unknown. Some troops returned by sea under Nearchus, while the rest returned by land through Gedrosia to Babylon, where Alexander died in 323 BC.

2/ A later depiction of Alexander the Great. In the 2nd century AD, Flavius Arrianus wrote his *History of Alexander* based on the writings of Alexander's contemporaries. These writings describe Alexander as clean-shaven with grey eyes, a fair complexion and a heavy mane of hair.

JEWISH WRITINGS

This was an age of Jewish expansion abroad, and many Mediterranean Hellenistic cities had a growing Jewish population, which began to adopt Greek as its own language. At Alexandria the Jewish Law was translated into Greek in the 3rd century BC; from the Alexandrine Jewish community in the 2nd century BC came the Greek *Letter of Aristeas*, the *Sibylline Oracles* (parts of Book III), the translation into Greek of *Ecclesiasticus*, and in the 1st century BC *2 Maccabees*, the *Wisdom of Solomon*, the romance of *Joseph and Aseneth*, and in the 1st century

AD the writings of Philo. (For other Alexandrian Jewish literature see pages 94-5.) Jewish literature in Greek was also found in Jerusalem; Judas Maccabeus' diplomat, Eupolemus, wrote a history of the Jews *c*158 BC; *2 Maccabees* is prefaced by letters written in Greek by Jewish leaders in Jerusalem to the Jewish community in Alexandria. The book *Esther* was translated into Greek in Jerusalem in 78/77 BC, as was *1 Maccabees* at much the same time. The coins of Alexander Jannaeus

(103-76 BC) had a Hebrew inscription on one side and a Greek inscription on the other. His contemporary, the Nabataean King Aretas III, called himself 'Philhellene' on his coins. By the 1st century AD Greek was written even at Qumran, the home of an Essene community, and Greek was spoken among the early Christian Hellenizers (ACTS 6:1). According to JOHN 19:20, Pontius Pilate used Greek, with Latin and Hebrew, for the title on the cross of Jesus.

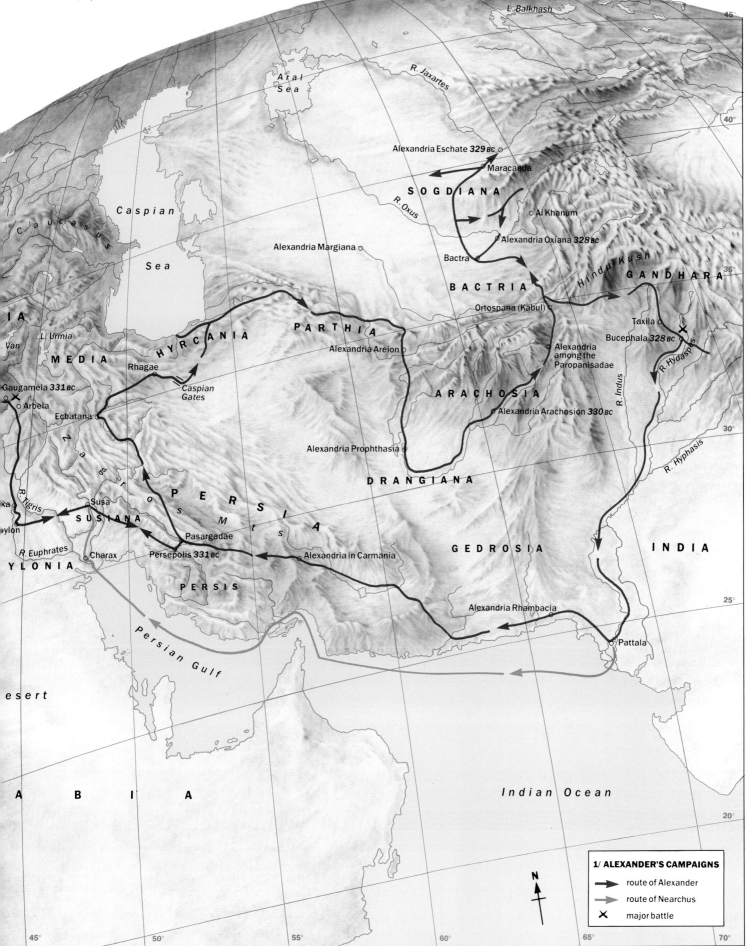

1/ ALEXANDER'S CAMPAIGNS
→ route of Alexander
→ route of Nearchus
✗ major battle

I N THE Intertestamental era Egypt once more played a crucial role in the history of the Jewish people. First, it was here that the Jewish scriptures were first translated into Greek – a translation which became known as the 'Septuagint' after its 70 (Greek *septuaginta*) translators. But secondly, Alexandria became the home of a very lively Jewish community, anxious to be included in the citizenship of the capital of Hellenistic Egypt. Contact between Alexandria and Jerusalem was easy, but the Ptolemies' administration and taxation of Judah were probably resented, and the change to Seleucid government in 200 BC welcomed, at least in its early years, though later it became oppressive.

Ptolemy I Soter was a Macedonian general of Alexander the Great. On the death of Alexander his empire was torn apart by his generals. Ptolemy seized Egypt as his portion of the spoil. The Ptolemies were Greeks, and they focused their kingdom on the Hellenistic world. At the height of their power, they held most of the Levant, the south and south-western coasts of Anatolia, Cyprus, and some coastal areas of Thrace.

PTOLEMAIC INTEREST IN THE LEVANT

Egypt had always coveted Palestine, but in Old Testament times its influence was often weak. Solomon married an Egyptian princess (I KINGS 3.1); after his death Pharaoh Shishak I briefly invaded Judah (pages 62-3) (I KINGS 14.25). Under Assyrian pressure Israel (724-2 BC) and Judah (701 BC) appealed for help to Egypt, but Egypt was 'a broken reed' (ISA 36.6). When Assyria fell, Pharaoh Nechoh took Judah (609 BC), but soon lost it to Nebuchadnezzar, king of Babylon (605 BC).

After Alexander's death (323 BC), Ptolemy took over Egypt as satrap, annexing Cyrenaica and then Syria and Phoenicia to improve his access to the Mediterranean and his defence against his rivals, Antigonus and Seleucus. He transferred the capital from Memphis to Alexandria, shifting Egypt's focus to the Mediterranean, occupied Coele-Syria and Judah (301 BC) and established control over Cyprus and the Aegean. In 288/7 BC he took Tyre and Sidon. In doing so, he not only secured a defensive ring of territory but also created close contacts with the Hellenistic world. Inevitably this led to collision with the Seleucid empire described in DAN 11.5-44.

After their defeat by Antiochus III at Panion in 200 BC the

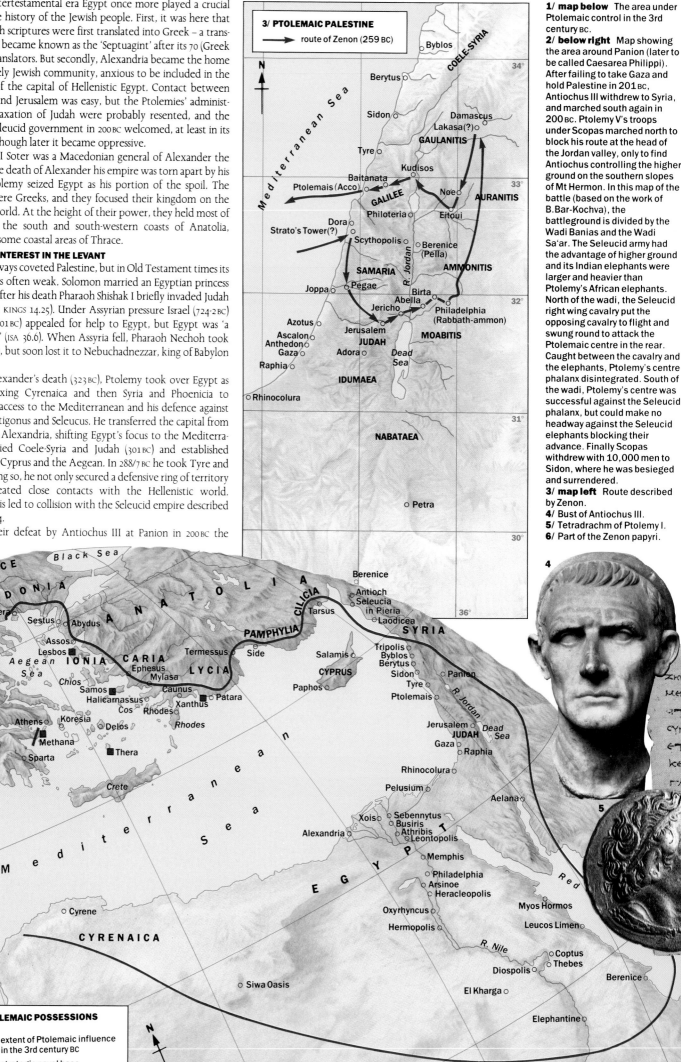

3/ PTOLEMAIC PALESTINE

→ route of Zenon (259 BC)

1/ map below The area under Ptolemaic control in the 3rd century BC.

2/ below right Map showing the area around Panion (later to be called Caesarea Philippi). After failing to take Gaza and hold Palestine in 201 BC, Antiochus III withdrew to Syria, and marched south again in 200 BC. Ptolemy V's troops under Scopas marched north to block his route at the head of the Jordan valley, only to find Antiochus controlling the higher ground on the southern slopes of Mt Hermon. In this map of the battle (based on the work of B. Bar-Kochva), the battleground is divided by the Wadi Banias and the Wadi Sa'ar. The Seleucid army had the advantage of higher ground and its Indian elephants were larger and heavier than Ptolemy's African elephants. North of the wadi, the Seleucid right wing cavalry put the opposing cavalry to flight and swung round to attack the Ptolemaic centre in the rear. Caught between the cavalry and the elephants, Ptolemy's centre phalanx disintegrated. South of the wadi, Ptolemy's centre was successful against the Seleucid phalanx, but could make no headway against the Seleucid elephants blocking their advance. Finally Scopas withdrew with 10,000 men to Sidon, where he was besieged and surrendered.

3/ map left Route described by Zenon.

4/ Bust of Antiochus III.

5/ Tetradrachm of Ptolemy I.

6/ Part of the Zenon papyri.

1/ PTOLEMAIC POSSESSIONS

—— extent of Ptolemaic influence in the 3rd century BC

■ strategic naval base

Ptolemies had little influence on Judah. In 150 BC the Seleucid pretender Alexander Balas, seeking help against his rival Demetrius, allied with Ptolemy VI, marrying his daughter Cleopatra; but the next year Ptolemy attacked Alexander, won the Levant, and had himself crowned in Antioch as king. Both Ptolemy and Alexander died as a result of the subsequent battle, and the Seleucid Demetrius regained the kingdom.

SYRIAN-EGYPTIAN WARS

274-271 BC. Ptolemy II fought Antiochus I. Ptolemy celebrated victory with a procession at the festival of Ptolemaieia in Alexandria, 271/270 BC.

260-253 BC. Ptolemy II fought Antiochus II. Antiochus gained new territory in Ionia, Pamphylia and Cilicia, and under the settlement terms repudiated his wife Laodicea for Ptolemy's daughter Berenice (DAN 11.6).

246-241 BC. Ptolemy III fought Seleucus II. Ptolemy attacked in order to support Berenice's son's claim to the Seleucid throne. He failed, but regained territory along the Anatolian seaboard, and captured Seleucia in Pieria (see DAN 11.7-9).

219-217 BC. Ptolemy IV fought Antiochus III. Antiochus had initial success, recapturing Seleucia, Ptolemais, Tyre and Gaza, but was defeated decisively at Raphia, 217 BC. Ptolemy regained most of his territory but left Seleucia in Seleucid hands (see DAN 11.10-12).

202-200 BC. Ptolemy V fought Antiochus III. Antiochus captured Coele-Syria at Panion, and took Sidon and Gaza, and annexed Judah (see DAN 11.13-16).

170-168 BC. Ptolemy VI fought Antiochus IV. Antiochus invaded Egypt in 169 and 168 BC, but in 168 BC was ejected by the Romans ('Kittim', DAN 11.30; see DAN 11.25-30; I MACC 1.16-20; II MACC 5.1).

JEWS IN EGYPT

Under the Ptolemies, the Jewish population in Egypt began to increase. Jews had settled in Egypt after the fall of Jerusalem in 587 BC (cf JER 43.5-7, 44.1), and the Elephantine Papyri reveal a Jewish colony near Aswan acting as a Persian frontier garrison. In 312 BC Ptolemy added Jewish captives from Jerusalem; some, according to the Letter of Aristeas, were later repatriated in exchange for a copy of the Torah which was taken from Jerusalem to Alexandria and translated into Greek for Ptolemy II's library (or, more likely, for the benefit of the growing Jewish population in Alexandria). In the mid-2nd century BC, Onias IV fled to Egypt and built a temple at Leontopolis, either for the local Jewish military garrison, or as a religious centre for all the Jews of the Nile Delta. Ptolemy III was well disposed towards the Jews, and in his reign many appear settled as farmers, artisans, soldiers, policemen, tax collectors, and administrators. Jewish synagogues are known at Alexandria, Crocodilopolis in the Fayum, Athribis, and elsewhere.

EGYPTIAN-JEWISH LITERATURE

Jewish writers flourished in Ptolemaic Alexandria. Demetrius (late 3rd century) wrote a chronology of Jewish history. In the 2nd century, Aristobulus was a teacher and philosopher (cf II MACC 1.10), Artapanus a religious propagandist who wrote a work called *Concerning the Jews*. Ezekiel dramatized the Exodus story in Greek verse, and Pseudo-Hecataeus wrote *On the Jews* and *On Abraham*. In 132 BC or soon after Ecclesiasticus was translated into Greek.

RELATIONSHIP OF JEWS AND GREEKS IN EGYPT

Some Jews favoured Hellenistic culture while others rejected it. But all Jewish writers were anxious to persuade fellow Jews and gentiles alike that the Jewish traditions compared well with those of the gentiles. Jews may boast of their contribution to the world of learning and of their loyalty to society, to demonstrate that persecution was unjustified. Yet, in III MACC, Ptolemy IV tried unsuccessfully to massacre Jews packed into a hippodrome by loosing on them intoxicated elephants. For all its improbabilities, this story reflects the fears of the Jews in alien surroundings.

THE ZENON PAPYRI

In 1915 papyri were found at the Hellenistic town of Philadelphia. These are the correspondence of Zenon, son of Agreophon, a native of Caunus who became the right-hand man of Ptolemy II's senior official Apollonius. Several documents concern the journey Zenon made through Judah, Transjordan and Galilee in 259 BC. One list gives the itinerary, another the travellers' names, and others details of rations supplied en route. Gifts to Ptolemy II are listed in a letter from Toubias, who commanded a small garrison of military settlers on his estate at Birta of Ammonitis (modern Arak el-Emir). His soldiers included an Athenian, a Macedonian, and a Cnidian; one of them sold Zenon a Sidonian slavegirl.

JOSEPHUS AND THE PTOLEMIES

There is little literary or archaeological evidence for Ptolemaic Judah. The main account is Josephus Ant XII, which tells only the translation of the Law into Greek (here following the Letters of Aristeas), Antiochus III's dealings with the Jews, and the activities of the Ptolemaic officials, Joseph and Hyrcanus, of the Oniad family.

THE PTOLEMIES

Ptolemy I Soter	305-283 BC
Ptolemy II Philadelphus	283-246 BC
Ptolemy III Euergetes I	240-221 BC
Ptolemy IV Philopator	221-204 BC
Ptolemy V Epiphanes	204-180 BC
Ptolemy VI Philometor	180-145 BC
with Ptolemy VIII Euergetes II and Cleopatra	170-164 BC
with Cleopatra II	163-145 BC
Ptolemy VIII Euergetes II (restored)	145-116 BC
Cleopatra III and Ptolemy IX Soter II (Lathyrus)	116-107 BC
Cleopatra III and Ptolemy X Alexander I	107-101 BC
Ptolemy X Alexander I and Cleopatra Berenice	101-88 BC
Ptolemy IX Soter II (restored)	88-81 BC
Cleopatra Berenice and Ptolemy XI Alexander II	80 BC
Ptolemy XII Neos Dionysus (Auletes)	80-58 BC
Berenice IV (at first with Cleopatra Tryphaena)	58-56 BC
Berenice IV and Archelaus	56-55 BC
Ptolemy XII Neos Dionysus (restored)	55-51 BC
Cleopatra VII Philopator	51-30 BC

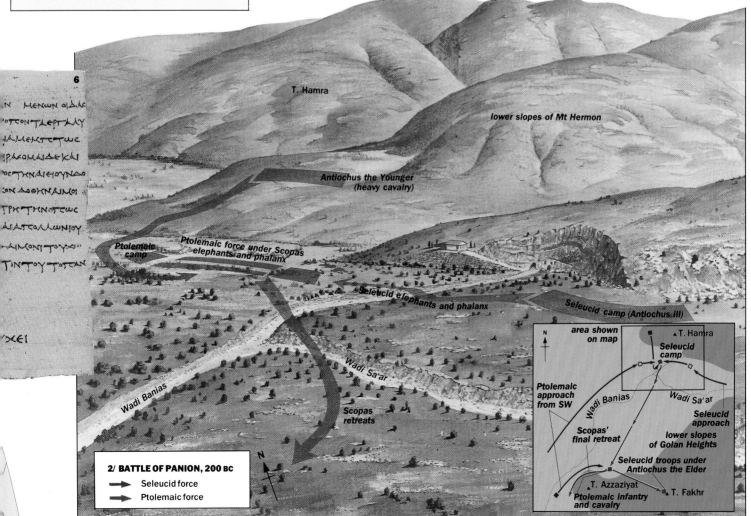

2/ BATTLE OF PANION, 200 BC

→ Seleucid force
→ Ptolemaic force

T. Hamra

lower slopes of Mt Hermon

Antiochus the Younger (heavy cavalry)

Ptolemaic camp

Ptolemaic force under Scopas elephants and phalanx

Seleucid elephants and phalanx

Seleucid camp (Antiochus III)

Wadi Banias

Wadi Sa'ar

Scopas retreats

area shown on map

Seleucid camp

T. Hamra

Ptolemaic approach from SW

Wadi Banias

Wadi Sa'ar

Scopas' final retreat

Seleucid approach lower slopes of Golan Heights

Seleucid troops under Antiochus the Elder

T. Azzaziyat

T. Fakhr

Ptolemaic infantry and cavalry

THE empire's first capital was the newly founded Seleucia on the Tigris; but Seleucus' political interests were in the west, where his main rival, Antigonus the One-eyed, aimed to reunite and rule Alexander's empire. In 301 BC, Seleucus and his son Antiochus together with Lysimachus of Thrace and Cassander of Macedon allied against Antigonus and his son Demetrius Poliorcetes. Seleucus, with 64,000 infantry, 10,500 cavalry, 400 elephants, and 120 chariots, aiming at conquest of west and southern Anatolia, was blocked by Antigonus with 70,000 infantry, 10,000 cavalry, but only 75 elephants at Ipsus. Antigonus was killed and his son Demetrius fled to Ephesus. The centre of the Seleucid empire now shifted west, and Seleucus moved his capital west, first to the port of Seleucia Pieria and then to Antioch on the Orontes in Syria.

THE EASTERN EMPIRE

The eastern empire was the Seleucid burden. In 308-3 BC Seleucus yielded the eastern provinces of Arachosia and Gedrosia to Chandragupta of India in exchange for 300 elephants. Bactria, however, well settled with Macedonian colonists and Hellenistic cities, and linked to the west by a good road, remained Seleucid until 250 BC, when it gained independence under Diodotus. In 247 BC the less Hellenized Parthia seized independence, but by 205 BC had lost it again to Antiochus III. However, after Antiochus' humiliation by the Romans in the Treaty of Apamea (188 BC), the Seleucids were unable to hold the east. Antiochus IV (166-5 BC; 1 MACC 3.30-37; 6.1-16), Demetrius II (141 BC; 1 MACC 14.1-2) and Antiochus VII (129 BC) all tried and failed to regain Parthia, whose king, Mithridates II (124-87 BC) welcomed ambassadors from China.

THE WESTERN EMPIRE

The Seleucids were equally unsuccessful in the west. They never controlled Armenia, Cappadocia, Pontus and Bithynia. They met opposition from the Galatians, from the growing states of Pergamum and Rhodes, from the Romans in Greece, and from the Ptolemies along the Mediterranean coasts. The Seleucids were effectively limited to Cilicia and Syria. The acquisition of Coele-Syria, Palestine and Transjordan after the battle of Panion (200 BC) was a major Seleucid success. Antiochus IV's anxiety to secure Judah as a buffer towards Egypt was probably a major factor in his reaction to the Maccabaean rebellion (pages 98-99).

SELEUCID ADMINISTRATION

The Seleucid rulers were of Macedonian origin; the subjects included both city-dwellers and nomads between the Aegean and India. The empire was divided into satrapies and eparchies. A

3/ Seleucus, a Macedonian general and satrap of Babylon, established rule over the eastern part of Alexander's empire in 312 BC, thus founding the Seleucid dynasty (table below left). He was one of the first commanders to realize the importance of elephants in battle, and they were an important factor in the victory at Ipsus in 301 BC.

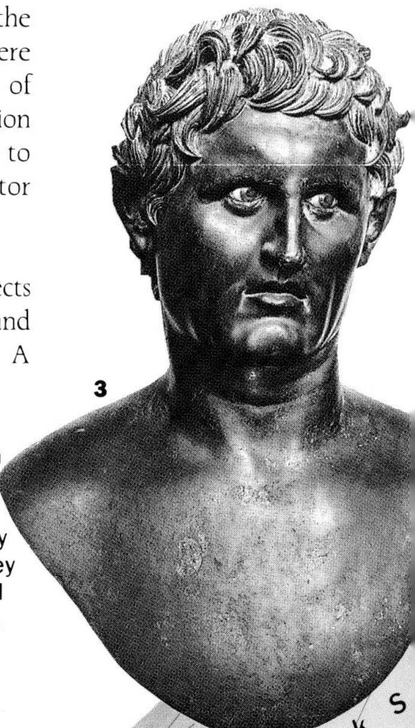

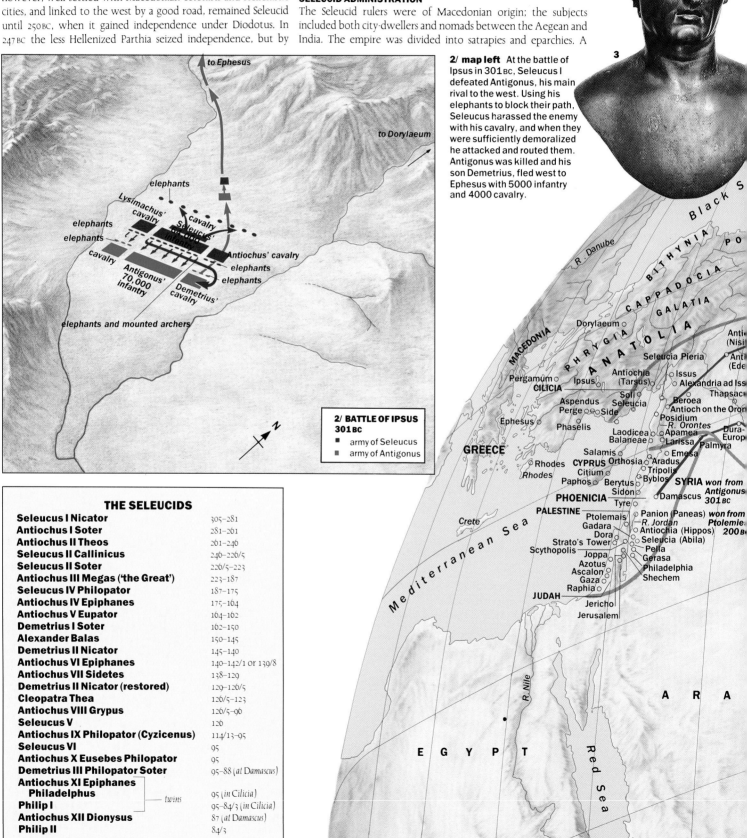

2/ map left At the battle of Ipsus in 301 BC, Seleucus I defeated Antigonus, his main rival to the west. Using his elephants to block their path, Seleucus harassed the enemy with his cavalry, and when they were sufficiently demoralized he attacked and routed them. Antigonus was killed and his son Demetrius, fled west to Ephesus with 5000 infantry and 4000 cavalry.

2/ BATTLE OF IPSUS 301 BC
- army of Seleucus
- army of Antigonus

THE SELEUCIDS

Seleucus I Nicator	305–281
Antiochus I Soter	281–261
Antiochus II Theos	261–246
Seleucus II Callinicus	246–226/5
Seleucus III Soter	226/5–223
Antiochus III Megas ('the Great')	223–187
Seleucus IV Philopator	187–175
Antiochus IV Epiphanes	175–164
Antiochus V Eupator	164–162
Demetrius I Soter	162–150
Alexander Balas	150–145
Demetrius II Nicator	145–140
Antiochus VI Epiphanes	140–142/1 or 139/8
Antiochus VII Sidetes	138–129
Demetrius II Nicator (restored)	129–126/5
Cleopatra Thea	126/5–123
Antiochus VIII Grypus	126/5–96
Seleucus V	126
Antiochus IX Philopator (Cyzicenus)	114/13–95
Seleucus VI	95
Antiochus X Eusebes Philopator	95
Demetrius III Philopator Soter	95–88 (at Damascus)
Antiochus XI Epiphanes Philadelphus	95 (in Cilicia)
Philip I	95–84/3 (in Cilicia)
Antiochus XII Dionysus	87 (at Damascus)
Philip II	84/3

(Antiochus XI Epiphanes Philadelphus and Philip I marked as twins)

Map labels: to Ephesus, to Dorylaeum, elephants, Lysimachus' cavalry, cavalry, Seleucus' infantry, elephants, elephants, cavalry, Antiochus' cavalry, Antigonus' 70,000 infantry, Demetrius' cavalry, elephants, elephants, elephants and mounted archers, N

Map labels (right): Black S, R. Danube, BITHYNIA, PO, CAPPADOCIA, GALATIA, MACEDONIA, PHRYGIA, ANATOLIA, Dorylaeum, Anti (Nisi), Seleucia Pieria, Anti (Ede), Pergamum, Antiochia (Tarsus), Issus, CILICIA, Ipsus, Alexandria ad Iss, Aspendus, Soli, Thapsac, Perge, Side, Seleucia, Beroea, Ephesus, Phaselis, Posidium, Antioch on the Oron, R. Orontes, Dura-Europ, Laodicea, Apamea, GREECE, Balaneae, Larissa, Palmyra, Salamis, Emesa, Rhodes, CYPRUS, Orthosia, Aradus, Citium, Tripolis, Rhodes, Paphos, Berytus, Byblos, SYRIA won from Antigonus 301 BC, Sidon, PHOENICIA, Damascus, Tyre, PALESTINE, Ptolemais, Panion (Paneas) won from Ptolemie, Crete, Gadara, R. Jordan, Dora, Antiochia (Hippos), Ptolemie 200 B, Strato's Tower, Seleucia (Abila), Scythopolis, Joppa, Pella, Azotus, Gerasa, Ascalon, Philadelphia, Mediterranean Sea, Gaza, Shechem, Raphia, JUDAH, Jericho, Jerusalem, A R A, R. Nile, EGYPT, Red Sea, A R A

20° 25° 30° 35° 40°

1/ map below The Seleucid empire was founded in 312 BC by Seleucus I. The capital was moved from Babylon to Antioch on the Orontes in 300 BC. Seleucus inherited the full extent of Alexander's eastern conquests, but Arachosia, Gedrosia, Bactria and Parthia were successively lost to the Seleucids. Antiochus III 'the Great' temporarily restored Seleucid control of Parthia. The Seleucids, however, were more interested in the west, but were checked by the rising power of Rome, which prevented Antiochus III from seizing Greece (189 BC) and Antiochus IV from seizing Egypt (169-168 BC).

major feature was the settlement of Macedonian soldiers into colonies, which developed into cities. New towns, usually with names taken from Macedonia (Larissa, Beroea) or from the Seleucid royal family (Antiochia, Laodicea), gave the king more direct control than the older, independent cities, with which to conclude an 'alliance' to proclaim the virtues of democracy and freedom. Temple cities also had a certain independence and the right of asylum (*cf.* Jerusalem, 1 MACC 10.43). The Seleucid aim was to make cities loyal to the crown, and so hold the empire together by peaceful rather than military means.

THE ARMY AND NAVY

The Seleucid army was composed of heavy infantry (originally drawn from Macedonian colonists) and local groups of light infantry and cavalry. The navy operated in the Mediterranean from Seleucia and Ephesus, and in the Persian Gulf. The Seleucid empire, however, never looked solid. Its eastern borders were too far from Antioch, its Greek colonists too insecure. From the mid-2nd century BC the Seleucids were under pressure from the Parthians and Armenians, east and north, and from Rome in the west. The empire fell to Rome with Pompey's arrival in 64 BC.

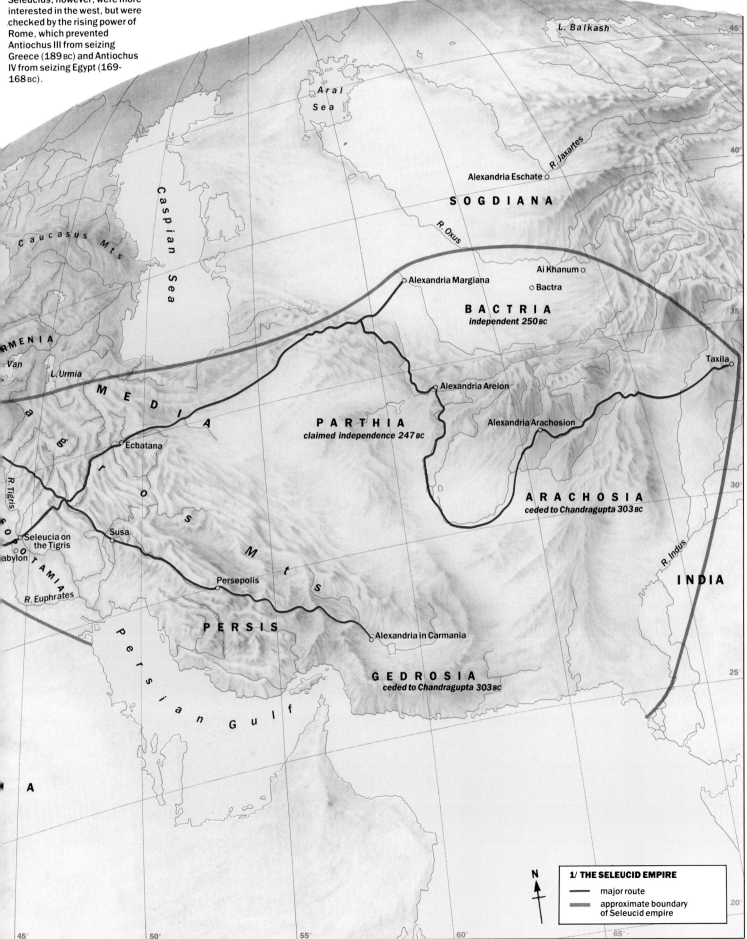

1/ THE SELEUCID EMPIRE

—— major route

—— approximate boundary of Seleucid empire

WHEN in 200 BC the Seleucids took Judah from the Ptolemies, some Jews may have preferred to remain under Egyptian rule, some may have fought for Judah's independence (cf. DAN 11.14), but most Jews probably welcomed the tax concessions and the freedom for them to live in accordance with the traditional Jewish Law granted by Antiochus III. Some Jews were in fact anxious to bring Judah into the cultural context of Hellenism via the Seleucid empire (1 MACC 1.11 portrays these as 'lawless men' who 'misled many'). Their political ambitions, coupled with Antiochus IV's ambition to rule Egypt, and the Seleucid need of money to pay off Roman war indemnities, combined to compel Judah from peace to civil war and direct Seleucid rule within a decade of Antiochus IV's accession in 175 BC.

The trouble began when Seleucus IV attempted to raise money by robbing the Jerusalem Temple (2 MACC 3). The high priest Onias resisted the attempt, but was deposed by his brother Jason, who offered Antiochus IV increased tribute in exchange for the high priesthood for himself and Greek city status for Jerusalem. Jason was soon similarly ousted by the priest Menelaus, but when Jason tried to regain his position by force, Antiochus (smarting from his recent eviction from Egypt by the Romans) saw this as rebellion, attacked Jerusalem and pillaged the Temple. There followed (autumn 167 BC) Antiochus' decree proscribing Jewish sacrifices, sabbath observance, circumcision, and the Jewish Law, and enforcing Gentile forms of cult (1 MACC 1.41-61); according to 2 MACC 6.2, the Temple was rededicated to Olympian Zeus. Antiochus thus cancelled the concession allowing Jews to govern themselves by their own Law, and made the Jerusalem Temple open to Gentiles, with their unclean offerings, as well as to Jews. The Jews saw this as religious persecution; Antiochus probably saw it as the political control of unruly subjects. Clearly, the ensuing Maccabean revolt was caused not so much by Hellenization of Judah as by the increasingly heavy-handed Seleucid treatment of Jewish opposition to the cynical misuse of the high-priesthood, both by Jews and Seleucids, for political ends.

THE MACCABEAN REBELLION

The Maccabees came from Modin, a village north-west of Jerusalem. The rebellion began when they killed a Jewish official as he committed an act of apostasy. The Maccabees had some initial success, killing the governor of Samaria as he led a small force against them, and ambushing a larger force in the pass of Beth-horon. In 165 BC the Maccabean leader, Judas, defeated a larger Seleucid army at Emmaus, and in Dec. 164 BC (just as Antiochus died) Judas seized the Temple area. The area was purged of its gentile cult and rededicated. In 162 BC Judas attacked the Seleucid garrison in Jerusalem, but Lysias, Antiochus V's vice-regent, invaded Judah, took Beth-zur, defeated Judas at Beth-zechariah (map 2), and besieged Judas' troops in turn, in the Temple. A threatened coup in Syria forced Lysias to abandon the siege; he repealed the decree of 167 BC, executed Menelaus but dismantled the Maccabean defences at the Temple and left the Syrian garrison in control of Jerusalem.

In 161 BC the new Seleucid king, Demetrius, appointed a new high priest, Alcimus, and a new general, Nicanor, who after initial attempts at peace was killed at Adasa (161-160 BC); Judas himself was killed at the battle of Elasa (160 BC). The new general, Bacchides, garrisoned the land effectively (1 MACC 9.50-53) but failed to defeat or capture Judas' successor Jonathan, who, after the death of Alcimus, was the only credible Jewish leader surviving.

TOWARDS INDEPENDENCE

Jonathan now bargained with successive contenders for the Seleucid throne to win political concessions. In 152 BC he supported the pretender Alexander Balas in return for the high-priesthood (to which he had no hereditary right). When Jonathan defeated Demetrius II in 147 BC Balas rewarded him with new honours and new territory, but on Balas' death (145 BC) Jonathan promptly allied with Demetrius II, acquiring thereby three Samaritan districts and their revenues. When Demetrius II was ousted by Balas' son, Antiochus VI, and his guardian Trypho, Jonathan maintained his position and with his brother Simon proceeded by various conquests to consolidate the Jewish position. This Jewish resurgence alarmed Trypho, who captured Jonathan treacherously at Ptolemais. Simon, however, took over the leadership, and continued to develop Judah's political and military strength, culminating in the expulsion of the Seleucid garrison from Jerusalem (141 BC). He renewed diplomatic relationships established earlier with Rome (1 MACC 8.17-32; 12.1-4) and Sparta (1 MACC 12.5-23), and negotiated the formal abolition of tribute with

Demetrius II. 1 MACC 13.41 notes that in 142 BC 'the yoke of the gentiles was removed from Israel, and the people began to write in their documents and contracts, "In the first year of Simon, the great high priest, commander and leader of the Jews"'.

The principal sources for the history of the Maccabean rebellion are 1 MACCABEES and 2 MACCABEES. These two books describe events from differing standpoints, 1 MACC emphasizing the political and military history and the importance of the Hasmonaean family, while 2 MACC underlines religious motivation. 1 MACC was originally written in Hebrew, perhaps in the reign of John Hyrcanus; 2 MACC was written in Greek, probably a little later. These books witness to the Hasmonaean understanding of the importance of the Maccabean rebellion for the future history and religion of the Jews.

1/ map below After the Maccabees' early campaigns against the Seleucids, their strategy changed under the leadership of Jonathan. Political manoeuvre worked where military action had been unsuccessful and Jonathan and his brother, Simon, were able to consolidate the Jewish position, culminating in 141 BC with the expulsion of the Seleucid garrison from Jerusalem.

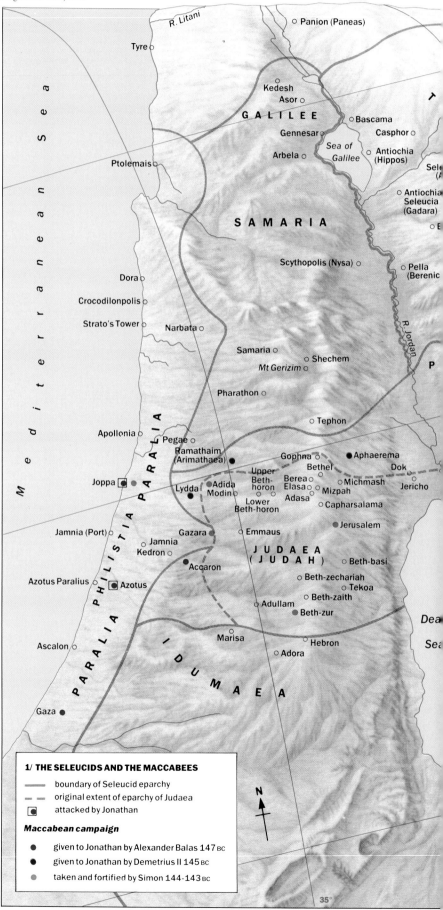

1/ THE SELEUCIDS AND THE MACCABEES

— boundary of Seleucid eparchy

-- original extent of eparchy of Judaea

▣ attacked by Jonathan

Maccabean campaign

● given to Jonathan by Alexander Balas 147 BC

● given to Jonathan by Demetrius II 145 BC

● taken and fortified by Simon 144-143 BC

THE MACCABEES

Judas ben Mattathias	died 166 BC
Judas the Maccabee	160 BC
Jonathan (high priest)	143 BC
Simon (high priest)	134 BC
John Hyrcanus I (high priest)	104 BC
Aristobulus I (high priest)	103 BC
Alexander Jannaeus (high priest)	76 BC
Alexandra Salome	67 BC
Aristobulus II	49 BC
Hyrcanus II (high priest)	30 BC
Antigonus	37 BC

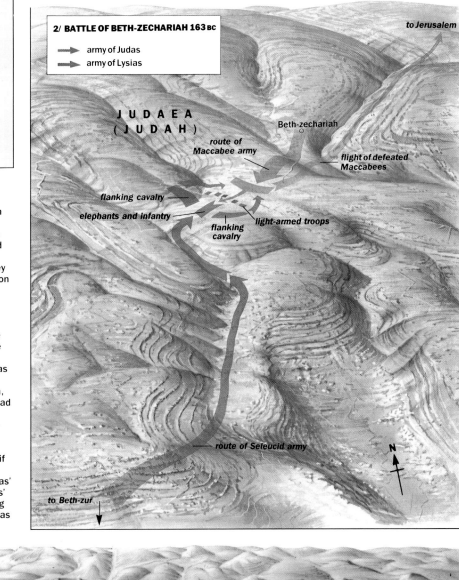

2/ BATTLE OF BETH-ZECHARIAH 163 BC
→ army of Judas
→ army of Lysias

2/ map right In 163 BC the Seleucid general, Lysias, with Antiochus V, campaigned against Judas Maccabaeus in Judaea. Lysias' elephants and infantry marched as a column through the centre of the valley protected by flanking cavalry on the hillsides and light-armed troops in front. Judas' troops attacked the heavy infantry phalanx head-on but were defeated by the cavalry on the high ground and forced to flee to Jerusalem and beyond.

3/ map below In 160 BC Judas camped at Elasa, and Bacchides faced him at Berea, half a mile away. Bacchides had 20,000 infantry and 2000 cavalry. Judas' army is said to have suffered loss of morale, his original 3000 men being reduced by desertion to 800; if so, his defeat of Bacchides' right wing is astonishing. Judas' men were pursuing Bacchides' army when the Syrian left wing swung round in their rear. Judas was among those killed.

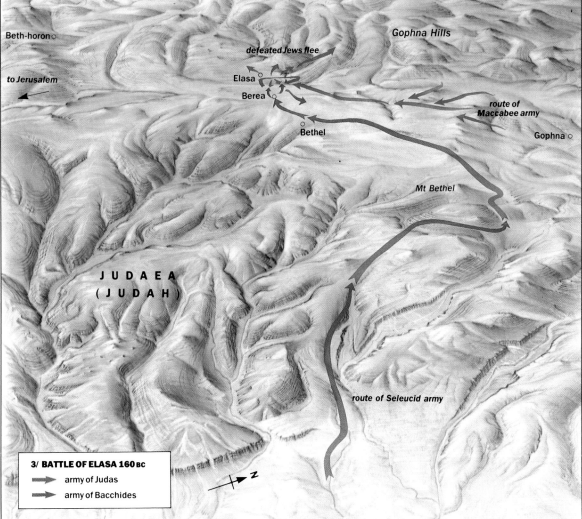

3/ BATTLE OF ELASA 160 BC
→ army of Judas
→ army of Bacchides

UNDER Simon, in the 170th year of the Seleucid era (142 BC), 'the yoke of the gentiles was removed from Israel' (I MACC 13.41), and the first year of a new era began. From now until the arrival of the Romans (63 BC) the Jews were free to develop their own independent state. The main features of the period are the final emancipation from Seleucid rule, the expansion of Judah's territory, the development of a monarchy, and opposition to this development.

Demetrius II (145-40 BC) exempted Judah from tribute (I MACC 11. 30-37), thus granting virtual independence, and Antiochus VII (138-29 BC) even granted Simon the right to mint coins (I MACC 15. 1-9). Antiochus soon reverted to hostility, however, demanding the return of disputed territory and attacking Simon. After Simon's death (134 BC) he successfully besieged Simon's son John Hyrcanus in Jerusalem, forcing from him hostages and tribute. In 129 BC, Antiochus died fighting the Parthians (129 BC) and thereafter the Seleucids were no threat to Judah.

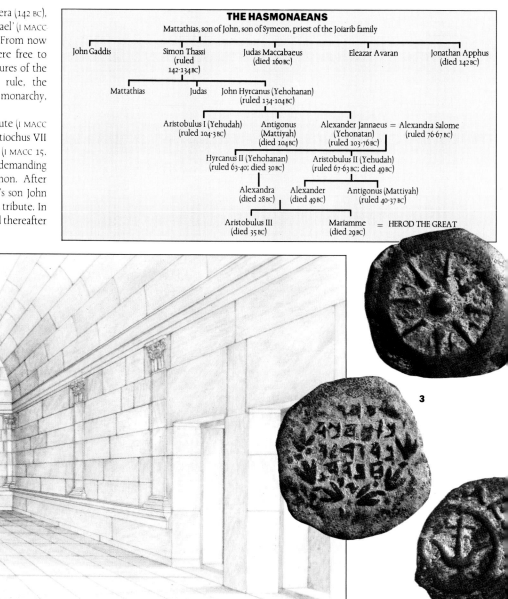

THE HASMONAEANS

Mattathias, son of John, son of Symeon, priest of the Joiarib family

John Gaddis — Simon Thassi (ruled 142-134 BC) — Judas Maccabaeus (died 160 BC) — Eleazar Avaran — Jonathan Apphus (died 142 BC)

Mattathias — Judas — John Hyrcanus (Yehohanan) (ruled 134-104 BC)

Aristobulus I (Yehudah) (ruled 104-3 BC) — Antigonus (Mattiyah) (died 104 BC) — Alexander Jannaeus (Yehonatan) (ruled 103-76 BC) = Alexandra Salome (ruled 76-67 BC)

Hyrcanus II (Yehohanan) (ruled 63-40; died 30 BC) — Aristobulus II (Yehudah) (ruled 67-63 BC; died 49 BC)

Alexandra (died 28 BC) — Alexander (died 49 BC) — Antigonus (Mattiyah) (ruled 40-37 BC)

Aristobulus III (died 35 BC) — Mariamme (died 29 BC) = HEROD THE GREAT

3

2/ THE MASONIC HALL

The Seleucid collapse gave Judah the opportunity to expand. Jonathan had already won some territory in the coastal region (Paralia) and Samaria (I MACC 10.30, 89; 11.28, 34), and Simon had annexed Gazara and Joppa (I MACC 10.76; 13.11; 14.5). Judah's expansion over the next 50 years is easily traced. Along the coast, Hyrcanus took Apollonia, Jamnia and Azotus, to which Jannaeus added Strato's Tower (the later Caesarea) and Dora to the north and Anthedon, Gaza, Raphia and Rhinocolura towards Egypt. Inland, to the north, Hyrcanus took Samaria in two stages, first defeating the people and destroying their temple on Mount Gerizim near Shechem, and later (108 BC) capturing the cities of Samaria and Scythopolis. This opened the way for Aristobulus (103 BC) to take Galilee and attack the Ituraeans further north. To the south, Hyrcanus invaded Idumaea, forcibly Judaizing the people (with the unexpected result that a century later an Idumaean, Herod, reigned in Jerusalem). This invasion threatened the Nabataeans (page 108), whose trading ambitions reached from Petra to the Mediterranean via Gaza, and to Syria via the Transjordan. Jannaeus cut Nabataean access to the Mediterranean by destroying Gaza; the route to Syria was cut when Hyrcanus seized Medeba and Jannaeus annexed towns in southern Moabitis and in Galaaditis, Gaulanitis and Syria to the north. However, the Nabataean, Obodas I, defeated Jannaeus in Gaulanitis c 93 BC, and his successor Aretas III took possession of Coele-Syria and Damascus in 85 BC. In 63 BC the Nabataeans aided Hyrcanus against Aristobulus, until forced home by the Romans. The location of forts at Alexandrium, Hyrcania, Masada and Machaerus reveals Jannaeus' concern for his southern and eastern borders.

In 142 BC Simon had been appointed high priest, military commander and civil ruler, offices inherited by his son Hyrcanus in 134 BC. If the coins inscribed 'Yehohanan the high priest and the congregation of the Jews' belong to Hyrcanus I, not Hyrcanus II, they show that he ruled as high priest, not as a king, a title which

first appears on coins of Jannaeus (103-76 BC) with the bilingual inscription 'Jonathan the king' (Hebrew) and 'King Alexander' (Greek). By the terms of Jannaeus' will, his wife Alexandra Salome succeeded him. Debarred as a woman from priesthood, she appointed her son Hyrcanus high priest. When she died, he succeeded, but almost immediately resigned his inheritance to his brother Aristobulus (67 BC). When Pompey removed Aristobulus (63 BC), he left Hyrcanus as high priest, without royal powers. It seems that only Jannaeus put 'king' on his coins.

The Hasmonaeans ruled with difficulty. Simon was assassinated and Hyrcanus I was opposed by the Pharisees, who objected to his high-priesthood. (The Maccabees and Hasmonaeans had no hereditary high-priestly rights, and Jonathan's assumption of the office in 152 BC probably caused the Qumran sect to call him 'the Wicked Priest'.) Later when Jannaeus presided as high priest at the feast of Tabernacles, he was pelted with citrons; his response was a massacre which led to civil war. The Pharisees enlisted the Seleucid Demetrius III against Jannaeus, who later revenged himself by crucifying 800 opponents and killing their families. On his deathbed he advised his wife Alexandra to make her peace with the Pharisees, which she did. After her death, her ambitious younger son, Aristobulus, forced his older brother, Hyrcanus, to resign the throne and the high-priesthood, but the even more ambitious Idumaean Antipater tried to re-establish Hyrcanus as his puppet with the help of Nabataean Aretas III, and they besieged Aristobulus in the Temple. Meanwhile the Romans under Pompey had taken over Syria, and both parties appealed to him. Pompey eventually supported Hyrcanus, successfully besieged Aristobulus in the Temple, paraded him in triumph in Rome, and left Hyrcanus as high priest (but not king). The Hasmonaean attempt to combine kingship and high-priesthood in one person contributed to the failure of Judah's brief period of independence in the midst of centuries of foreign rule.

1/map right The Hasmonaeans (see chart above) expanded Judah's territory considerably. Hyrcanus captured surrounding cities in Samaria, Idumaea and Ammonitis. Aristobulus was able to strike north into Galilee, and Jannaeus consolidated the kingdom by extending Judaean control down to the southern end of the Dead Sea and by building fortresses at strategic locations on the southern and eastern borders.

2/above left The Masonic Hall is one of the most beautifully preserved stone constructions of the late Hellenistic period in Jerusalem. The interior measures 60 x 85 ft and it is part of a system of underground chambers west of Wilson's Arch in Jerusalem. The Masonic Hall takes its name from the Masons, who for many years used it as a meeting place in the belief that it had been used for arcane religious rites in the days of Solomon.

3/above The first coins of the independent kingdom of Judah were struck by Hyrcanus, or, according to some scholars, by Jannaeus.

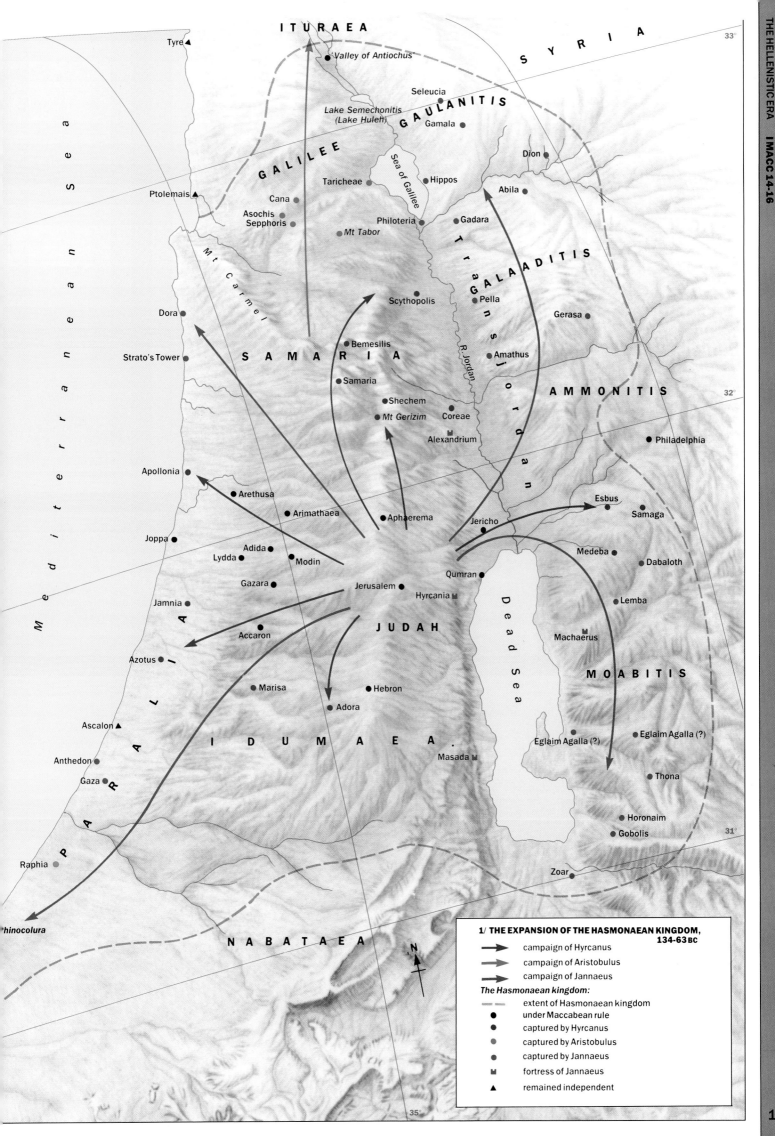

ITURAEA

Tyre ▲

SYRIA

33°

'Valley of Antiochus'

Seleucia

GAULANITIS

Lake Semechonitis
(Lake Huleh)

Gamala

Dion

GALILEE

Taricheae

Sea of Galilee

Hippos

Abila

Cana

Philoteria

Gadara

Asochis
Sepphoris

Mt Tabor

TRANSJORDAN

GALAADITIS

Scythopolis

Pella

Dora

Gerasa

Mt Carmel

SAMARIA

Bemesilis

Amathus

Strato's Tower

Samaria

AMMONITIS

32°

Shechem

Mt Gerizim

Coreae

Philadelphia

Alexandrium

Apollonia

Arethusa

Esbus

Samaga

Arimathaea

Aphaerema

Jericho

Medeba

Joppa

Dabaloth

Adida

Qumran

Lydda

Modin

Lemba

Gazara

Jerusalem

Hyrcania 🏰

Jamnia

JUDAH

Dead Sea

Accaron

MOABITIS

Azotus

Marisa

Hebron

Machaerus 🏰

Adora

Ascalon ▲

IDUMAEA

Eglaim Agalla (?)

Eglaim Agalla (?)

Anthedon

Masada 🏰

Thona

Gaza

Horonaim

Gobolis

31°

Raphia

Zoar

hinocolura

NABATAEA

N

Mediterranean Sea

PARALIA

R. Jordan

1/ THE EXPANSION OF THE HASMONAEAN KINGDOM,
134-63 BC

→ campaign of Hyrcanus

→ campaign of Aristobulus

⇒ campaign of Jannaeus

The Hasmonaean kingdom:

– – – extent of Hasmonaean kingdom

● under Maccabean rule

● captured by Hyrcanus

● captured by Aristobulus

● captured by Jannaeus

🏰 fortress of Jannaeus

▲ remained independent

WHEREAS the Greek monarchies had partitioned the Eastern Mediterranean, the west had remained under the sway of several powerful city-states. By the end of the 3rd century BC, one of these – Rome – gradually expanded its power over all of Italy and surrounding regions and confronted its chief rival in the west, Carthage. After the Third Punic War (146 BC), Rome was left master in the west and began to establish a provincial system to control its far-flung holdings.

Rome's conquests and trading interests brought increasing diplomatic interests in the east. Most notably Achaea (167 BC) and Macedonia (148 BC) became Roman provinces as a result of the Carthaginian Hannibal's association (202-197 BC) with the Greek rulers, including the Seleucid monarch Antiochus III, who had been defeated in 190 and pushed out of western Asia Minor. Rome thereby gained a foothold in Asia Minor by serving as protector of the client kingdom of Pergamum. When the last Attalid ruler of Pergamum died in 133 BC, its territories were bequeathed to Rome and were reconstituted as the Province of Asia. Gradually, much of the east came under Roman provincial organization through similar diplomatic measures. Rome's policy was to weaken the strong powers and to enlist the favour of local rulers who might be allied to Rome. Thus, in 168 BC Rome had interceded by forcing the Seleucid Antiochus IV to retire from his campaign on Ptolemaic Egypt. This intervention probably had an impact in Judah at the beginning of the Maccabean revolt.

POMPEY'S EASTERN SETTLEMENT

During the first century BC Rome faced new resistance in the east as the Seleucid power waned. Mithridates VI, king of Pontus, had formed an alliance through marriage with Tigranes of Armenia. Together they sought to expand their territories, with Mithridates raiding western Asia Minor and the Aegean while Tigranes moved into Syria, reaching Damascus (72 BC), before the Roman Lucullus pushed them back into Armenia (69 BC).

In 67 BC a new crisis faced Rome when pirates from Cilicia threatened to disrupt the corn fleets from Egypt. The Senate granted 'extraordinary' powers to the general Pompey, who pressed on the victories of Lucullus. He consolidated power in Asia Minor and forced Armenia to sue for peace. He then marched on Syria, reaching Damascus in 64 BC. Pompey formed a line of provinces along the coastline of Asia Minor and around to Syria. Beyond this, allied kingdoms with the status of *clientela* served as buffer states. Local rulers became 'client-kings' and were diplomatically termed 'friends' (*amici*) or 'allies' (*socii*) of Rome.

Judaea, too, came under Pompey's control. Just as Pompey was moving from Asia Minor into Syria, the Hasmonaean state fell into a civil war (page 100). To ensure peace, Pompey reorganized Palestine and deposed Aristobulus II in favour of Hyrcanus II, who ruled as High Priest and Ethnarch from 64-40 BC. The extensive Hasmonaean state, however, was reduced to three areas: Judaea (including Idumaea), Galilee and Peraea. Samaria was partitioned as a separate client state, while the territories of Chalcis and Nabataea had powerful trading interests in the east (page 108).

JUDAEA DURING THE ROMAN CIVIL WAR

The contest for power between Pompey and Julius Caesar further strained the old Republican political structure. Pompey's victories were matched by Caesar's conquests in Gaul, which became a province in 49 BC. In the following year Pompey was killed in Egypt by Ptolemy XIII. Julius Caesar, pursued to Alexandria, avenged Pompey's death, and began his fateful encounter with Ptolemy's sister, Cleopatra VII. Julius Caesar was assassinated (44 BC) by Republican sympathizers, who in turn were defeated by Marc Antony and Caesar's nephew, Octavian. Finally, Antony and Octavian fell out, with Antony seceding to Egypt and Cleopatra. In 31 BC Octavian defeated the forces of Antony and Cleopatra and by 27 BC had claimed for himself the title of Augustus, in Greek *Sebastos*, Emperor of Rome.

During this time of unrest and factionalism, the client-king of Judah, Hyrcanus, employed as his chief adviser a prince called Antipater. At the right moment, they switched allegiance from Pompey to Caesar and were duly rewarded. Following the nomination of Marc Antony, Antipater's son, Herod, was declared 'King of Judaea' by the Senate in 37 BC. When the political wind shifted yet again, Herod sided with Octavian against Antony and Cleopatra. As a result of this 'loyalty' Octavian confirmed and rewarded Herod as client-king, thus producing the new Jewish state that existed under the early Roman empire.

1/ map below In the 2nd century BC Rome was at war on every front. To the west as a result of the wars with Carthage, she gained the provinces of Spain (Hispania) in 197 BC and Africa in 146 BC. In the east Roman legions defeated the Seleucids in 190 BC, and Macedonia and Asia were annexed in 148 BC and 133 BC. Under Sulla Lucullus and Pompey, the Romans gradually defeated the princedoms of Asia Minor and extended their control of Bithynia, Pontus Cilicia, Syria, Crete and Cyprus.

2/ map right The decline of Seleucid rule had allowed the Hasmonaean Jewish state under Jannaeus (103-76 BC) to expand. In 64 BC the Roman general Pompey and his successor Gabinius reduced the kingdom to Judaea, Galilee and Peraea, and allowed the 20 or so Greek cities which Jannaeus had captured to become independent. Under Gabinius (57-55 BC) a short-lived attempt was made to divide up the Jewish state yet further into five *synedria* (districts).

3/ map far right Herod became king of Judaea in 40 BC, and soon found favour with Augustus. He was given back Gaza and the coastal cities which had been ceded to Cleopatra. In later years Herod's kingdom included Batanaea, Gaulanitis, Trachonitis and Auranitis as rewards for his loyalty to Rome

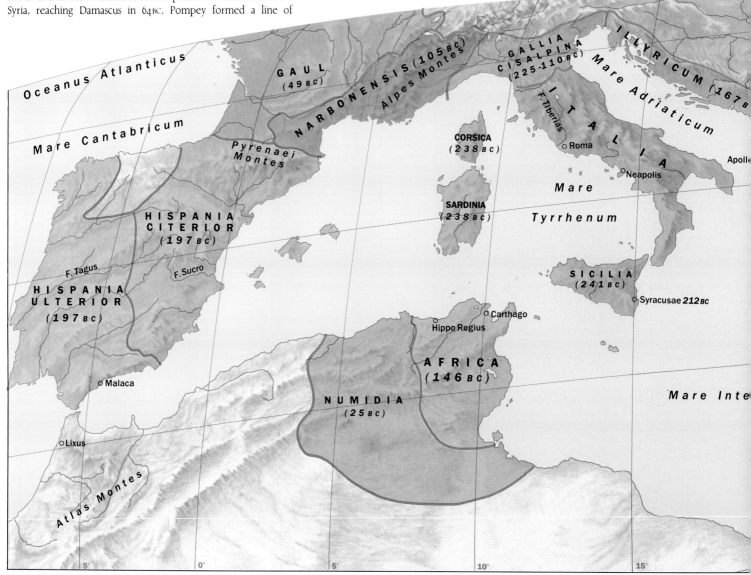

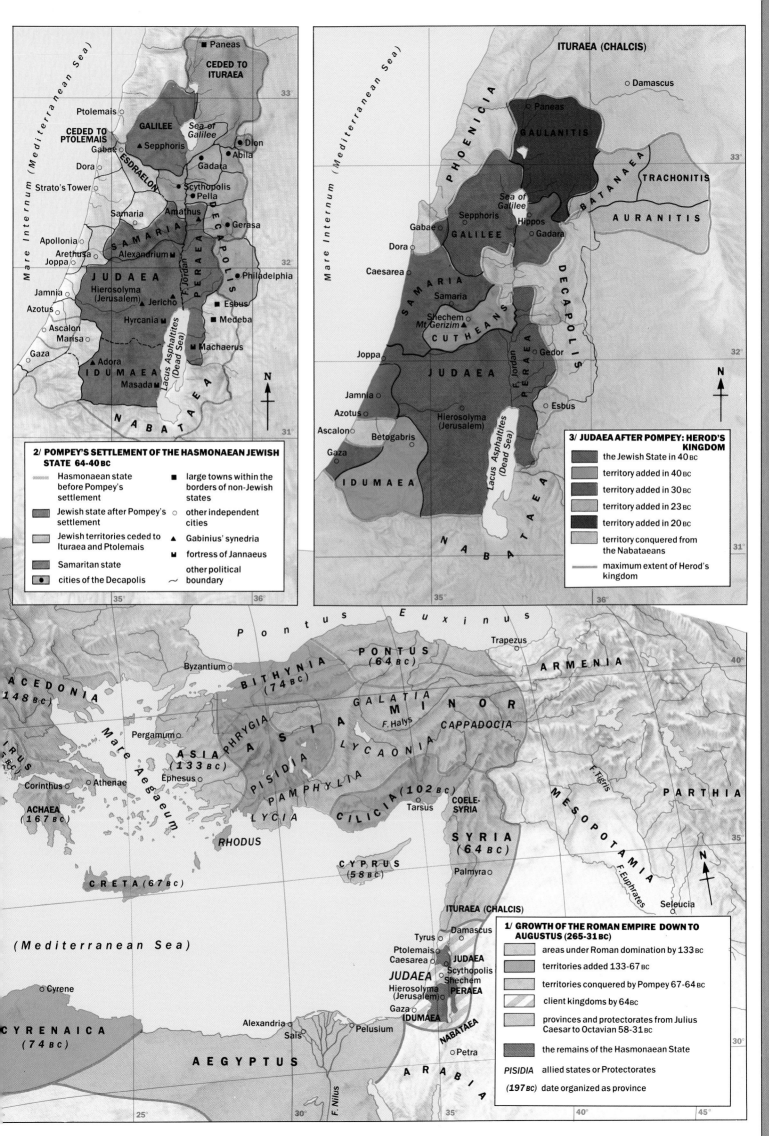

Map 2 (top left)

Paneas ■

CEDED TO ITURAEA

CEDED TO PTOLEMAIS

Mare Internum (Mediterranean Sea)

33

GALILEE
▲ Sepphoris
Sea of Galilee
Ptolemais ○
Gabae ○
Dora ○
● Dion
● Abila
Strato's Tower ○
ESDRAELON
● Gadara
● Scythopolis
● Pella
Samaria ○
Amathus ▲
SAMARIA
Apollonia ○
Arethusa ○
Joppa ○
Alexandrium ▥
● Gerasa
DECAPOLIS
JUDAEA
PERAEA
F. Jordan
32
Jamnia ○
Hierosolyma (Jerusalem) ▲
▲ Jericho
● Philadelphia
Azotus ○
Hyrcania ▥
■ Esbus
Ascalon ○
Marisa ○
■ Medeba
Lacus Asphaltites (Dead Sea)
▲ Machaerus
Gaza ○
▲ Adora
IDUMAEA
Masada ▲
NABATAEA
N

2/ POMPEY'S SETTLEMENT OF THE HASMONAEAN JEWISH STATE 64-40 BC

- ∿∿∿ Hasmonaean state before Pompey's settlement
- (hatched) Jewish state after Pompey's settlement
- (light) Jewish territories ceded to Ituraea and Ptolemais
- (dark) Samaritan state
- ●○ cities of the Decapolis
- ■ large towns within the borders of non-Jewish states
- ○ other independent cities
- ▲ Gabinius' synedria
- ▥ fortress of Jannaeus
- ∿ other political boundary

Map 3 (top right)

ITURAEA (CHALCIS)

○ Damascus

Mare Internum (Mediterranean Sea)

PHOENICIA
● Paneas
GAULANITIS
33
BATANAEA
TRACHONITIS
Sea of Galilee
Sepphoris ○
Hippos ○
GALILEE
● Gadara
AURANITIS
Gabae ○
Dora ○
DECAPOLIS
Caesarea ○
SAMARIA
Samaria ○
Shechem ○
Mt. Gerizim ●
CUTHEANS
● Gedor
32
Joppa ○
PERAEA
F. Jordan
JUDAEA
Jamnia ○
Azotus ○
Hierosolyma (Jerusalem) ○
■ Esbus
Ascalon ○
Betogabris ○
Lacus Asphaltites (Dead Sea)
Gaza ○
IDUMAEA
NABATAEA
31
N

3/ JUDAEA AFTER POMPEY: HEROD'S KINGDOM

- the Jewish State in 40 BC
- territory added in 40 BC
- territory added in 30 BC
- territory added in 23 BC
- territory added in 20 BC
- territory conquered from the Nabataeans
- maximum extent of Herod's kingdom

Map 1 (bottom)

Pontus Euxinus
Trapezus ○
Byzantium ○
BITHYNIA (74 BC)
PONTUS (64 BC)
ARMENIA
MACEDONIA (148 BC)
PHRYGIA
GALATIA
ASIA MINOR
CAPPADOCIA
Pergamum ○
ASIA (133 BC)
F. Halys
EPIRUS
Athenae ○
Ephesus ○
PISIDIA
LYCAONIA
PARTHIA
Corinthus ○
Mare Aegaeum
PAMPHYLIA
ACHAEA (167 BC)
LYCIA
CILICIA (102 BC)
COELE-SYRIA
Tarsus ○
RHODUS
F. Tigris
MESOPOTAMIA
SYRIA (64 BC)
CYPRUS (58 BC)
Palmyra ○
35
CRETA (67 BC)
F. Euphrates
Seleucia ○
ITURAEA (CHALCIS)
(Mediterranean Sea)
Tyrus ○
Damascus ○
Ptolemais ○
Caesarea ○
JUDAEA
Cyrene ○
JUDAEA
Scythopolis ○
Shechem ○
PERAEA
Hierosolyma (Jerusalem) ○
Gaza ○
IDUMAEA
Alexandria ○
NABATAEA
Sais ○
Pelusium ○
CYRENAICA (74 BC)
AEGYPTUS
Petra ○
F. Nilus
ARABIA
30

1/ GROWTH OF THE ROMAN EMPIRE DOWN TO AUGUSTUS (265-31 BC)

- areas under Roman domination by 133 BC
- territories added 133-67 BC
- territories conquered by Pompey 67-64 BC
- client kingdoms by 64 BC
- provinces and protectorates from Julius Caesar to Octavian 58-31 BC
- the remains of the Hasmonaean State
- *PISIDIA* allied states or Protectorates
- *(197 BC)* date organized as province

HEROD the Great, and his brother Phasael, were the sons of Antipater, the Idumaean who had risen to prominence under Hyrcanus II (64-40 BC). Antipater had been instrumental in brokering alliances throughout the region, to ensure the stability of Judaea. He had interceded with Pompey to install Hyrcanus II as king and high priest of Judaea over and against his rival Aristobulus II. Antipater had further orchestrated the political manoeuvring of Judaea over to Julius Caesar and as a result gained great favours. Hyrcanus II retained the title of high priest, but Antipater was named procurator (governor), and he named his sons *strategoi* ('commanders'). However, there was continuing unrest in the Hasmonaean realm. Within a year of Julius Caesar's death in 44 BC, Antipater had been assassinated by supporters of Aristobulus II. In 42 BC Marc Antony designated Phasael and Herod as tetrarchs ('rulers') over Judaea and Galilee respectively. In 41 BC Antigonus, the son of Aristobulus II, enlisted the help of Parthian armies to besiege Jerusalem, where he captured and disfigured Hyrcanus II. In the meantime, Phasael had been captured and executed. Antigonus then claimed the titles king and high priest (40-37 BC).

In Galilee Herod escaped and made his way to Rome. Once there Herod was introduced to the Senate by Antony and Octavian and was made King of Judaea. Herod thus returned to Judaea with a mandate and military support from Rome to pacify the region and expel the Parthians. By 37 BC Herod had captured all of Judaea (with Idumaea), Samaria, Peraea, and Galilee. The Galilee campaign had involved a particularly bloody resistance led by Hasmonaean partisans from Sepphoris (Josephus, *Antiquities* 14.416-430). Antigonus was captured and executed along with 45 Sadducean priests who had supported him. In the meantime, Herod had married the Hasmonaean princess Mariamne, grand-daughter of both Hyrcanus II and Aristobulus II, while her brother, Aristobulus III, was eliminated (page 100). This tie to the Hasmonaean line, along with the patronage of Rome, helped secure his power.

ORGANIZATION OF HEROD'S KINGDOM

From 37-27 BC Herod set about consolidating his kingdom (page 103, map 3). When Marc Antony assumed control over the east, Herod was forced to cede several territories to Cleopatra, including Ituraea and Nabataea along with the city-territories of Jericho, Gaza, Joppa, Gabae, and Sebaste (Samaria). These territories were eventually returned to Herod in 30 BC by Octavian, after Herod denounced Cleopatra in the wake of the battle of Actium (31 BC). Shortly thereafter the aged Hyrcanus II along with the remaining members of the Hasmonaean line, including Mariamne and her mother, were quietly eliminated on Herod's orders. As a result, Herod took possession of the vast Hasmonaean estates. In 23 BC Octavian, now the Emperor Augustus, conferred on Herod the territories of Batanaea, Trachonitis, and Auranitis, and in 20 BC Gaulanitis was added to his realm of Ituraea. Augustus saw in Herod's rule the chance to secure the region, with its strategic and profitable trade-routes, against Nabataean and Bedouin elements. With this,

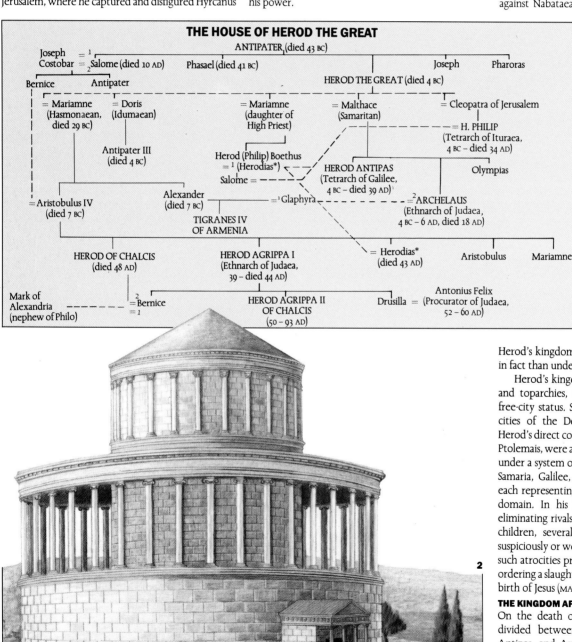

THE HOUSE OF HEROD THE GREAT

(Genealogical chart showing the descendants of Antipater, died 43 BC, including Joseph, Costobar, Salome (died 10 AD), Phasael (died 41 BC), Joseph, Pharoras, Herod the Great (died 4 BC); Bernice, Antipater; Mariamne (Hasmonaean, died 29 BC), Doris (Idumaean), Mariamne (daughter of High Priest), Malthace (Samaritan), Cleopatra of Jerusalem; Antipater III (died 4 BC); Herod (Philip) Boethus = 1 (Herodias*), Salome; H. PHILIP (Tetrarch of Ituraea, 4 BC – died 34 AD); HEROD ANTIPAS (Tetrarch of Galilee, 4 BC – died 39 AD), Olympias; Aristobulus IV (died 7 BC), Alexander (died 7 BC), Glaphyra, ARCHELAUS (Ethnarch of Judaea, 4 BC – 6 AD, died 18 AD); TIGRANES IV OF ARMENIA; HEROD OF CHALCIS (died 48 AD), HEROD AGRIPPA I (Ethnarch of Judaea, 39 – died 44 AD), Herodias* (died 43 AD), Aristobulus, Mariamne; Mark of Alexandria (nephew of Philo) = Bernice, HEROD AGRIPPA II OF CHALCIS (50 – 93 AD), Drusilla = Antonius Felix (Procurator of Judaea, 52 – 60 AD))

1/ map right Herod probably distinguished between the Greek cities, which possessed defined territories, and the Jewish areas, which he administered as toparchies. Most boundaries are known from 4th-century records and some may differ from Herod's time, as a number of cities were founded after his reign and that of his sons. On the other hand the administrative boundaries in Auranitis, Batanaea and Trachonitis are well authenticated by rabbinical sources or by Greek and Roman inscriptions.

2/ below left Two circular walls of curved ashlar blocks and *opus reticulatum* construction found north-west of the Damascus Gate of Jerusalem provide the basis for this reconstruction of a monument or mausoleum dated to the time of Herod.

Herod's kingdom reached its greatest extent, greater in fact than under the Hasmonaean kings.

Herod's kingdom was divided into city-territories and toparchies, regions without any settlement of free-city status. Some cities, such as Ascalon and the cities of the Decapolis, remained independent of Herod's direct control, while others, such as Gabae and Ptolemais, were autonomous. The rest were organized under a system of five meridarchies: Idumaea, Judaea, Samaria, Galilee, and Peraea. Herod had five wives, each representing alliances with major factions of his domain. In his later years Herod was ruthless in eliminating rivals for his throne, even among his own children, several of whom (like Mariamne's) died suspiciously or were executed for treason. Rumours of such atrocities probably contributed to the legend of ordering a slaughter of children around the time of the birth of Jesus (MATT 2.16).

THE KINGDOM AFTER HEROD

On the death of Herod in 4 BC, the kingdom was divided between his three surviving sons: Philip, Antipas, and Archelaus. Philip received Ituraea and Trachonitis (including Batanaea, Auranitis, and Gaulanitis); Antipas received Galilee and Peraea, while Archelaus received Judaea, Idumaea, and Samaria. Some city territories, such as Gabae, Hippos, Gadara, Gaza, and Esbus, were placed under direct Roman control by ceding them to the province of Syria. While Antipas and Philip had long and prosperous reigns in their respective tetrarchies, the reign of Archelaus was unsatisfactory in Judaea. In AD 6, Archelaus was removed from office and his territories placed under the direct Roman administration of a military procurator who answered to the Legate of Syria.

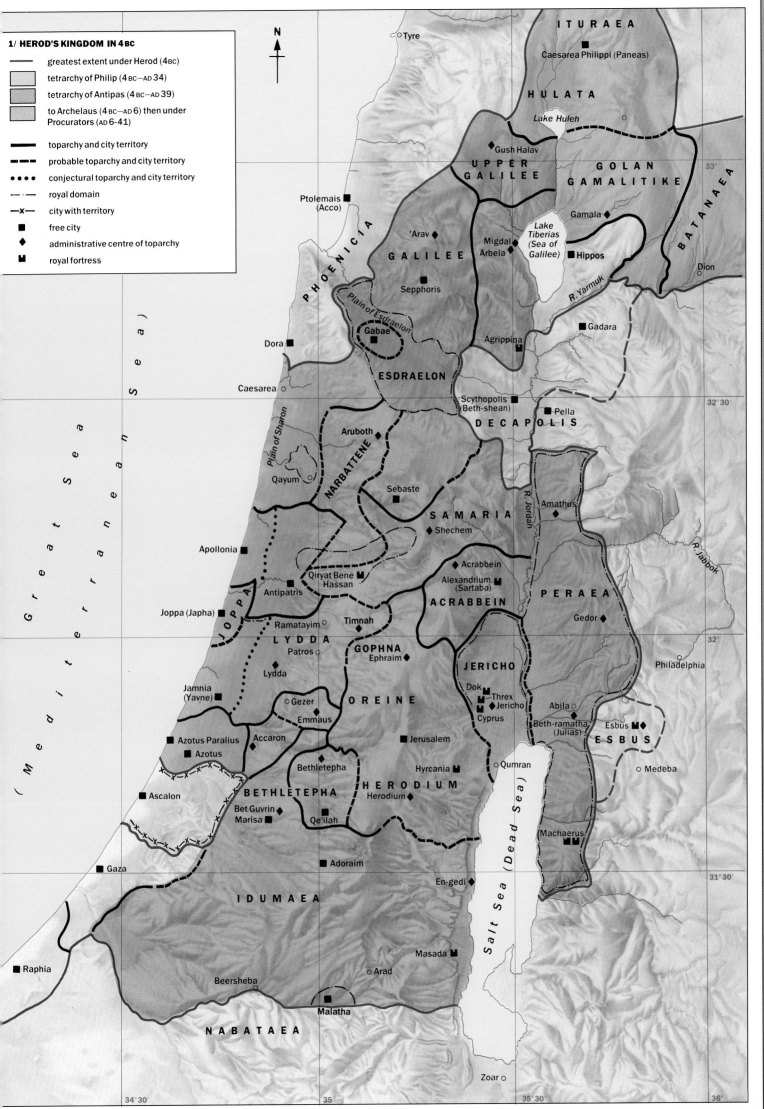

1/ HEROD'S KINGDOM IN 4 BC

— greatest extent under Herod (4 BC)

▨ tetrarchy of Philip (4 BC–AD 34)

▨ tetrarchy of Antipas (4 BC–AD 39)

▨ to Archelaus (4 BC–AD 6) then under
   Procurators (AD 6-41)

▬▬ toparchy and city territory

▬ ▬ probable toparchy and city territory

•••• conjectural toparchy and city territory

▬·▬ royal domain

—x— city with territory

■ free city

◆ administrative centre of toparchy

⬚ royal fortress

N

ITURAEA

○ Tyre

■ Caesarea Philippi (Paneas)

HULATA

Lake Huleh

◆ Gush Halav

UPPER GALILEE

GOLAN GAMALITIKE

BATANAEA

'Arav ◆

Migdal ◆ Gamala ◆

Arbela ◆ *Lake Tiberias (Sea of Galilee)*

GALILEE

○ Ptolemais (Acco)

■ Hippos

○ Dion

■ Sepphoris

R. Yarmuk

○ Dora

■ Gadara

Gabae ⬚

Plain of Esdraelon

Agrippina ◆

PHOENICIA

ESDRAELON

○ Caesarea

Scythopolis (Beth-shean) ■

DECAPOLIS

■ Pella

Plain of Sharon

Aruboth ◆

Amathus ◆

○ Qayum

NARBATTENE

Sebaste ■

R. Jordan

SAMARIA

Shechem ◆

R. Jabbok

■ Apollonia

Acrabbein ◆

Alexandrium (Sartaba) ⬚

PERAEA

Qiryat Bene Hassan ⬚

ACRABBEIN

■ Antipatris

JOPPA

Joppa (Japha) ◆

○ Ramatayim   Timnah ◆

LYDDA

GOPHNA

Ephraim ◆

Gedor ◆

Patros ○

○ Philadelphia

◆ Lydda

JERICHO

Jamnia (Yavne) ■

OREINE

Dok ⬚

Threx ⬚

○ Gezer   Emmaus ◆

Jericho ⬚

Cyprus ⬚

○ Abila

Esbus ⬚ ◆

■ Accaron

■ Jerusalem

Beth-ramatha (Julias) ⬚

ESBUS

■ Azotus Paralius

Bethletepha ◆

Hyrcania ⬚

○ Qumran

■ Azotus

Hyrcania ⬚

○ Medeba

■ Ascalon

BETHLETEPHA

HERODIUM

Herodium ◆

Bet Guvrin ◆

Marisa ■   Qe'ilah ◆

Salt Sea (Dead Sea)

Machaerus ⬚⬚

■ Adoraim

IDUMAEA

En-gedi ◆

■ Raphia

Masada ⬚

○ Arad

Beersheba ○

Zoar ○

Malatha ◆

NABATAEA

33°

32° 30'

32°

31° 30'

34° 30'   35°   35° 30'   36°

IN Jewish and Christian tradition Herod the Great is remembered with contempt due either to his role as Roman collaborator and puppet or to Gospel legends of his ruthless mania. However, Herod's reign was long and politically successful. He governed a large and diverse region and curried favour from many subjects, both Jewish and non-Jewish. The social and political unrest that characterized Judaea in the period of the two Jewish revolts (page 128), though often blamed on Herod, was really more the result of mismanagement on the part of his heirs or the Roman administration. Herod's success may be based in large measure on the degree of stability and economic growth that he generated in the region. Certainly, Herod ruled with an iron hand and tolerated no political unrest. As client-king responsible for collecting the state taxes due to Rome, he also became wealthy and created a civil bureaucracy in Judaea that could be inclined toward abuses. However, unlike its neighbours, Syria and Egypt, which became imperial provinces, the Judaean state remained a semi-autonomous client-kingdom through much of the 1st century AD, the legacy of Herod the Great. By virtue of his alliances through marriage and his statecraft as friend and benefactor well beyond his realm, he built a network of power for his Judaean state in the early Roman empire.

Herod, like his father Antipater, was an Idumaean,

a remnant of the Edomites, who in the Persian and Hellenistic periods had been pushed from the Negeb into southern Judah by the expanding Nabataean kingdom. In the Hasmonaean expansion of John Hyrcanus (134-104 BC) Idumaea was annexed to Judaea and its population was forcibly Judaized. Thus, Herod was socially and ethnically of mixed background, while a Jew in religion. This background must have influenced Herod's governance of his realm's diverse population, which included many non-Jews (goyim or 'gentiles') as well as other sub-ethnic groups, such as the Samaritans, Ituraeans or Galileans, whose Jewish lineage was likewise mixed during the Hellenistic period. Following the lead of his imperial benefactor, Augustus, Herod inaugurated a programme of royal bequests to these various groups and regions in order to ensure their loyalty. Chief among these bequests was an elaborate building programme in major cities, such as Jerusalem, Jericho and Masada. Herod also had other motivations of his own, including a taste for Roman style and luxury and a sense of strategic defence. Thus, in addition to many temples, civic buildings and public works projects, Herod built several palaces and fortresses for himself and his family.

JERUSALEM

At Jerusalem Herod took over and renovated the Hasmonaean palace and built a new palace on the western wall of the city (page 117). He further fortified

the walls of the city and added three defence towers (named Hippicus, Phasael and Mariamne) near the western palace. To the north of the Temple complex and near the pool of Bethzatha he built the fortress Antonia. All these royal apartments communicated through the temple complex itself by a series of porticoes or subterranean passages. Herod also refurbished the Hellenistic theatre and added a stadion or hippodrome. To ensure the water supply to the city he brought in Roman engineers to erect an aqueduct; fed from two springs south of Bethlehem, it ran through the city from the south-west, terminating at the Temple complex.

The most famous of Herod's projects was the rebuilding of the Temple itself, to replace the 'inglorious' structure built after the return from Babylon. The new Temple was built on a platform of massive quarried blocks, still visible at the so-called 'Wailing Wall' (the Kotel or 'Western Wall') and on the southern end of the Temple mound. The platform was surmounted on all sides by porticoes with Corinthian colonnades. The east colonnade, overlooking the Mount of Olives, was called Solomon's Portico (or 'porch'). The southern rampart overlooked the massive steps that led up through the Hulda Gates from the old city of David. Atop it stood the Royal Portico (or 'Basilica') with audience halls. The Temple complex, though overshadowed by the Antonia, towered over

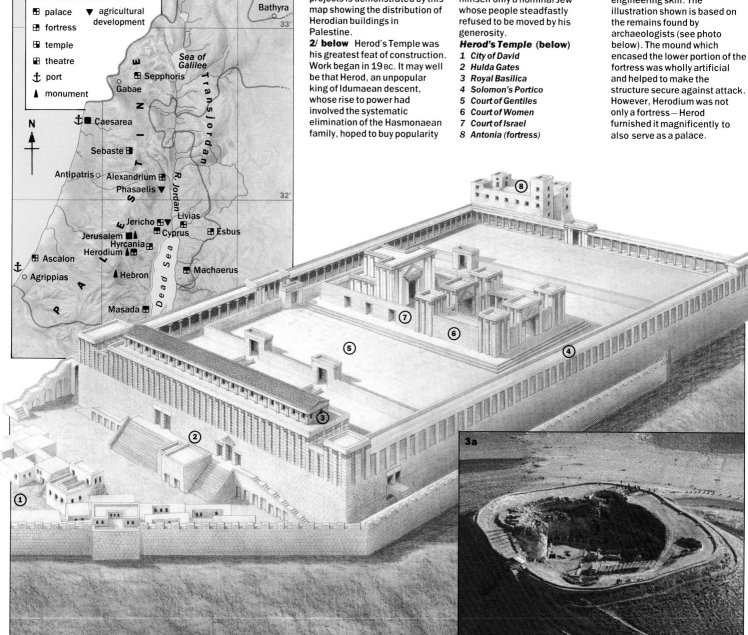

1/ **map left** The great variety and quantity of Herod's building projects is demonstrated by this map showing the distribution of Herodian buildings in Palestine.

2/ **below** Herod's Temple was his greatest feat of construction. Work began in 19 BC. It may well be that Herod, an unpopular king of Idumaean descent, whose rise to power had involved the systematic elimination of the Hasmonaean family, hoped to buy popularity

by providing a splendid temple for the Jews. However, he was himself only a nominal Jew whose people steadfastly refused to be moved by his generosity.

Herod's Temple **(below)**
1 *City of David*
2 *Hulda Gates*
3 *Royal Basilica*
4 *Solomon's Portico*
5 *Court of Gentiles*
6 *Court of Women*
7 *Court of Israel*
8 *Antonia (fortress)*

3/ **and 3a** The fortress of Herodium was a triumph of engineering skill. The illustration shown is based on the remains found by archaeologists (see photo below). The mound which encased the lower portion of the fortress was wholly artificial and helped to make the structure secure against attack. However, Herodium was not only a fortress – Herod furnished it magnificently to also serve as a palace.

1/ HEROD'S BUILDINGS
⊞ palace ▼ agricultural development
⊞ fortress
⊞ temple
⊞ theatre
‡ port
▲ monument

Paneas
Bathyra
Sea of Galilee
Sepphoris
Gabae
Caesarea
Sebaste
Antipatris
Alexandrium
Phasaelis
Jericho
Livias
Jerusalem
Cyprus
Esbus
Hyrcania
Herodium
Ascalon
Agrippias
Hebron
Machaerus
Masada
Transjordan
R. Jordan
Dead Sea

3a

2/ HEROD'S TEMPLE

the rest of the city and was reached from all sides by steps, stairs, bridges or ramps. In the open centre of the complex (called the 'Court of Gentiles') stood the Temple proper, which was enlarged and refurbished to include an outer court (the 'Women's Court') and an inner court (the 'Court of Israel'). It is indicative of the scale of this project that the Temple complex was constantly under construction for over 80 years (from c 19 BC to AD 64). While work on the sacred areas of the Temple itself was carefully supervised by the priests, huge numbers of construction workers found employment through Herod's largesse.

HEROD AS CIVIC BENEFACTOR

Through his benefactions to Jerusalem, Herod was concerned to show his support for Judaism and to make the Temple a showplace. He similarly adorned other traditional Jewish sites, as in the building of monumental enclosures for the tombs of the patriarchs at Hebron and nearby Mamre. In other areas of his domain, however, he showed equal care for local traditions. At Paneas (later called Caesarea Philippi), a Seleucid city located at one of the springs that feeds the River Jordan, Herod built a temple dedicated to the satyr Pan, the city's patron deity. At Samaria, which he rebuilt as Sebaste in honour of the Emperor, the Hellenistic city was enhanced with a huge Greek-style temple dedicated to Augustus, whose gleaming marble, according to Josephus, could be seen from the

sea, over 20 miles away. Herod also built pagan temples and public buildings in many cities both in his realm and outside, for example, in Sidon, Berytus (modern Beirut) and the cities of the Decapolis.

PALACES AND FORTRESSES

Among the most visible of Herod's engineering feats were his palaces and fortresses scattered throughout his lands, for example, the palaces at Sepphoris, the capital of Galilee. Other lavish Herodian palaces were built at Livias, in the free city of Ascalon, Herod's birth-place, and at Jericho (the so-called 'Winter Palace'). Herod's fortresses, usually built on strategic mountain locations are found at Alexandrium, Herodium, Machaerus and Masada. At Masada, and elsewhere, Herod made use of existing Hasmonaean construction and added an elaborate system of cisterns and storehouses. He then fortified the perimeter and built a small, self-contained city on the top of the mountain. At the northern end of Masada, overlooking the Dead Sea, a unique palace, with audience halls and thermal baths, was constructed on three natural rock terraces down the face of the cliff (page 128).

One of Herod's outstanding projects was the fortress named after him, the Herodium, where he was also to be buried. On the edge of the desert near the Dead Sea, the complex incorporated a summer palace with gardens and pools and the district capital for southern Judaea. At the centre of the complex was

a conical artificial mountain which was capped by a palatial multi-storied fortress with defence towers (as described by Josephus, WARS 1.419-421).

CAESAREA BY THE SEA

Other than Jerusalem itself, perhaps Herod's most ambitious project was the port and city at Caesarea Maritima (page 108). The small natural inlet had long been used and came to be known as Strato's Tower in Hellenistic times, but there was no adequate harbour for Roman shipping needs anywhere along Herod's coast. So, Herod commissioned the engineering of an artificial breakwater, similar to others from the Roman world. It was built by depositing large quarried blocks and a Roman technique of concrete construction down to a depth of c 37 metres to form a mole around the harbour entrance. The harbour itself was named Sebastos in honour of the Emperor, while the city proper was named Caesarea, in honour of Augustus' uncle. A temple dedicated to Roma and Augustus rose above the harbour at the entrance to the city. Other Herodian constructions at Caesarea included a theatre, amphitheatre, hippodrome, two aqueducts, Roman-style baths, warehouses, administrative buildings and a seaside palace. In Herod's day Caesarea was to be the trade centre with the rest of the Roman world. In subsequent years, it would also become the centre of the Roman provincial administration, the military command and capital for the procurators of Judaea.

defence tower

upper chambers (bedrooms)

peristyle courtyard (garden)

glacis (rampart)

sitting rooms

baths

stairs to palace grounds below

3/ FORTRESS OF HERODIUM

THE harbour at Caesarea became the gateway for an extensive shipping trade between the Near East and the rest of the world. From the east, caravans brought goods; incense from Dhofar, pearls from the Persian Gulf, silk from China, and spice and cotton from India, all found their way to Roman markets. The Roman taste for such exotic luxury items made both the camel caravans of the Nabataeans and efficient shipping indispensable in the Roman management of the east. But there was also a taste for things Roman in the provinces. Combined with the constant travel of soldiers and bureaucrats, trade and commerce from east and west linked the various parts of the Empire together. After Judaea came under procuratorial administration (in AD 6) Caesarea would serve as the provincial capital and military headquarters. Thus, the port at Caesarea was to serve through the Byzantine period as a major outpost of Roman culture in the east.

Analysis of pottery found in excavations of Caesarea reveal the extent of its contacts with the rest of the Roman world. Many goods were shipped in pots made near the point of production or the point of shipping. Often the exact claybed from which the pots were made can be identified. Ships from Italy came bearing foodstuffs and other goods packed in large red amphorae made near Pompeii. Other shipping amphorae found at Caesarea also came from Yugoslavia, Spain and the Aegean. They carried wine, olive oil, fish (or fish sauce) and grape syrup. Goods were off-loaded into the seaside warehouses (*horrea*) at Caesarea and were either parcelled out there or reloaded for shipment to other locations, such as Jerusalem. In turn, goods brought overland to Caesarea were packed in a local type of urn for shipping out to various parts of the Mediterranean.

Josephus notes that there was a substantial Jewish population in 1st-century Caesarea. Yet it was part of a cosmopolitan environment. Like any port city of the age, the landscape of the city bears the marks of both local and Roman culture, with theatre, hippodrome, marketplace and temples. In later centuries both a Jewish synagogue and a Christian church were built, but in the 1st century Caesarea was a cultural and religious melting-pot. The temple overlooking the harbour was dedicated by Herod to Roma and Augustus. The harbour itself was personified as the deity Sebastos who stands alongside the goddess Fortune (Tyche) of the city. Figures of most of the major deities of the Greek and Roman pantheon were found as well. Also found at Caesarea, though from later periods, were a statue of the Ephesian Artemis (page 127) and a sanctuary of the cult of Mithras. While Judaea was never a major province in the Roman empire, it served as an important crossroad in the administration of the eastern frontier.

THE NABATAEANS

Moving into the Negeb and the Wadi Arabah in the 4th century BC, the Nabataeans began to distinguish themselves as a force among the nomadic Arab clans of the region. They quickly adopted Aramaic language and were nominally under the Persian satraps, who allowed them to move further into the Syro-Palestinian and Sinai regions. After the conquests of Alexander the Great, they gradually developed a sedentary life by taking over the remnants of older Moabite and Edomite sites and building new cities in the desert through which they fostered an extensive caravan network. To support these isolated desert outposts highly developed water gathering and farming systems were invented which allowed them to exploit the resources of the Negeb.

The early Nabataean kings, beginning with Aretas I who ruled *c* 169 BC, during the time of the Seleucid Antiochus IV and the Maccabean revolt, seemed to have employed their strategic position between the Seleucid and Ptolemaic kingdoms to advantage. While sometimes allied with Hasmonaean interests (1 MACC 5.25, 9.35), they were often competitors, especially during the Hasmonaean expansion under Alexander Jannaeus. With the waning of Seleucid control the Nabataeans gradually took most of the province of Hauran, when, after killing the Seleucid Antiochus XII, Aretas III became king of Damascus. With the arrival of the Romans in 64 BC, however, the Nabataeans were once again pushed farther south for a time.

Both Antipater and Herod had extensive dealings with the Nabataean kings. Antipater had enlisted the aid of their king, Malichus, in favour of Hyrcanus, and he married a Nabataean woman, Kufra, the mother of Phasael and Herod the Great. Eventually, an alliance was formed when Herod's son Antipas (the future Tetrarch of Galilee) married the daughter of Aretas IV (9 BC–AD 40). Relations were strained once again when Antipas divorced her to marry Herodias, the event which also led to the fateful denunciations of John the Baptist. This same Aretas was the king of Damascus who attempted to arrest Paul (2 COR 11.32). Under Aretas IV Nabataean commerce and influence with Rome reached its zenith. Under Hellenistic and Roman influence the chief Nabataean god, Dushara, was identified with Dionysus while the goddess el-Uzza was identified with the syncretistic Attargatis. Finally, in AD 106 the Nabataean kingdom was reorganized into the Province of Arabia with Bostra as capital; it remained an important frontier to the Roman empire throughout the Byzantine period.

NABATAEAN TRADE AND COMMERCE

Much of the Nabataeans' wealth and power came from duties on the increasing caravan traffic through the Arabian peninsula and beyond the Persian Gulf. The Nabataeans also mined minerals on their own from the harsh terrain of the Arabian and Sinai peninsulas or collected bitumen from the Dead Sea and Arabah. By far their greatest asset was the network of caravan cities, ranging from Gaza and Rhinocolura on the Mediterranean coast to Al Jawf and Egra in the Arabian Desert and north to Bostra and Damascus. For a time, after Gaza was taken over by Herod, Oboda (modern 'Avedat) in the Negeb was the capital; it was built in honour of King Obodas II (30-9 BC), Herod's chief rival and the father of Aretas IV. Perhaps the most famous and spectacular Nabataean site is Petra, the city cut out of red rock. Petra, however, seems to have been more of a religious centre rather than commercial capital, as it lay several miles off the main trade route leading from Philadelphia to Aqaba. Most of the spectacular architecture was created for the rock-cut tombs of the Nabataean royalty.

FARMING AND IRRIGATION

The Nabataeans thrived in their harsh climate by successful management of their agricultural resources and by developing a sophisticated and efficient irrigation system. Seen from the air, many wadis resemble a staircase. In reality each step was created artificially by the construction of low stone retaining walls (*c* 2-2.5ft) to form a series of terraces spread some 40-50ft apart. The irrigation system works on the 'runoff' of rainwater not absorbed directly by the soil. The terrace walls catch some of the water and hold it so that it may be absorbed later. Excess water flows into the next lower terrace so more of the precious water can be retained and managed.

The Nabataeans also developed runoff farms, which used side retaining walls to create catchment areas around the terraced wadi. By gradually improving on the water catchment system the management and yield were significantly increased. In the runoff farm the terraces and side walls were about 5ft high, and a stepped spillway allowed for the runoff to lower areas. By piling up stones on the slopes of the wadi further collection could be attained. The ratio of catchment area to cultivated land was roughly 20:1, but it made possible substantial crop production in a climate with less than 4in of annual rainfall. Small farm settlements grew up around these terraced wadis, and documents from the Byzantine period indicate the major crops to include wheat, barley, figs, grapes, olives, almonds, pomegranates and dates.

2/ ROMAN CAESAREA

to Ptolemais

Mediterranean

Sebastos

Tetrapylon

Forum

Temple of Roma & Augustus

Mithraeum

Sea

Horrea

ornamental pool

theatre

to Joppa

1/ map right The Nabataeans made their living by taxing international trade caravans. The map shows the network of land and sea trade routes which covered the ancient Near East at that time. It also indicates the waxing and waning of Nabataean influence in the area over *c* 500 years.
2/ above Plan of Herod's harbour (Sebastos) and the Roman city of Caesarea.

3/ The Royal Tombs at Petra. One of the largest cemeteries in the ancient Near East, these rock-cut tombs form part of a complex cut into the cliffs to the east of the city. Some of the largest and most magnificent funerary monuments at Petra appear in this rock wall.
4/ Aerial view of the theatre at Caesarea, built by Herod the Great.

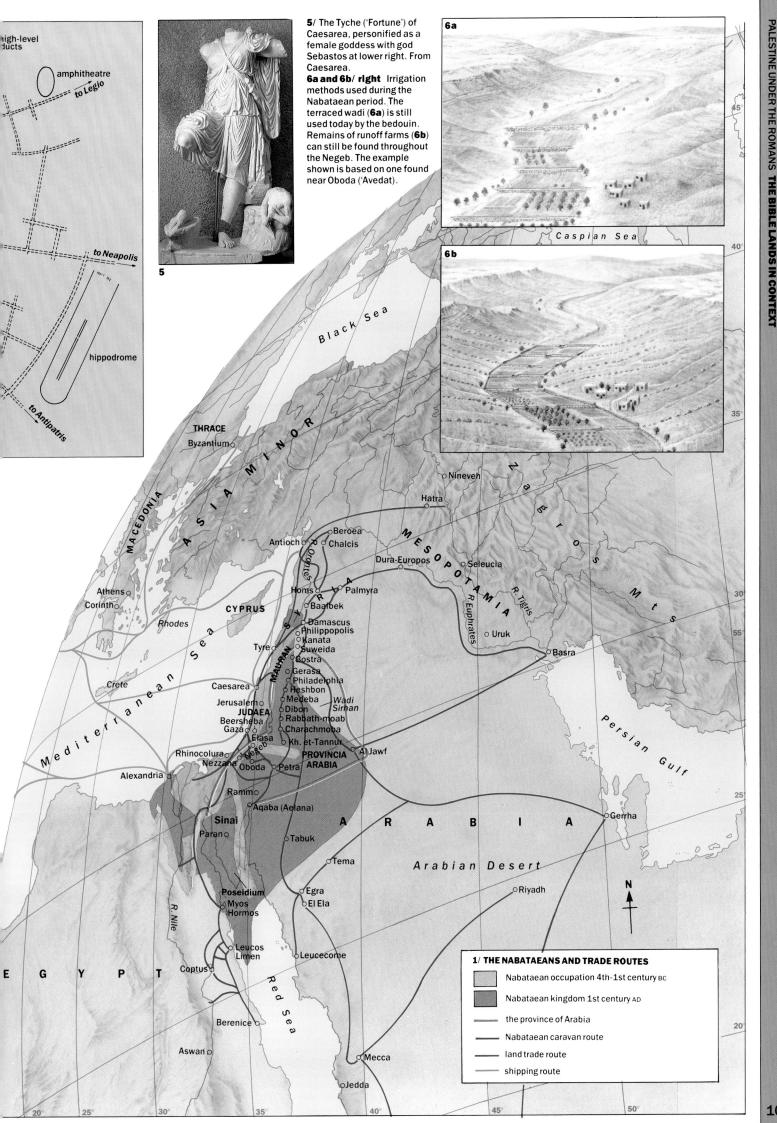

high-level
ducts

amphitheatre
to Legio

to Neapolis

hippodrome

to Antipatris

5/ The Tyche ('Fortune') of Caesarea, personified as a female goddess with god Sebastos at lower right. From Caesarea.
6a and 6b/ right Irrigation methods used during the Nabataean period. The terraced wadi (**6a**) is still used today by the bedouin. Remains of runoff farms (**6b**) can still be found throughout the Negeb. The example shown is based on one found near Oboda ('Avedat).

5

6a

6b

THRACE
Byzantium

MACEDONIA

ASIA MINOR

Black Sea

Caspian Sea

Nineveh

Hatra

Beroea
Antioch · Chalcis
Orontes
Dura-Europos · Seleucia
Homs · Palmyra
Baalbek
Damascus
Philippopolis
Kanata
Suweida
Bostra
Gerasa
Philadelphia
Heshbon
Medeba
Dibon
Rabbath-moab
Charachmoba
Kh. et-Tannur
Al Jawf

Athens
Corinth
Rhodes
CYPRUS
Crete
Tyre
Caesarea
Jerusalem
JUDAEA
Beersheba
Gaza
Elasa
Negeb
Rhinocolura
Nezzana
Oboda
Petra
PROVINCIA
ARABIA

MESOPOTAMIA
R. Euphrates
R. Tigris
Uruk
Basra

SYRIA
HAURAN
Wadi Sirhan

Zagros Mts

Mediterranean Sea

Persian Gulf

Alexandria

Ramm

Aqaba (Aelana)

Sinai

Paran

Tabuk

A R A B I A

Gerrha

Tema

Arabian Desert

Riyadh

N

EGYPT

Poseidium
Myos
Hormos

Egra
El Ela

R. Nile

Leucos
Limen
Coptus
Leucecome

Red Sea

Berenice

Aswan

Mecca

Jedda

1/ THE NABATAEANS AND TRADE ROUTES

Nabataean occupation 4th–1st century BC

Nabataean kingdom 1st century AD

the province of Arabia

Nabataean caravan route

land trade route

shipping route

IN 1947 a cache of scrolls was discovered in caves along the Wadi Qumran overlooking the Dead Sea and near the ruins of Khirbet Qumran. It has generally been concluded that it belonged to a 1st-century sect known as the Essenes. Although their origins are obscure, it appears that the Essenes split off from a conservative faction, known as the *Hasidim* (or 'pious ones') in the Maccabean revolt (1 MACC 2.42). They came from a priestly order who abandoned the temple after the Hasmonaean kings became high priests, sometime between 150 and 134 BC. The founder, probably a deposed Zadokite priest known as the Teacher of Righteousness, fled to the wilderness of Judah to fulfill the words of Isaiah (40.3), 'In the wilderness, prepare the way of the Lord'. They established the New Covenant to study the law night and day until the advent of two Messiahs: one a royal figure, called the Messiah of Israel; the other a priestly figure, called the Messiah of Aaron, who would restore the pure temple.

The sect went through several phases. Declining in the later Hasmonaean period, the settlement was abandoned after an earthquake (c 31 BC). Sometime after Herod there was a new phase of occupation and growth which lasted until the community was destroyed in AD 68, during the First Revolt (page 128). Other members of the sect probably lived in nearby farming settlements, while some documents suggest that there were enclaves living in distant towns that would gather periodically for a covenant renewal. The sect provided their own livelihood by herding or farming on the plain above the cliffs and at the nearby oasis of 'Ain Fashkha.

The scrolls reflect one of the major concerns of the religious life of the sect in 'studying the law night and day' (Rule of the Community 6.6-8). Among the scrolls were copies of all books of the Hebrew scriptures (with the exception of Esther), plus an extensive set of commentaries (called *pesharim*) on key prophetic texts. They also produced liturgical hymns for their communal worship. Information about their organization comes from several other scrolls that deal with community discipline (The Rule of the Community), the plan for the ideal temple (The Temple Scroll), and a plan for the eschatological battle (The War Scroll). The latter was taken very seriously, as the community was wiped out during the First Revolt. The settlement itself was burned, and eventually became a military camp (c AD 70-74). It is usually suggested that the scrolls, if not already stored in the caves, were hidden there in anticipation of this final confrontation.

1/ map right The settlement at Khirbet Qumran was founded by a religious sect known as the Essenes, who broke off from Jerusalem sometime during the early Hasmonaean period (c 150-134 BC). Excavations revealed an extensive community at Qumran itself, and there were several nearby farming settlements at 'Ain Fashkha and 'Ain Ghuweir that may have supplied the community.
2/ Part of the Isaiah Scroll, written on leather and hidden by the Essenes to protect it from the Roman advance in AD 68.
3/ Aerial view of Qumran. Excavation has shown that it was a very complex settlement. The discovery of the Dead Sea Scrolls illustrate how much emphasis the Essenes put on the study of Scripture, and archaeologists have uncovered a large 'scriptorium' at Qumran complete with bronze inkwells.

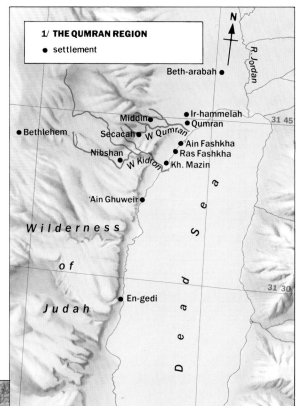

1/ THE QUMRAN REGION
● settlement

AFTER Herod's death his kingdom was divided among his three sons, but Judaea was under rule of a Roman military procurator who answered to the Legate of the province of Syria from AD 6-37 (page 104). The First Revolt (AD 66-70) would precipitate major changes in the administration of the provinces, which continued into the 4th century.

PROVINCIA JUDAEA

After the First Revolt Judaea was reorganized as an independent province under a governor of higher rank (*legatus Augusti pro praetore*), with headquarters at Caesarea Maritima. A full legion, initially the Tenth Fretensis which had served during the revolt, was assigned to the province and stationed at Jerusalem. Much of the area of Trachonitis was ceded to Agrippa II, while most of the region of the Decapolis was ceded directly to the province of Syria. In AD 106 Trajan organ-ized the remainder of the Nabataean kingdom into the Provincia Arabia.

Under Emperor Vespasian (AD 69-79) and later under Hadrian (AD 117-138) a new programme of 'urbanization' was begun in the north, partly in recognition that many of the free cities had not supported the Jewish revolt. As these city territories were organized a growing class of provincial aristocrats and merchants helped in the administration through the collection of taxes. Vespasian restored Gabae, Apollonia, Antipatris (Pegae), Joppa (Flavia Joppe), Jamnia (Jabneh), Azotus (Ashdod), and, in Galilee, Sepphoris and Tiberias as autonomous, self-governing city-territories. Sebaste (Samaria) was reconstituted as Flavia Neapolis. Jerusalem remained the legionary headquarters until Hadrian reconstituted the city as Aelia Capitolina (at the start of the Second Revolt).

PROVINCIA SYRIA PALAESTINA

During the Second Revolt (AD 132-135) Roman control was disrupted for a short time as a new state, with its capital at Jerusalem, was established by Bar Kokhba (page 129). After the revolt was put down the Emperor Hadrian proceeded with his plans to reconstitute Jerusalem as a Roman colony called Aelia Capitolina and dedicated to Capitoline Jupiter. At this time the provincial administration was upgraded to the highest consular rank as Provincia Syria Palaestina and assigned two legions. One legion (the Sixth Ferrata) was assigned to the Valley of Jezreel with headquarters at Capercot-nei. Subsequently the entire region, which became veterans' lands (*campus maximus legions*), was known as Legio, from which comes the modern name Lejjun.

Emperor Septimius Severus (AD 193-211) furthered 'urbanization' in the south by advancing the district

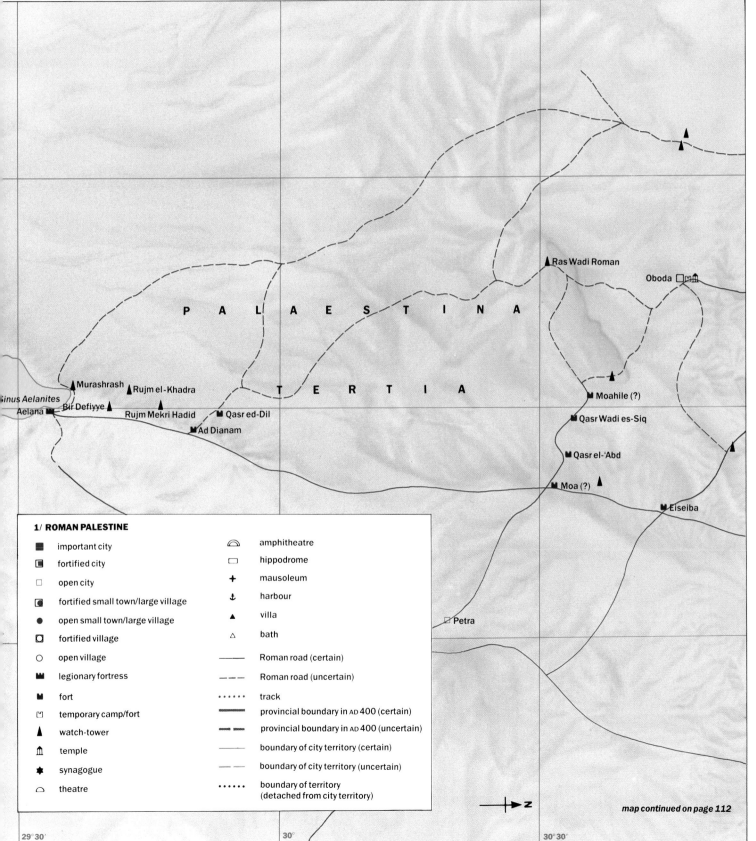

P A L A E S T I N A

T E R T I A

Ras Wadi Roman

Oboda

Murashrash
Rujm el-Khadra
Sinus Aelanites
Aelana
Bir Defiyye
Rujm Mekri Hadid
Qasr ed-Dil
Ad Dianam

Moahile (?)
Qasr Wadi es-Siq
Qasr el-'Abd
Moa (?)
Eiseiba

Petra

1/ ROMAN PALESTINE

■ important city	⌒ amphitheatre
▣ fortified city	▭ hippodrome
☐ open city	✚ mausoleum
◪ fortified small town/large village	⚓ harbour
● open small town/large village	▲ villa
⬕ fortified village	△ bath
○ open village	
㎭ legionary fortress	—— Roman road (certain)
◪ fort	--- Roman road (uncertain)
⌘ temporary camp/fort	⋯⋯ track
▲ watch-tower	━━ provincial boundary in AD 400 (certain)
🏛 temple	━ ━ provincial boundary in AD 400 (uncertain)
✦ synagogue	—— boundary of city territory (certain)
⌒ theatre	— — boundary of city territory (uncertain)
	⋯⋯ boundary of territory (detached from city territory)

→ N

map continued on page 112

29°30'   30'   30°30'

of Idumaea (including En-gedi) to city status under the name Eleutheropolis and the district of Lydda and Thamna under the name Diospolis. Meanwhile, after a revolt under the Legate of Syria, Severus reorganized and subdivided the province of Syria. The districts of Phoenicia, including the coastal cities from Tyre to Ptolemais and Dora, which had previously been under Syria were now made a separate province of Phoenicia. Eventually the coastal region was designated Phoenicia Prima, while the interior region, with its capital at Damascus, was designated Phoenicia Libanensis. In AD 220-221 the Emperor Heliogabalus promoted Emmaus to the city-territory of Nicopolis, and thus the entire province of Syria Palaestina (except for some imperial estates in the Jordan valley and in Upper Galilee known as Tetracomia) had been transformed into a net of larger and smaller city-territories.

THE THREE PALESTINES OF THE LATER EMPIRE

Emperor Diocletian (AD 284-305) reorganized the provinces of the entire Roman empire into four prefectures, which were divided into dioceses and subdivided by provinces. The province of Palaestina fell under the Diocese of the Oriens (along with Syria, Phoenicia and Osrhoene) in the prefecture of the East (which also included the Dioceses of Aegyptus, Pontus, Asiana, and Thracia). Diocletian established a strip of military territory called the Limes Palaestina along the southern border of Idumaea with the old Nabataean territories, previously part of Provincia Arabia. During this period Provincia Arabia was further developed in its urban centres while reinforced with military garrisons against the eastern frontier, the Limes Arabicus. About AD 358 the region south of Idumaea was reorganized and added to the province as Palaestina Salutaris, with its capital at Petra. Eventually, it was called Palaestina Tertia, after the remainder of the province was subdivided into a southern and northern district as Palaestina Prima (with a capital at Caesarea Maritima) and Palaestina Secunda (with a capital at Scythopolis), respectively. This organization of the region remained essentially intact throughout the Byzantine period and down to the time of the Arab conquests.

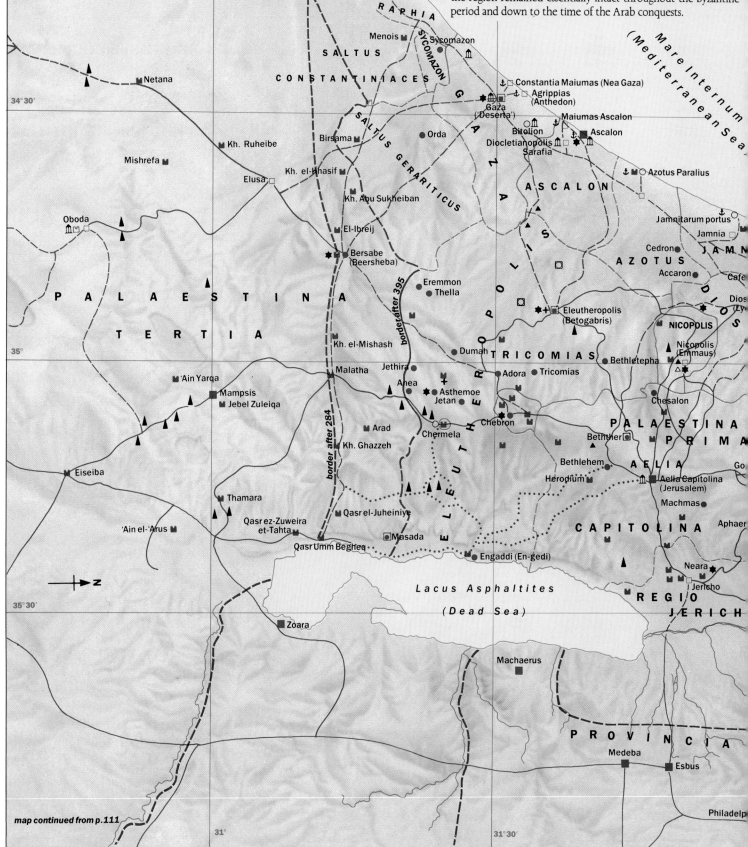

map continued from p.111

1/ map below The administrative districts of the Roman province of Palestine in c AD 400. Under the reorganization of Diocletian (AD 284) Palestine was subdivided into three regions governed as a consular province in the prefecture of the East.

2 and 3/ maps right These maps show the shifting provincial boundaries of Judaea–Palestine in the period after the death of Herod Agrippa I (AD 44), when procurators resumed command. Some of Agrippa's territories in the north were given to his son Herod Agrippa II (c AD 52-94). After his death most of his kingdom reverted directly to the province of Syria. Part of the territory of Agrippa II was taken by Jewish rebels in the First Revolt (AD 66-70), but afterward remained under Judaea. The territorial boundaries remained substantially the same through most of the 2nd century. After the Second Revolt (AD 132-135) the province was elevated in rank to Provincia Syria Palaestina with its own legate. Territorial boundaries shifted again in the reign of Septimius Severus (AD 193-211) when the new province of Phoenicia was established (separate from Syria) while much of the Transjordan (under Syria) was ceded to Provincia Arabia.

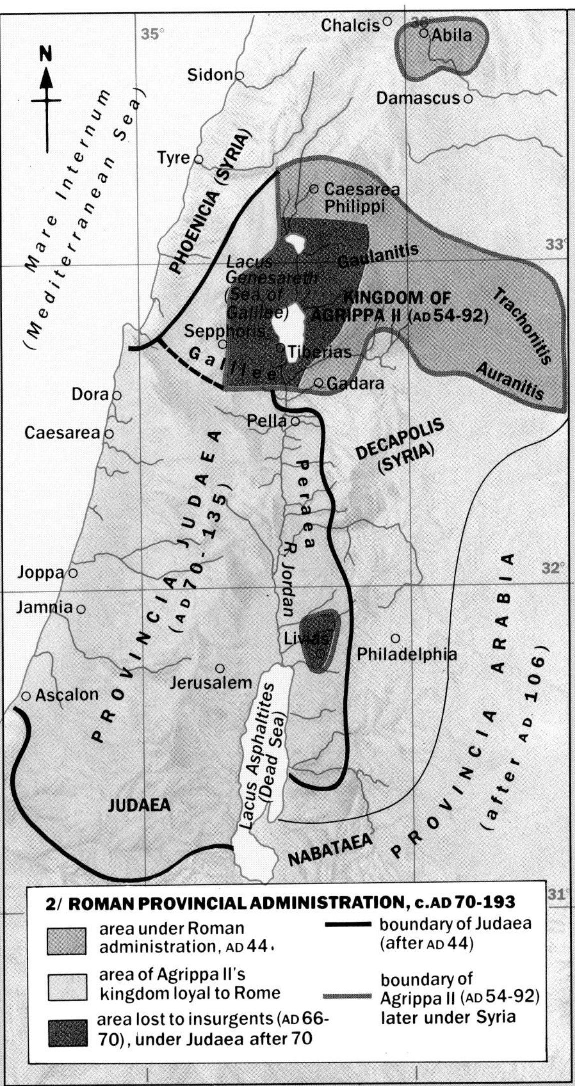
2/ ROMAN PROVINCIAL ADMINISTRATION, c.AD 70-193
area under Roman administration, AD 44.
area of Agrippa II's kingdom loyal to Rome
area lost to insurgents (AD 66-70), under Judaea after 70
boundary of Judaea (after AD 44)
boundary of Agrippa II (AD 54-92) later under Syria
Mare Internum (Mediterranean Sea)
PHOENICIA (SYRIA)
Chalcis
Abila
Sidon
Damascus
Tyre
Caesarea Philippi
Gaulanitis
Lacus Genesareth (Sea of Galilee)
KINGDOM OF AGRIPPA II (AD 54-92)
Trachonitis
Sepphoris
Tiberias
Galilee
Gadara
Auranitis
Dora
Pella
Caesarea
DECAPOLIS (SYRIA)
Peraea
PROVINCIA JUDAEA (AD 70-135)
R. Jordan
Joppa
Jamnia
Livias
Philadelphia
Jerusalem
Ascalon
Lacus Asphaltites (Dead Sea)
JUDAEA
NABATAEA
PROVINCIA ARABIA (after AD 106)
35°
36°
33°
32°
31°

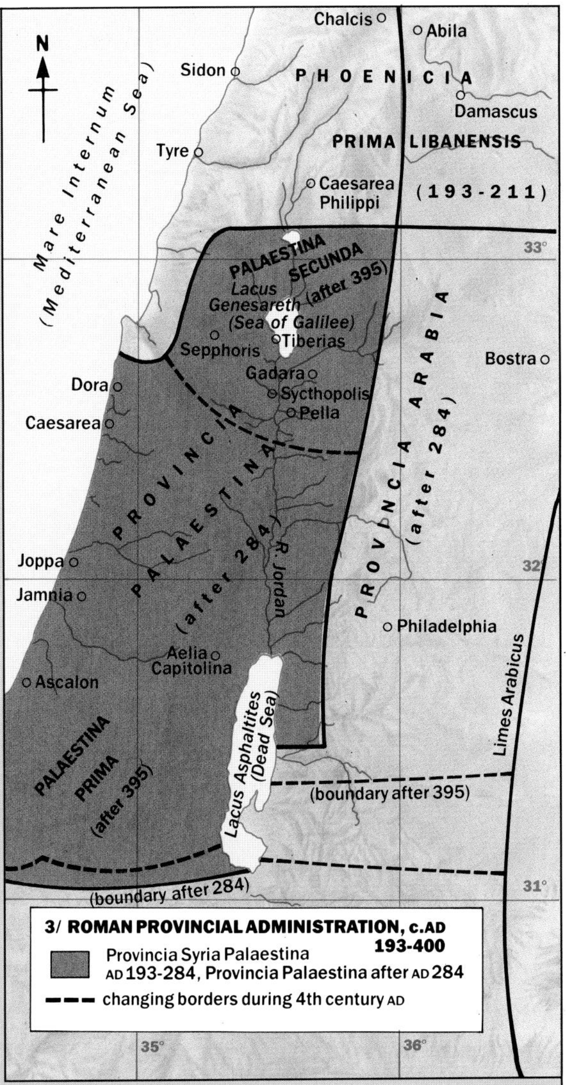
3/ ROMAN PROVINCIAL ADMINISTRATION, c.AD 193-400
Provincia Syria Palaestina AD 193-284, Provincia Palaestina after AD 284
changing borders during 4th century AD
Chalcis
Abila
Sidon
PHOENICIA
Damascus
PRIMA LIBANENSIS
Tyre
Caesarea Philippi
(193-211)
Mare Internum (Mediterranean Sea)
PALAESTINA SECUNDA (after 395)
Lacus Genesareth (Sea of Galilee)
Sepphoris
Tiberias
Gadara
Scythopolis
Pella
Dora
Bostra
Caesarea
PROVINCIA PALAESTINA (after 284)
PROVINCIA ARABIA (after 284)
R. Jordan
Joppa
Jamnia
Philadelphia
Aelia Capitolina
Ascalon
Limes Arabicus
PALAESTINA PRIMA (after 395)
Lacus Asphaltites (Dead Sea)
(boundary after 395)
(boundary after 284)
33°
32°
31°
35°
36°

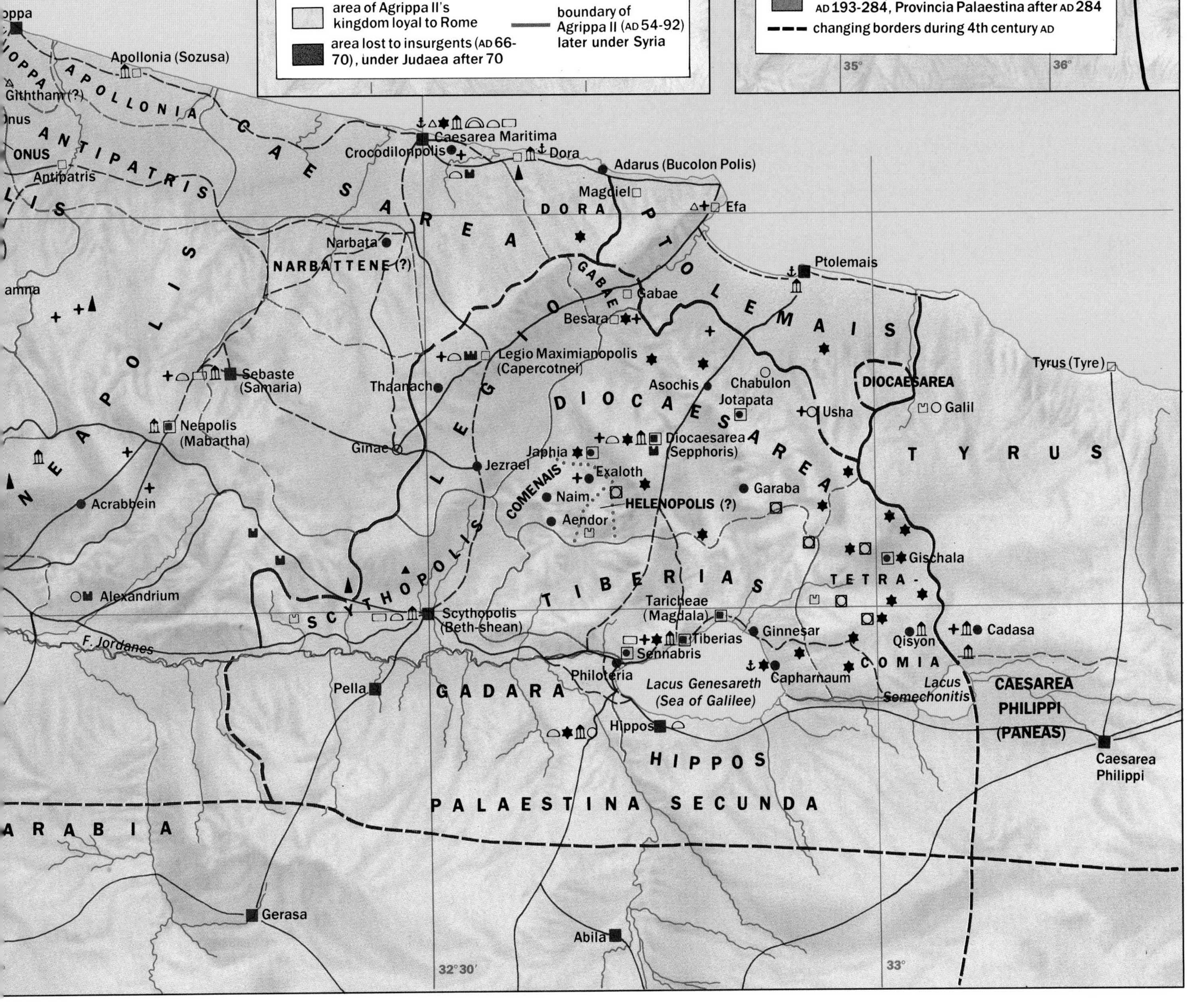
Joppa
Apollonia (Sozusa)
APOLLONIA
Gilththam (?)
ANTIPATRIS
Antipatris
CAESAREA
Caesarea Maritima
Crocodilonpolis
Dora
Adarus (Bucolon Polis)
Magdiel
DORA
Efa
Narbata
NARBATTENE (?)
PTOLEMAIS
Ptolemais
GABAE
Gabae
Besara
Legio Maximianopolis (Capercotnei)
Sebaste (Samaria)
Thaanach
Asochis
Chabulon
Jotapata
Usha
DIOCAESAREA
Galil
Tyrus (Tyre)
Neapolis (Mabartha)
NEAPOLIS
Ginae
Diocaesarea (Sepphoris)
Japhia
Jezrael
Exaloth
COMENAIS
Naim
HELENOPOLIS (?)
Garaba
TYRUS
Aendor
Acrabbein
LEGIO
Gischala
Alexandrium
TIBERIAS
TETRACOMIA
SCYTHOPOLIS
Scythopolis (Beth-shean)
Taricheae (Magdala)
Ginnesar
Cadasa
Qisyon
F. Jordanes
Tiberias
Sennabris
Capharnaum
Pella
GADARA
Philoteria
Lacus Genesareth (Sea of Galilee)
Lacus Semechonitis
CAESAREA PHILIPPI (PANEAS)
Hippos
HIPPOS
Caesarea Philippi
PALAESTINA SECUNDA
ARABIA
Gerasa
Abila
32°30′
33°

JESUS was a Galilean from the village of Nazareth, born during the last years of Herod the Great (died 4 BC). The Gospel of Matthew suggests that Jesus' family was from Judaea, near Bethlehem, and fled to Egypt to escape Herod. Afterwards they resettled in Galilee to avoid returning to Judaea under Archelaus (4 BC-AD 6). The Gospel of Luke differs, since it makes Nazareth the hometown of Joseph. According to later tradition, nearby Sepphoris was the hometown of Mary. Luke also associates the journey to Bethlehem with a census under P. Sulpicius Quirinius, the legate of Syria (AD 6-7?) after Archelaus was deposed. The family then returned by way of Jerusalem to Nazareth.

Until the Hasmonaean period, the northern hill country was not considered part of the Jewish homeland; instead, 'Galilee of the Gentiles' (ISAIAH 8.23/9.1; cf. MATT 4.15) was hostile to Judaea (1 MACC 5.15). After annexation under Aristobulus (104 BC), Jewish settlement was promoted by Alexander Jannaeus (103-76 BC). Following Pompey's conquests (64 BC) Galilee was reorganized as a separate administrative unit under Gabinius (57 BC). Its first capital was Sepphoris, the largest free city, situated between the Sea of Galilee and the coast at Ptolemais. A few miles south-east towards the Valley of Jezreel, was the village of Nazareth.

GEOGRAPHY

In Jesus' day, the Galilean highlands, with their deep, fertile valleys and passes, were surrounded by Greek cities. On the Phoenician coast, Ptolemais, Tyre and Sidon were independent city-territories under the province of Syria. At the headwaters of the River Jordan, below Mt. Hermon, was Paneas (named for the god Pan), later renamed Caesarea Philippi when it became a part of the tetrarchy of Philip (4 BC–AD 34). In the Valley of Jezreel, separating Galilee from Judaea-Samaria, lay Scythopolis, one of the independent city-states of the Decapolis (including Hippos, Gadara, Pella, Gerasa and Philadelphia).

While Galilee remained an administrative unit (except for a time under Agrippa II, c AD 52-66), it was marked by regional diversity. Josephus, who commanded the region during the First Revolt (page 128), assumes a geographical division between Upper and Lower Galilee (WAR 3.39). The boundary was marked by the Valley of Bet HaKerem on the west and the Nahal 'Ammud on the east, where the mountains of Meron rise up sharply and trail off northward into the Lebanon range. Because of its remoteness, the region remained more rural, a haven for refugees from the time of Herod until after the First Revolt. It was also known as Tetracomia ('Four Villages'), as there was no major free city, only larger villages such as Gischala (Gush Halav) and Meron.

The valleys of Lower Galilee provided the major trade route (called the Via Maris or 'Way of the Sea') around the Sea of Galilee

1/ map right The Synoptic Gospels – Matthew, Mark and Luke – represent the ministry of Jesus as being based around the Sea of Galilee.
2/ Mosaic from Sepphoris, an elaborate Roman city, depicting the 'Mona Lisa' of Galilee. From a large house, the floor mosaic depicts the four seasons with scenes from Roman mythology.

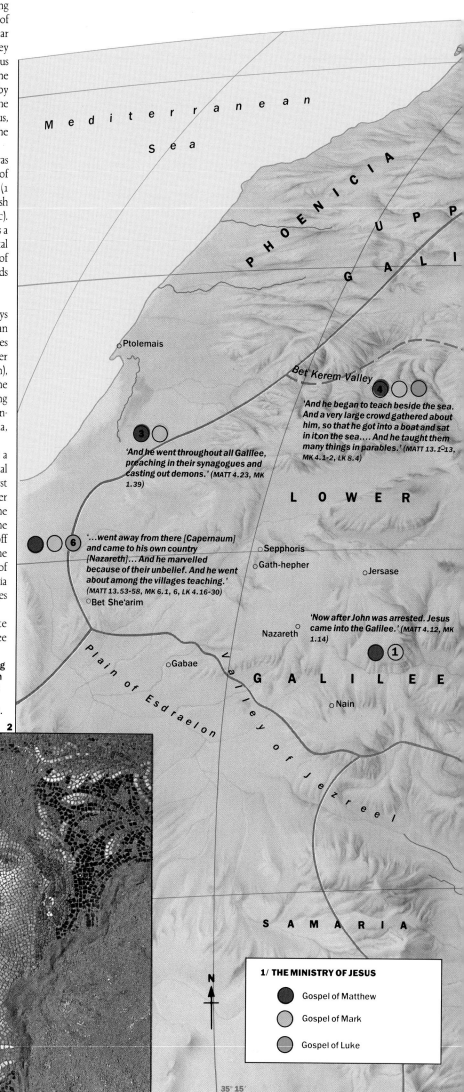

'And he went throughout all Galilee, preaching in their synagogues and casting out demons.' (MATT 4.23, MK 1.39)

'And he began to teach beside the sea. And a very large crowd gathered about him, so that he got into a boat and sat in it on the sea.... And he taught them many things in parables.' (MATT 13.1°13, MK 4.1-2, LK 8.4)

'...went away from there [Capernaum] and came to his own country [Nazareth]... And he marvelled because of their unbelief. And he went about among the villages teaching.' (MATT 13.53-58, MK 6.1, 6, LK 4.16-30)

'Now after John was arrested. Jesus came into the Galilee.' (MATT 4.12, MK 1.14)

1/ THE MINISTRY OF JESUS

- Gospel of Matthew
- Gospel of Mark
- Gospel of Luke

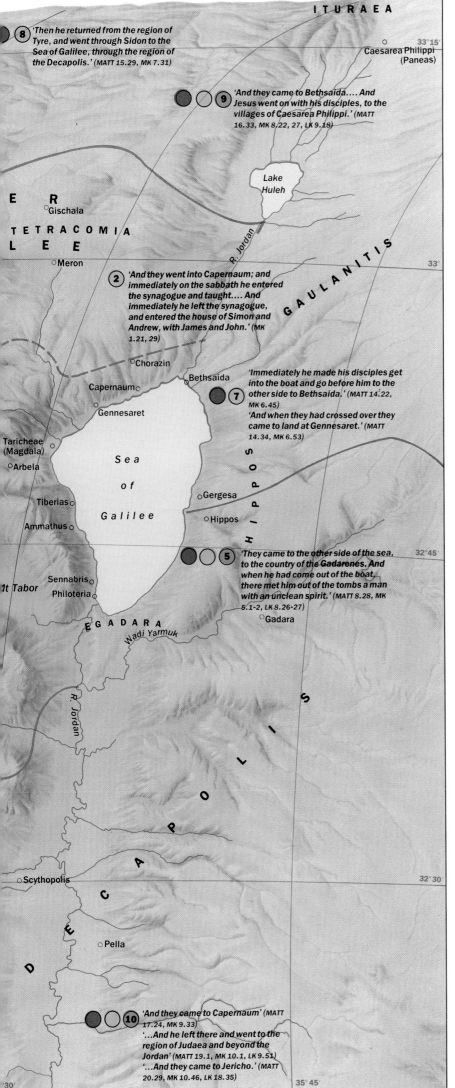

ITURAEA

⑧ *'Then he returned from the region of Tyre, and went through Sidon to the Sea of Galilee, through the region of the Decapolis.' (MATT 15.29, MK 7.31)*

Caesarea Philippi (Paneas)   33°15'

⑨ *'And they came to Bethsaida…. And Jesus went on with his disciples, to the villages of Caesarea Philippi.' (MATT 16.33, MK 8.22, 27, LK 9.18)*

Lake Huleh

E   R
Gischala

T E T R A C O M I A
L E E

Meron

② *'And they went into Capernaum; and immediately on the sabbath he entered the synagogue and taught…. And immediately he left the synagogue, and entered the house of Simon and Andrew, with James and John.' (MK 1.21, 29)*

G A U L A N I T I S   33°

Chorazin

Bethsaida

Capernaum

Gennesaret

⑦ *'Immediately he made his disciples get into the boat and go before him to the other side to Bethsaida.' (MATT 14.22, MK 6.45)*
'And when they had crossed over they came to land at Gennesaret.' (MATT 14.34, MK 6.53)

Taricheae (Magdala)

Arbela

S e a
o f
G a l i l e e

H I P P O S

Gergesa

Hippos

Tiberias

Ammathus

⑤ *'They came to the other side of the sea, to the country of the Gadarenes. And when he had come out of the boat, there met him out of the tombs a man with an unclean spirit.' (MATT 8.28, MK 5.1-2, LK 8.26-27)*   32°45'

Gadara

1t Tabor

Sennabris

Philoteria

E G A D A R A
Wadi Yarmuk

R. Jordan

D   E   C   A   P   O   L   I   S

Scytholpolis   32°30'

Pella

⑩ *'And they came to Capernaum' (MATT 17.24, MK 9.33)*
'…And he left there and went to the region of Judaea and beyond the Jordan' (MATT 19.1, MK 10.1, LK 9.51)
'…And they came to Jericho.' (MATT 20.29, MK 10.46, LK 18.35)

30'   35°45'

---

and across the Mediterranean coast or turning south to the Valley of Jezreel. Between AD 17-20 Herod Antipas founded Tiberias (in honour of the Emperor) as the new capital of his tetrarchy. Josephus reports some 204 villages in Galilee (LIFE 235), grouped for the most part as administrative districts or toparchies around free cities, Sepphoris and Tiberias.

ECONOMY AND SOCIETY
The social organization of Galilee was built around village economies and trade networks. The terrain, especially in Lower Galilee, was productive for farming or herding, and produce was sold in local village markets. Some villages specialized in other goods, such as coarseware pottery produced from local claybeds.

The Sea of Galilee (also called Lake Chinnereth, Gennesaret or Tiberias) supported a thriving fishing industry, centred at Magdala, on the *Via Maris*. The city was also known by the Greek name Taricheae, derived from its export of salted or pickled fish. During the First Revolt Josephus commandeered 230 (or 330) fishing boats from Taricheae for a naval assault on Tiberias (WAR 2.634-38).

The entire region was greatly influenced by Graeco-Roman culture. Aramaic was the vernacular, though classical Hebrew was still in restricted use. Official Latin was limited, but Greek was common, even in village life. Documents have been found in duplicate, one copy in Aramaic and another in Greek. Weights used in the market were stamped in Greek. Tomb inscriptions from catacombs at Bet She'arim assume that Greek was the first tongue for many Galilean Jews.

SEPPHORIS
Josephus calls Sepphoris 'the ornament of Galilee' (ANT 18.26). Antipas had moved the provincial capital from Sepphoris to Tiberias (AD 17). Under the procurator Felix (c AD 52-60), when Galilee was reapportioned, Sepphoris was once again made capital of the Roman province. The city also had its Greek names: Autokratis or Eirenopolis ('City of Peace'), referring to its posture toward Rome in the First Revolt (cf. WAR 3.30 and page 128). Later called Diocaesarea, the city was granted favoured status by the Emperor and senate. For 17 years it was the seat of Rabbi Judah the Prince, who codified the Mishnah there in c AD 200.

Excavations of Sepphoris have revealed an elaborate Roman city - a palace, theatre and fortress from the 1st century and extensive construction continuing through the time of Constantine. The city was built over a network of underground cisterns carved into the bedrock and supplied by aqueduct. While there was clearly a prominent Jewish population throughout the Roman period, Sepphoris was a centre for Roman administration and Hellenistic culture as well. Archaeological finds include small figurines of pagan gods and an elaborate mosaic floor depicting the personified seasons and other mythical scenes.

JESUS THE GALILEAN
To some, Galilean meant 'extremist' (LK 13.1). Herod had routed out Hasmonaean nationalists at Sepphoris and Arbela. The tax census of AD 6 precipitated rioting at Sepphoris led by Judah the Galilean (cf. ACTS 5.37; WAR 1.204, 2.56, 7.253), and John of Gischala was a force in the First Revolt. To others, being from Galilee might mean that Jesus was among the 'people of the land' (*amme ha-aretz*) who did not observe Torah scrupulously. But it seemed doubtful in any case that messianic claims should come from Galilee.

Jesus' public ministry began c AD 27-29, when Galilee and Peraea were ruled by Herod Antipas (4 BC-AD 39) and Judaea was under the procurator Pontius Pilate (AD 26-36). After John the Baptist was executed by Antipas (c AD 27-28; cf. MK 6.17-29 – MATT 14.1-12), Jesus returned to his home territory and Capernaum became the centre of his early activity (MK 2.1).

JESUS' MINISTRY IN THE SYNOPTIC GOSPELS
It appears from the Synoptic Gospels (MATT, MK and LK) that most of Jesus' public career occurred in the villages of Lower Galilee. Many events are impossible to locate with certainty and no mention is made of specific sites in Upper Galilee. The Synoptic Gospels generally present a geographical progression, seen especially in MARK. Jesus began in the region from Nazareth up to Capernaum, or along the *Via Maris*, only once leaving to cross over to the other side of the Sea of Galilee (MK 5.1). But then, after being rejected at Nazareth (MK 6.1-6), Jesus and his followers began to move more broadly in the region surrounding Lower Galilee, frequently crossing the sea. He also ventured to Tyre and Sidon (MK 7.24), perhaps hinting contact with Upper Galilee (cf. 6.53). After returning by way of the Decapolis or Ituraea (MK 7.31), Jesus moved from Capernaum to Bethsaida and Caesarea Philippi (MK 8.27). He journeyed to Judaea only at the end of his brief career.

THE Synoptic Gospels – Matthew, Mark and Luke – place the ministry of Jesus exclusively in the region around the Sea of Galilee, until, driven by the inevitability of his cause, he turns toward Jerusalem. Afterward his attack on merchants in the Temple angers the leaders (MK 11.15-19). The triumphal entry just a week before his death (MK 11.1-10 – MT 21.1-9 – LK 19.28-38) marks his first appearance in Jerusalem. All this leads up to the celebration of Passover, at which Jesus, after eating the Passover meal, is arrested and tried throughout the night and crucified on the following day just outside the city. In the Synoptics this is the only Passover mentioned during Jesus' career.

In the appearances following Jesus' resurrection the Synoptic Gospels show much greater diversity. In both Matthew and Mark the disciples were advised at the empty tomb to go to Galilee to see Jesus (MT 28.7–MK 16.7). In Luke, however, all the post-resurrection appearances occur in and around Jerusalem itself (LK 24.13-53, ACTS 1.4-12).

THE GOSPEL OF JOHN

The fourth Gospel, which was written later, presents a different chronology. In John, Jesus visits Jerusalem from the beginning of his career, and three different Passover feasts are mentioned. The first of these occurs in JN 2.13-21, at which Jesus cleanses the Temple. In the third feast Jesus eats the last supper and is crucified on the day of preparation just before the Passover is to begin (JN 13.1,18,28, 19.14). Thus, the traditional three-year ministry of Jesus is the scenario of John's Gospel, and in it Jerusalem plays a

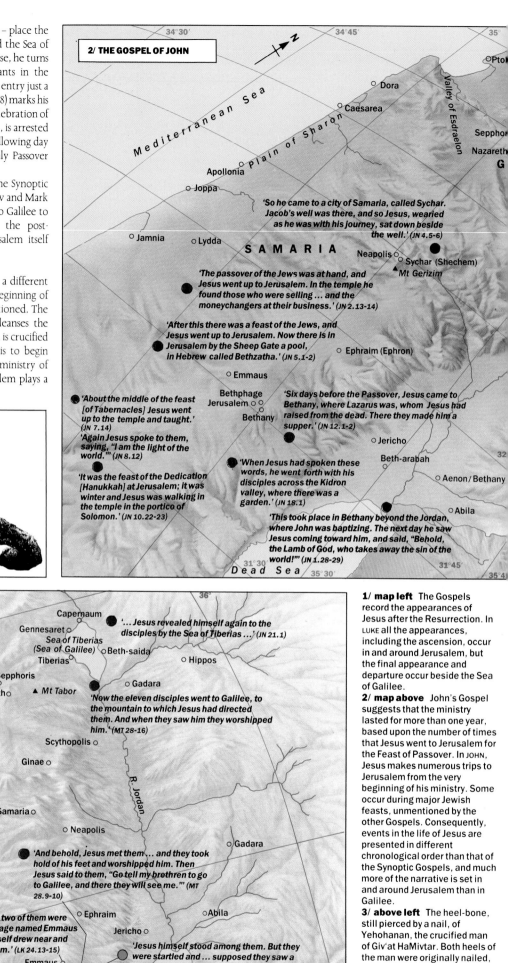

2/ THE GOSPEL OF JOHN

'So he came to a city of Samaria, called Sychar. Jacob's well was there, and so Jesus, wearied as he was with his journey, sat down beside the well.' (JN 4.5-6)

'The passover of the Jews was at hand, and Jesus went up to Jerusalem. In the temple he found those who were selling … and the moneychangers at their business.' (JN 2.13-14)

'After this there was a feast of the Jews, and Jesus went up to Jerusalem. Now there is in Jerusalem by the Sheep Gate a pool, in Hebrew called Bethzatha.' (JN 5.1-2)

'About the middle of the feast [of Tabernacles] Jesus went up to the temple and taught.' (JN 7.14)
'Again Jesus spoke to them, saying, "I am the light of the world."' (JN 8.12)

'It was the feast of the Dedication [Hanukkah] at Jerusalem; it was winter and Jesus was walking in the temple in the portico of Solomon.' (JN 10.22-23)

'Six days before the Passover, Jesus came to Bethany, where Lazarus was, whom Jesus had raised from the dead. There they made him a supper.' (JN 12.1-2)

'When Jesus had spoken these words, he went forth with his disciples across the Kidron valley, where there was a garden.' (JN 18.1)

'This took place in Bethany beyond the Jordan, where John was baptizing. The next day he saw Jesus coming toward him, and said, "Behold, the Lamb of God, who takes away the sin of the world!"' (JN 1.28-29)

'… Jesus revealed himself again to the disciples by the Sea of Tiberias …' (JN 21.1)

'Now the eleven disciples went to Galilee, to the mountain to which Jesus had directed them. And when they saw him they worshipped him.' (MT 28-16)

'And behold, Jesus met them … and they took hold of his feet and worshipped him. Then Jesus said to them, "Go tell my brethren to go to Galilee, and there they will see me."' (MT 28.9-10)

'That very day two of them were going to a village named Emmaus … Jesus himself drew near and went with them.' (LK 24.13-15)

'Jesus said to her' [Mary Magdalene], "Woman, why are you weeping? Whom do you seek?" (JN 20.15)

'On the evening of that day, the first day of the week, Jesus came and stood among them …' (JN 20.19)

'Jesus himself stood among them. But they were startled and … supposed they saw a spirit.' (LK 24.36-37)

'Then he led them out as far as Bethany … While he blessed them he parted from them, and was carried up into heaven. And they returned to Jerusalem.' (LK 25.50-52)

'Eight days later, his disciples were again in the house, and Thomas was with them … Then he said to Thomas, "Put your finger here, and see my hands."' (JN 20.26-27)

1/ JESUS' APPEARANCES AFTER THE RESURRECTION

● Gospel of Matthew ● Gospel of Luke ● Gospel of John

1/ map left The Gospels record the appearances of Jesus after the Resurrection. In LUKE all the appearances, including the ascension, occur in and around Jerusalem, but the final appearance and departure occur beside the Sea of Galilee.

2/ map above John's Gospel suggests that the ministry lasted for more than one year, based upon the number of times that Jesus went to Jerusalem for the Feast of Passover. In JOHN, Jesus makes numerous trips to Jerusalem from the very beginning of his ministry. Some occur during major Jewish feasts, unmentioned by the other Gospels. Consequently, events in the life of Jesus are presented in different chronological order than that of the Synoptic Gospels, and much more of the narrative is set in and around Jerusalem than in Galilee.

3/ above left The heel-bone, still pierced by a nail, of Yehohanan, the crucified man of Giv'at HaMivtar. Both heels of the man were originally nailed, and tearing occurred upon his removal from the cross. The nail which pierced the heelbone had evidently struck a knot in the wood and bent, so that the nail could not be removed without causing severe damage. Other evidence for the use of nails in crucifixion has not been found. The arms might have been tied to the cross with ropes.

4/ right A reconstruction of Herodian Jerusalem from archaeological findings.

'On the third day there was a marriage feast in Cana in Galilee, and the mother of Jesus was there.' (JN 2.1)

'So he came again to Cana in Galilee, where he had made the water into wine. And at Capernaum there was an official whose son was ill.' (JN 4.46)

'After this Jesus went to the other side of the Sea of Galilee ... And a multitude followed him, because they saw the signs he did.' (JN 6.1-2)

greater role, while the Galilean links are somewhat blurred. Instead, in John, Jesus' early ministry is spent travelling between Galilee and Jerusalem, while the final days in Jerusalem (JN 12.1) take up more of the narrative. Thus, in reporting events after the resurrection, John's Gospel mentions appearances both in Jerusalem and, sometime later, beside the Sea of Galilee.

THE TRIAL OF JESUS

The sequence of events surrounding the arrest and death of Jesus is unclear. A trial before the Jewish council on the first day of Passover would seem to be contrary to Torah. Thus, John's chronology, which places the meal, trial and crucifixion prior to the beginning of Passover, may be correct. However, John, like the Synoptics has a theological motive in presenting the events. For in John, Jesus hangs on the cross while the Passover lambs are being slaughtered in preparation for the feast, harking back to the words of John the Baptist (JN 1.29).

The charges on which Jesus was condemned reflect Jewish concerns over messianic expectation, but ultimately they were politically motivated. Crucifixion was a punishment meted out by the Romans to rebels. Jesus was perceived as a seditious threat (LK 23.5), claiming to be the King of the Jews, as the plaque on the cross proclaims the charge (MK 15.26). The Gospels seek to exonerate the Romans from responsibility for the crucifixion – probably from a later apologetic interest – but the mode of execution indicates that the responsibility had to rest with the Roman procurator. The Romans did not invent crucifixion as a mode of execution, but they employed it especially to make an example, as in cases of slave revolt. Josephus notes that several revolutionaries in the period before the First Revolt were executed in this manner. In 1968 excavation of Jewish burials at Giv'at HaMivtar unearthed an ossuary bearing the name Yehohanan. The bones are those of a young man who was apparently crucified, the only direct archaeological evidence. Although one of the heel bones still has the nail in it, it is uncertain whether nails or ropes were used to secure the arms to the cross. How much it is possible to generalize from this case to that of Jesus is difficult to say.

THE PLACE OF CRUCIFIXION

The location of the praetorium where Jesus was tried is disputed. As with many sites associated with the life of Jesus, tradition has fixed the locality while there is little or no archaeological proof. According to legend the praetorium is associated with the fortress Antonia, adjacent to the Temple, and the traditional steps of the 'Via Dolorosa' begin there. However, some scholars think that the procurator, on visits to Jerusalem from Caesarea, would have used the Hasmonaean palace. Having been enlarged by Herod, it was accessible by the Gennath Gate, on the road to Joppa and the coast.

The execution took place in an old quarry, which in Jesus' day was just outside the city walls. In the angle of the first and second walls, marked by the Gennath Gate, was a quarry dating to the 7th century BC. It was not brought within the bounds of the city until Herod Agrippa I (AD 41-44) extended the city to the north. The present day Church of the Holy Sepulchre, which was built in the 4th century AD, stands over the northern section of this quarry. In excavations it was found that a protrusion on the southern side was never quarried, and this may have been the place known as Golgotha, resembling a 'skull' (MK 15.22 – LK 23.33). Facing it were several tombs cut out of the cliff dating from the 1st century AD.

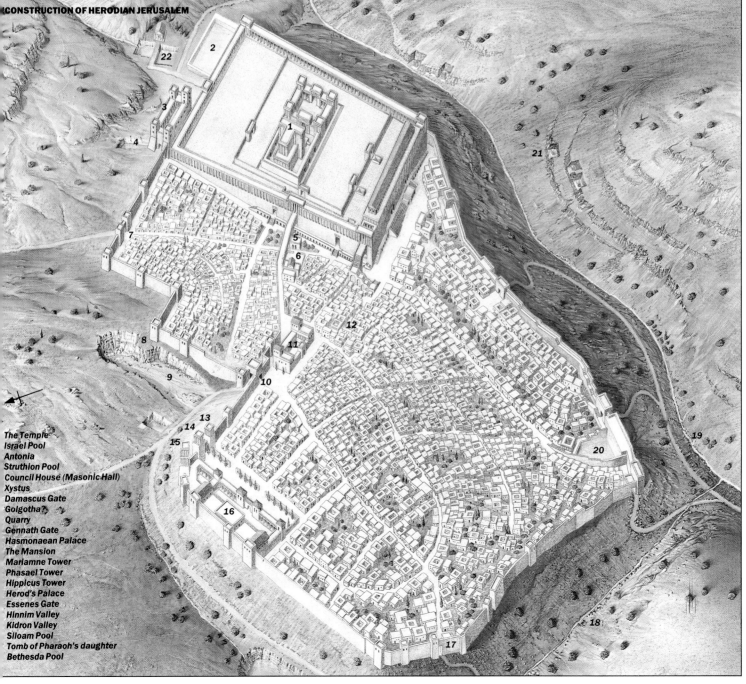

CONSTRUCTION OF HERODIAN JERUSALEM

1 The Temple
2 Israel Pool
3 Antonia
4 Struthion Pool
5 Council House (Masonic Hall)
6 Xystus
7 Damascus Gate
8 Golgotha?
9 Quarry
10 Gennath Gate
11 Hasmonaean Palace
12 The Mansion
13 Mariamne Tower
14 Phasael Tower
15 Hippicus Tower
16 Herod's Palace
17 Essenes Gate
18 Hinnim Valley
19 Kidron Valley
20 Siloam Pool
21 Tomb of Pharaoh's daughter
22 Bethesda Pool

IN the days of Jesus, the Kingdom of Herod was administered piecemeal as three separate districts. Herod Antipas ruled as Tetrarch of Galilee and Peraea from 4 BC to AD 37. The region of Gaulanitis, Ituraea, and Trachonitis was under Herod Philip from 4 BC to AD 34. Judaea (including Samaria and Idumaea), however, had been under direct Roman rule since Herod's son Archelaus was deposed in AD 6. In his place a Roman military procurator administered Judaea from Caesarea under the direct authority of the Province of Syria. Pontius Pilate was procurator of Judaea from AD 26-36.

The powerful Parthian empire forced the Emperor Tiberius (AD 14-37) to strengthen his eastern frontier by annexing a number of the client-kingdoms under direct rule. In AD 18 Commagene was incorporated into Syria, and Cappadocia (including Lesser Armenia) was made a province (page 102).

With the demise of Herod's sons, the entire region might have come under procuratorial control; however, Tiberius' successor, Gaius (AD 37-41), reversed this trend. He favoured personal friends to serve as client-kings in the east. Among these was Herod Agrippa I, grandson of Herod the Great and an heir of the Hasmonaean line, brought to Rome by his mother Berenice, Herod's niece. Agrippa I was well connected both at Rome and in the east. A cousin was client-king of Armenia and a brother the client-king Herod of Chalcis. His sister was Herodias, who had married Herod Antipas in AD 28, and her daughter (his niece) was married to Herod Philip. In AD 37 Gaius bequeathed to Agrippa the tetrarchies of Philip and Lysanias, and in AD 40 Galilee and Peraea.

When Gaius was assassinated in AD 41 Agrippa supported the accession of Claudius (AD 41-54), another of his companions from days in Rome. Claudius ceded the procuratorial territory of Judaea to Agrippa I; his kingdom now equalled that of Herod the Great and his Hasmonaean ancestors. His pro-Jewish policies favoured the old aristocrats as well as the Pharisees, and, according to Josephus, his rule was popularly acclaimed. Only the story of his role in ordering

1/ map below Claudius placed Judaea under Herod Agrippa I in AD 41 as a gesture of reconciliation after the cruelty of Gaius Caesar (Caligula). Agrippa II was granted much of his father's northern territory under Claudius and Nero.

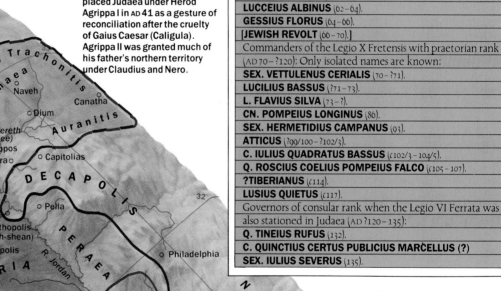

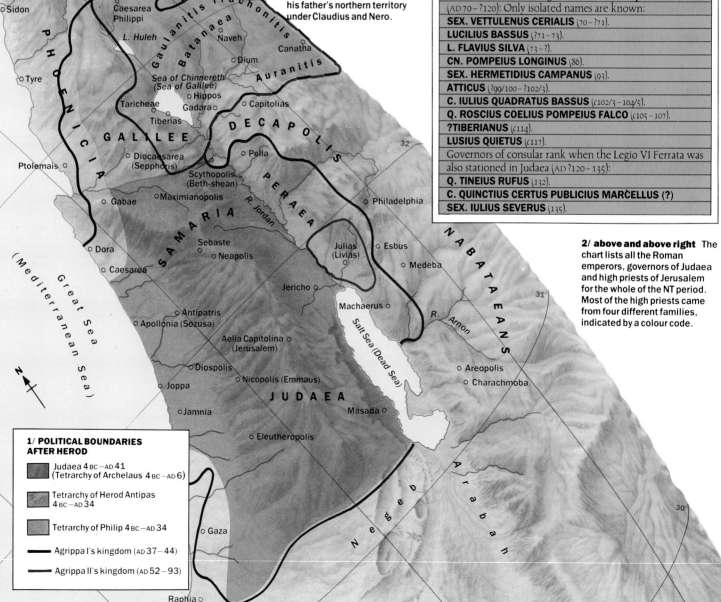

ROMAN EMPERORS

AUGUSTUS (16 January 27 BC – 19 August AD 14).	
TIBERIUS (17 September 14 – 16 March 37).	
GAIUS (16 March 37 – 24 January 41).	
CLAUDIUS (24 January 41 – 13 October 54).	
NERO (13 October 54 – 9 June 68).	
GALBA (10 June 68 – 15 January 69).	
OTHO (15 January 69 – 14 April 69).	
VITELLIUS (2 January 69 – 20 December 69).	
VESPASIAN (1 July 69 – 24 June 79).	
TITUS (24 June 79 – 13 September 81).	
DOMITIAN (14 September 81 – 16 September 96).	
NERVA (16 September 96 – 25 January 98).	
TRAJAN (25 January 97 – 8 August 117).	
HADRIAN (11 August 117 – 10 July 138).	

ROMAN GOVERNORS OF JUDAEA (AD 6–132)

Prefects/Procurators subject to supervision by the Imperial Legate in Syria (AD 6–66):

COPONIUS (c6–9)	
MARCUS AMBIBULUS (c9–12)	
*ANNIUS RUFUS** (c12–15).	
VALERIUS GRATUS (15–26).	
PONTIUS PILATE (26–36).	
MARCELLUS/MARULLUS (36–41).	
KING HEROD AGRIPPA I (41–44).	
CUSPIUS FADUS (44–?46).	
TIBERIUS IULIUS ALEXANDER (?46–48).	
VENTIDIUS CUMANUS (48–c52).	
ANTONIUS FELIX (c52–?60).	
PORCIUS FESTUS (?60–62).	
LUCCEIUS ALBINUS (62–64).	
GESSIUS FLORUS (64–66).	
[JEWISH REVOLT (66–70).]	

Commanders of the Legio X Fretensis with praetorian rank (AD 70–?120): Only isolated names are known:

SEX. VETTULENUS CERIALIS (70–?71).	
LUCILIUS BASSUS (?71–73).	
L. FLAVIUS SILVA (73–?).	
CN. POMPEIUS LONGINUS (86).	
SEX. HERMETIDIUS CAMPANUS (93).	
ATTICUS (?90/100–?102/3).	
C. IULIUS QUADRATUS BASSUS (c102/3–104/5).	
Q. ROSCIUS COELIUS POMPEIUS FALCO (c105–107).	
?TIBERIANUS (c114).	
LUSIUS QUIETUS (c117).	

Governors of consular rank when the Legio VI Ferrata was also stationed in Judaea (AD ?120–135):

Q. TINEIUS RUFUS (132).	
C. QUINCTIUS CERTUS PUBLICIUS MARCELLUS (?)	
SEX. IULIUS SEVERUS (135).	

2/ above and above right The chart lists all the Roman emperors, governors of Judaea and high priests of Jerusalem for the whole of the NT period. Most of the high priests came from four different families, indicated by a colour code.

1/ POLITICAL BOUNDARIES AFTER HEROD

Judaea 4 BC – AD 41 (Tetrarchy of Archelaus 4 BC – AD 6)

Tetrarchy of Herod Antipas 4 BC – AD 34

Tetrarchy of Philip 4 BC – AD 34

— Agrippa I's kingdom (AD 37–44)

— Agrippa II's kingdom (AD 52–93)

HIGH PRIESTS

Appointed by King Herod the Great (37–4 BC):
ANANEL (37–36, and again from 34 BC).
ARISTOBULUS III (35 BC).
JESUS SON OF PHIABI (to c 23 BC).
SIMON SON OF BOETHUS (c23–5 BC).
MATTHIAS SON OF THEOPHILUS (5–4 BC).
JOSEPH SON OF ELLEM (one day).
JOAZAR SON OF BOETHUS (4 BC).
Appointed by the Tetrarch Archelaus (4 BC–AD 6):
ELEAZAR SON OF BOETHUS (from 4 BC).
JESUS SON OF SEE (to AD 6).
Appointed by Quirinius, Legate of Syria (AD 6):
ANANUS/ANNAS SON OF SETHI (AD 6–15).
Appointed by Gratus, Procurator of Judaea (AD 15–26):
ISMAEL SON OF PHIABI (15–16).
ELEAZAR SON OF ANANUS (c16–17).
SIMON SON OF CAMITHUS (17–18).
JOSEPHUS CAIAPHAS (18–37).
Appointed by Vitellius, Legate of Syria (AD 35–39):
JONATHAN SON OF ANANUS/ANNAS (two months in 37).
THEOPHILUS SON OF ANANUS/ANNAS (from 37).
Appointed by King Agrippa I (AD 41–44):
SIMON CANTHERAS SON OF BOETHUS (from 41).
MATTHIAS SON OF ANANUS/ANNAS.
ELIONAEUS SON OF CANTHERAS (c44).
Appointed by Herod of Chalcis (AD 44–48):
JOSEPH SON OF KAMI.
ANANIAS SON OF NEDEBAEUS (47–c59).
Appointed by King Agrippa II (AD 50–?92):
ISMAEL SON OF PHIABI (c59–61).
JOSEPH CABI SON OF SIMON (61–62).
ANANUS SON OF ANANUS/ANNAS (three months in 62).
JESUS SON OF DAMNAEUS (62–63).
JESUS SON OF GAMALIEL (c63–64).
MATTHIAS SON OF THEOPHILUS (65–?   ).
Appointed by people during the Revolt (AD 66–70):
PHANNIAS/PHANNI/PHANASOS SON OF SAMUEL.

▨ House of Phiabi		▨ House of Ananus/Annas	
▨ House of Boethus		▨ House of Kamith	

the death of James and the arrest of Peter (ACTS 12.1-23) suggests a less favourable picture.

When Agrippa I died suddenly at Caesarea in AD 44, his son and heir Agrippa II was only 17. Consequently, Claudius transferred the entire kingdom (much of it for the first time) to procuratorial control as the Province of Judaea. In AD 50 Agrippa II was made client-king of Chalcis. Then, in AD 53 Claudius gave him the territories of Abila and Arca along with all the Tetrarchy of Philip in exchange for Chalcis. After the accession of Nero to power (AD 54-68), eastern Galilee, including the cities of Tiberias and Taricheae, and the territory of Julias in Peraea were ceded to Agrippa II. He would have been granted the remainder of Herodian lands, had it not been for the outbreak of hostilities in Judaea leading up to the First Jewish Revolt in AD 66 (page 128). Agrippa II favoured the Romans throughout. His sister Drusilla was married to the Roman procurator Antonius Felix (AD 52-60), and both are reported to have dealt with Paul after his arrest (ACTS 24.24, 25.13). In the Revolt, Agrippa II lost much of his territory to the rebels, but it was restored afterward, with the exception of eastern Galilee. He was further rewarded with other territories which he ruled until c AD 93. While Agrippa II never ruled Judaea proper, he was accorded the hereditary right to appoint the high priest in Jerusalem throughout much of his reign, until the destruction of the Temple in AD 70. During the First Revolt there was considerable resistance to Agrippa's pro-Roman policies, and his appointed high priest, a descendant of the House of Annas, was replaced by a supporter of the revolutionary party.

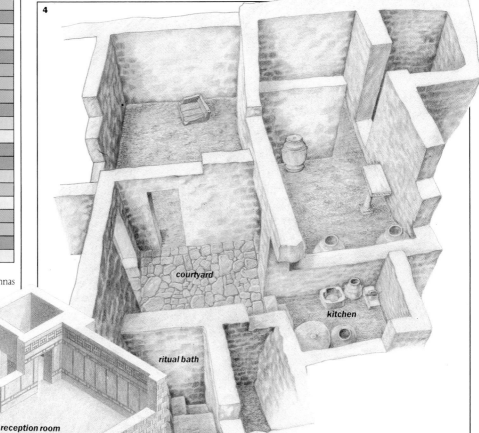

4

courtyard

kitchen

ritual bath

reception room

antechamber

courtyard

4/ above The Burnt House
The Burnt House lies slightly to the north on the same street as the Mansion House. There survives the basement level area of a much larger building —

3/ right The Mansion House
Recent excavations have uncovered a number of Herodian houses which were destroyed in AD 70, when the Roman forces under Titus captured Jerusalem and destroyed it. The Mansion particularly bears witness to the wealth and splendour of the city at that time. It overlooked the Temple Mount and occupied an area of more than 700 sq yds, comprising a series of rooms around a central courtyard. The decoration of the public rooms consisted of plaster shapes to resemble bossed Herodian masonry.

with evidence that grinding, measuring, weighing and cooking took place there. A weight, found there, bears the inscription 'Bar Kathros'. The Talmud refers to the House of Kathros as a high priestly family.

WHILE contacts with other lands had been common since Solomon's day, the sense of national identity for the people of Israel remained intact. But with the Assyrian conquest of northern Israel (722 BC), and even more so with the Babylonian conquest of Judah (586 BC), many Israelites were deported, exiled, or 'dispersed' to other lands. These communities striving to maintain their heritage and identity in alien contexts came to be known in later times as the Jews of the diaspora (from the Greek word for dispersion). While some of the Babylonian exiles returned to rebuild Jerusalem, others remained in the Mesopotamian regions through the Persian period and after to make it a centre of Jewish culture and tradition. Nor were all diaspora Jews forcibly removed from their homeland. During the Babylonian period many Judahites fled to Egypt. Later Jewish mercenaries of the Persian state commanded a garrison (5th-4th centuries BC) at Elephantine, in Upper Egypt, and from it an archive of correspondence (in Aramaic) has been preserved (page 90).

The great expansion of the diaspora occurred after the conquests of Alexander the Great (332-323 BC, page 92), especially from Jews who had once again become associated with the homeland and the new Temple. Moreover, Alexander's victories fused the entire eastern Mediterranean (as far as the Persian Gulf) into a single political entity and fostered the development of Hellenistic culture. Thus, some Jews were again carried off as war captives under Ptolemy I Soter (323-285 BC), and again after the siege of Pompey (64 BC). Others emigrated voluntarily as the political unification of Mediterranean lands provided ample opportunities abroad, either as merchants or mercenaries. In the 3rd-2nd centuries BC Jewish mercenaries under a rival priest, Onias IV, were commissioned by the Ptolemaic court and founded a colony at Leontopolis, where they built their own temple. The apocryphal book of *Tobit* and the *Letter of Aristeas* give further glimpses of the contacts between such diaspora Jewish communities by the 2nd-1st centuries BC.

THE ROMAN DIASPORA

By the end of the 1st century BC, when Rome had taken over the eastern Mediterranean, Jewish communities could be found in many cities of the east. The nearer regions of Syria and Egypt had sizable Jewish populations where proximity to the homeland made travel and commerce profitable. Two of the most prominent diaspora communities were located in the capital cities, Antioch and Alexandria. From the hellenistic period, enclaves followed Ptolemaic and Seleucid trade to other centres of the Greek world. Already in the later Hasmonaean period and during the time of Julius Caesar Jewish communities were thriving in Asia Minor and Greece. The growth of communities outside the homeland would be expanded through the 1st and 2nd centuries AD as a result of the two Jewish Revolts. By the 3rd-4th centuries, well-established Jewish communities could be found in most major cities of the eastern Empire and through the western provinces as well.

It is impossible to guess the population of the homeland or the diaspora by the 1st century AD; however, Philo, the Jewish philosopher of Alexandria, claims that there were a million Jews in Egypt alone. Estimates place the Jewish population of Alexandria at over 100,000, or approximately 12% of the total inhabitants. The percentage of Jewish residents at Antioch was probably higher, though the total population was smaller. By the 2nd-4th centuries AD it is estimated that the Jewish population of the city of Rome might have been approaching 100,000 as well, and after the two Jewish Revolts it is likely that more Jews lived in the diaspora than in the homeland.

JEWISH LIFE IN THE DIASPORA

The evidence for Jewish life in the diaspora is scattered, and the picture must take account of Jewish literature as well as inscriptions and archaeological remains. One of the prime sources is the New Testament itself, especially for example, Paul, a diaspora Jew from Tarsus in Cilicia, who travelled

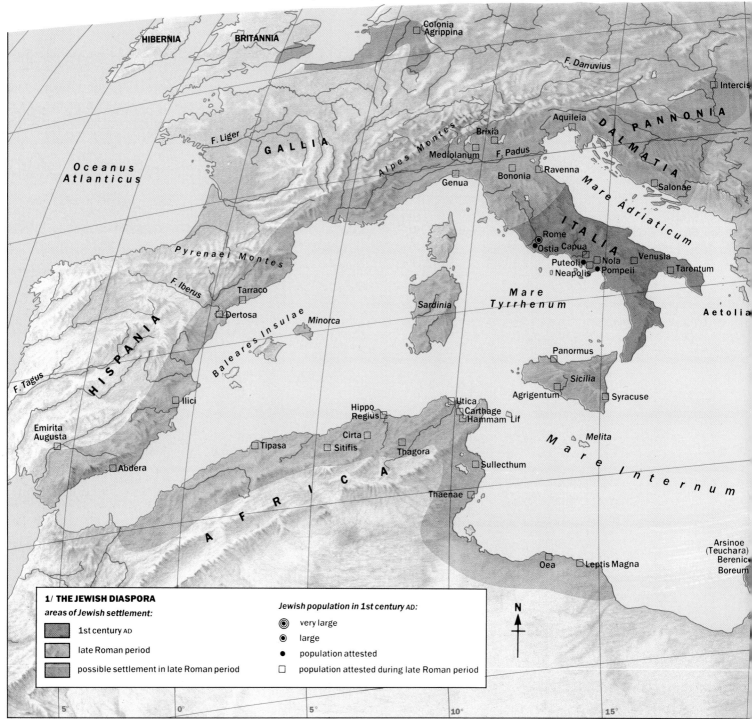

1/ THE JEWISH DIASPORA
areas of Jewish settlement:

- 1st century AD
- late Roman period
- possible settlement in late Roman period

Jewish population in 1st century AD:

- ◉ very large
- ◉ large
- ● population attested
- □ population attested during late Roman period

through Asia Minor and Greece. Josephus also gives scattered information about diaspora communities, and he lived out his life as a retainer of the emperors at Rome, while maintaining contacts with Jews in Cyrene and Egypt. Other occasional pieces of Jewish literature come from the diaspora, including *The Epistle of Jeremiah*, *Joseph and Asenath*, *The Wisdom of Jesus son of Sirach*, the Greek additions to the book of Daniel, and others. Unfortunately, the authors are seldom known, but often these writings were preserved and transmitted by later Christian usage.

Perhaps the best known Jewish writer of the diaspora, other than Paul, is Philo of Alexandria (*c* 25 BC-AD 50). From him we have not only a sizable quantity of writings preserved but also substantial personal information. He was born into a wealthy Jewish family which was already well-established in Alexandrian society. His elder brother served as *alabarch* (the official government tax agent) for Alexandria, and the family made a huge donation of gold for the decoration of Herod's temple. Philo's nephew Mark was married to a daughter of Herod Agrippa I. Another nephew, Tiberius Julius Alexander, abandoned his Jewish faith to enter Roman civil service; he served as procurator of Judaea (*c* AD 46-48) before becoming prefect of Egypt. Philo himself seems to have resisted public life for his scholarly and philo-sophical pursuits. He blends a strong devotion to Jewish tradition and observance with a liberal strain of Stoic and Middle Platonic thought to present both exposition of Jewish scriptures and defence of their faith. Still, Philo was drawn into political life, especially after pogroms against the Jews of Alexandria in AD 37-38. He led a delegation to Rome and secured from the Emperor Claudius an official rescript protecting the rights of Alexandrian Jews.

Like Philo, most Jews of the diaspora spoke Greek and participated to some extent in the surrounding culture. By the first century, the Jewish scriptures (and other writings) had been rendered into Greek, in a version from Egypt which came to be known as the *Septuagint*. This would be the Bible of the diaspora, for Jews and Christians alike. The social standing of diaspora Jews varied from place to place. Some communities faced prejudice and sporadic persecution, and many notices of Jews from pagan authors perpetuate hostility or misinformed rumours. Other Jewish communities enjoyed a favourable social position. Jews participated regularly in theatre and gymnasia and could aspire to the ranks of local aristocracy, city councillors, or magistrates. Extensive Jewish papyri (from Egypt) and inscriptions (as in the Roman catacombs) from across the Empire show that Jewish activities stretched across all walks of life and social levels. In many cases, Jewish residents were given equal citizenship (*isopoliteia*) status with the Greek residents, while in other cases they were given a measure of autonomy in dealing with internal Jewish affairs.

Much of the evidence for Jewish religion in the diaspora comes either from the literary remains, such as the writings of the Jewish philosopher Philo, or from the archaeological evidence for synagogues. It would be inappropriate to make a distinction between diaspora and homeland Judaism on the basis of the former's acculturation to Hellenistic ideas. Both show a high degree of Hellenistic influence, while devotion to Temple and Torah were the central marks of Jewish faith for both. Many diaspora Jews attempted to make the pilgrimage to Jerusalem for one of the major feasts so long as the Temple stood, and in later generations it became common among more wealthy Jews to be reburied in the homeland. However, among diaspora Jews there is still a tension of living in an alien environment and trying to balance their tradition with culture. The result is that there were many diverse forms of Jewish theological reflection in the diaspora, with greater or lesser degrees of pagan influence. The community itself, eventually becoming identified with its place of assembly (in Greek, *synagoge*), became the focus of Jewish identity for the diaspora.

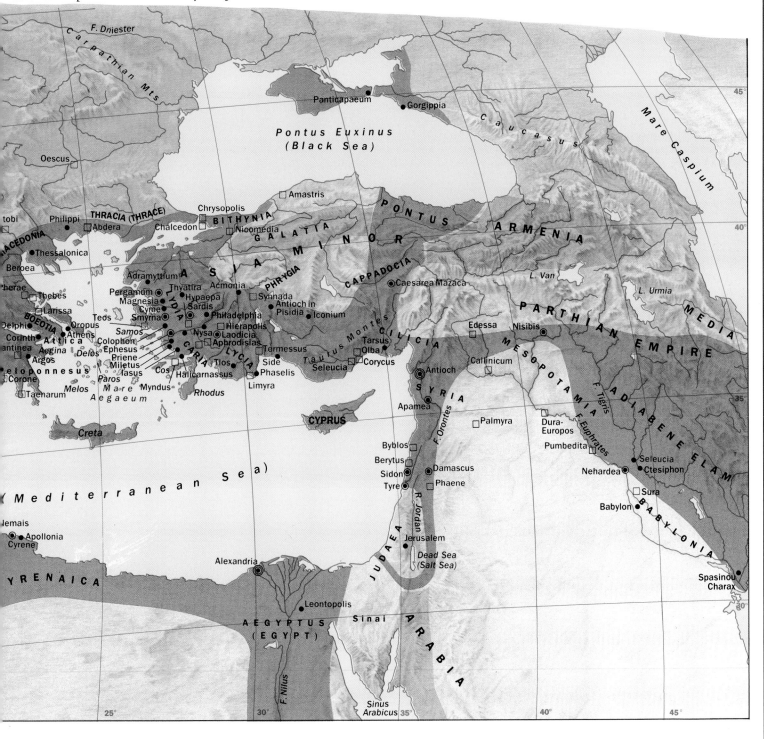

THE Greek word *synagoge* means 'assembly' and originally was used to translate the Hebrew idea of the 'congregation' of Israel. Over time, however, it came to be used both of the assembled group and the place of assembly, much like a synonymous Greek word, *ekklesia* ('church'). Neither term was used for 'temple', which designated a dwelling for the divine rather than a place of congregational assembly. As in most of the surrounding cultures, the Temple at Jerusalem held the central place for Jewish worship through the priesthood and the sacrificial cult. After AD70, when Herod.'s Temple was destroyed, new modes of worship were needed, and the synagogue would then emerge as the central institution of Jewish prayer and study of Torah.

Just when the institution of the synagogue first began is uncertain. Some have suggested that it arose after the destruction of Solomon's Temple among the Babylonian exiles; others, that it came from the Second Temple period as part of Ezra's reform in Judah. Neither seems likely, and in general the evidence points to the Hellenistic period.

Although synagogues are portrayed as a common feature of Jesus' day, there is no archaeological evidence of synagogue buildings in 1st-century Palestine. Several buildings thought to be synagogues at Gamla, Masada and Herodium are more properly identified as audience halls associated with Herodian palaces. Most archaeological evidence for synagogue buildings (including building remains, inscriptions and papyri) during the 2nd century AD comes from the diaspora. Synagogue remains from Palestine come from the 3rd century and later. Thus, traditional assumptions regarding synagogue architecture and worship in the 1st century must be used with caution. Instead, it is likely that there were probably two distinct lines of development: one from the diaspora, the other from the homeland. In the diaspora, the needs of minority Jewish enclaves seeking to maintain their worship and identity in an alien environment gave rise to communal centres as places of prayer. In the homeland, local places of civic assembly (*beth ha-knesset*) and small associations for the study of Torah (*beth ha-midrash*) were brought together under the new religious leadership of the Pharisees. After AD 70 these distinct lines of development began to merge.

ARCHITECTURE

Jewish places of prayer (*proseuchai*) are known from inscriptional and literary references in the diaspora, from Egypt to Greece, during the Hellenistic period. Most of the excavated synagogues from the diaspora have been renovated from houses. The earliest of these comes from the island of Delos in the Aegean, where a private residence was converted into a plain assembly hall. Recently discovered inscriptions also indicate a Samaritan 'prayerhall' nearby.

In urban centres such as Alexandria, where the Jewish population was substantial, there were several synagogues. These probably served as neighbourhood community centres as well as places of assembly and worship. Philo also indicates that these congregations were loosely organized under a governing 'council of elders' (*gerousia*). At Rome, over eleven synagogues are known after the 1st century AD, but there is no indication of a central governing body. While there is ample evidence for these local congregations in many towns of the diaspora, very few synagogue buildings have been discovered. This may be due to small gatherings still being held in houses or undecorated buildings, as may also be suggested for the city of Corinth in Paul's day (ACTS 18.7-8). The evidence of a synagogue building at Corinth called 'Synagogue of the Hebrews' appears to be a later development.

In the 2nd and 3rd centuries AD, houses where congregations had held casual assembly were taken over and renovated. At Dura-Europos, a Roman garrison on the Euphrates, such a building has been found. The private house was first converted into a

2

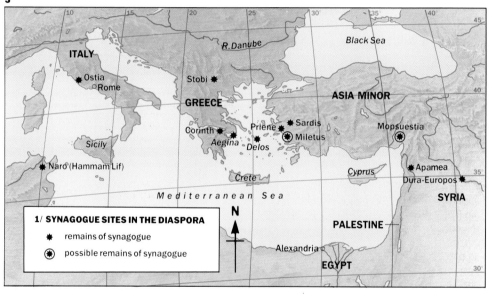

3

1/ map below The great majority of synagogue remains throughout the diaspora date from the late Roman and Byzantine periods.
2/ Detail of the Torah shrine from the Dura-Europos synagogue showing the artistic representations: a menorah with ethrob and lulab, the Temple, and the sacrifice of Isaac.
3/ Paintings from the West Wall of the later synagogue at Dura-Europos. The paintings are grouped around the central Torah shrine.
4/ Torah Ark lintel stone, from the Nabratein synagogue.
5/ map right Distribution of synagogue remains in Roman Palestine. There are no remains of identifiable synagogue buildings from the 1st century or before. Most of the sites shown date from the 4th to 6th centuries AD, though there are some indications that architectural development had begun by the end of the 2nd century, and a few date to the 3rd century.

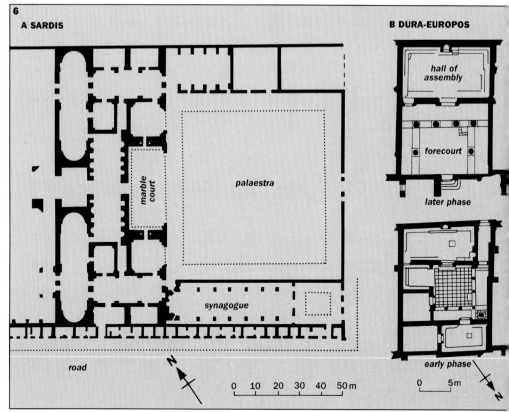

1/ SYNAGOGUE SITES IN THE DIASPORA

✶ remains of synagogue

✶ possible remains of synagogue

6

A SARDIS

marble court

palaestra

synagogue

road

0 10 20 30 40 50m

B DURA-EUROPOS

hall of assembly

forecourt

later phase

early phase

0 5m

small synagogue building in the late 2nd century AD. Then, in AD 244 the house-synagogue was entirely refurbished into a larger and more opulent synagogue hall with forecourt. It is clear too that the hall of assembly was designed for formal Jewish worship, as a Torah shrine (or 'holy ark') was built and the walls were lavishly painted with biblical scenes.

In excavations of Sardis, in Asia Minor, a magnificent basilical synagogue was uncovered. Dating from the 3rd-6th centuries, the enormous hall was part of the municipal bath-gymnasium complex, lavishly decorated inside with mosaic floors and marbled walls. Inscriptions indicate that the congregation numbered several prominent citizens as members. Here the synagogue building was a manifestation of the wealth and social acceptance of the local Jewish community.

Synagogue buildings in Palestine, though greater in number, come from the 3rd-6th centuries AD, when rabbinical Judaism was being consolidated with the compilation of the Mishnah and the Talmud. Many buildings come from Galilee and Gaulanitis. While strict architectural forms or orientation were not enforced, some regional patterns were evolving, as reflected at Horbat Shema' (4th century AD). A raised platform (or *bema*) and Torah shrine stood on the side or at one end of the rectangular hall. Some buildings show elaborate artistic decorations, such as the mosaic floors from Bet Alfa or Tiberias, including a central zodiac and depictions of the Torah shrine, menorah and other Jewish symbols.

WORSHIP

Over time the rabbinical organization came to dominate, but great variety existed in worship and order. Women were not excluded from the assembly until later times, and often served in leadership roles, especially in the diaspora. Organization and worship were further developed after the destruction of the Temple in AD 70, and even more so in the later 2nd century. With the demise of the sacrificial cult, weekly prayers and annual feasts were centred in the synagogue; however, the synagogue liturgy did not have a fixed form in the 1st century.

Reading of scripture became a central act of worship. Depending on location, the scriptures were read in Greek translation (the Septuagint) or were paraphrased in Aramaic vernacular (Targum). Two of the major synagogue prayers (the *Shema* and Eighteen Benedictions) were already in use by the end of the 1st century, though not in their later fixed forms.

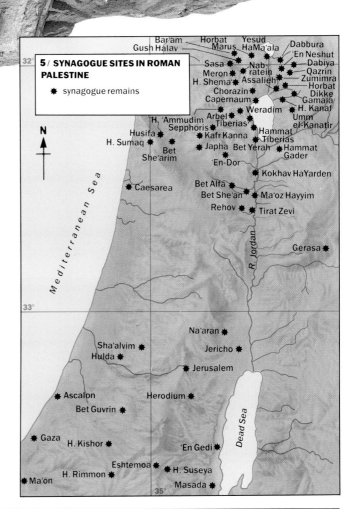

4

6/ bottom A Plan of the municipal complex of Sardis (Asia Minor), showing the position of the basilical hall that was taken over and renovated as a synagogue (3rd-6th centuries). B Plan of the synagogue at Dura-Europos (Roman Syria), in two phases of development. In the earlier phase (*bottom*), it was a typical house where one room served as a hall of assembly. In the later phase (*top*), the entire structure was renovated into a formal hall with forecourt (mid-3rd century). C Plan of the Bet Alfa synagogue, showing the mosaic floor decorations, including the Torah shrine flanked by menorahs, a central zodiac medallion and the biblical scene of the 'Sacrifice of Isaac' (4th-5th centuries).

7/ below right An artist's reconstruction, based on the archaeological remains of the mid-4th century AD synagogue at Horbat Shema'.

5/ SYNAGOGUE SITES IN ROMAN PALESTINE

✱ synagogue remains

7/ RECONSTRUCTION OF HORBAT SHEMA'

ET ALFA

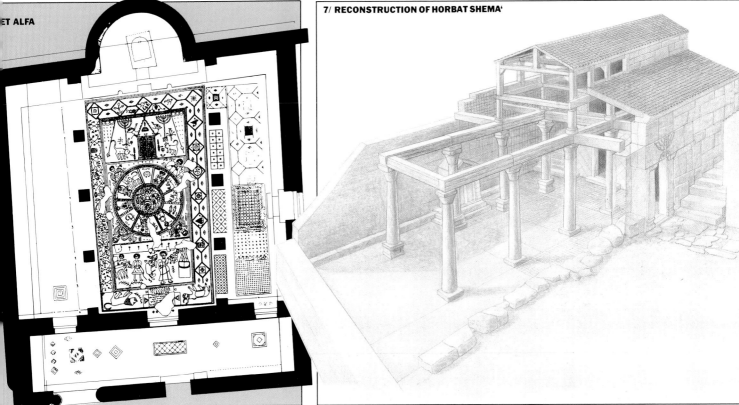

PERHAPS more than any other figure in the New Testament, the spread of Christianity to non-Jews was the achievement of Paul. While he was not the first Christian to work outside of Jewish networks, Paul the 'missionary' (Greek *apostolos*), opened new doors in the urban environment of the Roman empire.

Paul himself was a diaspora Jew from Tarsus, a cosmopolitan trade centre in Cilicia. He had received a Greek education but also studied in Jerusalem as a Pharisee. He first comes to historical notice in the years after the death of Jesus. He becomes the exemplar of the spreading church in the ACTS OF THE APOSTLES. For, after initially resisting the Christian movement, he experiences a call to spread the word. Paul's first work occurred in and around the city of Damascus, but he soon moved back to the region of Cilicia and Syria. He was associated with Antioch, the capital of Syria and the centre for a large Jewish community through which Christian groups had spread, and where the name 'Christian' was first used (ACTS 11.26). This phase is reflected in the so-called 'first missionary journey' (ACTS 13-14).

THE GENTILE MISSION

This early phase of Paul's career covers the period from his call (in the mid-30s) up to *c* AD 48. During this time Paul had only limited contacts with the the church at Jerusalem (GAL 1.16-22). Meanwhile, concerns had been brewing among the Jewish-Christians of Antioch over the inclusion of Gentile converts. Paul and a delegation from Antioch went to Jerusalem to consult with Peter and James (the brother of Jesus) on this matter (GAL 2.1-10; ACTS 15). Even though they agreed with Paul, upon returning to Antioch a serious rift developed.

After this confrontation, which involved Peter (GAL 2.11-14), Paul left Antioch for good and embarked on a mission of his own in the coastal regions of western Asia Minor and Greece. This Aegean phase of Paul's career is reflected in ACTS on the so-called 'second' and 'third' missionary journeys (ACTS 16-20). Paul himself treats it as one phase, during which he was completely independent of either Jerusalem or Antioch, and his efforts were directed toward Gentile converts. It covers the period from *c* AD 49-60, during which time most of the known letters of Paul were written. At the end of this phase he had planned to embark on a new mission through Rome to Spain, after visiting Jerusalem with a collection for the poor (ROM 15.22-29). Apparently, it was on this visit (which was probably his first since the beginning of the Aegean mission) that Paul was arrested and eventually taken to Rome (ACTS 21-28), where tradition holds that he was martyred under the Emperor Nero.

TRAVELS AND LETTERS IN THE AEGEAN

It has been estimated that Paul logged some 10,000 miles during his

1/ map below The map shows the missionary activities of Paul as depicted in ACTS. They lasted for some 16-18 years and carried Paul around the Mediterranean littoral beginning at Antioch, the capital of Syria. Paul's first missionary activities were carried on among Gentile sympathizers in the areas around Antioch and Tarsus, his home town (ACTS 13-14). Paul's own letters often give a different or more detailed picture of his extensive travels. After leaving Antioch Paul moved into the Aegean coastal regions where he spent the rest of his known career. Instead of distinct missionary journeys, Paul treats the Aegean period (*c* AD 49-60) of his ministry as one phase, during which he made numerous visits with his local congregations.

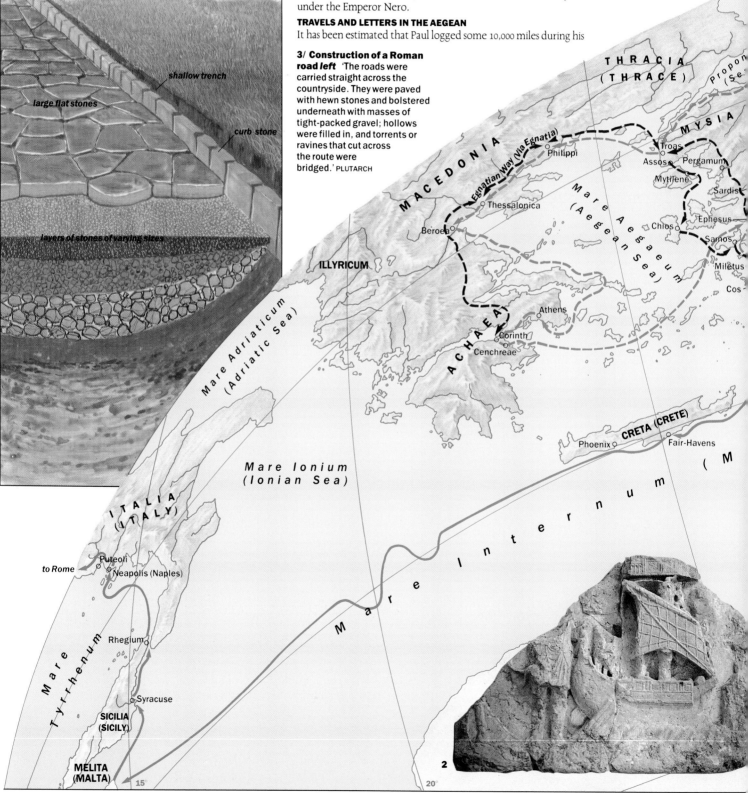

3/ Construction of a Roman road left 'The roads were carried straight across the countryside. They were paved with hewn stones and bolstered underneath with masses of tight-packed gravel; hollows were filled in, and torrents or ravines that cut across the route were bridged.' PLUTARCH

2/ bottom left A Mediterranean trading ship from the time of Paul, taken from part of a sarcophagus from Sidon. The safe sailing season ran from 27 May to 14 September.

missionary travels. The picture described by Paul's letters is one of a tireless worker who moves from city to city along the major highways of the Roman world. ACTS portrays a series of individual stops during an extended travelogue. His letters indicate that Paul followed the major highways to leading urban centres, where he then sought hospitality from which to begin his work of setting up local congregations of followers. Paul was concerned to keep in contact with his congregations, either through visits or by sending his co-workers letters. Paul's letters in the New Testament reflect the widely-used conventions of his day.

Paul visited Corinth at least three times, Timothy and Titus were sent on other occasions, and Paul wrote them at least four letters (and perhaps as many as six). The Corinthians also sent letters to Paul in Ephesus, and several times groups of individuals from Corinth or Philippi conferred with Paul there. Thus, the two letters to Corinth in the New Testament preserve only a part of his extensive dealings with them, and all the letters reflect similar activities as Paul, his helpers, and letters to and from him criss-crossed the Aegean. In this the focus of Paul's missionary work was on the organization of local churches in these major cities.

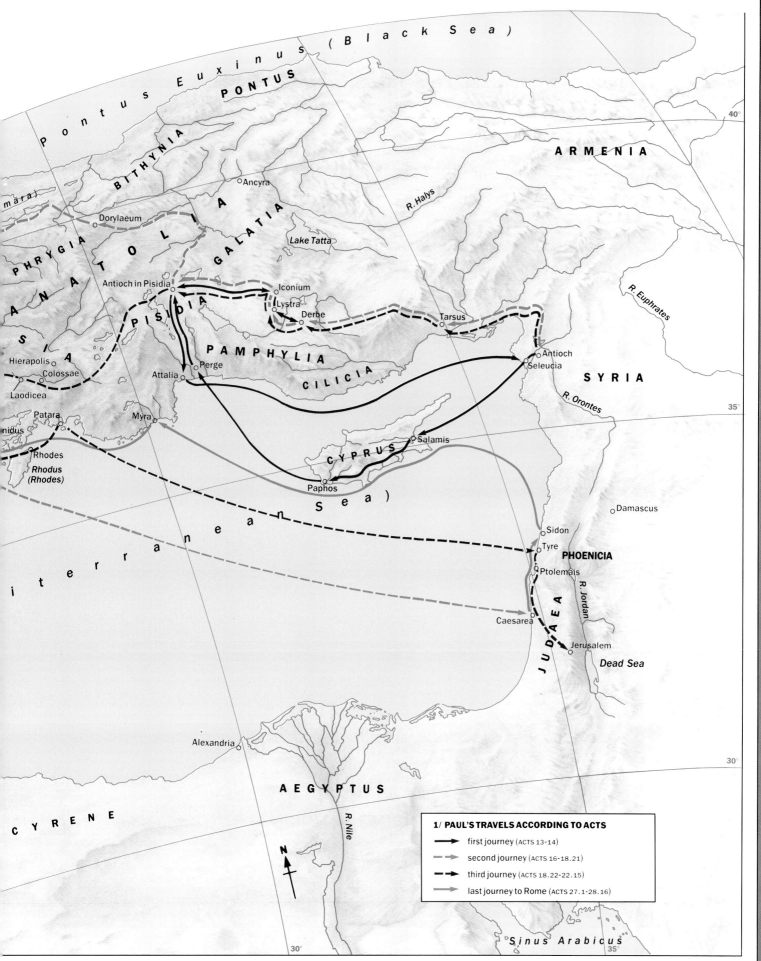

1/ PAUL'S TRAVELS ACCORDING TO ACTS

→ first journey (ACTS 13-14)

→ second journey (ACTS 16-18.21)

→ third journey (ACTS 18.22-22.15)

→ last journey to Rome (ACTS 27.1-28.16)

WHEN Paul left Antioch for his new mission in the Aegean, he headed west through Asia Minor, probably stopping at Ephesus and Troas. From there he went by boat across to Macedonia, landing at the port of Neapolis, where he caught the Egnatian Way, the major overland route across Greece connecting the Levant with the Adriatic coast. Two of the major cities on the Egnatian Way were Philippi and Thessalonica.

PHILIPPI AND THESSALONICA

Philippi lies about nine miles inland from Neapolis at a strategic location through the mountains. The older Greek city, named after Philip of Macedon, was the site of Antony and Octavian's victory over Brutus and Cassius in 42 BC. Afterwards it became an Italian colony under imperial favours, and the bulk of the official inscriptions were in Latin. Greek and Roman gods blended with local Thracian deities, such as the Bendis-Diana. In addition there was a sanctuary to the Egyptian gods Isis and Sarapis.

Little is known of the city in the 1st century AD, as it was largely rebuilt by the Romans from the 2nd century through the Byzantine period. The forum sits alongside the Egnatian Way but was rebuilt in the later 2nd century BC by the Antonine emperors. The new building included elements from the earlier Hellenistic city, but the city itself took on the air of a Roman imperial outpost. As the district capital it controlled all of the towns from Neapolis to Apollonia.

Thessalonica is the main city on the Egnatian Way as it turns across the mainland of Greece. Named after the daughter of Philip II, the city was the first capital of the Roman province of Macedonia (146 BC). With some 36 villages and towns in its administrative district it held a prominent position in the economy of the region. In addition to both local and foreign cults, Thessalonica could boast a major imperial cult centre as well as Samaritan and Jewish enclaves.

When Paul came to Philippi and Thessalonica he worked largely among the local Greek population (1 THESS 1.9). He may have faced local opposition in Philippi (1 THESS 2.2, cf. ACTS 16.24-34), and quickly moved on to Achaea (1 THESS 2.17-3.1). Paul's first letter (1 THESS) was written to Christians at Thessalonica (c AD 50) to encourage and instruct them in his absence. Later he would make several more visits, and the church in Philippi continued to be a major financial supporter of his work (PHIL 4.10-20; cf. 2 COR 8.1).

CORINTH

From Macedonia Paul stopped in Athens for a short time (1 THESS 3.1-6, ACTS 17.16-34) before moving on to Corinth. He remained in Corinth for some months during the year 50-51, while L. Junius Gallio was proconsul of Achaea (cf. ACTS 18.12). Under Rome the ancient city of Corinth had been destroyed (146 BC). Julius Caesar had the city rebuilt and refounded (44 BC) as a Roman colony; under Augustus it became capital of the province of Achaea. In Paul's day, Athens remained an intellectual and tourist centre, alongside the famous sanctuaries of Eleusis and Delphi, but Corinth was the leading administrative and economic centre of the region.

Paul's missionary efforts in the cosmopolitan city of Corinth resulted from its peculiar position as a trade centre in the Aegean. Religious and ethnic groups from across the Mediterranean moved through Corinth. It was especially known as a centre for the healing cult of Asklepios (which had a sanctuary in the city's Lerna district), whose most important sanctuary was at nearby Epidaurus. Also prominent was the worship of the Egyptian Isis cult, which had several temples and smaller sanctuaries in Corinth and Cenchreae. A prominent feature in Corinthian religious life was cultic dining, that is meals in dining halls attached to temples and dedicated to the worship of a particular deity. The Egyptian cults were especially known for this practice. Archaeological work has also revealed that traditional Greek cults were expanded to include dining facilities, as seen at Corinth in the Temple of Demeter.

The city proper sits away from the shore and up against a mountain citadel (the Acrocorinthus) overlooking the isthmus to the mainland. What gave the city its unique position was its two ports, one on each side of the isthmus so that it served as the major shipping centre between the Adriatic (and Italy) and the Aegean (and Asia Minor). The western port at Lechaeum was connected to Corinth by a major road and protected by extensions of the city walls. The eastern port lay at Cenchreae, an artificially constructed harbour, which was connected by roadway to the city and to Isthmia, Epidaurus, and other parts of the administrative district.

Paul apparently spent some time in Corinth on his first visit. He then left for Ephesus which would become his mission base for the next few years (cf 1 COR 16.5-8), while he continued to visit his local churches whenever possible. Paul also wrote letters, delivered by one of his co-workers, giving advice or exhortation in his absence. Paul visited Corinth at least three times and wrote at least four (and possibly six) different letters. During these years the church at Corinth was

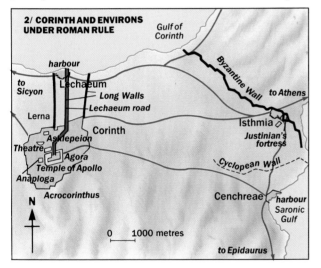

2/ CORINTH AND ENVIRONS UNDER ROMAN RULE

Gulf of Corinth

harbour
to Sicyon
Lechaeum
Long Walls
Lechaeum road
Lerna
Corinth
Asklepeion
Theatre
Agora
Temple of Apollo
Anaploga
Acrocorinthus
N
0 1000 metres

Byzantine Wall
to Athens
Isthmia
Justinian's fortress
Cyclopean Wall
Cenchreae
harbour Saronic Gulf
to Epidaurus

1/ map right Paul's new mission in the Aegean took in cities from Asia Minor, Macedonia, and Achaea.
2/ plan left Capital of the province of Achaea, Corinth held a unique position with its two ports either side of the isthmus.
3/ below Reconstruction based on archaeological evidence of a Hellenistic villa recently excavated at Anaploga in Corinth. Christian congregations may have gathered in such houses to listen to Paul.

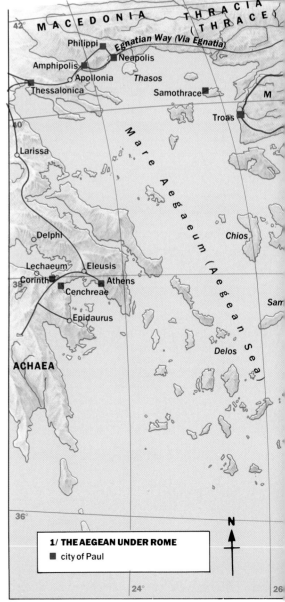

1/ THE AEGEAN UNDER ROME
■ city of Paul

MACEDONIA THRACIA / THRACE
Philippi
Egnatian Way (Via Egnatia)
Amphipolis
Neapolis
Apollonia
Thasos
Thessalonica
Samothrace
Troas
Mare Aegaeum (Aegean Sea)
Larissa
Delphi
Chios
Lechaeum
Eleusis
Corinth
Athens
Cenchreae
Epidaurus
ACHAEA
Delos
Sam

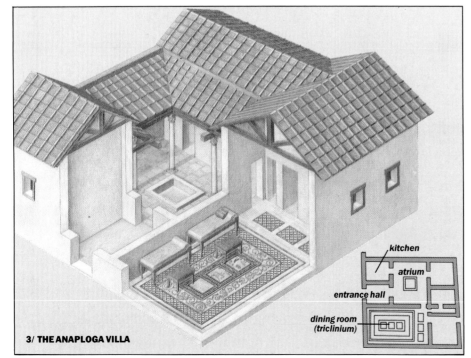

kitchen
atrium
entrance hall
dining room (triclinium)

3/ THE ANAPLOGA VILLA

beset by a number of social, ethical and theological problems that Paul tried to address in his visits and letters. At times the exchanges became heated and discord reigned.

There were several Christian groups in greater Corinth in Paul's day. A lintel stone inscribed in Greek identifies a later Jewish synagogue that stood somewhere along the Lechaeum road. Paul met Prisca and Aquila, who is called a Jew from Pontus, at Corinth after they had come from Italy (ACTS 18.2). Paul stayed with them, and their home became the meeting place for Christians (1 COR 16.19; ROM 16.3). There were several other such 'house churches' (ROM 16.23). Paul notes another Christian group at Cenchreae in the house of a wealthy woman Phoebe, whom he calls deacon and patroness (ROM 16.2).

The fact that these early Christian congregations met in the homes of leading members is important. Each group was relatively small and derived in part from the social makeup of the household, including family, relatives, clients, friends, and slaves of the owners. For this reason, too, factionalism could be a problem (1 COR 1.11-14). A villa found in the excavations of the Anaploga neighbourhood of Corinth may reflect something of the scale of domestic life in which these early Pauline congregations gathered. Paul's remarks (1 COR 11.17-34) make it clear that the eucharist and worship were held around the dinner table, in the dining room (*triclinium*) of each house church. Under prevailing social conventions, it would have been normal to rank the guests in importance at the dinner table by where they sat and what they were served. Paul argued that the disruptive effects of such social stratification in the fellowship meal was inappropriate to Christian communion and worship.

EPHESUS

Ephesus was the capital of the Roman province of Asia and a leading port city. It stood on the highway that ran down the Maeander valley from Colossae and Hierapolis; turning south the road ran to Miletus and Halicarnassus, and north to Ephesus, Smyrna, and Pergamum. The Hellenistic city, famed for its magnificent temple of Ephesian Artemis, had been moved by the general Lysimachus (287 BC) to higher ground between Mts. Pion and Coressos. New Roman construction in honour of the imperial family was begun shortly after the accession of Augustus. The city faced the harbour along a colonnaded thoroughfare, the Arcadian Way, that proceeded to the theatre. Excavations of the commercial market (*agora*), a Temple of the Egyptian Gods, the Library of Celsus, the Hadrianic Temple of Artemis, fountains of Trajan, and a lavish residential quarter reflect the great growth of the Roman city, especially from the 2nd century AD. By the Byzantine period the city had become a large Christian centre associated not only with the work of Paul but also with the traditions of the apostle John and the mother of Jesus.

Ephesus became Paul's base of operation for several years during his Aegean mission, and from it he travelled and wrote many of his letters to other churches (1 COR 16.5-8). Here too there were several house churches; one met with Prisca and Aquila who, like Paul, moved about frequently (1 COR 16.19).

Also, Paul and his co-workers established churches in other nearby cities, including Colossae, Laodicea, and Hierapolis (COL 4.12-16). ACTS 19 records a riot, instigated by silversmiths engaged in production of statues of Artemis, that brought Paul before the city magistrates (the 'Asiarchs') in the theatre of Ephesus. From Paul's own letters it seems that he spent some time in legal detention at Ephesus, probably as a result of his preaching activities (2 COR 1.8-10). Subsequently, he left Ephesus for Troas and Macedonia, before moving on to Corinth (2 COR 2.12-13, 7.5-16). It was from Corinth on this last visit that Paul wrote his letter to the church at Rome in planning his mission to Spain (ROM 15.22-27, 16.1-24).

4/ The theatre at Ephesus.
5/ plan below right Ephesus was the capital of the Roman province of Asia and a major port city.
6/ View of 1st century AD street of the Curetes, at Ephesus.
7/ Artemis, the Asian goddess of fertility. Paul preached against worship of this goddess at Ephesus and nearly incited a riot as a result.

5 / EPHESUS IN ROMAN TIMES

ancient harbour

Temple of Artemis (Old City)

Arcadian Way

outer wall

Sarapeion and Agora

Theatre

Mt Pion

Hadrian's Temple

Mt Coressos

Library of Celsus

Curetes Street

0   500
metres

N

Pontus Euxinus (Black Sea)

Chalcedon

Nicomedia

Propontis (Sea of Marmara)

Dorylaeum

BITHYNIA

F. Sangarius

GALATIA

F. Rhyndacus

Amastris

cus

F. Macestus

Pergamum

PHRYGIA

F. Cogamis

Sardis

ASIA

Smyrna

Philadelphia

LYDIA

Ephesus

Magnesia ad Meandrum

Hierapolis

Laodicea ad Lycum

Colonia Antiochia

Priene

Aphrodisias

Colossae

Miletus

CARIA

PISIDIA

Myndus

Malicarnassus

Cos

PAMPHYLIA

LYCIA

Xanthus

Patara

Rhodus (Rhodes)

28°   30°

JUDAEA was often racked by political unrest, punctuated by two bloody revolts against Rome, and fuelled by religious fervour and expectation of messianic deliverance. The First Revolt (AD 66-74) would result in the destruction of Herod's Temple (in AD 70). The Second Revolt (AD 132-135) dashed hopes of restoring the state and the Temple. The disastrous outcomes forced both political reorganization under the Romans and religious reconstruction among Jews and Christians alike.

THE FIRST REVOLT

Much of the information for this period comes from the Jewish historian Flavius Josephus, who commanded the Jewish armies in Galilee. Following a decisive defeat and realizing the futility of the war, Josephus elected surrender rather than suicide. From Rome he wrote his account of *The Jewish War* and his voluminous *Antiquities of the Jews*.

Procuratorial administration of Judaea produced resentment and resistance, nourished by nationalistic and messianic hopes. Josephus places equal blame on the mismanagement of the last Roman procurators, Albinus (AD 62-64) and Gessius Florus (64-66). The spark came in the late spring of AD 66, after riots at Caesarea, when Florus confiscated the Temple treasury. The governor of Syria, Cestius Gallus (AD 63-66) then marched with reinforcements to Caesarea and Jerusalem. On his return (in October), the Roman forces were routed in an ambush near Beth-horon. Taking this as a sign of divine favour, revolution swept through Jerusalem. The leaders divided the country into military districts, each with its own commander, among them Ananus the High Priest (Jerusalem) and Josephus (Galilee).

The Jewish forces spent the winter consolidating their districts. Having taken much of the kingdom of Agrippa II, Josephus fortified several cities (WAR II.573-74). In spring AD 67 Nero dispatched Vespasian, who marshalled his troops at Ptolemais. Vespasian first attacked Galilee, and it fell without much resistance. As the insurgents scattered, Sepphoris (and other cities) capitulated eagerly. Josephus retreated to Tiberias and then to the strongholds of Gamala and Jotapata, but resistance was futile.

After Josephus surrendered, John of Gischala, his rival, fled to Jerusalem. Meanwhile Samaria fell, and by the end of AD 67 Judaea and Peraea were left alone. Vespasian spent the next months 'pacifying' the outlying territories, from Jamnia (Jabneh) to Idumaea and Peraea as far south as the Dead Sea. As the Romans marched on Jericho, it appears that the Essenes took up arms and Qumran was destroyed.

In AD 68 Vespasian retired to Caesarea to plan the final siege of Jerusalem. Just then news came that Nero had been killed and civil war was threatening at Rome. The 'year of four Emperors' produced a hiatus in the war, as Vespasian was recalled by the Senate to help restore peace. By July of AD 69 Vespasian himself had been named Emperor.

With Vespasian in Rome, his son Titus resumed the war in AD 70. The ravages wrought by Roman attacks were matched by the increasing starvation and the in-fighting between the rebel factions. In August Jerusalem fell in a final assault during which the Temple and much of the old city were destroyed while the population was decimated.

From AD 71-73 the commanding general Lucilius Bassus subdued the fortresses of Herodium and Machaerus. Only the followers of Eleazar ben Jair held out in the imposing fortress of Masada. Encircled by Roman forces, now under Flavius Silva (AD 73-81), the Masada group watched as an earthen assault ramp was constructed. At the final assault (in spring, AD 74) the Romans found that the group had committed suicide rather than face capture.

BEGINNINGS OF THE SECOND REVOLT AD 115-132

The province of Judaea remained 'peaceful' under Vespasian (AD 69-79) and his sons, Titus (AD 79-81) and Domitian (AD 81-96). The Jewish population was resettled, especially in Galilee. New Jewish apocalyptic writings (4 EZRA and 2 BARUCH) predicted coming messianic events, and the Christian gospels viewed the Revolt in light of Jesus' teaching (MK 13 – MATT 24). During the last years of Trajan (AD 98-117) there would be uprisings among the Jews of Egypt, Cyrene, Cyprus and Mesopotamia. The apocalyptic fervour of the First Revolt still persisted in some quarters.

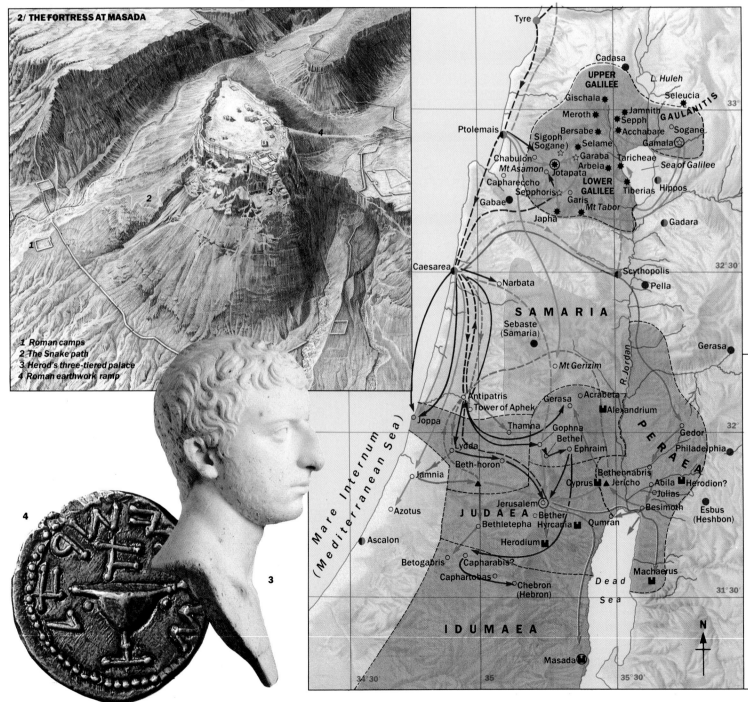

2/ THE FORTRESS AT MASADA

1 Roman camps
2 The Snake path
3 Herod's three-tiered palace
4 Roman earthwork ramp

The precise causes of the Second Revolt are uncertain. The accession of Hadrian (AD 117-138) brought a new period of imperial building. While visiting the east (AD 129-131) Hadrian announced a plan to rebuild Jerusalem as a Roman city called Aelia Capitolina, with a temple of Jupiter built on the Herodian ruins. Combined with other edicts against Jewish practices, this prospect sparked a new revolt.

The leader of the revolt was Simon bar Kosiba, commonly called Bar Kokhba, a messianic title meaning 'Son of the Star' (cf. NUM 24.17). He was supported by Rabbi Akiba. The rebels took Jerusalem and held it for two years. Coins struck under Bar Kokhba are regularly dated according to the year 'of the freedom of Israel' or 'the freedom of Jerusalem'. In response Hadrian called Julius Severus, another veteran of British wars, to command the legions. The final battle took place in AD 135 at Bether, south of Jerusalem. Both Bar Kokhba and Akiba were killed, many towns destroyed and survivors deported as slaves.

Many caves have been found near the Dead Sea containing archives, coins and other goods stored during the Revolt. Four caves at Wadi Murabba'at yielded documents in Hebrew, Aramaic, Greek and Latin. The Cave of the Pool from Nahal Dawid could have sheltered an entire family for some time. The five caves from Nahal Hever, however, yielded some of the most poignant remnants. The Cave of Letters contained letters of Bar Kokhba and the personal accounts of a woman named Babata, as well as 18 skeletons. In the Cave of Horrors, it appears that 40 persons, men, women and children died of starvation, as a Roman camp sat on the ridge above.

THE AFTERMATH OF REVOLT
After the revolt collapsed, Hadrian proceeded with plans for the rebuilding of Jerusalem (Aelia Capitolina), and Jews were excluded from that immediate region of Judaea (from Acrabeta to near En-gedi). Under Antoninus Pius (AD 138-161) some of the restrictions were lifted, but Jewish population shifted either to the diaspora or to Galilee. From Usha, rabbis led the reconstruction, reflected in the codification of the Mishnah by Judah the Prince at Sepphoris in c AD 200.

5/ Bust of the Emperor Hadrian, whose actions sparked off the Bar Kokhba revolt.
6/ **left to right** Coin of Titus (AD 77-78) and coin of Vespasian (AD 71) both showing Judaea Capta legends and indicating the climate of Judaea in the period between the two Revolts; the Shimeon coin (a reference to Bar Kokhba), and a coin with the legend 'For the Freedom of Jerusalem' are both restruck from Roman silver coins.
7/ **map below** The Judaean Desert contained many caves of refuge and Roman camps.
8/ **bottom** The Cave of Letters, over 450 ft long, contained remains of the Bar Kokhba rebels.

1/ **map left** The first Jewish war against Rome resulted from nationalist fervour and exacerbation of the last procurators. Jerusalem was captured and destroyed by Titus in AD 70. Of the few remaining strongholds, Masada was the last to fall in AD 74.
2/ **far left** The fortress at Masada is described by Josephus in *The Jewish War* book VII. Situated on a rock surrounded by ravines, it became a last refuge for Jewish zealots after the First Revolt had been quashed by the Romans.
3/ Much of the information about this period comes from the historian Josephus. Born a Jew, he fought against Rome, but was eventually captured and chose to accept service under the Romans.
4/ A shekel dating from the time of the First Revolt. A Roman silver coin was restamped with a Jewish legend by the revolutionary regime.

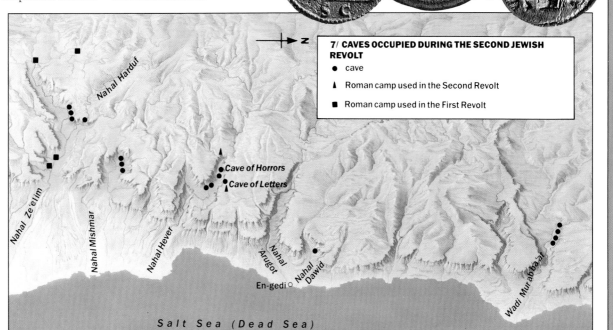

7/ CAVES OCCUPIED DURING THE SECOND JEWISH REVOLT
● cave
▲ Roman camp used in the Second Revolt
■ Roman camp used in the First Revolt

Nahal Harduf
Nahal Ze'elim
Nahal Mishmar
Nahal Hever
Cave of Horrors
Cave of Letters
Nahal Arugot
Nahal Dawid
En-gedi
Wadi Murabba'at
Salt Sea (Dead Sea)

E FIRST JEWISH REVOLT
an military operations:
Cestius Gallus AD 66
AD 67
AD 68
AD 69
AD 70
after AD 70
non-hostile troop movement
attack
major Roman camp
major siege
sh defences:
rebel military district
primarily Jewish population
primarily Samaritan population
gentiles attack Jews AD 66
Jews attack gentiles AD 66
Hasmonaean or Herodian fortress used by rebels
site probably fortified by rebels
site possibly fortified by rebels

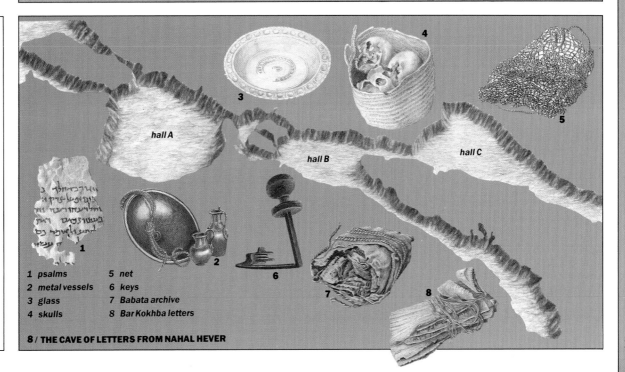

1 psalms
2 metal vessels
3 glass
4 skulls
5 net
6 keys
7 Babata archive
8 Bar Kokhba letters

hall A
hall B
hall C

8 / THE CAVE OF LETTERS FROM NAHAL HEVER

THE First Jewish Revolt against Rome (AD 66-74) (page 128) proved to be significant for the development of both Christianity and Judaism. The period of reconstruction following the war forced a new religious outlook and stimulated new missionary activities. Other than the writings of Paul, all the documents of the New Testament come from after AD 70. During this period the Christian movement would also begin to split apart from Judaism as a separate religion in the eyes of the Roman world.

When Paul wrote to the church at Rome there were already several thriving Christian congregations, even though Paul had never been there. This church may have been founded by diaspora Jews who, like Paul, moved about freely in the Roman world. Likewise, other major cities such as Alexandria had early Christian communities whose beginnings are now lost. By the 2nd century Christian groups were flourishing in Egypt and Syria. The Syrian tradition of Edessa held that Didymas Thomas and Addai (or Thaddaeus) first carried the message there. The impact of travel may be seen in the letters addressed to the seven churches of Asia Minor at the beginning of REVELATION and in the proposed itinerary through Cappadocia, Bithynia, Galatia and Asia of 1 PETER. About AD 96, Clement of Rome wrote a letter to the church at Corinth to deal with organizational matters. Other writings such as the Didache (or 'Teaching of the Twelve Apostles') from Syria also reflect the importance of travelling Christian missionaries in the early 2nd century.

In the first decades of the 2nd century, the first official notice of Christians was beginning to produce persecution. Clement of Rome, his wife Flavia Domitilla and John of Ephesus all faced persecution in the last years of Domitian (AD 81-96). Under Trajan (AD 98-117) more direct notice was taken. Letters written by Pliny the Younger, as imperial legate of Bithynia-Pontus (C AD 110-112), show both the extent of Christian growth in those regions and the beginning of Roman response. At about the same time, the Christian bishop of Antioch, Ignatius, was arrested and transported to Rome, where he was eventually martyred. En route Ignatius was allowed to visit several churches in Asia Minor, particularly Smyrna. From there he wrote letters to Philadelphia, Magnesia, Tralles and Ephesus. After his departure, he wrote to Smyrna, a separate letter to its bishop Polycarp, and to Rome.

By the 2nd century, Christianity outside the Jewish homeland was becoming mainly gentile. It would soon spread to other regions of the Roman empire, especially to Gaul (from Asia Minor) and to North Africa (from Rome). Yet the dominant language continued to be Greek, even in Rome, up through the 3rd century. The first Latin Christian literature comes from Carthage near the end of the 2nd century. North Africa was also the place where the Christian scriptures were first translated from Greek into Latin. In the east they would eventually be rendered into Syriac, Armenian and Coptic (Egyptian) versions as well.

By the beginning of the 3rd century Christians were spreading into more cities, and with it came further acculturation to the Roman world. Christian teachers – Justin Martyr at Rome, Clement and Origen at Alexandria and Tertullian at Carthage –

1/ map below The spread of Christianity between the 1st and 3rd centuries AD.
2/ map right Between the reign of Constantine and the Muslim onslaught in the 630s, there was a spate of new religious buildings in Palestine. However, most churches and monasteries were built in the 4th century becoming important centres during the 6th and 7th centuries.
3/ below Synagogue and church at Capernaum (in a retouched photo). The synagogue (right) dates from the 4th century; the church (left) was built in the 5th century to commemorate the house of St Peter in which Jesus stayed, built on the same spot.
4/ The Colosseum in Rome, scene of many early Christian martyrdoms, was officially opened in AD 80. It was 164 ft high and could hold up to 70,000 spectators.
5/ Baptistry room of Christian building at Dura-Europos, renovated from a private house C AD 241.

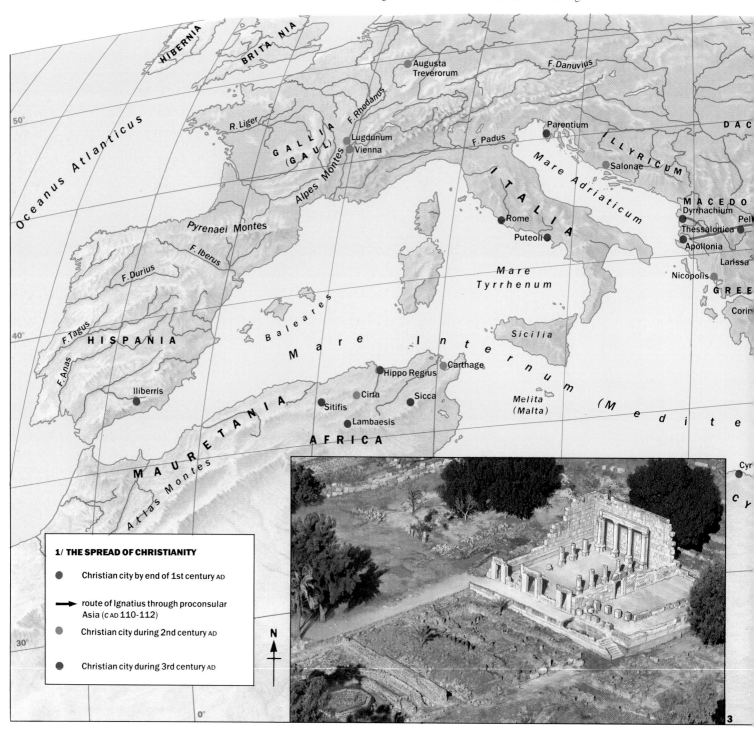

1/ THE SPREAD OF CHRISTIANITY

- Christian city by end of 1st century AD
- → route of Ignatius through proconsular Asia (C AD 110-112)
- Christian city during 2nd century AD
- Christian city during 3rd century AD

N

interpreted the scriptures in the light of Greek philosophy. Further interpretation also produced theological controversies as Christian thought was pulled in different directions. Gnosticism inclined toward a Greek mythological understanding of the created order. Jewish-Christians favoured literal interpretation and complete adherence to Torah, while Marcion rejected Judaism and its scriptures altogether. Greater growth produced greater diversity as the church went 'unto all the world'.

During this period both Jewish and Christian groups in the diaspora began to develop distinctive burial sites, including the catacombs in Rome. Artistic decorations and inscriptions bear testimony to the preservation of the biblical traditions overlaid with a veneer of Roman culture. They also began to expand social organizations and build separate, identifiable religious buildings.

Prior to the 3rd century Jewish and Christian congregations still met in private homes or assembly halls. From the 3rd century onward, new, more elaborate religious architecture began to develop. The earliest known Christian building yet excavated, from Dura-Europos in Syria, illustrates the process of converting a house into a distinctive place of worship. Nearby, another house had been converted into a large and opulent synagogue with painted walls (page 122). Here, as in many areas, Jews and Christians coexisted side by side, although they still faced sporadic persecution from local opposition groups. However, after the two Jewish Revolts there was no wholesale pogrom against Jews or Christians until the later 3rd century. This period of relative peace contributed to their growth and establishment throughout the Roman world.

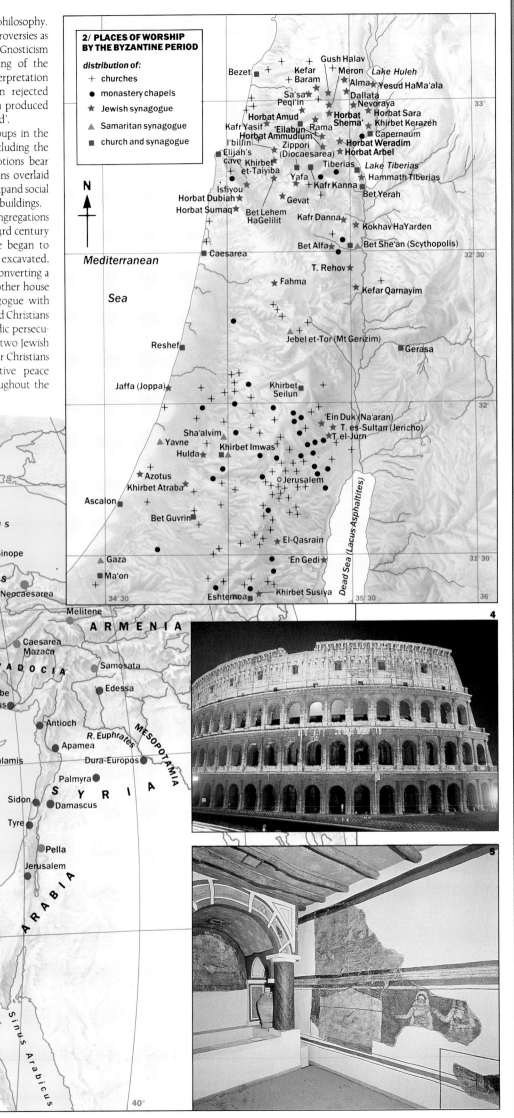

2/ PLACES OF WORSHIP BY THE BYZANTINE PERIOD

distribution of:
+ churches
● monastery chapels
★ Jewish synagogue
▲ Samaritan synagogue
■ church and synagogue

THE Bible presupposes a first-hand knowledge of the geography and place-names of ancient Palestine, since most of the biblical materials emerged from people who were living on the land. The stories in I-II SAM about Eli, the prophet Samuel, and the kings Saul and David, are especially attentive to geographical detail and refer to numerous local places by names which would have been well known to the ancient Israelites.

Unfortunately, it is difficult to map the biblical stories, to the extent that all such maps are hypothetical in varying degrees. Locations of the major cities of ancient Palestine can be established with a reasonable degree of certainty. Difficulties often arise, however, with less prominent villages and landmarks. One example is the story of Saul's search for his father's asses in I SAM 9-10. According to verses 4-5 he passed through the hill country of Ephraim, the lands of Shalishah, Shaalim and Benjamin, and eventually reached the land of Zuph. Except for the references to Ephraim and Benjamin, which point to the central hill country north of Jerusalem as the general setting of the story, none of the 'lands' mentioned in these three verses can be located with confidence.

Further problems arise in cases where the ancient manuscripts of the Bible are difficult to translate, or where they present variant readings. II SAM 24 reports that David conducted a census of his kingdom, for example, and verses 5-7 describe the area covered by the census officials. Unfortunately, the syntax of these verses seems garbled in the standard Hebrew manuscripts, and it is unclear whether some of the words should be translated as proper names (for example, Tahtim-hodshi and Dan-yaan).

The story of how David killed the giant Goliath in I SAM 17 is not so difficult to follow geographically. Most of the places mentioned are well known. However, the story reflects a common folk theme and includes details which conflict with information provided in other biblical passages. For example, I SAM 16.14-23 states that David had already left Bethlehem and joined Saul's court before the Goliath incident. II SAM 21.19 credits another Bethlehemite, Elhanan, with killing Goliath. According to II SAM 5, Jerusalem (to which David brought the head of Goliath) did not fall into Israelite hands until after Saul's death. In short, the story poses another mapping difficulty – how to treat stories which are of doubtful historicity. That both scholars and general readers differ on the historicity of biblical events further complicates the matter.

Often the question to be posed is not whether a particular story *is* legend or history, but whether it mixes legend *with* history. The account of the travels of the Ark in I SAM 4.1-7.2 is a case in point. The narrative begins with the Ark at Shiloh in the charge of the old priest Eli and his two ill-behaved sons. Then the scene shifts to Aphek and Ebenezer, where the Israelite and Philistine armies are camped in preparation for battle. Battle is joined and it appears that the Philistines will be victorious, whereupon the Israelites bring the Ark into the fray in the hope that this will turn the tide. It does not; the Philistines rout the Israelites. Eli's sons are killed, and Eli himself dies upon hearing the news. What is worse, the Philistines capture the Ark and take it to Ashdod, one of the chief cities. Now the Ark begins to bring trouble upon the Philistines – the statue of their god Dagon collapses before it and the people of Ashdod are struck by a plague. The Ark is transferred to Ekron, another Philistine city, with similar results. Finally, in desperation, the Philistines place the Ark on a cart yoked to two milch cows who pull the Ark to Beth-shemesh, where it is taken into custody by Levites. The Levites take it to the house of Abinadab at Gibeah (or 'the hill') near Kiriath-jearim. There it remains, presumably, until David transfers it to Jerusalem (the story seems to continue in II SAM 6).

However, if the Ark was with the Philistines or at Kiriath-jearim from Eli's death until David transferred it to Jerusalem, how can it also be at one of Saul's

battles and in the hands of one of Eli's descendants (see I SAM 14.3)? Furthermore, the story includes motifs and details which other stories in I SAM associate with Samuel and/or Saul. Samuel is also reported to have had two ill-behaved sons who misused their priestly office. Samuel and Saul are both involved in major battles with the Philistines – Samuel's occurred at Ebenezer, Saul's near Aphek. Saul's battle also ended with

disastrous defeat for Israel, including the death of Saul and his sons. Did the careers of Eli, Samuel and Saul actually include these striking similarities? Or do these stories present a somewhat garbled folk memory which blends together three of Israel's early heros?

THE JOURNEY OF EDWARD ROBINSON

It is not until 1838 that modern research in biblical geography really began. In that year Edward Robinson,

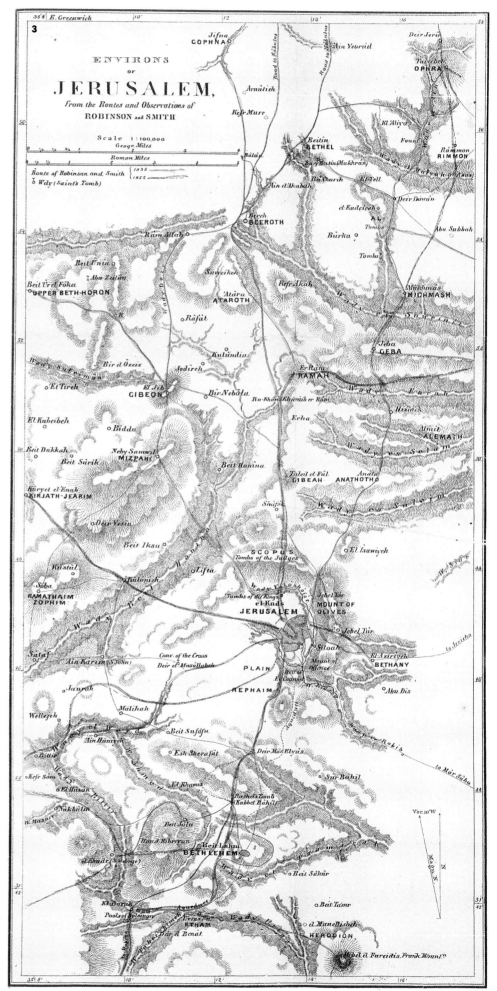

an American scholar who had a thorough training in the Bible, travelled the country recording accurately the modern names of towns and villages; in 1852 he made a similar expedition. Thus with a detailed knowledge of modern Arabic place-names he proceeded to propose biblical names based on his belief that ancient names cling tenaciously to places even when peoples and languages change. The echo of ancient Hebrew names, he maintained, could frequently be heard in the sounds by which villagers identified their home. For example, in the name of Anata he could hear Anathoth, the home of Jeremiah; (el-) Jib he took as a shortened form of Gibeon, where the sun was said to have stood still; er-Ram was Ramah; Jeba' was probably the site of Geba; Mukhmas was Michmash, the place of Jonathan's victory over the Philistines; Beitin, the site of Bethel.

Since Robinson's day archaeology has produced further evidence for identifications. The discovery of ruins dated to periods when a site is said to have been inhabited, increases the probability of equating ancient place-names with the modern. In some few instances the actual name of the site has emerged from the ground being excavated.

1/ map right The route of the ark of the covenant from Shiloh, where it was in possession of the old priest Eli, to the Philistine cities and its return to the house of Abinadad at Gibeah near Kiriath-jearim, can be traced by the narrative in I SAM 4-7. Yet the seemingly clear geographical and historical picture is confronted by divergent traditions in the books of SAMUEL.

2/ map below The description of Saul's search for his father's asses found in I SAM 9.10 locates the area around Ephraim and Benjamin and mentions several familiar cities. However, the three 'lands' of Shalishah, Shaalim and Zuph cannot be located on a map, since they are not mentioned elsewhere in the Bible.

3/ map left The route taken on May 4-5, 1838, by Edward Robinson and Eli Smith over the area immediately north of Jerusalem. They attempted to identify biblical places on the basis of similarity between the ancient name (in capitals) and the name which has survived in Arabic (in italics).

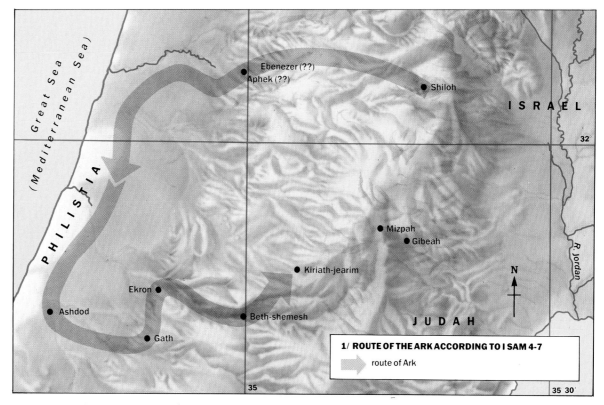

1/ ROUTE OF THE ARK ACCORDING TO I SAM 4-7

→ route of Ark

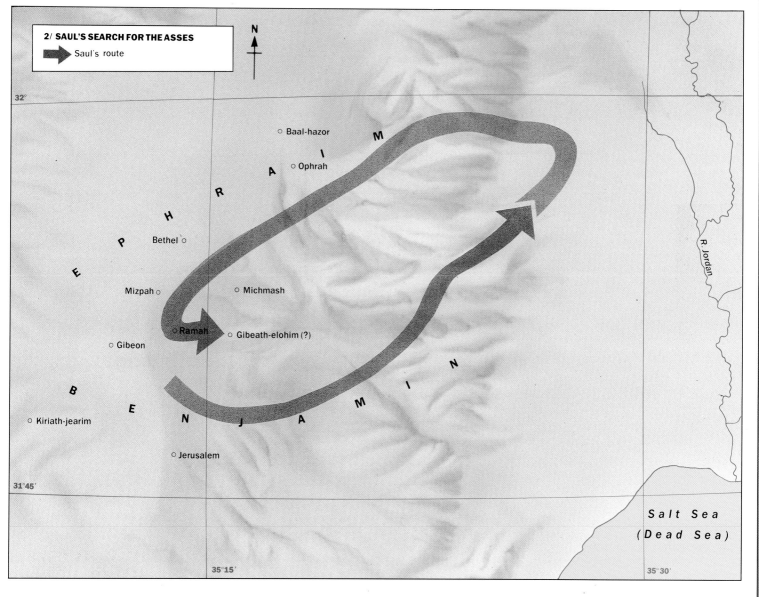

2/ SAUL'S SEARCH FOR THE ASSES

→ Saul's route

ARCHAEOLOGICAL field work can be divided into two main activities: survey and excavation. The earliest surveys were made by Edward Robinson and Eli Smith in 1838 and 1852 to identify places mentioned in the Bible (page 132). The crowning achievement of the 19th-century Palestinography was the *Survey of Western Palestine* made by a team of Royal Engineers sponsored by the Palestine Exploration Fund. During the years 1872-1877 they prepared a 26-sheet set of maps covering the entire country. During the 1920s and 30s attention began to be given to the datable potsherds found on the surface of sites as clues for the dates of settlements. In the past decade surveys have been carried out with different objectives. Assuming that human settlements are not scattered over an area haphazardly or established by chance, it is important to discover the advantages offered by a particular location. Was the spot favourable for defence, subsistence, trade, transport? Was it one with a good water supply or in proximity to other settlements connected by bonds of kinship or religion? These and other questions have prompted many careful surveys of large areas for answers.

EXCAVATION

Scientific excavations began in 1890 with Sir Flinders Petrie's stratigraphic excavations at Tell el-Hesi. There he demonstrated that the ancient mound, or *tell*, was composed of layers of debris deposited by successive occupations often over long periods of time. In general it could be assumed that unless the deposits had been disturbed, the upper layer was later in time than the lower. The layers of deposits, however, are difficult to distinguish because of the digging of pits and foundation trenches into earlier layers, and the robbing of stones from earlier structures for use in later buildings. Yet the principle of stratigraphy established in 1890 is the basic practice of modern archaeology.

A record of the vertical arrangement of what remains of ancient occupation of a site is made on a carefully measured drawing of the face of the cut made into a *tell*. On the 'cross-section', as it is called, appear such details as floors, layers of ash (from a destruction, possibly), sand or organic matter (representing, perhaps, a period of desertion), walls, storage pits, and other features that show along the face of the cut made through the superimposed layers of debris. The horizontal dimensions of buildings, fortifications, ovens, as well as the exact location of artefacts, are surveyed and drawn to scale. It is from these two types of drawings and the photographs taken from the ground and from the air that conclusions are arrived at about the plan and architecture of the superimposed settlements.

The most common artefact from a site is the ceramic vessel, or potsherds from it. Because a pot was fragile and had to be replaced frequently, styles were often changed by potters as they sought to attract buyers. Great quantities of these indestructible potsherds, with such wide differences in form and decoration, provide various kinds of information about ancient life. One is the dating of the stratum in which they were found. Since changes in styles were gradual and some styles survived longer than others a quantitative record of the number of sherds of a type provides an accurate picture of change from one period to another. The data obtained by classifying potsherds according to a typology and then counting examples are suitable for processing in a computer and displaying in bar graphs. Evolution is observed in other forms as well. Typologies of tools, weapons, jewellery, ivory and bone carvings are useful in charting changes through time and serve to strengthen chronological conclusions based on pottery types. More precise means for dating are provided by coins of a known mint, scarabs, inscriptions and the identification of imports of a known date from neighbouring civilizations. Examples of close dating of destructions wrought by invaders like Shishak, Sennacherib or Nebuchadnezzar, or others for whom written records are available, are useful in pin-pointing dates for artefacts found in the ruins. Yet even here there is debate among scholars over identification of a particular destruction with a specific event mentioned in the Bible or other texts.

USE OF SCIENCE IN ARCHAEOLOGY

During the past half-century science has provided new means for dating objects and the context in which they were found. Most notable is radiocarbon dating from samples of carbon such as wood, grain or bone. The isotope Carbon-14 is absorbed from the atmosphere by all living things. Upon the death of the organism the C-14 begins to decay and continues at a steady rate, halving every 5730 years. The remaining C-14 in an object thus provides a measure of the time elapsed since the tree was cut or the animal died. Tree-ring dating is another device useful for chronology. The

pattern of the rings in the trunk of a tree, each representing a year's growth, can be matched with those in a long series which had been established from samples of ancient wood with overlapping ring patterns, whose dating has been obtained by C-14 analysis. A further contribution of science to the dating of objects is that of thermoluminescence. It relies upon the low level of radioactivity in fired clay. Over a period of time electrons are trapped within the clay. When it is again heated the electrons are released as light, which can be measured to determine how much time has elapsed since the original firing of the pottery. New information about the past comes from yet another field of science. Grains of pollen, which are virtually indestructible, can be extracted from soil by the 'flotation' process. The identification of specific plants can throw valuable light on the vegetation of a region or of a particular period of occupation at a site.

NEW OBJECTIVES

Archaeological field work long restricted to the land has recently been extended to include the sea as well. Wrecks of ancient ships, filled with valuable cargo (for example at Cape Gelidonya and Ulu Burun in Turkey and Kyrenia in Cyprus) have documented ancient trade and revealed the construction of the ships which made it possible. The development of techniques like the lifting balloon, the small submarine for deep waters, and means for adapting the grid technique used on land to underwater archaeology have all created a new chapter in the discovery of man's past.

The objectives of archaeological research in Palestine in its earlier days have included the identification of ancient places, the political and social history of the land in various periods and the testing of traditions preserved in written sources, such as the Bible, with what could be deduced from the archaeological record. More recently new questions are being asked. Was there a stratification of society? What are the evidences for the accumulation of wealth, power and position? How has society adapted to its environment at various periods of its history? Other concerns of a socio-anthropological nature exploit the floral and faunal resources of an area. To answer questions of this kind specialists are needed from a variety of disciplines, such as zoology, botany, hydrology and geology. The layout of human settlements is important for a knowledge of ancient behaviour. Similarly the organization of space within the walls of a city provides evidence for what might be termed micro-environment. Fortunately the distribution of artefacts designed for specific uses, such as ritual, cooking, weaving and metalworking, can produce a plan of relationships between those who work at various activities within a city or settlement. Human society and its organization in ancient Palestine throughout its history has become an important objective of archaeological research.

1/ map right The change in settlement patterns has been charted for the sites appearing on the map of the coastal plain for three periods of occupation: Early Bronze II-III (c 2850-2350 BC), Middle Bronze IIA (c 2000-1750 BC) and Middle Bronze IIB (c 1750-1550 BC). The bar graph at the bottom shows comparisons of settlements for each of these periods. For comparisons with the pattern of settlements for the same periods in the area of the central mountain area and in the middle and lower Jordan Valley the quantity of sites occupied is also indicated by bar graphs (sites not shown on the map).

2/ above The *tell* at Beersheba (Tell es-Seba'), about 2.5 acres in area, as seen from the air after the excavations made by Tel Aviv University, which began in 1969, under the direction of

metres above sea-level	18
30	5 metres
29	
28	
27	
26	
25	
24	Late Bronze Age II
23	Late Bronze Age I
22	Middle Bronze Age III
21	
20	
19	
18	
17	
16	
15	**3/ CROSS SECTION THROUGH T.MIKHAL**
14	
13	1664 locus no

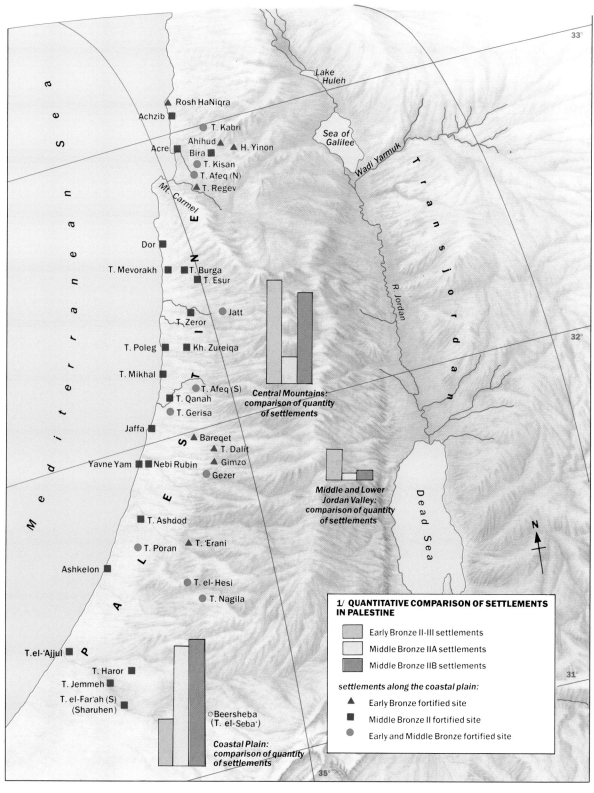

A. Aharoni. The extensive area excavated disclosed the horizontal arrangement of various sections of the city and its buildings in addition to the vertical record of the successive layers of occupation.

3/ below A vertical view of the layers of Tel Mikhal, revealing a system of superimposed earthen ramparts dating from the MBA IIB-LB II (c1750-1200BC). Each deposit uncovered in the excavation was designated separately according to its colour and composition. The thick black lines represent the upper surfaces of the various archaeological features of a period. The broken lines represent the hypothetical continuation of these archaeological features.

1/ QUANTITATIVE COMPARISON OF SETTLEMENTS IN PALESTINE

- Early Bronze II-III settlements
- Middle Bronze IIA settlements
- Middle Bronze IIB settlements

settlements along the coastal plain:

- ▲ Early Bronze fortified site
- ■ Middle Bronze II fortified site
- ● Early and Middle Bronze fortified site

Central Mountains:
comparison of quantity of settlements

Middle and Lower Jordan Valley:
comparison of quantity of settlements

Coastal Plain:
comparison of quantity of settlements

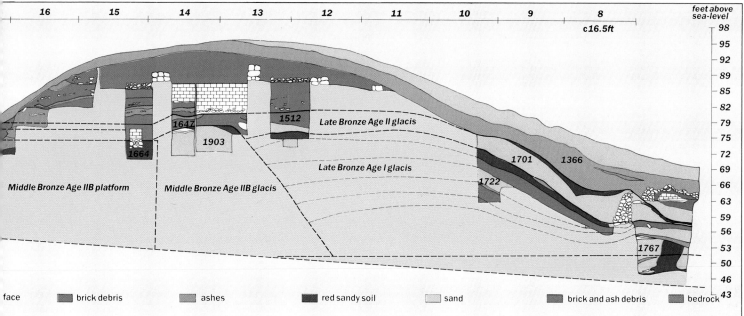

| face | brick debris | ashes | red sandy soil | sand | brick and ash debris | bedrock |

Middle Bronze Age IIB platform

Middle Bronze Age IIB glacis

Late Bronze Age I glacis

Late Bronze Age II glacis

c16.5ft

feet above sea-level

PALESTINE is a small country. When one measures distances between prominent cities in the Old Testament they are separated by miles that can generally be expressed in figures of only one or two digits. Journeys were slow and usually covered but a few miles.

The following list gives the distances in miles between places mentioned in biblical narratives about journeys, marches and other movements of people. A selection of distances outside Palestine, has also been added to the list to set journeys mentioned in the New Testament in a wider context. Since the routes taken from one point to another are not generally known, distances are those of a straight line. This approximation serves for comparative purposes and to provide an idea of the length of a journey. Only those ancient places that can be identified with reasonable certainty are included.

From	To	Miles
Abel-beth-maacah	Gibeon	103
	Jerusalem	105
Abel-meholah	Succoth	13
Abel-shittim	Jericho	14
Adullam	Bethlehem (Judah)	13
	Gath	10
Ai	Jericho	11
Aijalon	Michmash	15
Anathoth	Jerusalem	3
Antioch	Acco	235
	Caesarea	55
	Ephesus	575
	Damascus	195
	Dura-Europos	310
	Jerusalem	330
Aphek (Sharon)	Ashdod	29
	Shiloh	22
Arad (Canaanite)	Hormah	4
Arumah	Shechem	5
Ashdod	Apphek (Sharon)	29
	Gath	12
	Jerusalem	34
Ashkelon	Azotus	10
	Gaza	12
	Joppa	30
	Timnah	23
Athens	Corinth	62
	Ephesus (by sea)	230
	Philippi	310
	Thessalonica	230
Azekah	Beth-horon	12
	Socoh (Shephelah)	8
Baalah (a/c Kiriath-jearim)	Jerusalem	8
Baal-hazor	Jerusalem	14
Beersheba	Bethel	53
	Dan	146
	Gerar	17
	Hebron	25
Bethel	Beersheba	53
	Bethlehem (Judah)	16
	Gibeah	5
	Haran	410
	Hebron	29
	Mizpah (Benjamin)	3
	Ramah (Benjamin)	5
	Shechem	19
	Shiloh	9
	Tekoa	20
Beth-horon (lower)	Jerusalem	12
	Azekah	12
Bethlehem (Judah)	Adullam	13
	Bethel	16
	Jerusalem	4
Beth-shean	Hebron	72
	Jabesh-gilead	13
Beth-shemesh (Judah)	Ekron	7
	Jerusalem	16
	Kiriath-jearim	9
Bezek	Gibeah	36
	Jabesh-gilead	17
	Jerusalem	42
Caesarea-Philippi	Damascus	40
	Capernaum	27
	Tyre	25
	Philadelphia	90
	Petra	260
Corinth	Alexandria (by sea)	600
	Caesarea (by sea)	750

From	To	Miles
Cunaxa	Sardis	1000
	Trapezus	630
Damascus	Antioch	195
	Dura-Europos	295
	Hamath	110
	Jerusalem	140
	Palmyra	135
	Tyre	65
Dan (a/c Laish)	Beersheba	146
	Hebron	123
	Shechem	75
	Sidon	28
Dothan	Samaria	10
	Shechem	14
Eglon	Gezer	24
	Hebron	23
Ekron	Beth-shemesh (Judah)	7
	Gath	5
Emmaus	Azotus	30
	Gazara	14
	Jamnia	28
En-gedi	Maon	16
Eshtaol	Laish	107
	Kiriath-jearim	6
	Zorah	2
Etam	Timnah	17
Gath	Adullam	10
	Ashdod	12
	Ekron	5
	Jerusalem	23
Gaza	Alexandria	270
	Hebron	38
	Hormah	36
	Jerusalem	48
	Joppa	38
	Petra	100
	Zorah	36
Geba (Benjaman)	Gezer	20
	Jerusalem	6
	Ramah (Benjamin)	2
Gerar	Beersheba	17
Gezer	Eglon	24
	Geba (Benjamin)	20
	Gibeon	15
	Jerusalem	19
	Lachish	21
Gibbethon	Tirzah	41
Gibeah	Bethel	5
	Bezek	36
	Jabesh-gilead	45
	Jerusalem	6
	Mizpah (Benjamin)	3
	Ramah (Benjamin)	1
	Rimmon	2
	Ziph	28
Gibeon	Abel-beth-maacah	103
	Gezer	15
	Jerusalem	6
	Kiriath-jearim	6
	Mahanaim	38
Haran	Bethel	410
	Shechem	390
	Ur	590
Hebron	Beersheba	25
	Bethel	29
	Beth-shean	72
	Dan	123
	Eglon	23
	Gaza	38
	Jerusalem	19
	Marisa	13
	Shechem	48
Heshbon	Kadesh-barnea	130
Hormah	Arad (Canaanite)	4
	Gaza	36
Ibleam	Jezreel	8
	Megiddo	12
Jabesh-gilead	Beth-shean	13
	Bezek	17
	Gibeah	45
	Rabbath-ammon	35
	Shiloh	33
Jericho	Abel-shittim	14
	Ai	11
	Gazara	32
	Jerusalem	14
	Samaria	31
Jerusalem	Abel-beth-maacah	105
	Alexandria	320
	Anathoth	3
	Antioch	330
	Ashdod	34
	Ashkelon	42
	Baalah	8
	Baal-hazor	14
	Beth-horon (lower)	12
	Bethlehem (Judah)	4
	Beth-shemesh (Judah)	16
	Bethzur	16
	Bezek	42
	Caesarea	54
	Damascus	140
	Dora	60
	Elephantine	740
	Gath	23
	Gaza	48
	Gazara	19
	Geba (Benjamin)	6
	Gezer	19
	Gibeah	6
	Gibeon	6
	Hebron	19
	Jamnia	30
	Jericho	14
	Jezreel	54
	Joppa	34
	Lachish	27
	Mahanaim	39
	Mareshah	23
	Masada	33
	Megiddo	57
	Michmash	8
	Mizpah (Benjamin)	8
	Modein	18
	Panion	102
	Persepolis	1020
	Rabbath-ammon	43
	Ramah (Benjamin)	6
	Ramoth-gilead	67
	Samaria	35
	Shechem	30
	Succoth	37
	Tekoa	10
	Tyre	104
Jezreel	Ibleam	8
	Jerusalem	54
	Ramoth-gilead	40
	Samaria	21
Jogbehah	Penuel	14
Joppa	Ashkelon	30
	Gaza	38
	Jerusalem	34
Kadesh-barnea	El-paran	80
	Heshbon	130
Kedesh-naphtali	Ramah	88
Kiriath-jearim	Beth-shemesh (Judah)	9
	Eshtaol	6
	Gibeon	6
	Laish	103
	Zorah	7
Lachish	Gezer	21
	Jerusalem	27
Laish (a/c Dan)	Eshtaol	107
	Kiriath-jearim	103
	Sidon	28
	Zorah	111
Mahanaim	Gibeon	39
	Jerusalem	39
Maon	En-gedi	16
	Ziph	5
Mareshah	Jerusalem	23
Megiddo	Ibleam	12
	Jerusalem	56
Michmash	Aijalon	15
Mizpah (Benjamin)	Bethel	3
	Gibeah	3
	Jerusalem	8
	Ramah	3
	Samaria	27
	Shechem	23
	Shiloh	13
Ophrah (Abiezer)	Shechem	27
Penuel	Jogbehah	14
	Shechem	24
	Succoth	5
Rabbath-ammon	Aroer (Reuben)	34
	Jabesh-gilead	34
	Jerusalem	43
Ramah (Benjamin)	Bethel	5
	Geba (Benjamin)	2
	Gibeah	1
	Jerusalem	6
	Kedesh-naphtali	88
	Mizpah (Bejamin)	3

From	To	Miles
(Ramah (Benjamin))	Shiloh	14
	Tirzah	30
Ramoth-gilead	Jerusalem	67
	Jezreel	40
	Samaria	50
Rimmon	Gibeah	64
Rome	Ostia	15
	Puteoli	125
Samaria	Dothan	10
	Jericho	31
	Jerusalem	35
	Jezreel	21
	Mizpah (Benjamin)	27
	Ramoth-gilead	50
	Tirzah	9
Sepphoris	Acco	19
	Caesarea	24
	Capernaum	20
	Gischala	22
	Nazareth	4
	Tiberias	15
Shechem	Arumah	5
	Bethel	19
	Dan	75
	Dothan	14
	Haran	390
	Hebron	48
	Jerusalem	31
	Mizpah (Benjamin)	23
	Ophrah (Abiezer)	27
	Penuel	24
	Shiloh	11
	Succoth	20
	Tirzah	7
Shiloh	Aphek (Sharon)	22
	Bethel	9
	Jabesh-gilead	33
	Mizpah (Benjamin)	13
	Ramah (Benjamin)	14
Sidon	Laish	28
Socoh (Shephelah)	Azekah	8
Succoth	Abel-meholah	13
	Jerusalem	37
	Penuel	5
	Shechem	20
Tamar	Jerusalem	66
Tekoa	Bethel	20
	Jerusalem	10
Timnah	Ashkelon	23
	Etam	17
	Zorah	5
Tirzah	Gibbethon	41
	Ramah (Benjamin)	30
	Samaria	9
	Shechem	7
Tyre	Damascus	65
	Jerusalem	104
Ur	Haran	590
Ziph	Gibeah	28
	Maon	5
Zorah	Eshtaol	2
	Gaza	36
	Kiriath-jearim	7
	Laish	111
	Timnah	5

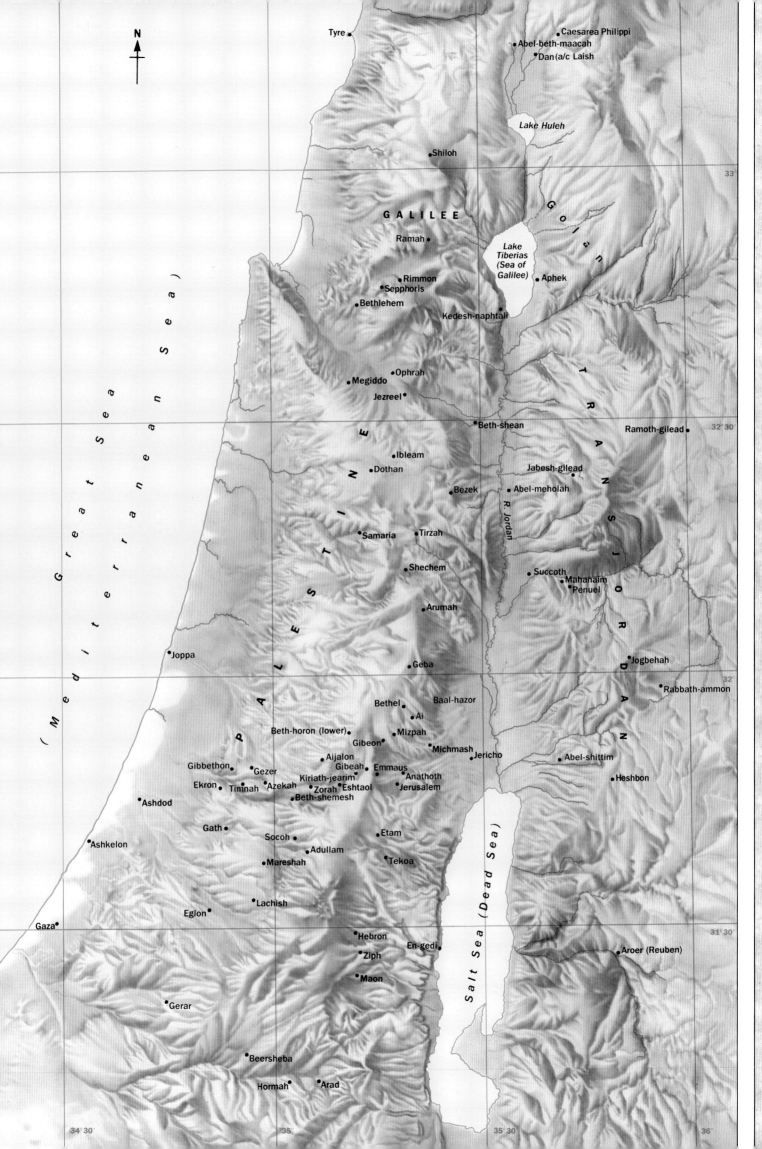

N

Tyre

Caesarea Philippi
Abel-beth-maacah
Dan (a/c Laish

Lake Huleh

Shiloh

GALILEE

Ramah

Lake
Tiberias
(Sea of
Galilee)

Rimmon
Sepphoris
Bethlehem
Kedesh-naphtali

Aphek

G
o
l
a
n

Ophrah
Megiddo
Jezreel

Beth-shean

Ramoth-gilead

Ibleam
Dothan

Bezek

Jabesh-gilead
Abel-meholah

Samaria
Tirzah

Shechem

Succoth
Mahanaim
Penuel

Arumah

Joppa

Geba

Jogbehah

Rabbath-ammon

Bethel
Ai

Baal-hazor

Beth-horon (lower)
Gibeon
Aijalon
Gibeah
Gibbethon
Gezer
Kiriath-jearim
Ekron
Timnah
Azekah
Zorah
Eshtaol
Beth-shemesh

Mizpah
Michmash
Jericho

Emmaus
Anathoth
Jerusalem

Abel-shittim

Heshbon

Ashdod

Gath

Socoh
Adullam
Etam
Tekoa

Ashkelon

Mareshah

Lachish

Eglon

Gaza

Hebron
Ziph
Maon

En-gedi

Aroer (Reuben)

Gerar

Beersheba

Hormah
Arad

Great Sea
(Mediterranean Sea)

R. Jordan

T R A N S J O R D A N

Salt Sea (Dead Sea)

P A L E S T I N E

33°

32° 30'

32°

31° 30'

34° 30'

35°

35° 30'

36°

THIS concise bibliography has been compiled for the reader who wishes to pursue further a geographical, archaeological or historical subject alluded to or dealt with in the text. In addition to more recent books there are included some that served as milestones in the progress of the historical geography of the Bible.

OLD TESTAMENT

Abel, F. -M. Géographie de la Palestine, vols. I-II, Paris 1933-38.

Ackroyd, P. R. Israel under Babylonia and Persia, London 1970

Aharoni, Y. The Land of the Bible, a Historical Geography, 2nd ed., London 1979

Ahituv, S. Canaanite Toponyms in Ancient Egyptian Documents, Jerusalem 1984

Albright, W. F. The Archaeology of Palestine, Harmondsworth 1960

Amiran, R. Ancient Pottery of the Holy Land, New Brunswick, N. J. 1970

Anati, E. Palestine before the Hebrews, New York 1963

Avi-Yonah, M., Stern, E. (eds.) Encyclopedia of Archaeological Excavations in the Holy Land, 4 vols., Jerusalem 1975-78

Baly, D. The Geography of the Bible, rev. ed., New York 1974

Beek, M. A. Atlas of Mesopotamia, New York 1962

Biran, A. Temples and High Places in Biblical Times, Jerusalem 1981

Braemer, F. L'archétecture domestique du Levant à l'âge du fer, Paris 1982

Bright, J. A History of Israel, 3rd ed., Philadelphia 1981

Busink, Th. A. Der Tempel von Jerusalem, von Salomo bis Herodes, 2 vols., Leiden 1970, 1980

The Cambridge History, 3rd ed., Cambridge 1970ff.

Davies, G. I. The Way of the Wilderness, Cambridge 1975

Desborough, V. R. d'A. The Last Mycenaeans and their Successors, Oxford 1964

Dothan, T. K. The Philistines and their Material Culture, New Haven 1982

Ehrich, R. W. (ed.) Chronologies in Old World Archaeology, Chicago 1965

Eph'al, I. The Ancient Arabs: Nomads on the Borders of the Fertile Crescent 9th-5th Centuries B.C., Jerusalem 1982

Finegan, J. Handbook of Biblical Chronology, Princeton 1964

Galling, Kurt (ed.) Biblisches Reallexikon, 2nd ed., Tübingen 1977

Gardiner, A. Egypt of the Pharaohs: An Introduction, Oxford 1961

Gurney, O. R. The Hittites, Harmondsworth 1981

Hallo, W. W., Simpson, W. K. The Ancient Near East: A History, New York 1971

Hammond, N. G. L. Atlas of the Greek and Roman World in Antiquity, Park Ridge, N. J. 1981

Harding, A. (ed.) Climatic Change in Later Prehistory, Edinburgh 1982

Harden, D. B. The Phoenicians, rev. ed., Harmondsworth 1980

Hawkins, J. D. (ed.) Trade in the Ancient Near East, London 1977

Helck, W. Die Beziehungen Ägyptens zu Vorderasien im 3. und 2. Jahrtausend v. Chr., Wiesbaden 1962

Heltzer, M. Goods, Prices and Organization of Trade in Ugarit, Wiesbaden 1978

Hennessey, J. B. The Foreign Relations of Palestine during the Early Bronze Age, London 1967

Jagersma, H. A History of Israel in the Old Testament Period, Philadelphia 1983

Keel, O. The Symbolism of the Biblical World, New York 1978

Kenyon, K. M. Archaeology in the Holy Land, 4th ed., London 1979

Macqueen, J. G. The Hittites and their Contemporaries in Asia Minor, London 1975

Mayes, A. D. H. Israel in The Period of the Judges, London 1974

Mellaart, J. The Chalcolithic and Early Bronze Ages in the Near East and Anatolia, Beirut 1966

The Neolithic of the Near East, London 1975

Miller, J. M., Hayes, J. H. A History of Ancient Israel and Judah, Philadelphia 1986

Moscati, S. The World of the Phoenicians, London 1968

Na'aman, N. Borders and Districts in Biblical Historiography, Jerusalem 1986

Naveh, J. Early History of the Alphabet, Jerusalem 1982

North, R. A History of Biblical Map Making, Rome

Noth, M. The History of Israel, 2nd ed., London 1960

O'Callighan, R. T. Aram Naharaim, Rome 1948

Oppenheim, A. L. Ancient Mesopotamia, Chicago 1964

Ottosson, M. Temples and Cult Places in Palestine, Uppsala 1980

Préhistoire du Levant, CNRS Paris 1981

Pritchard, J. B. The Ancient Near East in Pictures Relating to the Old Testament, 2nd ed., Princeton 1969

(ed.) Ancient Near Eastern Texts Relating to the Old Testament, 3rd ed., Princeton 1969

Robinson, E. Biblical Researches in Palestine, 3 vols, Boston 1874

Rowley, H. H. From Joseph to Joshua, London 1950

Saggs, H. W. F. The Greatness that was Babylon, rev. ed., London 1988

The Might that was Assyria, London 1984

Sanders, N. K. The Sea Peoples, London 1978

Simons, J. The Geographical and Topographical Texts of the Old Testament, Leiden 1959

Handbook for the Study of Egyptian Topographical Lists Relating to Western Asia, Leiden 1937

Jerusalem in the Old Testament, Leiden 1952

Stern, E. The Material Culture of the Land of the Bible in the Persian Period 538-332 B.C., Warminster 1982

Stubbings, F. H. Mycenaean Pottery from the Levant, Cambridge 1951

Supplément, Dictionnaire de la Bible, Paris 1928-

Thiele, E. The Mysterious Numbers of the Hebrew Kings, rev. ed., Grand Rapids, Michigan 1984

Thompson, T. L. The Historicity of the Patriarchal Narratives, Berlin 1974

The Settlement of Palestine in the Bronze Age, Wiesbaden 1979

Tübinger Atlas des Vorderen Orients, Wiesbaden

Van Seters, J. The Hyksos, A New Investigation, New Haven 1966

de Vaux, R. Ancient Israel: Its Life and Institutions, 2 vols., New York 1965

The Early History of Israel, London 1978

Weippert, M. Edom. Studien..., Tübingen 1971

The Settlement of the Israelite Tribes in Palestine, London 1971

Welten, P. Die Königs-Stempel, 1969

Wiseman, D. J. (ed.) Peoples of Old Testament Times, Oxford 1973

Yadin, Y. The Art of Warfare in Biblical Lands, 2 vols., New York 1963

Zohary, M. Plants of the Bible, Cambridge 1982

Vegetation of Israel and Adjacent Areas, 1981

INTER-TESTAMENT

Aharoni, Y. The land of the Bible, Cambridge 1985

Baines, J., Malek, J. Atlas of ancient Egypt, Oxford 1980

Bar-Kochva, B. Judas Maccabaeus: the Jewish struggle against the Seleucids, Cambridge 1989

Bartlett, J. R. Jews in the Hellenistic world, Cambridge 1985

Bartlett, J. R. The Bible: faith and evidence, London 1990

Bickermann, E. J. From Ezra to the last of the Maccabees, New York 1962

Bickermann, E. J. Four strange books of the Bible, New York 1967

Bickermann, E. J. The Jews in the Greek age, Cambridge, Mass. 1988

Coggins, R. J. Samaritans and Jews, Oxford 1975

Davies, W. D., Finkelstein, L. (eds.) The Cambridge History of Judaism, I: Introduction: The Persian period,, Cambridge 1984, II: The Hellenistic age, Cambridge 1990

Fraser, P. M. Ptolemaic Alexandria, I-III, Oxford 1972

Hadas, M. Hellenistic culture: fusion and diffusion, New York 1959

Hengel, M. Judaism and Hellenism, London 1974

Hengel, M. Jews, Greeks and Barbarians, London 1980

McNamara, M. Intertestamental literature, Wilmington, Delaware 1983

Momigliano, A. Alien wisdom: the limits of Hellenisation, Cambridge 1975

Nickelsburg, G. W. E. Jewish literature between the Bible and the Mishnah, London 1981

Porten, B. Archives from Elephantine, Los Angeles & London 1968

Schalit, A. (ed.) The World History of the Jewish People, VI: The Hellenistic Age, Jerusalem 1972

Stern, E. The material culture of the land of the Bible in the Persian period, Warminster & Jerusalem 1982

Stone, M. E. Scriptures, sects and visions, Oxford 1982

Tarn, W. W., Griffith, G. T. Hellenistic civilisation, 3rd ed., London 1952

Tcherikover, V. Hellenistic civilisation and the Jews, Philadelphia & Jerusalem 1961

Vermes, G. The Dead Sea Scrolls in English, 3rd ed., Harmondsworth 1987

Wallbank, F. E. The Hellenistic world, London 1981

NEW TESTAMENT

Akurgal, E. Ancient Civilizations and Ruins of Turkey, 6th ed., Istanbul 1985

Brooten, B. Women Leaders in Ancient Synagogues, Brown Judaic Studies 36, Chico (Atlanta) 1982

Cook, S. A., Adcock, F. E., Charlesworth, M. P. (eds.) The Cambridge Ancient History, vols. 8-11, Cambridge 1930-36

Freyne, S. Galilee from Alexander the Great to Hadrian: A Study of Second Temple Judaism, Wilmington 1980

Goodenough, E. R. Jewish Symbols in the Graeco-Roman Period, 12 vols., New York 1954-67

Holum, K. G., Hohlfelder, R. L., Bull, R. J., Raban, A. King Herod's Dream: Caesarea on the Sea, New York and London 1988

Jeremias, J. Jerusalem in the Time of Jesus, London 1969

Jones, A. H. M. The Cities of the Eastern Roman Provinces, 2nd ed., Oxford and New York 1971

Koester, H. Introduction to the New Testament, 2 vols., Philadelphia 1982

Leaney, A. R. C. The Jewish and Christian World: 200 BC to AD 200, Cambridge 1984

Meeks, W. A. The First Urban Christians: The Social World of the Apostle Paul, New Haven and London 1983

Meyers, E. M., Strange, J. F. Archaeology, the Rabbis, and Early Christianity, Nashville 1981

Murphy-O'Conner, J. St. Paul's Corinth: Texts and Archaeology, Wilmington 1983

Reicke, B. The New Testament Era, Philadelphia 1974

Safrai, S., Stern, M. (eds.) The Jewish People in the First Century, 2 vols., Assen & Philadelphia 1974-1976

Stambaugh, J. E., Balch, D. L. The New Testament in its Social Environment, Philadelphia 1986

Stambaugh, J. E., The Ancient Roman City, Baltimore 1988

Van der Meer, F., Mohrmann, C. Atlas of the Early Christian World, London 1966

Vermes, G. The Dead Sea Scrolls: Qumran in Perspective, rev. ed., Philadelphia 1981

White, L. M. Building God's House in the Roman World: Architectural Adaptation among Pagans, Jews and Christians, Baltimore 1990

Yadin, Y. The Bar Kochba Revolt, London 1971

Masada, London 1966

This atlas covers the Mediterranean world, the Near East and southwest Asia as they occur in biblical history over a period of several thousand years. The names on the maps, therefore, reflect the different languages involved over this time-span: ancient Egyptian, Akkadian, Greek, Latin, Hebrew and Arabic. In the interests of simplicity diacritics have been omitted in the transliteration of modern Hebrew and Arabic names, e.g. Zippori appears as Zippori, Taffūḥ as Taffuh.

This index includes the names of all those countries, regions, places and physical features shown in the atlas which carry an annotation on the maps or which bear a symbol explained in the legend of the relevant map; not indexed are those names shown on the maps for locational purposes. Entries are of four types:-

1 The names of Old and New Testament sites, given as they are spelled in the Revised Standard Version of the Bible. Following the entry in brackets are given: variant spellings and forms of the biblical name; earlier Egyptian and Akkadian and later Greek and Latin names by which the place was also known; the modern Arabic name (preceded by a question mark if identity is uncertain) and the modern Hebrew name of the site if it has one. Location of these sites is given generally as N(orthern) Palestine, C(entral) Transjordan, etc., and specifically by use of a six-figure grid reference to the end-paper maps. The grid coordinates should be read in the conventional manner: the first three numbers refer to the north-south axis, the second three to the east-west axis. A six-figure grid reference *not* followed by a sub-entry and a page number means that the main-entry name occurs only on the end-paper maps and does not appear in the body of the atlas.

2 Other early names (and their variants), mainly Latin or Greek, which do not occur in the Bible; modern Arabic and/or Hebrew names of archaeological sites; historical names of places outside the Holy Land. Variant names, if any, are shown in brackets. Location is by general geographical reference, as C(entral) Palestine, W(est-ern) Syria, E(astern) Asia Minor, S(outhern) Mesopotamia; L(ower) and U(pper) in the case of Egypt, etc.

3 A bracketed variant name given in bold type indicates that that name also appears in primary position on a map and that there is a separate reference to it in the index. In such subordinate entries identity with the biblical or principal name is indicated by use of the equals sign =

4 All other variant forms and spellings of names which are not found in primary position on any of the maps are cross-referred to main entries by the use of *see*.

Note In alphabetizing compound Arabic names the lower-case form of definitive article is ignored, e.g. Khirbet el-'Ater comes before Khirbet Atraba.

Note The final part of each entry indicates the page number on which the name will be found. When there is more than one map on a page, the entry refers to the map number, e.g. 129/2.

ABBREVIATIONS

a/c	also called
Akk.	Akkadian
Anc.	ancient
Ar.	Arabic
a/s	also spelled
Bibl.	biblical
EBA	early Bronze Age
Eg.	Egyptian
Eng.	English
Gk.	Greek
G/L	Greek and Latin
H.	Horbat
Heb.	modern Hebrew
Kh.	Khirbet
Lat.	Latin
LBA	Late Bronze Age
MBA	Middle Bronze Age
Mod.	modern
n/c	now called
n/s	now spelled
Per.	Persian
T.	Tel (Hebrew)
	Tell (Arabic)

GLOSSARY OF GEOGRAPHICAL TERMS

'AIN (Ar)	spring
BE'ER (Heb)	well
BEIT (Ar)	house
BET (Heb)	house
BIR (Ar)	well
BURJ (Ar)	fort
'EIN (Ar)	spring
'EN (Heb)	spring
HAMMAM (Ar)	hot springs
HORBAT (Heb)	ruins
JEBEL (Ar)	mountain
KAFR (Ar)	village
KEFAR (Heb)	village
KHIRBET (Ar)	ruins
NAHAL (Heb)	river, stream
QAL'AT (Ar)	fort
QARN (Ar)	hill
QASR (Ar)	palace, fort
RAS (Ar)	headland, summit
ROSH (Heb)	headland, summit
RUJM (Ar)	mound, cairn
TEL (Heb)	mound
TELL (Ar)	mound
WADI (Ar)	watercourse

A

Abar Nahara (*a/c* Province Beyond the River) Persian province of Syria 91

Abdera NE Greece Jewish diaspora 121

Abdera (*mod*. Adra) S Spain Phoenician city 56; Jewish diaspora 120

Abdon (*Ar.* Kh. 'Abdeh, *Heb.* T. 'Avdon) N Palestine 165272

Abel (in Galilee) (*Ar.* 'Ain Ibl) N Palestine 188279

Abel (in Gilead) (*a/c* **Abila, Seleucia**, *Ar.* T. Abil) N Transjordan 231231

Abel-beth-maacah (*a/c* Abel-maim, *Eg.* Abilum, *Ar.* Abil el-Qamh, *Heb.* T.Avel Bet Ma'akha) N Palestine 204296 42

Abel-keramim (*Ar.?* Na'ur) N Palestine 228142 44/1

Abella C Transjordan 94/3

Abel-maim *see* **Abel-beth-maacah**

Abel-meholah (*Ar.* T. Abu Sus) N Palestine 203197 Elisha 75

Abel-shittim (*a/c* Shittim, *Ar.* T. el-Hammam) C Transjordan 214138

Abiezer C Palestine clan-district of Israel 74

Abila = **Abel** captured by Jannaeus 101; Roman city 113

Abila (*a/c* Abel, *Ar.* Suq Wadi Barada) S Syria in Kingdoms of Agrippas I and II 118

Abila C Transjordan Jewish revolts 128

Abil el-Qamh *see* **Abel-beth-maacah**

Abilum = **Abel-beth-maacah** MBA town 16/3

Abimael tribe of S Arabia 59

Abu Ghosh = **Gibeah of Kiriath-jearim** early settlement 11

Abu Shahrain *see* **Eridu**

Accad (*a/s* Akkad) region of C Mesopotamia early trade 15/1; early writing 60; conquests in Judah 71

Accaron = **Ekron** given to Jonathan 98; captured by Jannaeus 101; Herod's kingdom 105; Roman town 112

Acchabare (*a/s* Acchabaron) N Palestine Jewish revolts 128

Acco (*Akk.* Akka, *Eg.* 'Akaya, *G/L* **Ptolemais**, *Eng.* Acre, *Ar.* T.el-Fukhkhar, *Heb.* T. 'Akko) N Palestine 158258 MBA site 16/1; Egyptian expansion 27,28; Mycenaean pottery 31; district of Solomon's kingdom 52; Phoenician influence 57/2; Iron Age site 62; captured by Assyrians 80/2; early settlement 135

Achaea Roman province of S Greece 103/1

Achshaph (*Akk.* Akshapa, *Eg.* Aksapa, *Ar.?*Kh. el-Harbaj, *Heb.* T.Regev) N Palestine 158240 Egyptian expansion 28; battle of Hazor 39/4; Canaanite royal city 39/5

Achzib (in Asher) (*Gk.* Ecdippa, *Ar.* Ez-zib, *Heb.* T.Akhziv) N Palestine 159272 MBA site 16/1; Phoenician finds 57/2; Iron Age site 62; captured by Assyrians 80/2; early settlement 135

Achzib (in Judah) (*a/c* Chezib, *Ar.?*Kh. T. el-Beida, *Heb.* H. Lavnin) C Palestine 145116 79/2

Acmonia W Asia Minor Jewish diaspora 121

Acrabbein (*a/s* **Acrabeta**, Acrabetta) N Palestine toparchy of Herod's kingdom 105; Roman town 113

Acrabeta = **Acrabbein** Jewish revolts 128

Acre *see* **Acco**

Adab (*mod*. Bismaya) S Mesopotamia ziggurat 14/2; local gods 69

Adadah *see* **Aroer** (in Negeb)

Adam (*Ar.* T. ed-Damiya) C Transjordan 201167 captured by Egyptians 63

Adamah (*a/c* Shemesh-adam, *Ar.?*Qarn Hattin, *Heb.* H. Qarne Hittim) N Palestine 193206

Adami-nekeb (*a/c* Adamim, *Ar.* Kh. et-Tell ed-Damiyeh, *Heb.* T.Adami) N Palestine 193239

Adarus (*a/c* Bucolon Polis) N Palestine Roman town 113

Adasa C Palestine 98

Ad Dianam S Palestine Roman fort 111

Ader S Transjordan MBA site 17/1

Adida = **Hadid** fortified by Simon 98,101

Adir S Transjordan Moabite site 66

Adora = **Adoraim** captured by Hyrcanus 101; Roman town 112

Adoraim (*a/c* **Adora**, *Ar.* Dura, *Heb.* Adorayim) C Palestine 152101 fortress of Rehoboam 78; free city of Herod's kingdom 105

Adra *see* **Abdera**

Adramyttium NW Asia Minor Jewish diaspora 121

Adullam (*Ar.* Esh-Sheikh Madkhur, *Heb.* H. 'Adullam) C Palestine 150117 Canaanite royal city 39/5; fortress of Rehoboam 78

Adummim N Palestine Egyptian expansion 28

Adurun N Palestine Egyptian expansion 28

Aegean Sea trade routes 22; Phoenician trade 57/1

Aegina SE Greece synagogue site 122

Aelana = **Elath** Nabataean trade 109; Roman fort 111

Aelia Capitolina = **Jerusalem** Roman city 112

Aendor = **En-dor** Roman town 113

Africa Roman province of Tunisia 102; growth of Christianity 130

'Afula = **Ophrah** (in Abiezer) Chalcolithic settlement 11; EBA city 12; Mycenaean pottery 31; Philistine remains 43;

Agade C Mesopotamia EBA city 13

Agrigentum (*Gk.* Akragas, *mod*. Agrigento) W Sicily Jewish diaspora 120

Agrippias = **Anthedon** Herodian port 106; Roman harbour 112

Agrippina = **Remeth** Herodian fortress 105

Ahihud N Palestine early settlement 135

Ahlab (*a/c* Mahalab, *Ar.* Kh. el-Mahalib) S Lebanon 172303 41/2

Ai (*Ar.* Kh. et-Tell) C Palestine 174147 EBA city 12; battle between Canaanites and Israelites 38/1; Canaanite royal city 39/5; LBA remains 41/3; Philistine remains 43; temple 53

Aiath (*Ar.?*Kh. Haiyan) C Palestine 175145

Aijalon (*Akk.* Ayaluna, *Ar.* Yalo) C Palestine 152138 Levitical city 50; captured by Egyptians 63; fortress of Rehoboam 78

Ain (*a/c* Ashan) S Palestine 50

Ain (*Ar.?*Kh. 'Ayyun) N Transjordan 212235

'Ain el-'Arus S Palestine Roman fort 112

'Ain Fashkha C Palestine Essene settlement 110

'Ain el-Gharabeh *see* **Beth-arabah**

'Ain Ghuweir C Palestine Essene settlement 110

'Ain Hod *see* **En-shemesh**

'Ain Ibl *see* **Abel** (in Galilee)

'Ain Jidi *see* **En-gedi**

'Ain Mallaha *see* **Enan**

'Ain Na'm N Palestine Egyptian expansion 27

'Ain el-Qudeirat *see* **Kadesh-barnea**

'Ain Sakhri C Palestine Natufian settlement 11

'Ain Shems *see* **Beth-shemesh** (in Judah)

'Ain Yarqa S Palestine Roman fort 112

'Akaya = **Acco** MBA town 16/3

Akka = **Acco** Egyptian rule 24

Akkad *see* **Accad**

Akragas *see* **Agrigentum**

Aksapa = **Achshaph** MBA town 16/3

Akshapa = **Achshaph** Egyptian rule 24

Alaca Hüyük NE Anatolia 33

Alalakh (*Ar.* Tell Atchana) NW Syria Egyptian expansion 21; trade with Hattushash and Que 33; early writing 60

'Aleiyan *see* **Kedemoth**

Alema N Transjordan 99/1

Alemeth *see* **Almon**

Aleppo (*Lat.* Beroea; *a/c* Khalab; *mod*. Halab) N Syria EBA city 12; early trade 14/1; Jacob's journey 17/2; Egyptian expansion 21; local gods 68; Egyptian expedition to Assyria 87;

Beroea – Dan

eroea N Greece Jewish diaspora 21; Paul's journeys 124
eroea =***Aleppo*** Nabataean trade 09
ersabe =***Beersheba*** Roman fort 12; Jewish revolts 128
ersinya see ***Rogelim***
eruta (*Lat.* ***Berytus***, *mod.* ***eirut***) C Lebanon Egyptian rule 1,25; Mycenaean pottery 31
erytus =***Beruta*** Jewish diaspora 21
esara N Palestine Roman city 13
esimoth =***Beth-jeshimoth*** Jewish evolts 128
et Alfa N Palestine synagogue ite 123,131/2
eta-shamshu =***Beth-shemesh*** (in Naphtali) MBA town 16/3
et Dagan see ***Beth-dagon***
eten (*Ar.*?Kh.Ibtin, *Heb.* H.Ivtan) Palestine 160241
et Guvrin =***Betogabris*** Herod's ingdom 105; synagogue site 23,131/2
eth-anath (*Ar.* Safed el-Battikh) Palestine 190289 Egyptian xpansion 27
eth-anoth (*Ar.* Kh.Beit 'Anun)) Palestine 162107
ethany (*a/c* Ananiah, *Ar.* El-Azariyeh) C Palestine 174130 visit f Jesus 116/2
eth-arabah (*Ar.* 'Ain el-Gharabeh) Palestine 197139 110
eth-arbel (*Ar.* Irbid) Transjordan 229218 in kingdom f Josiah 86
eth-aven see ***Bethel***
eth-azmaveth see ***Azmaveth***
eth-baal-meon (*a/c* Baal-meon, *r.* Ma'in) C Transjordan 219120 iblical city in Moab 66
eth-basi C Palestine 98
eth-dagon (*Ar.* Beit Dajan, *Heb.* et Dagan) C Palestine 134156 esieged by Assyrians 80/2
eth-diblathaim see ***Almon-diblathaim***
eth-eden see ***Bit-adini***
eth-eglain see ***Tell el- 'Ajjul***
ethel (*a/c* Beth-aven, *a/c* Luz, *Lat.* ethela, *Ar.* ***Beitin***) C Palestine 72148 MBA site 16/1; Canaanite oyal city 39/5; Philistine remains 3; Iron Age site 62; Israel's attack n Judah 70/1; Amos 75; Jewish evolts 128
eth-emek (*Ar.* T. Mimas, *Heb.* T. et Ha'Emeq) N Palestine 164263
ethennabris C Transjordan ewish revolts 128
ether (*a/s* ***Bethther***, *Ar.* Kh.el-ehud) C Palestine 162126
eth-gamul (*Ar.* Kh. el-Jumeil) Transjordan 235099 biblical city Moab 66
eth-haccherem (*a/s* Beth-accerem, *Ar.* Kh. Salih, *Heb.* ***Ramat ahel***) C Palestine 170127 Iron ge site 79/3
eth-haggan (*a/c* Gina, ***Ginae***; *Ar.* enin) N Palestine 178207
eth-haram (*a/s* Beth-haran, *Ar.* ***T. ktanu***) C Transjordan 214136 istrict of Solomon's kingdom 52; iblical city in Moab 66
eth-hoglah (*Ar.* Deir Hajlah) Palestine 197136
eth-horon (*Akk.* ***Bit-ninurta***) evitical city 50; captured by gyptians 63; Jewish revolts 128
eth-jeshimoth (*a/c* Besimoth, *Ar.* . el- 'Azeimah) C Transjordan 08132 biblical city in Moab 66
eth-leaphrah (*Ar.* ?Et-Taiyibeh) Palestine 153107
ethlehem (in Judah) (*Ar.* Beit ahm) C Palestine 169123 MBA ite 17/1; Phoenician finds 57/2; ortress of Rehoboam 78; Roman own 112
ethlehem (in Zebulun) (*Ar.* Beit ahm, *Heb.* ***Bet Lehem HaGelilit***) Palestine 168238 44
ethletepha (*mod.* Beit Natif) Palestine toparchy of Herod's ingdom 105; Roman town 112; ewish revolts 128
eth-nimrah (*a/c* Nimrah, *Ar.* T.el-leibil) C Transjordan 210146
ethogabri see ***Betogabris***
eth-pelet (*Ar.* ?T.es-Saqati) Palestine 79/2
ethphage C Palestine 116/2
eth-ramatha =***Bethsaida*** Herod's ingdom 105
Bethsaida (*a/c* ***Beth-ramatha***, Julias Livias, ***Livias***) N Palestine 209256 ministry of Jesus 115
Beth-shean (*a/s* Beth-shan, *a/c* Nysa, *Akk.* Bet-Shani, *Gk.* ***Scythopolis***, *Ar.* T.el-Husn, *Heb.* ***Bet She'an***) N Palestine 197212 EBA city 12, 27; MBA site 16/1; Midianite traders 19; Amarna tablets 24; Egyptian expansion 27,28; Mycenaean pottery 31; Philistine remains 43; 47/3; district of Solomon's kingdom 52; temple 53; Iron Age site 62; captured by Egyptians 63
Beth-shemesh (in Issachar) (*Ar.*? Sheikh esh-Shamsawi, *Heb.* H. Shemesh) N Palestine 199232 40
Beth-shemesh (in Judah) (*a/c* ***Har-heres***, 'Ain Shems, Ir-shemesh; *Ar.* T.er-Rumeileh, *Heb.* T.Bet Shemesh) C Palestine 147128 EBA city 12; MBA site 17/1; find of Ugaritic text 23; Mycenaean pottery 31; Levitical city 50; district of Solomon's kingdom 52; Iron Age site 79/3; captured by Assyrians 80/2; lamelech seal 82; route of the Ark 133/1
Beth-shemesh (in Naphtali) (*Eg.* ***Beta-shamshu***, *Ar.* ***T.er-Ruweiseh***, *Heb.* T.Rosh) N Palestine 181271 40
Beth-tappuah (*Ar.* Taffuh) S Palestine 154105 79/2
Bethther =***Bether*** Roman town 112
Beth-yerah (*a/c* ***Philoteria***, *Ar.* Kh. el-Kerak, *Heb.* T.Bet Yerah) N Palestine 204235 EBA city 12; MBA site 16/1
Beth-zacariah C Palestine battle between Judas and Lysias 99/2
Beth-zaith (*Ar.* Zeita) C Palestine 98
Beth-zur (*Ar.* Kh. et-Tubeiqeh) C Palestine 159110 MBA site 17/1; LBA remains 41/3; Philistine remains 43; Phoenician finds 57/2; fortress of Rehoboam 78; Iron Age site 79/3; lamelech seal 82; fortified by Simon 98
Bet Lehem HaGelilit =***Bethlehem*** (in Zebulun) synagogue site 131/2
Betogabris (*a/c* Bethogabri, ***Eleutheropolis***; *Ar.* Beit Jibrin, *Heb.* ***Bet Guvrin***) S Palestine Jewish revolts 128
Betonim (*Ar.* Kh.Batneh) C Palestine 217154
Bet-Shani see ***Beth-shean***
Bet She'an =***Beth-shean*** Chalcolithic settlement 11; synagogue site 123,131/2
Bet She'arim N Palestine synagogue site 123
Bet Yerah =***Beth-yerah*** synagogue site 123,131/2
Bezek (*Ar.* Kh. Ibziq) N Palestine 187197 47/2
Bezer (*Ar.*? Umm el- 'Amad) C Transjordan 235132 biblical city in Moab 66
Bezet N Palestine synagogue site 131/2
Bilean see ***Ibleam***
Bira N Palestine early settlement 135
Bir Defiyye S Palestine Roman watchtower 111
Birsama S Palestine Roman fort 112
Birta C Transjordan 94/3
Bisitun see ***Behistun***
Bismaya see ***Adab***
Bit-adini (*Bibl.* Beth-eden) region of C Syria in Assyrian Empire 72/1, 72/2;
Bit-bakhiani region of N Mesopotamia in Assyrian Empire 72/2
Bithynia Roman province of N Asia Minor 103/1
Bit-ninurta =***Beth-horon*** Egyptian rule 24
Bitolion S Palestine Roman village 112
Bit-zitti S Lebanon captured by Assyrians 81/2
Böğazköy see ***Hattushash***
Bononia (*mod.* Bologna) N Italy Jewish diaspora 120
Boreum E Libya Jewish diaspora 120
Borim (*Ar.* Kh. Burin, *Heb.* H. Borin) N Palestine 153203 captured by Egyptians 63
Borsippa (*Akk.* Barsip) C Mesopotamia early trade 14/2; local gods 69
Bosor N Transjordan 99/1
Bostra S Syria Nabataean trade 109
Bouqras (*mod.* Buqrus) E Syria early settlement 10
Bozrah (in Edom) (*Ar.* Buseirah) S Transjordan Iron Age site 79/3
Bozrah (*a/c* ***Busranu***, ***Busruna***) S Transjordan Iron Age site 79/3
Brescia see ***Brixia***
Brixia (*mod.* Brescia) N Italy Jewish diaspora 120
Bubastis (*Bibl.* Pibeseth) L Egypt campaigns of Amosis 20/1
Bucephala NW India Alexander's campaigns 93
Buculon Polis see ***Adarus***
Buqei'a see ***Peqi'in***
Buqrus see ***Bouqras***
Burj el-Isaneh see ***Jeshanah***
Burquna N Palestine Egyptian rule 24
Buseirah see ***Bozrah*** (in Edom)
Busiris L Egypt 91
Busranu =***Bozrah*** MBA town 16/3
Busruna =***Bozrah*** Egyptian rule 24
Butartu C Transjordan Egyptian expansion 27
Byblos (*Bibl.* ***Gebal***, *Akk.* ***Gubla***, *mod.* Jbail, Jubail, Jebail, Jebeil) N Lebanon early settlement 11; EBA city 12; early trade 14/1; Egyptian expansion 21, 27; trade with Mycenae and Cyprus 30; Mycenaean pottery 31; journey of Wen-amon 42; Phoenician trade 57/1; early writing 60; local gods 68; Jewish diaspora 121
Byzantium (*mod.* Istanbul) Christian city 131/1

C

Cabul see ***Chabulon***
Cadasa =***Kedesh-naphtali*** Roman town 113; Jewish revolts 128
Cádiz see ***Gades***
Caditis see ***Gaulanitis***
Caesarea (*a/c* Caesarea Maritima, ***Strato's Tower***, *a/s* Straton's Tower) N Palestine 140212 Herod's kingdom 105,106; plan of harbour of Sebastos 108; Nabataean trade 109; Roman city 113; synagogue site 123,131/2; Paul's journeys 125; Jewish revolts 128
Caesarea Mazaca (*mod.* Kayseri) E Asia Minor Jewish diaspora 121; Christian city 131/1
Caesarea Philippi =***Paneas*** free city of Herod's Kingdom 105; Roman town 113
Caferdago C Palestine Roman town 112
Cagliari see ***Caralis***
Calah (*a/s* Kalah, *Akk.* ***Kalkhu***, *mod.* Nimrud) N Mesopotamia ziggurat 14/2; early trade 15/1
Callinicum N Syria Jewish diaspora 121
Calneh see ***Kullania***
Cana =***Kanah*** (in Galilee) captured by Aristobulus 101; visit of Jesus 117/2
Canaan (*Akk.* ***Kina'ni***, *Eg.* ***Retenu***) country of C Palestine EBA cities 12; MBA towns and sites 16-17; Hyksos rule 19; Egyptian expansion 20-21; trade with Ugarit 23; Egyptian province 27,28,29; trade with Mycenae and Cyprus 30; Mycenaean pottery 31; cities unconquered by Israelites 41/2; early tribes 59
Canatha (*a/c* Kenath, Nobah; *Akk.* ***Qanu***, *Ar.* Qanawat) N Transjordan 118
Capercotnei see ***Legio Maximianopolis***
Capernaum (*a/s* ***Capharnaum***) N Palestine 204254 ministry of Jesus 115; synagogue site 123,131/2
Capharabis C Palestine Jewish revolts 128
Caphareccho N Palestine Jewish revolts 128
Capharnaum =***Capernaum*** Roman town 113
Capharsalama C Palestine 98
Caphartobas C Palestine Jewish revolts 128
Caphtor see ***Crete***
Caphtorites (*a/c* Caphtorim) tribe of Egypt 58
Capitolias N Transjordan 118
Cappadocia (*Per.* Katpatuka) country of NE Asia Minor Persian province 91
Capua C Italy Jewish diaspora 120
Caralis (*a/s* Carales, *mod.* Cagliari) S Sardinia Phoenician city 56
Carchemish (*Akk.* ***Gargamish***, *Ar.* Jarabulus, Jerablus, Jerabish) NE Syria EBA city 12; early trade 14/1; Jacob's journey 17/2; captured by Assyrians 72/2; tribute to Assyria 76; Egyptians defeated by Babylonians 84/2,87,89
Carmel (*Ar.* Kh. el-Kirmil) C Palestine 162092
Carmel, Mt N Palestine Elijah 65
Carnaim see ***Karnaim***
Carthage (*Lat.* Carthago) Tunisia Phoenician city 56; Jewish diaspora 120; Christian city 130
Casluhites (*a/c* Casluhim) tribe of Egypt 58
Casphor (*a/c* Chaspho) N Transjordan 98
Caspian Gates N Persia Alexander's campaigns 93
Çatal Hüyük C Anatolia early settlement 10
Cave of Horrors C Palestine Jewish revolts 129
Cave of Letters C Palestine Jewish revolts 129
Çayönü E Anatolia early settlement 10
Cedron (*a/c* Kedron, Kidron) C Palestine Roman town 112
Celaenae W Asia Minor Cyrus 91
Cenchreae C Greece Paul's journeys 124,126/1,126/2
Cephalonia (*a/s* Cephallenia) island of W Greece Mediterranean trade 32
Chabulon (*a/c* Cabul) N Palestine Roman village 113; Jewish revolts 128
Chagar Bazar NE Syria EBA city 13
Chalcedon NW Asia Minor Jewish diaspora 121
Chalcis N Syria Nabataean trade 109
Chaldaea region of S Mesopotamia attacked by Assyrians 76
Charachmoba =***Kir-hareseth*** Nabataean trade 109
Charax S Mesopotamia Alexander's campaigns 93
Chasalon see ***Chesalon***
Chaspho see ***Casphor***
Chebron =***Hebron*** Roman town 112; Jewish revolts 128
Chephirah (*Ar.* Kh. el-Kefireh) C Palestine 160137 79/2
Cherem-hattel C Palestine 74
Chermela C Palestine Roman fort 112
Chesalon (*a/c* Chasalon, *Ar.* Kesla, *Heb.* Kesalon) C Palestine 154132 Roman town 112
Chesulloth (*a/c* ***Exaloth***, Chisloth-tabor; *Ar.* Iksal) N Palestine 180232
Chezib see ***Achzib*** (in Judah)
Chinnereth (*a/s* Chinneroth, *Ar.* Kh. el- 'Oreimeh, *Heb.* T.Kinrot) N Palestine 200252 MBA site 16/1; battle of Hazor 39/4; Aram-Israel conflicts 70/1
Chinnereth, Sea of see ***Galilee, Sea of***
Chios island of E Aegean Paul's journeys 124
Chisloth-tabor see ***Chesulloth***
Chorazin (*mod.* Korazim) N Palestine 203257 synagogue site 123
Chorsia see ***Gergesa***
Chrysopolis NW Asia Minor Jewish diaspora 121
Cilicia (*a/c* ***Khilakku***, ***Kizzuwadna***, ***Que***) country of S Anatolia trade with Ugarit 22; seeks protection of Assyria 84/1; Roman province 103/1
Cimmerians see ***Gomer***
Cirta N Algeria Jewish diaspora 120; Christian city 130
Cisalpine Gaul see ***Gallia Cisalpina***
Citium =***Kition*** captured by Assyrians 84/1;
City of Moab (*Ar.* Kh. el-Medeiyineh) S Transjordan 232076 biblical city in Moab 66
City of Salt (*Ar.* ?Kh. Qumran) C Palestine 193127
Cnidus SE Aegean Paul's journeys 124
Cnossus (*Gk.* Knossos) Crete exports to Canaan 30; Mediterranean trade 33; Christian city 131/1
Colonia Agrippina (*mod.* Cologne) NW Germany Jewish diaspora 120
Colophon W Asia Minor Jewish diaspora 121
Colossae SW Asia Minor Paul's journeys 127/1; Christian city 131/1
Constantia Maiumas (*a/c* Maiumas, Nea Gaza) S Palestine Roman harbour 112
Coptus (*Gk.* Koptos) U Egypt Nabataean trade 109
Corinth (*Lat.* Corinthus) C Greece Jewish diaspora 121; synagogue site 122; Paul's journeys 124,126/1,126/2; Christian city 130
Corone S Greece Jewish diaspora 121
Corsica Roman province 102
Corycus S Asia Minor Jewish diaspora 121
Cos (*a/s* Kos) SE Aegean Paul's journeys 124
Cossyra (*n/c* Pantelleria) island of C Mediterranean Phoenician city 56
Creta =***Crete*** Roman province 103/1
Crete (*Akk.* Kaptaru, *Bibl.* Caphtor, *Lat.* ***Creta***) island of E Mediterranean trade with Ugarit 22; exports to Canaan 30; Mediterranean trade 32-33; early writing 60; Ptolemaic rule 94/1; Christian city 130
Crocodilonpolis C Palestine Roman town 113
Crocodilopolis see ***Arsinoe***
Ctesiphon C Mesopotamia Jewish diaspora 121
Cunaxa C Mesopotamia Cyrus attacks Artaxerxes 91; Alexander's campaigns 93
Cush (*Akk.* Kashi, *mod.* Nubia) country of NE Africa 24,58
Cuthah (*a/s* Kuta) C Mesopotamia local gods 69; deportations to Israel 77/4
Cutheans people of N Palestine 103/3
Cydrara see ***Hierapolis***
Cyme W Asia Minor Jewish diaspora 121
Cyprus (*Akk.* Yadnanu, *anc.* Alashiya, *a/c* Elishah) early settlements 10; trade with Ugarit 22; Mediterranean trade 33; Phoenician trade 57/1; early writing 60; in Assyrian Empire 72/1; Ptolemaic rule 94/1; Seleucid rule 96/1; Paul's journeys 125
Cyprus C Palestine Herodian fortress 105,106; Jewish revolts 128
Cyrenaica Roman province of N Africa 103/1
Cyrene Libya Jewish diaspora 121; Christian city 130

D

Dabaloth C Transjordan captured by Jannaeus 101
Dabaritta see ***Daberath***
Dabbesheth (*Ar.* ?T.esh-Shammam, *Heb.* T.Shem) N Palestine 164230
Dabbura N Transjordan synagogue site 123
Daberath (*a/c* Dabaritta, *Ar.* Daburiyeh) N Palestine 185233 Levitical city 50
Dabiya N Transjordan synagogue site 123
Daburiyeh see ***Daberath***
Dahshur U Egypt campaigns of Kamosis 20/1
Damascus (*Akk.* Dimashqa, *mod.* Esh-Sham, Dimashq) S Syria early trade 14/1; Jacob's journey 17/2; Egyptian expansion 27,28; Elisha 65; local gods 68; Aram-Israel conflicts 70; captured by Assyrians 73/4; tribute to Assyria 76; anti-Assyrian activities 77/3; captured by Babylonians 88; Nabataean trade 109; Jewish diaspora 121; Christian city 131/1
Damascus, Kingdom of S Syria Assyrian vassal state of 77/2
Dan (*a/c* ***Laish***, Leshem, ***Leshi***; *Ar.* T. el-Qadi, Heb ***T. Dan***) N Palestine 211294 Canaanite royal city 39/5; new Iron Age site 41/3,62;

Lydites – Palestine

Lydites (*a/c* Ludim) tribe of Egypt 58
Lyon *see* ***Lugdunum***
Lystra C Asia Minor Paul's journeys 125; Christian city 131/1

M

Maa-Palaiokastro W Cyprus trade with Canaan and Syria 30
Ma'barot N Palestine MBA site 16/1
Mabartha *see* ***Neapolis***
Macedonia Alexander 92; Roman province of N Greece 103/1
Machaerus C Transjordan fortress of Jannaeus 101,103/2; Herodian fortress 105,106; Roman town 112; Jewish revolts 128
Machmas =***Michmash*** Roman town 112
Mada *see* ***Media***
Madaba *see* ***Medeba***
Madai =***Medes*** people of NW Persia 59
Madmannah (*Ar.* Kh.Tatrit) S Palestine 143084
Madmen (*Ar.* Kh. Dimneh) S Transjordan 217077 biblical city in Moab 66
Madon N Palestine battle of Hazor 39/4; Canaanite royal city 39/5
Magdalu =***Migdol*** Egyptian rule 24
Magdiel N Palestine Roman city 113
Magiddu =***Megiddo*** Egyptian rule 24; Assyrian vassal 77/2
Magnesia W Asia Minor Jewish diaspora 121; Christian city 131/1
Magog people of the Caucasus 59
Mahalab =***Ahlab*** captured by Assyrians 81/2
Mahanaim (T. edh-Dhahab el-Gharbi) C Transjordan 214177 captured by Egyptians 63
Mahoza *see* ***Muhhazi***
Ma'in *see* ***Beth-baal-meon***
Maiumas *see* ***Constantia Maiumas***
Maiumas Ascalon S Palestine Roman harbour 112
Maked N Transjordan 99/1
Makhadu (*mod.* Minet el-Beida) NW Syria port of Ugarit 23
Makhneh el-Foqa *see* ***Michmethath***
Makkah *see* ***Mecca***
Makkedah C Palestine imprisonment of Canaanite King 39/3; Canaanite royal city 39/5
Maktulya C Palestine MBA town 16/3
Malaca (*mod.* Málaga) S Spain Phoenician city 56
Malatha =***Moladah*** free city of Herod's kingdom 105
Malta *see* ***Melita***
Malthi S Greece 32
Mampsis S Palestine Roman city 112
Manahath (*Ar.* El-Malhah, *Heb.* Manahat) C Palestine 167128
Manasseh tribe of C Palestine 40;45/3
Mansuate city and region of SW Syria captured by Assyrians 73/4; Assyrian vassal state 77/2
Mantinea C Greece Jewish diaspora 121
Maon (*Ar.* Kh.Ma'in, *Heb.* Ma'on) S Palestine 162090 synagogue site 123,131/2
Ma'oz Hayyim N Palestine synagogue site 123
Maracanda (*mod.* Samarkand) C Asia Alexander's campaigns 93
Marah W Sinai route of Exodus 35
Maralah (*Ar.* ?T.Thorah, *Heb.* T.Shor) N Palestine 166228 40
Marathus W Syria Persian rule 90/2
Mareshah (*G/L* ***Marisa***, *a/s* Marissa) S Palestine Phoenician influence 57/2; fortress of Rehoboam 78; lamelech seal 82
Mari (*mod.* Tell Hariri) NW Mesopotamia EBA city 13; early trade 14/1; ziggurat 14/2; find of cuneiform text 23; early writing 60; local gods 68
Marisa =***Mareshah*** captured by Hyrcanus 101; free city of Herod's kingdom 105
Masa region of S Anatolia 33
Masada C Palestine fortress of Jannaeus 101,103/2; Herodian fortress 105,106; Roman town 112; synagogue site 123; Jewish revolts 128
Maximianopolis N Palestine 118
Mecca (*Ar.* Makkah) W Arabia Nabataean trade 109
Medeba (*Ar.* Madaba) C Transjordan 225124 biblical city in Moab 66; Iron Age site 79/3; Roman city 112
Medes (*Per.* Madai) people of NW Persia 59
Media (*Per.* Mada) country of NW Persia in Assyrian Empire 73/1; deportations from Israel 77/4; allied with Babylon against Assyria 84/2; Persian province 91; Alexander's campaigns 93; Seleucid rule 97
Median Wall C Mesopotamia defensive line 89
Medina *see* ***Yatribu***
Mediolanum (*mod.* Milan) N Italy Jewish diaspora 120
Mediterranean Sea early trade routes 32-33; Phoenician trade 56-57
Megiddo (*Akk.* ***Magiddu***, *Ar.* T.el-Mutesellim, *Heb.* T.Megiddo) N Palestine 167221 Chalcolithic settlement 11; EBA city 12; MBA site 16/1; Jacob's journey 17/2; battle against the Egyptians 20/3; find of cuneiform text and Ugaritic text 23; Egyptian expansion 27,28; Mycenaean pottery 31; route of Exodus 34; Canaanite royal city 39/5; Philistine remains 43; district of Solomon's kingdom 52; temple 53; city gate 54/1; Phoenician finds 57/2; Iron Age site 62; captured by Egyptians 63; Josiah defeated by Egyptians 86
Melid city & region of E Asia Minor in Assyrian Empire 73/1,76
Melita (*mod.* Malta) C Mediterranean Phoenician city 56; Paul's journeys 124
Melitene E Asia Minor Christian city 131/1
Melukkha (*a/c* Nubia) region of Egypt 24
Memphis (*Bibl.* Moph, ***Noph***) L Egypt Hyksos capital 19; campaigns of Amosis 20/1; Egyptian capital 26; captured by Assyrians 72/1, 84/1; Alexander's campaigns 92
Me-Neftoah *see* ***Waters of Nephtoah***
Menois S Palestine Roman fort 112
Mephaath (*Ar.* ?T.Jawah) C Transjordan 239140
Mérida *see* ***Emerita Augusta***
Merneptah in Pi-Aram =***Kumudi*** Egyptian fort 29
Merom (*a/c* ***Meroth***, *Ar.* T. el-Khirbeh?, *Heb.* ***Meron***) N Palestine 190275 Egyptian expansion 27
Meron =***Merom*** synagogue site 123,131/2
Meroth =***Merom*** Jewish revolts 128
Mesad Hashavyahu C Palestine 86
Meser *see* ***Mezer***
Meshech tribal region of S Anatolia 58
Meskene *see* ***Emar***
Mesopotamia early settlements 10; EBA cities 13; Abraham's migration 14-15; S 14/2; early trade 15/1; early writing 60; pagan cults 68-69; Nabataean trade routes 109; Jewish diaspora 121
Methana SE Greece Egyptian naval base 94/1
Mevasseret Ziyyon *see* ***Mozah***
Mevo Dotan N Palestine Chalcolithic settlement 11
Mezer (*a/c* Meser) N Palestine Chalcolithic settlement 11; EBA city 12
Michmash (*a/s* Michmas, ***Machmas***; *Ar.* Mukhmas) C Palestine 176142 battle between Israelites and Philistines 46/1
Michmethath (*Ar.* Makhneh el-Foqa) C Palestine 175176 40,74
Middin (*Ar.* ?***Kh.Abu Tabaq***) C Palestine 188127 110
Midian country of NW Arabia early trade 14/1
Midianites tribe of N Transjordan defeated by Gideon 45/3
Migdal N Palestine Herod's kingdom 105
Migdal-gad (*Ar.* ?Kh.el-Mejdeleh, *Heb.* H.Migdal Gad) S Palestine 140105
Migdol (*Akk.* ***Magdalu***) L Egypt route of Exodus 35; captured by Assyrians 84/1;
Mikhmoret N Palestine Phoenician influence 57/2
Miletus SW Asia Minor trade with Mycenae 30; Alexander's campaigns 92; Jewish diaspora 121; synagogue site 122; Paul's journeys 125,127/1; Christian city 131/1
Minet el-Beida *see* ***Makhadu***
Mira-Kuwaliya region of W Anatolia 33
Mishal (*Ar.* ***T.Kisan***, *Heb.* T.Kison) N Palestine 164253
Mishrefa S Palestine Roman fort 112
Misrephoth-maim N Palestine 39/4
Mitanni country of N Mesopotamia early trade 15/1
Mizpah (in Benjamin) (*a/s* Mizpeh, *Ar.* ***T. en-Nasbeh***) C Palestine 170143 LBA remains 41/3; Iron Age site 79/3; lamelech seal 82; captured by Babylonians 88
Mizpah-gilead *see* ***Ramath-mizpeh***
Mizpeh =***Ramath-mizpeh*** MBA site 16/1. *See also* Mizpah
Mizraim people of Egypt 58
Moa S Palestine Roman fort 111
Moab (*a/c* Moabitis) country of C Transjordan early trade 14/1; Egyptian subject state 27; biblical routes 37/3; partly conquered by David 50; biblical cities and sites of excavation 66; pagan cults 68; invaded by Aram 70/2; tribute to Assyria 76; Assyrian province 77/2; Iron Age sites 79/3
Moabites tribe of C Transjordan defeated by Ehud 45/4
Moabitis =***Moab*** Seleucid rule 99/1; in Hasmonaean Kingdom 101
Moahile S Palestine Roman fort 111
Mohenjo-Daro NW India early writing 61
Moladah (*a/c* ***Malatha***, *Ar.* ? Khereibet el-Waten, *Heb.* H.Yittan) S Palestine 142074 79/2
Moph *see* ***Memphis***
Mopsuestia SE Asia Minor synagogue site 122
Moreh, Hill of N Palestine 46/3
Moresheth-gath (*Akk.* ***Mu'rashti***, *Ar.*? T.el-Judeidah, *Heb.* T. Goded) C Palestine 141115 Micah 75; fortress of Rehoboam 78; lamelech seal 82
Morocco Phoenician trade 56
Motya W Sicily Phoenician city 56
Moukhtara N Lebanon early settlement 11
Mouliana E Crete Mediterranean trade 33
Mozah (*Ar.* Qalunyah, *Heb.* Mevasseret Ziyyon) C Palestine 165134 Persian rule 90/2
Mudraya *see* ***Egypt***
Muhhazi (*a/c* Mahoza, *Akk.* ***Mu'khaza***, *Ar.* T.Abu Sultan, *Heb.* T.Mahoz) C Palestine 125147
Mu'khaza =***Muhhazi*** Egyptian rule 24
Mukhmas *see* ***Michmash***
Munhatta N Palestine Chalcolithic settlement 11
Murashrash S Palestine Roman watchtower 111
Mu'rashti =***Moresheth-gath*** Egyptian rule 24
Mureybat (*a/s* Mureybit) N Syria early settlement 10
Mycenae S Greece exports to Canaan 30/2
Myndus SW Asia Minor Jewish diaspora 121
Myos Hormos NE Egypt Nabataean trade 109
Myra S Asia Minor Paul's journeys 125
Mytilene E Aegean Paul's journeys 124

N

Naarah (*a/s* Naarath, *Lat.* ***Neara***, *Ar.* T.el Jisr, *Heb.* ***Na'aran***) C Palestine 190144
Na'aran =***Naarah*** synagogue site 123
Nabataea country of S Transjordan 103
Nabataeans people of the Negeb trade 109
Nabi Yunis C Palestine Phoenician influence 57/2
Nablus *see* ***Neapolis***
Nabratein N Palestine synagogue site 123
Nahal 'En Gev N Palestine Natufian settlement 11
Nahal Gerar S Palestine MBA site 17/1
Nahal Mishmar S Palestine Chalcolithic settlement 11
Nahal Oren N Palestine early settlements 11
Nahal Rabba C Palestine Chalcolithic settlement 11
Naharaim *see* ***Naharima***
Naharima (*a/s* Naharina, *a/c* Naharaim) region of NE Syria 25
Nahariyya N Palestine temple 53
Naim =***Nain*** Roman town 113
Nain (*a/s* ***Naim***) N Palestine 183226
Naphtali tribe of N Palestine 40
Naphtuhites (*a/c* Naphtuhim) tribe of Egypt 58
Naples *see* ***Neapolis***
Narbata N Palestine Roman town 113; Jewish revolts 128
Narbattene region of C Palestine toparchy of Herod's kingdom 105; Roman district 113
Narbonensis Roman province of S France 102
Naro (*mod.* Hammam Lif) Tunisia synagogue site 122
Nasibina *see* ***Nisibis***
Naucratis L Egypt 91; Christian city 131/1
Na'ur *see* ***Abel-keramim***
Naveh (*Ar.* Nawa) N Transjordan 248255 118
Nawa *see* ***Naveh***
Nazareth N Palestine 178234 ministry of Jesus 114
Nea Gaza *see* ***Constantia*** Maiumas
Neapolis (*a/c* Mabartha, Flavia Neapolis; *mod.* Nablus) N Palestine Roman city 113; Christian city 131/1
Neapolis NE Greece Paul's journeys 126/1
Neapolis (*mod.* Naples) C Italy Jewish diaspora 120; Paul's journeys 124
Neara =***Naarah*** Roman fort 112
Neballat (*Ar.* Beit Nabala, *Heb.* Nevallat) C Palestine 146154
Nebo (*Ar.* 'Ayun Musa) C Transjordan 220131 biblical city in Moab 66
Nebi Rubin C Palestine early settlement 135
Nefrusy U Egypt campaigns of Kamosis 20/1
Negeb (*a/s* Negev) region of S Palestine biblical routes 37/3; fortresses of the wilderness 79/3
Negev *see* ***Negeb***
Nehardea C Mesopotamia Jewish diaspora 121
Neiel (*Ar.* Kh.Ya'nin, *Heb.* H.Ya'anin) N Palestine 171255
Neocaesarea N Asia Minor Christian city 131/1
Nesana *see* ***Nessana***
Nessana (*a/s* Nesana, *Heb.* Nizzana) S Palestine Nabataean trade 109
Netana S Palestine Roman fort 112
Netophah (*Ar.* ?Kh.Bedd Faluh) C Palestine 171119
Newe Ur N Palestine Chalcolithic settlement 11
Nezib (*Ar.* Kh.Beit Nesib) C Palestine 151110 79/2
Nibru *see* ***Nippur***
Nibshan (*Ar.* ?Kh. el-Maqari) C Palestine 186123 110
Nicomedia NW Asia Minor Jewish diaspora 121; Christian city 131/1
Nicopolis =***Emmaus*** Roman city 112
Nicopolis W Greece Christian city 130
Nimrah *see* ***Beth-nimrah***
Nimrud N Mesopotamia inscriptions concerning Israel 71
Nina (*mod.* Surghul) S Mesopotamia ziggurat 14/2
Nineveh (*Akk.* Ninua, *mod.* Quyunjiq) N Mesopotamia EBA city 13; ziggurat 14/2; early trade 15/1; early writing 60; local gods 68; inscriptions concerning Judah 71; besieged by Ummanmanda 84/2
Ninua *see* ***Nineveh***
Nippur (*Akk.* Nibru, *mod.* Nuffar) C Mesopotamia EBA city 12; ziggurat 14/2; local gods 69
Nisibis (*a/c* Nisibin, ***Antiochia***; *Akk.* Nasibina, *Turk.* Nusaybin) SE Asia Minor captured by Assyrians 72/2,73/3; Jewish diaspora 121
Niyi (*mod.* Qal'at el-Mudiq) N Syria Egyptian rule 25,27
Nizzana *see* ***Nessana***
Noah C Palestine clan-district of Israel 74
Nob (*Ar.* ?El- 'Isawiyeh) C Palestine 173134
Nobah *see* ***Canatha***
Noe N Transjordan 94/3
Nola C Italy Jewish diaspora 120
Noph =***Memphis*** journey of Wen-amon 42
Nora S Sardinia Phoenician city 56
Nubia *see* ***Melukkha***
Nuffar *see* ***Nippur***
Nugasse *see* ***Nukhashshe***
Nukhashshe (*a/s* Nugasse) region of N Syria 25; Egyptian expansion 21
Numeira S Transjordan Moabite site 66
Nusaybin *see* ***Nisibis***
Nuzi (*a/s* Nuzu, *mod.* Yorghan Tepe) N Mesopotamia EBA city 13; early writing 60
Nysa W Asia Minor Jewish diaspora 121

O

Oak of Zaanannim N Palestine Sisera slain by Jael 44/2
Obal tribe of S Arabia 59
Oboda (*a/s* Obodo) S Palestine Roman city 112
Oea W Libya Jewish diaspora 120
Oescus N Bulgaria Jewish diaspora 121
Olba SE Asia Minor Jewish diaspora 121
Olisipo (*mod.* Lisbon) Portugal Phoenician trade 56
Olives, Mount of C Palestine 173132
On (*a/c* Heliopolis) L Egypt Hyksos empire 19; captured by Assyrians 84/1; attacked by Babylonians 88;
Ono (*Lat.* ***Onus***, *Ar.* Kafr'Ana) C Palestine 137159 in kingdom of Josiah 86
Onus =***Ono*** Roman town 113
Ophir tribe of Red Sea area 59
Ophrah (in Abiezer) (*Ar.*? El-'Affuleh, *Heb.* ***'Afula***) N Palestine 177223 44/2
Ophrah (in Benjamin) (*Ar.* Et-Taiyibeh) C Palestine 178151 133/2
Orchomenus C Greece 32
Orda S Palestine Roman town 112
Oreine district of C Palestine toparchy of Herod's kingdom 105
Oropus E Greece Jewish diaspora 121
Orthosia =***Ullaza*** Persian rule 90/2
Ortospana (*mod.* Kabul) Afghanistan Alexander's campaigns 93
Ostia C Italy Jewish diaspora 120; synagogue site 122

P

Palaestina Prima Roman province of C Palestine 112
Palaestina Secunda Roman province of N Palestine 113
Palaestina Tertia Roman province of S Palestine 111-112
Palermo *see* ***Panormus***
Palestine (*Lat.* Palaestina) early settlements 10,11; Abraham's migration 14/1; early trade 14/1; MBA towns and sites 16-17; Egyptian expansion 20,27,28; trade with Ugarit 23; Egyptian rule 24; geology 36/1; Biblical routes 37/3; the twelve tribes of Israel 40; Philistine remains 43; Phoenician influence 57/2; Phoenician trade 57/1; Iron Age II sites 62; pagan cults 68; under Persian rule 90-91; Alexander's campaigns 92; Ptolemaic rule

Shaveh-Kiriathaim – Tell Jemmeh

expansion 20,21; captured by Egyptians 63; Iron Age site 79/3
Shaveh-Kiriathaim C Transjordan MBA site 17/1
Sheba tribe of SW Arabia 59
Shechem (*a/c* Sekmen, *Akk.* ***Shakmi***, *Ar.* ***T.Balatah***) N Palestine 176179 early trade 14/1; MBA site 16/1; Jacob's journey 17/2; sale of Joseph 19; find of cuneiform text 23; Egyptian expansion 28; Levitical city 50; district of Solomon's kingdom 52; temple 53; Phoenician influence 57/2; Iron Age site 62; clan-district of Israel 74; captured by Hyrcanus 101; Herod's kingdom 105
Sheikh Abu Zarad *see* ***Tappuah***
Sheikh 'Ali N Palestine early settlement 11
Sheikh esh-Shamsawi *see* ***Beth-shemesh*** (in Issachar)
Sheikh Sa'd =***Karnaim*** Egyptian expansion 27
Sheleph tribe of S Arabia 59
Shem tribal grouping of Arabia 59
Shemesh-adam *see* ***Adamah***
Shemida C Palestine clan-district of Israel 74
Shephelah region of C Palestine conquered by Israelites 39/3
Sheri =***Seir*** 24
Shianu W Syria battle of Qarqar 73/3
Shikmona (*a/s* Shikimonah, *Ar.* T. es-Samak, *Heb.* ***T. Shiqmona***) N Palestine Phoenician influence 57/2
Shikkeron (*Ar.* T.el-Ful) C Palestine 132136
Shiloh (*Ar.* ***Kh.Seilun***) C Palestine 177162 MBA site 16/1; LBA remains 41/3; Iron Age site 62; route of the Ark 133/1
Shimron (*Akk.* ***Sham'una***, *a/s* Shim'on, *a/c* Simonias, *Ar.* Kh. Sammuniyeh *Heb.* ***T. Shimron***) N Palestine 170234 battle of Hazor 39/4; Canaanite royal city 39/5
Shinar tribal region of Babylonia 59
Shittim *see* ***Abel-shittim***
Shosu region of SW Syria 16/2
Shufah *see* ***Siphtan***
Shunama =***Shunem*** Egyptian rule 24
Shunem (*a/c* ***Shunama***, *Ar.* Solem) N Palestine 181223 captured by Egyptians 63
Shuqba C Palestine Natufian settlement 11
Shur wilderness of W Sinai route of Exodus 35
Shuruppak (*mod.* Tell Fara) S Mesopotamia EBA city 13; ziggurat 14/2
Shush *see* ***Susa***
Shutu region of C Palestine 16/2
Sicca Tunisia Christian city 130
Sicilia (*Eng.* Sicily) Phoenician trade 56; Roman province 102
Side S Asia Minor Alexander's campaigns 92; Jewish diaspora 121
Sidon (*Akk.* ***Siduna***, *Ar.* Saida) S Lebanon Egyptian expansion 21,27 Mycenaean pottery 31; journey of Wen-amon 42; Phoenician trade 57/1; local gods 68; tribute to Assyria 72/2,73/4; captured by Assyrians 81/2,84/1; ministry of Jesus 115; Jewish diaspora 121; Paul's journeys 125; Christian city 131/1
Siduna =***Sidon*** Egyptian rule 25
Sigoph N Palestine Jewish revolts 128
Sile (*Eg.* ***Sillu***) NE Egypt base for invasion of Canaan 20; fort 28,29
Sillu =***Sile*** Egyptian rule 24
Siloam Pool Jerusalem 83
Simeon tribe of S Palestine 40
Simirra (*a/s* Simyra, *Bibl.* Zemer) Assyrian vassal state of W Syria 77/2
Simyra (*a/c* Simyra of Ramesses, *a/s* Simirra, *Akk.* ***Sumur***, Sumura) W Syria Egyptian provincial centre 27,28; anti-Assyrian activities 77/3
Sinai Egyptian empire 27; routes of Exodus 34-35
Sinai, Mount (*a/c* Mount Horeb) S Sinai route of Exodus 35
Sinites tribe of Syria 59
Sinope NE Asia Minor Xenophon's retreat 91; Christian city 131/1
Sinzar W Syria Egyptian rule 25
Siphtan (*Ar.*? Shufah) C Palestine 157186 74
Sippar (*a/c* Sepharvaim) C Mesopotamia local gods 69; deportations to Israel 77/4
Siracusa *see* ***Syracuse***
Sitifis N Algeria Jewish diaspora 120; Christian city 130
Siwa W Egypt Alexander's campaigns 92
Smyrna (*mod.* Izmir) W Asia Minor Jewish diaspora 121; Christian city 131/1
Socoh (near Mt. Judah) (*Ar.* Kh.Shuweikeh) S Palestine 150090
Socoh (in Sharon) (*Ar.* Kh. Shuweiket er-Ras) N Palestine 153194 district of Solomon's kingdom 52; captured by Egyptians 63; royal winery 82
Socoh (in Shephelah) (*Ar.* Kh. 'Abbad, *Heb.* H.Sokho) C Palestine 147121 79/2
Sodom and Gomorrah S Transjordan MBA site 17/1
Sogdiana country of C Asia Alexander's campaigns 93
Solem *see* ***Shunem***
Soli (*a/c* Pompeiopolis) S Asia Minor Alexander's campaigns 92; Seleucid rule 96/1
Sorek, *Valley of* C Palestine Philistine attack on Jerusalem 48/1
Soûr *see* ***Tyre***
Sousse *see* ***Hadrumetum***
Sozusa *see* ***Apollonia***
Spain Phoenician trade 56; Jewish diaspora 120
Sparda *see* ***Lydia***
Spasinou Charax S Mesopotamia Jewish diaspora 121
Stobi Macedonia Jewish diaspora 121; synagogue site 122
Strato's Tower =***Caesarea***
Suba *see* ***Zobah***
Suberde C Anatolia early settlement 10
Succoth (*Ar.* ***T Deir 'Alla***) 208178 MBA site 16/1; attacked by Gideon 45/3; Iron Age site 62; captured by Egyptians 63; Aram-Israel conflicts 70/1
Succoth L Egypt route of Exodus 34;
Sufunim N Palestine Natufian settlement 11
Sullecthum C Tunisia Jewish diaspora 120
Sumer country of S Mesopotamia early trade 15/1; early writing 61;
Sumur =***Simyra*** Egyptian rule 25
Supite (*Bibl.* ***Zobah***) Assyrian vassal state of C Syria 77/2
Suq Wadi Barada *see* ***Abila***
Sura C Mesopotamia Jewish diaspora 121
Suraya N Palestine MBA town 16/3
Surghul *see* ***Nina***
Surri =***Tyre*** Egyptian rule 24
Susa (*mod.* Shush) W Persia EBA city 13; ziggurat 14/2 early trade 15/1; early writing 61; destroyed by Assyrians 85/1; Alexander's campaigns 93; Seleucid rule 97
Susiana region of SW Persia Alexander's campaigns 92
Sutu Bedouin tribe of Syria 24-25
Suweima C Transjordan Chalcolithic settlement 11
Sychar C Palestine 177180 visit of Jesus 116/2
Sycomazon S Palestine Roman city 112
Synnada C Asia Minor Jewish diaspora 121
Syracuse (*Lat.* Syracusae, *mod.* Siracusa) E Sicily Jewish diaspora 120; Paul's journeys 124
Syria early settlements 10,11; Abraham's migration 14/1; EBA cities 12-13; Egyptian expansion 21,28; Egyptian rule 25; trade with Mycenae, Crete and Cyprus 30,33; Mycenaean pottery 31; Phoenician trade 57/1; early writing 60; pagan cults 68; conquered by Asssyria 72-73; under Persian rule 90-91; Alexander's campaigns 92; Seleucid rule 96/1; Roman province 103/1; Nabataean trade routes 109
Syria Palaestina Roman province 113/3

T

Taanach (*a/s* ***Thaanach***, *Akk.* Ta'(nuk)a, *Ar.* Tell Ti'innik) N Palestine 171214 EBA city 12; MBA site 16/1; battle of Megiddo 20/3; find of Ugaritic text 23; Mycenaean pottery 31; Canaanite royal city 39/5; Philistine remains 43; Levitical city 50; district of Solomon's kingdom 52; Iron Age site 62; captured by Egyptians 63
Taanath-shiloh (*Ar.* Kh. Ta'na el-Foqa) C Palestine 185175 74
Tabal city and region of E Asia Minor in Assyrian Empire 72/1,76; 85/1
Tabaqat Fahl N Transjordan early settlements 11; Mycenaean pottery 31
Tabeh *see* ***Jotbathah***
Tabor, Mt. N Palestine Jewish revolts 128
Tabuk NW Arabia Nabataean trade 109
Tadmor =***Palmyra*** early trade 14/1
Taenarum S Greece Jewish diaspora 121
Taffuh *see* ***Beth-tappuah***
Taiyiba N Transjordan Natufian settlement 11
Takhsi region of S Syria Egyptian rule 25,28
Takrit N Mesopotamia captured by Assyrians 84/2
Tamar (*Ar.* 'Ein Husb, *Heb.* Hazeva) S Palestine 173024 captured by Egyptians 63
Taminta region of C Syria Egyptian expansion 28
Tananir N Palestine temple 53
Tanis =***Avaris*** trade with Ugarit 23
Taphnith (*Ar.* Tibnin) N Palestine 188288
Tapika (*mod.* Maçat) E Anatolia 33
Tappuah (*Ar.* Sheikh Abu Zarad) N Palestine 172168
Tarbisu N Mesopotamia captured by Babylonians 84/2
Taricheae N Palestine captured by Aristobulus 101; Roman city 113; Jewish revolts 128
Tarraco (*mod.* Tarragona) NE Spain Jewish diaspora 120
Tarshish people of the Mediterranean 58
Tarsus (*a/c* ***Antiochia***) SE Asia Minor Mediterranean trade 33; Cyrus 91; Alexander's campaigns 92; Jewish diaspora 121; Paul's journeys 125; Christian city 131/1
Tauchira *see* ***Arsinoe***
Taxila NW India Alexander's campaigns 93; Seleucid rule 97
Teichos Dymeion W Greece 32
Tekoa (*Ar.* Kh. Tequ') C Palestine 170115 Amos 75; fortress of Rehoboam 77
Tel Adami *see* ***Adami-nekeb***
Tel Afeq (N) =***Aphek*** (in Asher) Philistine remains 43; early settlement 135
Tel Afeq (S) =***Aphek*** (in Sharon) early settlement 135
Tel 'Akko *see* ***Acco***
Tel 'Akhziv *see* ***Achzib*** (in Asher)
Tel 'Alil *see* ***Hali***
Tel Ashdod =***Ashdod*** early settlement 135
Tel 'Ashir C Palestine MBA site 16/1
Tel Ashqelon *see* ***Ashkelon***
Tel 'Avdon *see* ***Abdon***
Tel Avel Bet Ma'akha *see* ***Abel-beth-maacah***
Tel Aviv C Palestine Chalcolithic settlement 11; EBA city 12
Tel 'Azeqa *see* ***Azekah***
Tel Aznot Tavor *see* ***Aznoth-tabor***
Tel Batash =***Timnah*** Chalcolithic settlement 11; Mycenaean pottery 31; Philistine remains 43
Tel Be'er Sheva' =***Beersheba*** Philistine remains 43
Tel Bet HaEmeq *see* ***Beth-emek***
Tel Bet Mirsham *see* ***Tell Beit Mirsim***
Tel Bet She'an *see* ***Beth-shean***
Tel Bet Shemesh *see* ***Beth-shemesh*** (in Judah)
Tel Bet Yerah *see* ***Beth-yerah***
Tel Bira =***Rehob*** (in Asher) MBA site 16/1
Tel Burga N Palestine MBA site 16/1; early settlement 135
Tel Burna *see* ***Libnah***
Tel Dalit C Palestine early settlement 135
Tel Dan =***Dan*** Mycenaean pottery 31; Philistine remains 43; temple 53
Tel Dor *see* ***Dor***
Tel 'En Hadda *see* ***En-haddah***
Tel 'Erani C Palestine Philistine remains 43; lamelech seal 82; early settlement 135
Tel Esur N Palestine MBA site 16/1; early settlement 135
Tel 'Eter *see* ***Ether***
Tel 'Eton (*Ar.* Tell 'Aitun) C Palestine Philistine
Tel Gamma *see* ***Yurza***
Tel Gat C Palestine EBA city 12
Tel Gat Hefer *see* ***Gath-hepher***
Tel Gerisa =***Gath-rimmon*** MBA site 16/1; early settlement 135
Tel Goded *see* ***Moresheth-gath***
Tel Hadid *see* ***Hadid***
Tel Halif =***En-rimmon*** EBA city 12; MBA site 17/1; lamelech seal 82
Tel Hannaton *see* ***Hannathon***
Tel Harashim N Palestine MBA site 16/1
Tel Haror =***Gerar*** early settlement 135
Tel Hasi *see* ***Eglon***
Tel Hazor *see* ***Hazor***
Tel Hefer N Palestine EBA city 12
Tel 'Ira C Palestine lamelech seal 82
Tel Jeshu'a *see* ***Jeshua***
Tel Kinrot *see* ***Chinnereth***
Tel Kison *see* ***Mishal***
Tel Lakhish *see* ***Lachish***
Tel Ma'aravim S Palestine Philistine remains 43
Tel Mahoz *see* ***Muhhazi***
Tel Malhata =***Arad*** MBA site 17/1
Tel Malot *see* ***Gibbethon***
Tel Masos =***Hormah*** MBA site 17/1; Philistine remains 43
Tel Megadim N Palestine Phoenician influence 57/2
Tel Megiddo *see* ***Megiddo***
Tel Mevorakh N Palestine MBA site 16/1; Mycenaean pottery 31; temple 53; Phoenician influence 57/2; Iron Age site 62; early settlement 135
Tel Mikhal C Palestine MBA site 16/1; Mycenaean pottery 31; Iron Age site 62; early settlement 135
Tel Miqne =***Ekron*** Philistine remains 43
Tel Mor C Palestine Mycenaean pottery 31; Philistine remains 43; Iron Age site 79/3
Tel Nagila *see* ***Tell Najileh***
Tel Poleg C Palestine MBA site 16/1; Phoenician influence 57/2; Iron Age site 62
Tel Poran C Palestine MBA site 17/1; early settlement 135
Tel Poreg N Palestine early settlement 135
Tel Qanah C Palestine early settlement 135
Tel Qashish *see* ***Helkath***
Tel Qasila C Palestine MBA site 16/1; new Iron Age city 41/3; Philistine remains 43; temple 53; Iron Age site 62
Tel Qedesh *see* ***Kedesh***
Tel Qeriyot *see* ***Kerioth*** (in Negeb)
Tel Qiryat Ye'arim *see* ***Kiriath-jearim***
Tel Qishyon *see* ***Kishion***
Tel Raqqat *see* ***Rakkath***
Tel Regev =***Achshaph*** early settlement 135
Tel Rehov =***Rehob*** synagogue site 131/2
Tel Rekhesh =***Anaharath*** MBA site 16/1
Tel Rosh *see* ***Beth-shemesh*** (in Naphtali)
Tel Sera' *see* ***Ziklag***
Tel Shalaf *see* ***Eltekeh***
Tel Sharuhen *see* ***Sharuhen***
Tel Shem *see* ***Dabbesheth***
Tel Shimron =***Shimron*** MBA site 16/1
Tel Shiqmona =***Shikmona*** Hyksos scarab 19
Tel Shor *see* ***Maralah***
Tel Yarmut *see* ***Jarmuth*** (in Judah)
Tel Yin'am *see* ***Jabneel*** (in Naphtali)
Tel Yizre'el *see* ***Jezreel***
Tel Yoqneam *see* ***Jokneam***
Tel Yosef N Palestine MBA site 16/1
Tel Zafit =***Gath*** MBA site 17/1
Tel Zefi *see* ***Zephath***
Tel Zeror C Palestine MBA site 16/1; Philistine remains 43; Iron Age site 62; early settlement 135
Tel Zippor C Palestine MBA site 17/2 Mycenaean pottery 31; Philistine remains 43
Tel Zova *see* ***Zobah***
Tel Zor'a *see* ***Zorah***
Teleilat el-Ghassul C Transjordan early settlement 11; EBA city 12; temple 53
Tell Abu Habil N Transjordan Chalcolithic settlement 11
Tell Abu Hawam =***Libnath*** Mycenaean pottery 31; Phoenician influence 57/2; Iron Age site 62
Tell Abu Hureira N Syria early settlement 10
Tell Abu Shusheh *see* ***Gezer***
Tell Abu Sultan *see* ***Muhhazi***
Tell Abu Sus *see* ***Abel-meholah***
Tell Ahmar *see* ***Til Barsip***
Tell 'Ain Jedur *see* ***Gedor*** (in Gilead)
Tell 'Aitun *see* ***Tel 'Eton***
Tell el-'Ajjul (*a/c* Beth-eglain) S Palestine Hyksos capital; MBA site 17/1; Mycenaean pottery 31; Philistine remains 43; early settlement 135
Tell el-'Amr (*a/c* Geba-somen) C Palestine MBA site 16/1
Tell 'Ashtarah *see* ***Ashtaroth***
Tell Asmar *see* ***Eshnunna***
Tell 'Asur *see* ***Baal-hazor***
Tell Atchana *see* ***Alalakh***
Tell el-'Azeimeh *see* ***Beth-jeshimoth***
Tell el-Balat *see* ***Rehob*** (in Galilee)
Tell Balatah =***Shechem*** EBA city 12
Tell el-Batashi *see* ***Timnah***
Tell el-Bedeiwiyeh *see* ***Hannathon***
Tell Beit Mirsim (*Heb.* Tel Bet Mirsham) S Palestine EBA city 12; MBA site 17/1; Hyksos scarab 19; Mycenaean pottery 31; Philistine remains 43; Iron Age site 79/3
Tell el-Bir el-Gharbi *see* ***Rehob*** (in Asher)
Tell el-Bleibil *see* ***Beth-nimrah***
Tell Bornat *see* ***Libnah***
Tell Brak E Syria EBA city 13; ziggurat 14/2
Tell ed-Damiya *see* ***Adam***
Tell Deir 'Alla =***Succoth*** Mycenaean pottery 31; Philistine remains 43
Tell edh-Dhahab el-Gharbi *see* ***Mahanaim***
Tell edh-Dhahab esh-Sherqiyah *see* ***Penuel***
Tell ed-Dibbin *see* ***Ijon***
Tell Dothan *see* ***Dothan***
Tell ed-Duweir *see* ***Lachish***
Tell Erfad *see* ***Arpad***
Tell Esdar S Palestine LBA remains 41/3
Tell Fara *see* ***Shuruppak***
Tell el-Far'ah (North) =***Tirzah*** EBA city 12; MBA site 16/1; LBA remains 41/3
Tell el-Far'ah (South) =***Sharuhen*** MBA site 17/1; Mycenaean pottery 31; Philistine remains 43; Phoenician find 57/2; early settlement 135
Tell el-Ful C Palestine Philistine remains 43; Iron Age site 79/3; lamelech seal 82.
Tell Ghanam C Transjordan Chalcolithic settlement 11
Tell el-Ghassul SW Syria Mycenaean pottery 31
Tell el-Hammam *see* ***Abel-shittim***
Tell Hamman S Mesopotamia ziggurat 14/2
Tell el-Hammeh *see* ***Hammath***
Tell Harari *see* ***Mari***
Tell el-Hesi =***Eglon*** MBA site 17/1; Mycenaean pottery 31; Philistine remains 43; early settlement 135
Tell el-Hibba *see* ***Urukug***
Tell el-Husn SW Syria MBA site 16/1
Tell Iktanu =***Beth-haram*** C Transjordan Chalcolithic settlement 11; MBA site 16/1
Tell Isdar S Palestine Chalcolithic settlement 11
Tell Jawah *see* ***Mephaath***
Tell Jemmeh =***Yurza*** MBA site 17/1; Mycenaean pottery 31; Philistine remains 43; Phoenician finds 57/2; Iron Age site 79/3; early settlement 135

MAPS

We have pleasure in acknowledging:

p.38   1   Based on *The Problem of Ai* by Z. Zevit in *Biblical Archaeology*

p.49   4   Based on photograph courtesy of Sonia Halliday Photographs, Weston Turville, England

p.62-3   1,2   Based on original material by Y. Aharoni, with permission of M. Aharoni and Burns & Oates Ltd, Tunbridge Wells, England and The Westminster Press, Philadelphia

p.122-3   1, 5   Based on *Ancient Synagogues Revealed* edited by L. I. Levine, published by Israel Exploration Society, Jerusalem

p.111-13   Based on original material by M. Avi-Yonah, and used by courtesy of the Israel Department of Antiquities and Museums, Jerusalem

p.109   1   Based on original information by A. Negev, Jerusalem

p.135   1   Based on Broshi and Gophna *Middle Bronze Age II Palestine – Its Settlements and Population* published in BASOR 261; 74-90 used by permission of American School of Oriental Research, Valpariso University, Indiana

Front end paper   Based on information published in *Land of the Bible*, by Y. Aharoni, and used by permission of M. Aharoni and Burns and Oates Ltd, Tunbridge Wells, England, and The Westminster Press, Philadelphia

ILLUSTRATIONS

Unless stated to the contrary, all the illustrations in this book are the work of the following artists: Irene Bates, Duncan MacKay, Rex Nicholls and Malcolm Swanston.
The publishers should like to thank the following museums, publishers and picture agencies for permission to base illustrations upon their photographs or to reproduce them. Where there is no such acknowledgement, we have been unable to trace the source, or the illustration is a composition by our illustrators and contributors.

p.10   3   Jericho Excavation Fund
     4   Palestine Exploration Fund
     8, 9   Professor B. Hennessy, Sydney, Australia

p.12   2   Based on fig. 3 pages 224-225 of *Israel Exploration Journal* Vol 2 1952, published by Israel Exploration Society, Jerusalem
     3   Based on excavation of Arad, courtesy of Ruth Amiran, Director, Arad Expedition, sponsored by the Israel Museum and the Israel Exploration Society; and drawing by L. Ritmeyer, Jerusalem

p.13   4   Based on excavation by W.F.M. Petrie, published by J.C. Hinrichs Verlag, Leipzig
     5   Based on excavation by R. De Vaux, published in *Revue Biblique* 69, 1962 planches XIX, XX and XXI, by Ecole Biblique et Archéologique Française, Jerusalem

p.14   British Museum (Michael Holford)

p.15   ET Archive

p.16   4   ACL, Brussels
     5   Giraudon, Paris
     6   Hirmer Verlag, Munich

p.18   2   Service des Antiquites, Cairo
     3   From *Late Middle Kingdom Papyrus* by William Hayes, published by The Brooklyn Museum, New York
     6   Kunsthistorisches Museum, Vienna

p.19   4   Courtesy of the Oriental Institute of the University of Chicago

p.21   4   Uni Dia Verlag, Munich
     5   Peter Clayton

p.22   4,5   Paolo Koch, Vision International

p.23   6   Damascus Museum, Syria
     7,8   Paolo Koch, Vision International
     9   Cliche Musees Nationaux, Louvre, Paris

p.24   2   British Museum (Michael Holford)
     3   ET Archive

p.25   4   Department of Antiquities, Israel Museum, Jerusalem
     5,6   British Museum (Michael Holford)

p.27   3   J. Vertut, Issy les Moulineaux, France
     4   Giraudon, Paris

p.28   2   British Museum

p.29   4   National Museum of Antiquities, Cairo
     4a   Professor K.A. Kitchen
     5   Peter Clayton

p.31   3   Vronwy Hankey
     4, 5   British Museum

p.33   3   Sonia Halliday Photographs
     4   British Museum
     5   Sonia Halliday Photographs

p.36   5   The Ancient Art and Architecture Collection
     6   British Museum (Michael Holford)

p.37   4   Courtesy of the University Museum, University of Pennsylvania

p.42   3   Courtesy of The Oriental Institute of the University of Chicago
     4   The Ancient Art and Architecture Collection

p.43   5   Werner Forman Archive

p.44   7   Department of Antiquities, Israel Museum, Jerusalem

p.51   1   Institute of Archaeology, University of London
     2   Z. Radovan, Jerusalem
     3   *(illustration)* Based on Jericho P19 tomb, excavated by Kathleen Kenyon, courtesy of the Trustees of the British Museum, London
     4   *(photograph)* Sonia Halliday Photographs
     5   Department of Antiquities, Israel Museum, Jerusalem

p.53   1F   Sonia Halliday Photographs

p.54   1   Based on *The City Gate in Eretz-Israel and its Neighbouring Countries* by Z. Herzog, published by The Institute of Archaeology, Tel Aviv
     2   Based on *King Solomon's Palaces* by D. Ussishkin, published in *Biblical Archaeologist*, 36:78-105 (ASOR)
     3   Based on L.K. Townsend in H. Shanks' *The City of David After Five Years Digging* published in *Biblical Archaeology Review* 11, 6:22-38

p.57   3, 5   British Museum (Michael Holford)

p.58   2, 3   Based on information in *History of Ancient Geography* by J. Oliver Thomson, 1948, published by Cambridge University Press, Cambridge

p.59   4   British Museum

p.62   3   Courtesy of The Oriental Institute of the University of Chicago
     4   British Museum

p.64   2   Based on *Revue Biblique* 58, 1952, published by Ecole Biblique et Archeologique Francaise de Jerusalem
     3   British Museum (Michael Holford)
     4   Based on information in *Samaria Sebaste 1: The Buildings* plates 1 and 2, by J.W. Crowfoot, K.M. Kenyon and E.L. Sukenik, published by The Palestine Exploration Fund, London, 1942

p.66   3   Cliche Musees Nationaux, Louvre, Paris

p.67   1   Mrs Rosalind Janssen, University College London
     2   Cliche Musees Nationaux, Louvre, Paris
     3   Mrs Rosalind Janssen, University College London
     4   Professor J.B. Pritchard

p.69   2   Department of Antiquities, Israel Museum
     3   Badisches Landesmuseum Karlsruhe, West Germany
     4,5   F. Roulet, Biblical Institute, Fribourg, Switz.
     6, 7   Z. Radovan, Jerusalem

p.70   6   Courtesy of the University Museum, University of Pennsylvania

p.75   3   Paul Jordan, Norwich
     4   Department of Antiquities, Israel Museum, Jerusalem
     5, 6, 7   Z. Radovan, Jerusalem

p.76   2   Holle Verlag, Baden-Baden
     3   The Ancient Art and Architecture Collection

p.78   *(Arad-rabbah fortress)* Based on *Ancient Arad* by Ruth Amiran and Y. Aharoni, used by permission of R. Amiran, Z. Herzog and M. Aharoni
     (Ezion-geber fortress) Based on fig.9, vol 28 of *Biblical Archaeologist* 1965 (ASOR)
     (Kadesh-barnea fortress) Based on information published by the Israel Museum, Jerusalem

p.81   3, 4, 5   British Museum (Michael Holford)

p.83   1   Palestine Exploration Fund
     3   British Museum (Michael Holford)

p.85   4   Michael Holford

p.86   2   Giraudon, Paris

p.87   3   Based on *Israel Exploration Journal*, 160, Vol 10, p.130, published by Israel Exploration Society, Jerusalem
     4   Michael Holford

p.89   2a   Courtesy of Professor D. Wiseman, Epsom

p.90   4   The MacQuitty International Photographic Collection

p.91   3   Robert Harding Picture Library

p.92   2   Giraudon, Paris

p.94   4   The Mansell Collection
     5   British Museum
     6   The British Library

p.96   3   The Mansell Collection

p.100   2   Based on drawing by L. Ritmeyer, Jerusalem
     3   British Museum

p.104   2   Based on a reconstruction by L. Ritmeyer, Jerusalem

p.108   3   Alan Hutchinson Library Ltd
     4   Sonia Halliday Photographs

p.109   5   c 1986 Aaron Levin

p.110   2   The Ancient Art and Architecture Collection
     3   Sonia Halliday Photographs

p.114   2   Joint Sepphoris Project

p.117   4   Based on a reconstruction by L. Ritmeyer, Jerusalem

p.119   4   Based on *Discovering Jerusalem* by N. Avigad, published by Basil Blackwell, Oxford

p.122   2, 3   c Professor L. Michael White

p.123   4   c Professor L. Michael White
     7   Based on information in *Ancient Synagogues Revealed*, compliments of the excavator, Eric M. Meyers

p.124   2   Sonia Halliday Photographs

p.126   3   Based on a reconstruction by L. Ritmeyer, Jerusalem

p.127   4, 6, 7   Sonia Halliday Photographs

p.128   2   Based on a reconstruction by L. Ritmeyer, Jerusalem
     3   N.Y. Carlsberg Glypotek, Copenhagen
     4   Z. Radovan, Jerusalem

p.129   5, 6   Z. Radovan, Jerusalem
     8   Based on information from *The Bar Kochba Revolt* by Y. Yadin, published by Weidenfeld & Nicholson, London

p.130   3   Sonia Halliday Photographs

p.131   4   Werner Forman Archive
     5   c Professor L. Michael White

p.134   2   Sonia Halliday Photographs